ENVIRONMENTAL MANAGEMENT IN ORGANIZATIONS

ENVIRONMENTAL MANAGEMENT IN ORGANIZATIONS

The IEMA Handbook

Edited by
John Brady

Institute of Environmental
Management & Assessment

London • Sterling, VA

First published by Earthscan in the UK and USA in 2005
Reprinted 2006

ISBN: 1-83383-976-0

Typesetting by Saxon Graphics Ltd, Derby
Printed and bound in the UK by CPI Bath
Cover design by Danny Gillespie

For a full list of publications please contact:

Earthscan
8–12 Camden High Street
London, NW1 0JH, UK
Tel: +44 (0)20 7387 8558
Fax: +44 (0)20 7387 8998
Email: earthinfo@earthscan.co.uk
Web: **www.earthscan.co.uk**

22883 Quicksilver Drive, Sterling, VA 20166–2012, USA

Earthscan is an imprint of James and James (Science Publishers) Ltd and publishes in association with the International Institute for Environment and Development

A catalogue record for this book is available from the British Library

Library of Congress Cataloging-in-Publication Data
Environmental management in organizations : the IEMA handbook / edited by John Brady
    p. cm.
  Includes bibliographical reference and index.
  ISBN 1-85383-976-0 (hardback)
    1. Environmental management. 2. Environmental sciences--Information resources. I.
  Brady, John, 1945- II. Institute of Environmental Management and Assessment.

  GE30.E568 2005
  658.4'083--dc22

                                                        2004019977

Printed on elemental chlorine-free paper

Contents

List of Figures, Tables and Boxes

Figures

Tables

Boxes

About the Contributors

Introduction – Robin Bloodworth
Robin is the manager of the HSE training and consultancy team at Woodland Grange Training and Conference Centre, and programme manager for the IEMA Certificate Course in Environmental Management. He also lectures on the Woodland Grange/Oxford Brookes University MSc programme in Health Safety and Environmental Management.

Chapters 1.1, 1.2 and 1.3 – Dr Mark Everard
Mark has worked in sustainable development and aquatic sciences in the academic, private, public and NGO sectors, and in both the developed and the developing world. He has contributed to numerous government advisory groups, held offices in various associations and universities, and is a fellow of the Linnean Society. Currently with the Environment Agency, Mark also served for six years as director of science for the international sustainable development charity The Natural Step.

Chapter 2.1 – Paul Stookes
Paul is a solicitor, member of the Institute of Environmental Management and Assessment and chief executive of the Environmental Law Foundation. He is co-author of *Environmental Action: A Guide for Individuals and Communities* and editor of the environmental sentencing guidelines *Costing the Earth* published by the Magistrates' Association. He is currently working with the United Nations Environment Programme on its Global Judges Programme based in Nairobi and has recently been appointed as special adviser to the government's Environmental Audit Committee. Paul has published numerous articles in the environmental and legal press.

Chapter 2.2 – Pamela Barnes
Pamela is the Jean Monnet Principal Lecturer in European Union Studies in the Faculty of Social Sciences and Law at the University of Lincoln. Pamela has published extensively on European matters.

Chapter 2.3 – David Holland
David is an Associate in Eversheds' environment, health and safety team. He has worked for the Environment Agency as a regional adviser on contaminated land and as a national adviser on international waste movements, sitting on the agency's national waste lawyers group.

Chapter 2.3 – Paul Winter
Paul is a partner with the law firm Eversheds. He has practised environmental law for a number of years and has written extensively on the subject.

Chapter 3.1 – Dr Kim Polgreen

Kim has ten years' experience working with business and the public sector as an environmental manager and a consultant on operational and strategic environmental management.

Chapter 3.2 – Martin Baxter

Martin is technical director of the Institute of Environmental Management and Assessment. He is responsible for the IEMA's membership, professional standards and communications. He provides input on environmental management issues to national and international standards bodies and is the UK EMAS expert to the EU.

Chapter 3.3 – Christopher Brown

Chris is procurement strategy manager with the Environment Agency. Chris leads sustainable procurement development within the Environment Agency and also supports the UK Government and the United Nations in driving this agenda.

Chapter 3.4 – Robert Nuij

Robert is a senior consultant at Environmental Resources Management with over seven years' experience in research, policy development and project management related to product stewardship and environmental product development. Prior to joining ERM he was a policy adviser with DG Environment of the European Commission, responsible for the development of integrated product policy at EU level.

Chapter 3.5 – Helen Woolston

Helen is head of environment at the Engineering Employers Federation, which represents 6000 companies in engineering, manufacturing and technology based industries. She is responsible for leading lobbying campaigns to put forward the interests of manufacturing, and directing initiatives to promote best practice in environmental and sustainable development performance.

Chapter 3.6 – Judith Lowe

Judith is the author of a number of guidance documents on land contamination and is currently an independent consultant advising public and private sector organizations on strategic and site specific solutions to land contamination issues.

Chapter 3.7 – Mark Yoxon

Mark has over 22 years' international experience as a trainer and writer on environmental management and stakeholder dialogue. He was awarded a national certificate of excellence from IPPR/*The Guardian* in 2001. He has worked with numerous organizations from small businesses to EU policy making. He now divides his time between The Open University and *IN*FORM Training & Communication.

Chapters 4.1 and 4.2 – Karl Fuller

Karl is the director of the Centre for Environmental Assessment and Management at the Institute of Environmental Management and Assessment. He has over ten years' experience in quality assurance in EIA and SEA.

Chapter 4.3 – Professor Simon Pollard

Simon holds the chair in waste technology at Cranfield University and has a background in environmental risk management gained in industry, regulation and academia. Prior to joining Cranfield University, Simon was the Environment Agency's risk analysis manager with responsibility for developing and implementing risk analysis across the agency's remit and producing, with others, guidance on environmental risk assessment across government. Simon is co-author of the text *Risk Assessment for Environmental Professionals* published by Lavenham Press.

Chapter 4.4 – Sarah Cowell
Sarah is senior lecturer at the Centre for Environmental Strategy, University of Surrey and director of the Environmental Life Cycle Management Programme. Her other responsibilities include chair of the SETAC Europe LCA Steering Group and membership of the editorial board of the International Journal of LCA. Sarah is grateful to Roland Clift, Robyn Fairman, Ragnar Lofstedt and Barbara Nebel who co-authored many of the technical publications that formed the basis of this chapter.

Chapter 5.1 – Malcolm Pratt
During nearly 30 years with Entec UK Limited and its predecessor companies, Malcolm has conducted and led a wide range of environmental projects in a number of countries. Specific issues that have been addressed include air quality measurement and assessment, odour and dust nuisance assessment and environmental impact assessment. He has provided expert evidence on air quality and general environmental impacts at a number of public inquiries in England and Scotland including Manchester Runway 2 and Heathrow Terminal 5. He has given evidence to a Royal Commission on Environmental Pollution and to the House of Commons Environmental Committee.

Chapter 5.1 – Phil Crowcroft
Phil is director of contaminated land at Entec UK Ltd, leading a multidisciplinary team dealing with all aspects of chemically and radioactively contaminated land. Prior to joining Entec, he was the contaminated land policy manager at the Environment Agency.

Chapter 5.1 – Peter Garbett
Peter is the principal adviser on environmental regulation for Severn Trent Water Limited. He is a graduate of the University of Plymouth (Environmental Science) and University of Bristol (Water and Environmental Management), and has been employed in the water industry for ten years.

Chapter 5.2 – Dr John Pullen
John is a chartered chemist, a member of the Royal Society of Chemistry and an environmental auditor (IEMA). He has been with Casella Stanger since 1991 and his main roles are in the development of guidance on industrial air quality, and the assessment of environmental risk. He is also chairman of the Source Testing Association.

Chapter 5.3 – Martin Houldin
Martin is a director of Entec UK, responsible for the EHS group. He has 16 years' experience in environmental management, covering environmental reporting and performance benchmarking, ISO 14001 and EMAS accreditation and certification, environmental reviews, development of policy and strategy, auditing, training, management systems implementation (including integration with health and safety management) and sustainability management.

Martin wishes to acknowledge the guidance he received from Chris Hoggart and the University of Bath's Centre for Distance Learning.

Chapter 6.1 – Etienne Yves Butruille

Etienne is an associate at White Young Green Environmental Ltd. He has developed performance measurement and evaluation systems for environment and CSR issues in various industry sectors. His experience includes benchmarking, analysis of indicators and target setting processes, and the design and implementation of management systems.

Chapter 6.2 – Professor Rob Gray

Rob is professor of accounting and director of the Centre for Social and Environmental Accounting Research at the University of Glasgow. He is the author/co-author of over 200 books, monographs, chapters and articles – mainly on social and environmental accounting, sustainability, social responsibility and education.

Chapter 6.3 – Professor Brian Clark

Brian is professor of environmental management and planning at the University of Aberdeen. He is on the board of the Scottish Environment Protection Agency (SEPA) and chairman of its North Region Board. He is also a member of the Committee of Radioactive Waste Management (CoRWM) and chairman of the IEMA's Technical Committee.

Chapter 7.1 – Dr Martin Bigg

Martin is head of process industries regulation at the Environment Agency. After working in the chemical industry he became a field inspector before establishing the Government/Agency Local Authority Unit and the Pollution Inventory. He currently manages the development and delivery of PPC, emissions trading and the modern regulation of industry.

Chapter 7.2 – Dr Helen Byron

Helen is a policy officer at the Royal Society for the Protection of Birds (RSPB). Her work concentrates on environmental assessment and regional policy issues. Helen is the author of the RSPB's Biodiversity Impact report, which provides best practice advice on the treatment of biodiversity in EIA. She is also chair of the Biodiversity and Ecology Section of the International Association for Impact Assessment.

Chapter 7.2 – Robin Wynde

Robin is a biodiversity policy officer at the RSPB. His work is focused on the bio-diversity action plan process in the UK. He is also the nominated lead partner for the stone-curlew and edited *Biodiversity Counts: Delivering a Better Quality of Life* for Biodiversity Challenge in 2001. He has been closely involved in the development of biodiversity reporting mechanisms in the UK.

Chapter 7.3 – Charlotte Jourdain

Charlotte is a specialist in climate change. Having worked as the coordinator of the Climate Strategies network, and as a research officer at Imperial College, she is now a consultant at ERM. Her current work involves providing quantitative assessments of greenhouse gas emissions and policy analysis to companies and governments.

Chapter 7.4 – Malcolm Fergusson

Malcolm is a senior fellow at the Institute of European Environmental Policy, specializing in transport. Recent work has addressed various aspects of transport policy at both the European and national levels, in particular the application of transport policy instruments for environmental purposes.

Chapter 7.4 – Dawn Haines

Dawn is a research officer at the Institute of European Environmental Policy, specializing in transport. She previously worked for various local authorities as a travel plan coordinator advising businesses on transport issues.

Chapter 7.4 – Ian Skinner

Ian is a research fellow at the Institute of European Environmental Policy and has ten years' experience of working on various aspects of transport and environment policy at local, national and European levels.

Chapter 7.5 – Charles Neame

Charles is an agricultural economist who has worked for Cranfield University since 1992. He has a particular interest in rural development and the Common Agricultural Policy. Before this he and his family ran a farming business in Kent.

Chapter 8.1 – Dr Michael Mason

Michael is a lecturer in environmental geography in the Department of Geography and Environment, London School of Economics and Political Science.

Chapter 8.2 – Chris Sheldon

Chris is an international policy consultant, trainer and author on environmental management and sustainable development issues. He has been involved in the highest levels of Environmental Management System development for over a decade through standards institutions, professional bodies, NGOs and commercial application.

Chapter 8.3 – Professor Ross King

Ross is committed to the development of a sustainable management profession. He has worked in ITT/STC, Lucas, Bosch, Communications in Business, and more recently as the senior professorial departmental head at Warwick University. He co-founded the Brunel Management Environmental Programme (now called CSEM), which was the first and largest broad senior environmental management programme in Europe. He has recently played a leading role in developing an Integrated Sustainable Management Modular Masters Programme.

Foreword

I can recall two personal milestones in my career as a water engineer. Together they signalled the transition from apprentice to fully fledged professional. The first occurred in 1976, when I was 30. With my lunch packed and my family's best wishes, I caught a train to Edinburgh to attend the professional interview for membership of the Institution of Civil Engineers. I was seeking that MICE qualification that would permit me to become a chartered engineer (CEng). This was an important moment. I couldn't progress as an engineer without the qualification and the implied approbation of my peers. At the time, not being MICE, CEng would have left my career blighted, or at least that is how it felt at the time.

The journey to Edinburgh was spent rehearsing all the possible questions that I might be asked. Had I missed some fundamental learning point? Was I worthy of chartered status? Would I be accepted into the club as a bona fide engineer, or would there be – forever – a question mark over my professional competence? It was a nervous time – a moment of truth.

About a month after my interview I received the letter telling me that I had passed the test. This was a special moment and the interview and the letter opening remain vivid memories to this day. The tens of thousands of people who have experienced the achievement of a professional qualification do not forget these moments. In one sense they are the closing pages of a book called 'formal education'. You remind yourself that you have been accepted into an association that has made an enormous contribution to improving the wellbeing of people all over the world. It is easy for these emotions and this pleasure to be discounted to zero over the years; but in that moment, the sense of achievement is quite profound.

My second milestone occurred shortly afterwards. It was a less tangible experience but real nevertheless. I remember being called into a meeting at Northumbrian Water to answer questions on proposals being formulated at the time for the clean up of the River Tees estuary. The technical details are not now important, but my ability to answer all the searching questions to the satisfaction of the external scrutineers was personally significant. For the first time I felt in total command of the subject and confident that I could respond meaningfully and intelligently to any enquiry. And 'I don't know but I'll find out' became a response that I could dare to give. Whereas MICE, CEng was my external rite of passage, the River Tees clean up meeting was a personal validation of my competence. At last I had the personal conviction that I was up to the job and felt I had become a true professional. The sense of achievement of CEng felt earlier was supplemented with a new confidence – a quiet and deeply reassuring moment.

This then is the baggage I carry when the conversation turns to what it means to be an environmental professional, as it has done on many occasions during the intervening years of the IEMA's development.

In the early 1990s I became involved in the creation of the Environmental Auditors Registration Association (EARA), a sister organization to the Institute of Environmental Assessment (IEA). Within five years about 2000 members had taken the various EARA examinations and become associate, full or principal auditors, and the IEA had become one of the centres of technical competence in the new field of environmental impact assessment. At the time of the merger of IEA/EARA and the Institute of Environmental Management in the late 1990s, the combined individual membership had increased to 4000 – today it stands at over 8000. The institute's growth over the last ten years is a reflection of the increasing importance of environmental issues and, more generally, sustainable development in our society. The range of interests of our members has steadily broadened as environmental professionals have found themselves playing an increasingly important role in the affairs of public and private sector organizations in the UK and around the world. We are witnessing the emergence of an environmental profession.

In the 1980s and as a result of the European EIA Directive we became interested in defining good practice for environmental impact assessment. Because of this, most of the early environmental professionals worked for environmental consultancies and were engaged in advising industry and government on how this new legislation should be implemented. In the 1980s, the notion of an environmental practitioner certainly didn't exist inside my employer's organization, Northumbrian Water – although ecology and landscape architecture were valued skills and much of the water industry's work was concerned with improving the quality of inland, coastal and estuarine waters. At about the same time, auditing and environmental management were beginning to make their presence felt on the corporate landscape.

Twenty years ago, environmental skills were about interpreting legislation and monitoring compliance with emission standards. Today, the environment and sustainable development are diverse areas of study, as this handbook testifies. The environmental field embraces management processes such as ISO 14001 and the European Eco-management and Audit Scheme (EMAS). There are many more standards to monitor against and comply with. Technology has developed in step with these new demands. Market instruments are being used, for example in connection with climate change agreements and the UK packaging regulations. Social responsibility initiatives are seeking to extend corporate and public sector responsibilities beyond environmental considerations, and conceptual models of sustainable development have been developed that allow us to begin to understand how biological and man made systems interact in the round.

The transformation has been astounding. Twenty years ago, the environment as a corporate responsibility was virtually non-existent, whereas today most organizations employing more than 200 people cannot manage without an environmental practitioner. And the change in skills requirements has also been quite remarkable. Twenty years ago all that was probably required was the close inspection of one or two acts of parliament and some technical adjustments to industrial processes. Today, the territory of environmental practice is very substantial, as this handbook illustrates.

The handbook contains core primer material for those who wish to make a career in the environmental field. The environmental brief is now diverse because governments and society more generally are alert to the fact that all organizations impact on this world of ours in many complex and poorly understood ways.

My rite of passage in the engineering profession to MICE and CEng can now be enjoyed by environmental practitioners. MIEMA is an internationally recognized professional qualification and I have no doubt that MIEMA together with the new chartered environmentalist qualification (CEnv) will become important milestones in the careers of many thousands of people in the UK and overseas. Fully qualified environmental practitioners should feel proud of their work and achievements, and this handbook and the qualifications it underpins should be of value to large numbers of people. I hope you enjoy reading it or find it useful as a reference text. In any event, enjoy your contribution to society as an environmental practitioner – the world needs you to help steer a more sustainable path.

John Brady
Editor
IEMA

Acknowledgements

A considerable number of people have been involved in developing and writing this handbook. Jonathan Sinclair Wilson, a director of James and James/Earthscan, had the original idea. The first drafts of the scope and index were discussed with Jonathan and Martin Baxter, a director of the Institute of Environmental Management and Assessment. The handbook's overall shape and content is largely due to their early contributions. Members of the IEMA's staff and council were invited to comment at this stage and I am particularly grateful to Karl Fuller, Raymond Hill and Ian Housley for their contributions.

Two meetings were held with colleagues to discuss the scope and index in detail, and my especial thanks go to Martin Houldin, Glynn Skerratt, Frank Taylor, Helen Woolston and Mark Yoxon for their valuable contributions at this stage.

I am also grateful to Akan Leander and his colleagues at James & James/Earthscan for their thorough attention to detail in copy-editing and proof-reading this book. And thanks to Brian Marshall who kindly offered to cast an environmental practitioner's eye over the whole document and to Peta Marshall.

I also need to extend my copious appreciation and thanks to the authors who have given their time freely to write the chapters. The authors are listed separately. Without them, this compendium of environmental knowledge and practice would not have been possible.

John Brady
Editor
IEMA

List of Acronyms and Abbreviations

AAS	atomic apsorption spectometry
ACCA	Association of Chartered Certified Accountants
ACEA	European Automobile Manufacturers Association
ALARA	as low as reasonably achievable
ALARP	as low as reasonably practicable
ALGE	Association of Local Government Ecologists
AP	acidification potential
AQMA	air quality management area
AQS	air quality strategy
AURN	Automatic Urban and Rural Network
AWSG	area waste strategy group
BAP	biodiversity action plan
BAT	best available technique; or best available technology
BATNEEC	best available techniques not entailing excessive cost
BiE	Business in the Environment
BOD	biochemical oxygen demand
BOD (ATU)	biochemical oxygen demand (allyl thiourea)
BPEO	best practicable environmental option
BRC	British Retail Consortium
BREF	BAT reference document
BSE	bovine spongiform encephalopathy
BSI	British Standards Institution
CAP	Common Agricultural Policy
CAS	Community Advisory Committee
CBD	Convention on Biological Diversity
CCLA	Climate Change Levy Agreement
CDM	clean development mechanism
CEC	Commission of the European Community
CEE	Central and Eastern Europe
CEM	continuous emissions monitoring system
CEN	European Committee for Standardization
CEnv	chartered environmentalist
CFC	chlorofluorocarbon
CIRIA	Construction Industry Research and Information Association
CITES	Convention on International Trade in Endangered Species
CLEA	contaminated land exposure assessment
CMP	catchment management plan

CMS	Convention on Migratory Species of Wild Animals
CNG	compressed natural gas
COD	chemical oxygen demand
COMAH	control of major accident hazards
COP	Convention of the Parties
CoRWM	Committee on Radioactive Waste Management
CRI	Corporate Responsibility Index
CSEAR	Centre for Social and Environmental Accounting Research
CSR	corporate social responsibility
Defra	Department for Environment, Food and Rural Affairs
DETR	Department of the Environment, Transport and the Regions
DfE	design for the environment
DJSI	Dow Jones Sustainability Index
DNA	deoxyribonucleic acid
DOAS	differential optical absorption spectrometry
DoE	Department of the Environment
DoH	Department of Health
DQRA	detailed quantitative risk assessment
DTI	Department of Trade and Industry
EA	Environment Agency
EAC	Environmental Audit Committee
EAEC	European Atomic Energy Community, EURATOM
EAF	electric arc furnace
EAP	environmental action plan; or environmental action programme
EC	European Commission
EC	European Community
ECCP	European Climate Change Programme
ECD	electron capture detector
ECI	environmental condition indicator
ECJ	European Court of Justice
ECSC	European Coal and Steel Community
EDTA	ethylenediamine tetra-acetic acid
EEA	environmental effect analysis
EEA	European Environment Agency
EEC	European Economic Community
EIA	environmental impact assessment
ELV	emission limit value
EMAS	Eco-management and Audit Scheme
EMIS	environmental management information system
EMS	environmental management system
EP	European Parliament
EPA	Environmental Protection Act 1990
EPE	environmental performance evaluation
EQS	environmental quality standard
ERDP	England Rural Development Programme
EU	European Union
EU-ETS	EU Emissions Trading Scheme
FAO	Food and Agriculture Organization of the United Nations

FEE	Fédération des Experts Comptables Européens
FID	flame ionization detector
FMEA	failure mode effect analysis
FP	flame photometry
FSC	Forest Stewardship Council
FSOS	First Secretary of State
FTIR	Fourier transform infrared
GATS	General Agreement on Trade and Services
GATT	General Agreement on Tariffs and Trade
GC	gas chromatography
GDP	gross domestic product
GHG	greenhouse gas
GM	genetically modified
GQA	general quality assessment
GRI	Global Reporting Initiative
GWP	global warming potential
HACCP	hazard analysis and critical control points
HCFC	hydrochlorofluorocarbon
HCl	hydrogen chloride gas
HCV	health criteria value
HIA	health impact assessment
HMIP	Her Majesty's Inspectorate of Pollution
HPLC	high pressure liquid chromatography
HSE	Health and Safety Executive
IAF	International Accreditation Forum
IC	ion chromatography
ICAO	International Civil Aviation Organization
ICC	International Chamber of Commerce
ICJ	International Court of Justice
ICMS	integrated catchment management systems
ICP	inductively coupled plasma
ICP-AES	inductively coupled plasma – atomic emission spectrometry
IEH	Institute for Environment and Health
IEMA	Institute of Environmental Management and Assessment
IER	initial environmental review
IFC	International Finance Corporation
IFM	integrated farm management
IIP	Investors in People
IMPEL	Network for Implementation and Enforcement of Environmental Law
IoP	Institute of Petroleum
IPC	integrated pollution control
IPCC	Intergovernmental Panel on Climate Change
IPPC	integrated pollution prevention and control
IQA	Institute of Quality Assurance
IR	infrared
IRCA	International Register for Certificated Auditors
ISE	ion selective electrode
ISEA	Institute for Social and Ethical Accountability

ISO	International Organization for Standardization
ISPA	Instrument for Structural Policies for Pre-accession
ITEQ	international toxic equivalent
IUCN	World Conservation Union
JAMA	Japan Automobile Manufacturers Association
JI	joint implementation
JIT	just in time
KAMA	Korea Automobile Manufacturers Association
LAAPC	local authority air pollution control
LAPC	local air pollution control
LAPPC	local air pollution prevention and control
LA 21	Local Agenda 21
LBAP	local biodiversity action plan
LC	liquid chromotography
LCA	life cycle analysis; or life cycle assessment
LCM	life cycle management
LCR	land condition record
LEAF	Linking Environment and Farming
LGA	Local Government Association
LGC	Laboratory of the Government Chemist
LiDS	life cycle design strategies
LIFE	Financial Instrument for the Environment
LPG	liquefied petroleum gas
MAFF	Ministry of Agriculture, Fisheries and Foods
MBA	Masters Degree in Business Administration
MCERTS	Monitoring Certification Scheme
MDI	mean daily intake
MET	material–energy–toxicity
MPI	management performance indicator
MS	mass spectrometry
MSC	Marine Stewardship Council
NASA	National Aeronautics and Space Administration
NDIR	non-dispersive infrared
NDUV	non-dispersive ultra-violet
NEPA	National Environmental Policy Act
NGO	non-governmental organization
NHBC	National House-building Council
NHS	National Health Service
NO_x	oxides of nitrogen
NRA	National Rivers Authority
NVQ	National Vocational Qualification
NVZ	nitrate vulnerable zone
ODPM	Office of the Deputy Prime Minister
OEC	occupational exposure limits
OES	optical emission spectrometry
OECD	Organisation for Economic Co-operation and Development
OFR	operating and financial review
OHSAS	occupational health and safety systems

OMA	operator monitoring assessment
OPI	operational performance indicator
OPRA	operator and pollution risk appraisal
OU	The Open University
PAH	polycyclic aromatic hydrocarbon
PCB	polychlorinated biphenyls
PEBLDS	Pan-European Biological and Landscape Diversity Strategy
PID	photo-ionization detector
PM	particulate material
PM_{10}	particulate material up to ten micrometers in size
POP	persistent organic pollutant
PPC	pollution prevention and control
PPG	planning policy guidance
ppm	parts per million
PRN	packaging waste recovery note
PSE	producer support estimate
QA	quality assurance
QC	quality control
QUEST	quite useful ecosystem scenario tool
RBM	river basin management
RCEP	Royal Commission on Environmental Pollution
RE	river ecosystem
REACH	registration, evaluation and authorization of chemicals
ROC	renewables obligation certificate
RoHS	restriction of hazardous substances
RQO	river quality objective
RSPB	Royal Society for the Protection of Birds
RTPI	Royal Town Planning Institute
SA8000	Social Accountability 8000
SAC	special area of conservation
SBC	Scottish Borders Council
SEA	Single European Act
SEA	strategic environmental assessment
SEPA	Scottish Environment Protection Agency
SETAC	Society of Environmental Toxicology and Chemistry
SGV	soil guideline value
SIGMA	Sustainability: Integrated Guidelines for Management
SiLC	specialist in land condition
SMART	specific, measurable, achievable, relevant and time related
SME	small and medium-sized enterprises
Soc Env	Society for the Environment
SO_x	oxides of sulphur
SPA	special protection area
SPG	supplementary planning guidance
SPS	sanitary and phytosanitary
SRI	socially responsible investment
SS	suspended solids
SSSI	site of special scientific interest

STA	Source Testing Association
TARGETS	Tool to Assess Regional and Global Environmental and Health Targets for Sustainability
TCPA	Town and Country Planning Act
TDI	tolerable daily intake
TEC	Treaty of the European Community
TEOM	tapering element oscillating microbalance
TEQ	toxic equivalent
TEU	Treaty on the European Union
TNS	The Natural Step
ToA	Treaty of Amsterdam
TOC	total organic carbon
ToN	Treaty of Nice
TRIPS	trade-related aspects of intellectual property rights
TS	total solids
TSP	total suspended particulates
UKAS	United Kingdom Accreditation Service
UK-ETS	UK Emissions Trading Scheme
UN	United Nations
UNCED	United Nations Conference on Environment and Development
UNCLOS	UN Convention on the Law of the Sea
UNEP	United Nations Environment Programme
UNESCO	United Nations Educational, Scientific and Cultural Organization
UNFCCC	UN Framework Convention on Climate Change
UTF	Urban Task Force
UV	ultra-violet
VED	vehicle excise duty
VOC	volatile organic compound
WAC	waste acceptance criteria
WCED	World Commission for Environment and Development
WDA	Welsh Development Agency
WEEE	waste electrical and electronic equipment
WIA	Water Industry Act 1991
WISARD	Waste: Integrated Systems Assessment for Recovery and Disposal
WMO	World Meteorological Organization
WQO	water quality objective
WRA	Water Resources Act 1991
WSSD	World Summit on Sustainable Development
WTO	World Trade Organization
WWF	World Wide Fund for Nature
WWS	World Water Summit
XRD	x-ray diffraction
XRF	x-ray fluorescence
YWS	Yorkshire Water Services

Introduction

This handbook is a comprehensive and practical reference covering all the main components of environmental management in public and private sector organizations in the UK. The focus is on building a solid broad based foundation of environmental management knowledge. Its purpose is to inform the reader across a wide range of topics, and explain methods and approaches to analysing and assessing environmental issues. The handbook includes examples to illustrate good practice and it should become a major reference document for environmental practitioners. It will be a valuable aid to anyone involved in learning about or managing environmental affairs in organizations.

It is only over recent years that organizations have felt it necessary to appoint specialists such as environmental managers to advise and help manage environmental issues. Challenges facing organizations can range from having to comply with legal requirements of integrated pollution prevention and control (IPPC) to setting up environmental management systems to meet the ISO 14001 standard in environmental management. Many organizations also have to deal with specific issues including contaminated land, the climate change levy and packaging regulations. Wider issues also have to be addressed such as sustainable development and corporate social responsibility. Organizations have also started to realize the benefits of effective environmental management in terms of the cost savings that can be made – for example, the savings that can be achieved through effective waste and energy management initiatives.

The trend towards integrating environmental practices into everyday management has in many cases created a training need for the specialist and generalist. This handbook will be of benefit to specialists, generalists and line managers alike and in particular to anyone who is:

- in an environment related position in the public or private sectors, is about to take on environmental responsibilities, or wishes to develop an understanding of the issues. This person will be interested in taking the IEMA's associate member and full member assessments. They might have taken a National Vocational Qualification (NVQ) and have a desire to broaden their understanding of environmental management;
- a full time or part time student at the undergraduate or graduate level in an environmental subject or who is making the transition from another academic discipline. The student is likely to be interested in taking the institute's associate member open-book examination. The handbook and the further reading cover significant elements of the syllabus;

- working as an environmental consultant, as a lecturer or researcher in a university or as an employee of a non-governmental organization. This person could be working closely with public and private sector clients and is likely to want to understand the broad range of environmental issues that organizations have to address;
- a training provider in the private sector or in a university who delivers environmental training courses to people from a wide range of backgrounds.

The IEMA has been leading the way in setting standards and competency requirements for environmental practitioners. One important initiative has been the establishment of assessment criteria for entry into membership of the IEMA. There are several routes to associate (AIEMA) and full (MIEMA) membership such as completing an open-book assessment paper or achieving qualifications such as the IEMA Certificate in Environmental Management.

The open-book assessment route requires the completion of a series of carefully set questions that cover a wide range of environmental topics. The qualification and experience route involves sitting examinations and completing projects. In both cases this handbook provides essential information – the material will also be of benefit to many other practitioners ranging from students taking environmental management degrees through to line managers having to implement environmental management systems within their organization.

The IEMA recognizes that competency is not based on knowledge alone. The entry criteria for full membership also require candidates to demonstrate experience in environmental management and assessment practice, and practitioners aspiring to become chartered environmentalists (CEnv) will be well placed to achieve this new qualification by following the IEMA's individual membership routes.

The training requirements for environmentalists are forever changing and the IEMA has a Professional Standards Committee to oversee and advise on the professional development requirements of members. This committee is responsible, among other things, for ensuring that training reeds are identified, standards are set and ways of meeting those standards are established. This book is seen by the institute as a key step forward in providing essential information and support material to its members. It will also be beneficial to those who have a wider remit and wish to add to their existing specialist roles in areas such as health and safety and quality management.

A number of organizations provide training in environmental management and related topics in both the public and private sector. Environmental management can be studied at undergraduate and postgraduate degree levels in many universities and higher educational establishments. Some organizations specialize in training for environmental management by delivering general courses such as the IEMA Certificate in Environmental Management and specialist courses on topics such as environmental auditing, waste management and environmental due diligence. Details of courses and training establishments that have been notified to the IEMA are normally listed in the institute's bi-monthly magazine, *the environmentalist*, and they can be found on the institute's web site at www.iema.net/.

Finally, this book will be of interest to anyone involved in environmental affairs whether it be to assist in the development of in-house or external environmental courses or as support material for those developing their competence in environmental management. Everybody within an organization should have some training on the environment ranging from awareness of local environmental issues for all employees to briefing the board of directors on their environmental responsibilities.

We hope you will find lasting value from the material in this handbook. The aim is to help individuals become more proficient in the way they discharge their environmental responsibilities, and in doing so help to deliver a more sustainable world.

Robin Bloodworth
Woodland Grange

Section 1

Environment and Sustainable Development

Chapter 1.1

The Earth's Natural Systems

With in excess of 220 definitions at the last count, it would be easy to assume that sustainability and sustainable development were arbitrary concepts. Nothing could be further from the truth. The supportive environment of planet Earth, which provides for our needs, present and future, works in definite ways circumscribed by the fixed rules of natural law. Stray outside of those rules and the global system suffers, decreasing its capacity to support all of life, including human wellbeing and economic activities.

The origins of the Earth

Best estimates place planet Earth at around 10 billion years old, condensed from the hot gases that were the primary constituents of the solar system. All of the matter comprising the early Earth is still with us today. Sedimentation, precipitation and other processes began to settle out the heavier fractions of this homogeneous amalgam as the Earth took form and cooled. Life was not possible on this proto-planet. Indeed, for most of the Earth's history, life has been absent. However, as cooling, sorting and solidifying progressed over geological time scales, conditions were at last possible for the origins of biological life.

Life itself put in its evolutionary debut some 3.85 billion years ago. All organisms make their living through reacting with chemicals in their environment, inevitably changing the chemistry of the world in which they occur. The arrival of living things instigated a new phase in Earth's evolution. They increased the rate at which some types of matter became 'locked away' into the Earth's crust (also known as the lithosphere), away from the biosphere (or living component of the planet comprising the land surface and soil, water and the atmosphere). Biomineralization processes locked away substances like heavy metals and phosphorus, and carbon too was sequestered into deposits in the growing crust of the Earth as dead creatures sank in the deep oceans or were buried as part of ancient forests. The biosphere of planet Earth was becoming an ever more complex place, but also an ever more clean place as substances toxic to life forms became progressively isolated from the biosphere.

The constitution of the atmosphere and the formation of stratospheric shields against ionizing radiation from space are also products of the collective action of living things. Each organism shapes the environment of which it is an inextricable part, and is shaped in turn by that environment. The co-evolution of all life forms as elements of tightly interdependent ecosystems vastly accelerated the throughput and the efficiency of processing of material resources. The sustainability of planet Earth rests upon the diversity, adaptability and efficiency of the ecosystems that it supports.

The living system of planet Earth

This seething mass of life, shaped by the finite biophysical limits of the biosphere, constantly adapts to changing conditions as part of a single unified planetary mega-ecosystem, or biosphere. In effect, the whole biosphere can be compared to a homeo-static organism, each component of which acts to maintain the stability of the whole upon which its survival depends.

This concept of the biosphere as a contiguous whole lies at the heart of the Gaia theory. British scientist James Lovelock is well known as the prime proponent of Gaia, along with the American evolutionary biologist Lynne Margulis. What is less well known is that James Lovelock was at the time an atmospheric scientist, and his formu-lation of Gaia arose from NASA sponsored research about the most effective means for detecting life on other planets. The presence of life on Earth, argued Lovelock, could be detected from afar by the instability of its atmosphere – free oxygen to name but one such indicator of instability – caused by the collective action of living things. The same principle should apply elsewhere in the universe, providing a diagnostic feature of other worlds upon which life may exist, or have existed.

But, closer to home, this promoted the concept of a homeostatic Earth biosphere of closely co-evolved ecosystems and species, each contributing to and benefiting from the stability of the whole. This whole-system perspective is indeed central to thinking about the workings of the Earth system, and therefore for sustainability. To seek to understand any element of nature, of which humanity is but a subset, out of the context of its ecosystem (at whatever scale) is to misunderstand its very essence, origins and future dependencies.

The development of systems thinking as a discipline over the past four decades has unlocked new understandings of complex systems. Systems thinking is based on understanding the properties of systems as a whole and the relationships of their components. These patterns and relationships within complex systems cannot neces-sarily be deduced by analysis of their constituent parts in isolation. By definition, a system will have emergent properties that exceed the sum of the parts, such as the catalytic properties of enzyme molecules, the capacity for consciousness of the mass of human brain cells, or the ecosystem functions provided by river catchments. Systems thinking focuses on whole dynamic systems, and the first-order principles that govern them, aiding understanding about and enabling strategic decision making affecting the system as a whole. It is essential for true sustainable development, which depends upon intervening in the right way in the highly complex human-ecological system of planet Earth.

Natural laws and living organisms

One of the characteristics of living organisms is their dependence upon chemical trans-formations of one type or another. All living things are therefore agents of change within the biosphere of this planet, as well as reflecting the evolutionary pressures that the evolving Earth system places upon them. And, within the complex system of the biosphere, all components act to maintain matter in constant circulation through the net capture of solar energy. The laws of nature that relate to flows of matter and energy throughout the biosphere are therefore of particular importance to understanding the workings of the system as a whole.

All interdependent elements of the biosphere – be that a bacterium, elephant, ocean, or economic decision – are indissoluble and interdependent elements of the whole. All affect, and are affected by, every other element of material and energy flows. And all elements, as indeed all interactions between them, are subject to the rules of natural law.

The laws of thermodynamics, together with the principle of matter conservation, collectively form some of the most important principles for understanding the sustainable Earth system. The purpose of this chapter is not to analyse these natural laws in huge detail, but to provide a working understanding of how they operate within the natural world of which we are an indissoluble part.

In essence, the principle of matter conservation tells us that matter cannot be created or destroyed. Paraphrased, one could describe this principle as 'everything's got to be somewhere'. Matter does not just appear or disappear. According to this principle, atoms are not lost or created in chemical reactions, though they can combine into new arrangements (molecules). Equally, wastes emitted to the environment on the 'dilute and disperse' principle do not simply stop existing, although many policymakers act as if this were true. We'll return to this point later.

The first law of thermodynamics – energy cannot be created or destroyed – tells us that this conservation principle also applies to energy. Put simply, all energy has to come from somewhere and (with the exception of nuclear reactions as discussed below) cannot be created or destroyed, though it may change its form. Heat dissipated to the atmosphere does not 'go away', and all inputs of energy into a system have to have a source.

Collectively, the principle of matter conservation and the first law of thermodynamics are known as the Conservation Laws. Of course, Einstein's now-famous (if little understood) equation $E=mc^2$ tells us that mass (i.e. matter) and energy are interconvertible in nuclear reactions, and this is particularly important in solar processes. But, boring and non-relative as they may be, the good old-fashioned Conservation Laws remain perfectly relevant to every aspect of the planet's cycles, our day-to-day lives, and pretty much every conceivable business and organizational decision on this planet! They therefore represent a sound basis for sustainable decision making.

The second law of thermodynamics is a little more esoteric but, in layman's terms, can be paraphrased as 'matter and energy tend to disperse spontaneously'. Energy will tend to flow from high to low states. The embodied energy within matter, such as the energy inherent within chemical bonds, means that physical substances will also tend to disperse and degrade as that energy tends to be released and dissipated. Gases spread out and intermingle, nutrients entering a river tend to become diluted throughout the whole system, cars rust, and jelly babies scatter everywhere when you drop a bag of them down the stairs. There are profundities hidden in the second law of thermodynamics, but it can be paraphrased as 'there's no such thing as a free lunch!' This is because, for everything, there has to be a net input of concentrated energy, in the form of the embodied energy within the structure of matter or direct input of other forms of energy. The payee of energy bills is often invisible, but always present.

The embodiment of energy in matter is an important principle emerging from these laws. In terms of their constituent atoms, there is no difference between the contents of one jar containing glucose (a sugar) and a little oxygen and a similar jar containing carbon dioxide and water. Yet we know that sugar powers our bodies and that oxygen is essential for us to breathe. The difference between the contents of our two theoretical jars is the way in which the carbon, oxygen and hydrogen atoms are arranged. It is in the concentration and structure of matter that the energy is embodied, hence sugars can be burned to release energy or eaten to power our muscles and minds.

Nature's cycles

The ecosystems of planet Earth have evolved over billions of years to capture solar energy and to keep matter in circulation. Life not only changes the world around it, but also maintains the stability of the biosphere in which it has evolved. And the cyclic processes within the biosphere of planet Earth are of fundamental importance to its sustainable operation.

In crude but relevant terms, photosynthetic processes are nature's innovation for the capture of energy, converting it through a series of biochemical pathways into the bonds within sugar molecules. The constituent atoms of these sugar molecules are derived from carbon dioxide and water. A huge diversity of other complex organic chemicals are also produced by cells, but ultimately the building blocks include sugars and the 'energy bills' are paid by solar energy captured in molecular bonds. While it is true that geothermal energy and various 'deep space' wavelengths of radiation also reach the planet's surface, the only substantive net input of energy driving the cyclical processes of the biosphere is derived from the sun. This photosynthetic production of sugars from simple molecular precursors is summarized by the chemical equation:

$$6H_2O + 6CO_2 + energy \rightarrow C_6H_{12}O_6 + 6O_2$$

While plant cells are able to photosynthesize, all cells have to respire. In simplistic terms, respiration is the process by which cells 'burn' these sugars (and other complex organic chemicals) in the presence of oxygen, liberating the energy embodied in molecular bonds for use in cellular processes, and producing waste carbon dioxide and water. This is summarized in the equation:

$$C_6H_{12}O_6 + 6O_2 \rightarrow 6H_2O + 6CO_2 + energy$$

The two equations above are, of course, mirror images. They demonstrate the elegance of natural design, producing no net waste and maintaining matter in continuous cyclic use through the capture and release of energy. These two processes of photosynthesis and respiration are fundamental building blocks within the cycling of carbon through the Earth's biosphere. Naturally, the carbon cycle is far more complex than this, and its details are beyond the scope and purpose of this book. However, it is the net input of solar energy and its capture in the form of carbon based molecules that create the building blocks of life and provide the fuel that drives natural cycles. Excess heat is re-irradiated into the atmosphere during the hours of darkness, from where it 'leaks' off into space, ensuring that the earth does not overheat through absorbing too much energy – unless, of course, we accidentally build a chemical greenhouse to prevent the escape!

Just as nature's cycling of carbon is continuous and waste free, so too are the cycles of nitrogen, phosphorus, and other natural chemical resources. Even chemotropic bacteria (bacteria that produce energy from chemical reactions such as in the nitrogen cycle), while not exploiting sunlight directly, are ultimately exploiting solar derived energy locked up in the chemical structure of their molecular 'foodstuff'. These cycles of matter and energy contribute cumulatively to the complex, multi-layered oxygen-rich atmosphere that supports life on Earth, and within which meteorological and geomorphological (Earth-building) processes occur, all of this paid for by the capture and redistribution of solar energy.

Biological diversity

The term 'biodiversity' relates to the diversity of life forms from viruses to whales, to the genetic strains within these groups, to age structures within populations, and to the ecosystems and habitats to which they are evolved. Nature's biological wealth is immense, and indeed remains substantially uncharted. This is not merely because scientists have yet to plot every last square inch upon which life may occur. It is because we actually know very little about the small and microscopic forms of life which, cumulatively, may account for the overwhelming majority of living things on this planet. And not only do we know little about them, we know next to nothing about how they interact with other livings things around them and the chemical world in which they thrive. We know almost nothing, in other words, about what they do.

Filling in the basic skeleton of nature's cycles – the revolution of energy and matter between the poles of photosynthesis and respiration discussed above – is a food web of extraordinary complexity, comprising a filigree network of interlinked and interdependent food chains. This food web comprises a diversity of functional groups adapted to all manner of modes of life. This ensures that there are multiple connections throughout different parts of the web. Herbivores eat plants ranging in size from microscopic algae to woodland trees, their predators are in turn consumed by other carnivores, and all beasts are host to parasites of staggering diversity. As leaves fall, shredders break them down into bite sized chunks, and decomposers then degrade them further to constituent chemicals. Fallen animals and plants are decomposed by micro-organisms of many types. Coprophytes subsist upon the faeces of the living, and saprophytes on the bodies of the dead and dying. The microbiological entourage living on and in macroscopic life forms and structures are the foodstuff of many other organisms. And green cells then once again reconstruct broken-down matter into more complex and energy rich substances through the net capture of solar radiation.

A direct analogy may be drawn between biodiversity and the road network. When a few major motorways link the big population centres, why bother with the plethora of A, B, C and D roads, the network of smaller lanes, trackways, bridle paths and footpaths? The 'Highway Code' of natural laws provides a simple set of rules, but the diversity of pathways and the freedom to navigate them ensure endless flexibility and adaptability to changing conditions and needs. For biodiversity, this multiplicity is an evolutionary innovation ensuring highly efficient processing of natural resources, resilience to pressures upon the ecosystem without diminishing its carrying capacity, and adaptation to changing conditions on a moment-by-moment, daily, lunar, seasonal and longer term basis. And of course, aside from supporting local needs, if a major motorway is out of action for any reason, there are numerous other ways of getting to your destination.

All of this biodiversity is of critical importance, albeit that most of its details remain at best poorly understood. There are no such things as redundant links in food chains as all contribute, for good if incompletely understood evolutionary purposes, to the complex pathways through which matter and energy can cycle on a habitat, regional and global basis.

Biodiversity is not just important for what it is, but also for what it does. Species, genetic strains, and assemblages of them within habitats represent not only the products of 3.85 billion years of evolution, but also the players within an elaborate theatre of living things that maintain the functions of ecosystems. And it is these natural functions that all living things in turn depend upon, including humanity and all of its activities.

Human ecology

Some of the assumptions upon which Western culture is built are fatally flawed. One of these is the assumed separateness of humanity and nature, which is at best misjudged and at worse disastrous. This division was most famously defined by René Descartes in his oft-quoted insight, 'I think therefore I am'. (This wisdom was, in good existentialist fashion, revealed to Descartes while sitting in a dark bread oven! This Cartesian division between 'us' and the rest of nature is even 'branded' with the man's name.) However, it did not begin with Descartes. It is even written in Chapter 1, Verse 28 of Genesis, the first book of the Bible, in the instruction from God to Adam and Eve to, 'Be fruitful and multiply, and replenish the earth, and subdue it: and have dominion over the fish of the sea, and over the fowl of the air, and over every living thing that moveth upon the earth'. The flawed notion of separateness from, and superiority to, nature has deep roots in our cultural psyche.

The reality of human existence is, in reality, less exalted. We are of nature, an evolved part of a biosphere within which we remain fully dependent. At the molecular level, the DNA (deoxyribonucleic acid which bears our genetic code) of a human is only 2 per cent distinct from that of a chimpanzee. Every day, our dependency upon the natural world forces us to stuff plant and animal remains into our mouths as a raw fuel, to replenish 3 per cent of the water in our bodies with new molecules, to breathe 9000 times, and to plug into the 'grid' of energy provided by natural cycles. In exchange, we excrete the spent products from each of these activities as nourishment for other parts of our host planetary system. There is not one thing that we are able to do that is not fully dependent upon the natural world, and that in turn does not influence that world and all of the rest of humanity.

Humanity has a range of unique biological attributes, including the year-round capacity for reproduction, opposable thumbs, and an upright gait. Yet there is a non-physical type of uniqueness peculiar to humanity. The fact that I have written these words, and that you are reading and comprehending them, is part of that uniqueness.

Our big brains, supporting a capacity to manipulate not only tools but also information, are what give us our evolutionary edge. We are natural-born communicators, and in this we have learned to break the bounds of space and time by verbal, written, electronic and other means of communication. The accumulated wisdom of one generation is available to the next, regardless of spoken language or physical location upon this Earth.

For much of our evolutionary history, spanning some 100,000 years since the appearance of *Homo erectus* in the Great Rift Valley of East Africa, we have been pre-occupied by physical survival. The utilization and innovation of tools is often seen as a physical artefact of our evolving mental abilities, as we used our reasoning to manipulate the world around us to our own ends. This attribute is of course not uniquely human. Chimpanzees and Japanese macaques use a variety of tools and the spine- or splinter-using woodpecker finch (one of Darwin's finches of the Galapagos Islands) are among today's larger-brained residents of planet Earth who show some sophistication in tool usage. Some small wasp species even use pebbles to tamp down earth over their nests. It is what we've done with those tools and their continued refinement that marks a step change in human capability.

The development of agricultural practices in the Middle East and Egypt at least 10 thousand years ago marked a revolution in human ingenuity, bringing into cultivation and domestication various plant and animal species comprising staple foods. It signalled an evolution in consciousness to the extent that farmers' decisions were premised upon future yields of food, rather than merely its current availability. It also provided an incentive for the establishment of permanent communities, new levels of social structure and communication, and for the transfer of knowledge between individuals and generations. This consciousness clearly deepened throughout the Agricultural Revolution, with its rapid advances in the development of agricultural methods over roughly two centuries from the 18th century onwards, in response to demand for food from a rapidly expanding population.

Our industrial legacy

The forefathers of Western industrialization set assiduously to the task of applying Cartesian thinking as the foundation for the Industrial Revolution from the latter half of the 18th century. The very notion of 'progress' was indeed often explicitly defined as 'fighting' or 'taming' nature, and human progress was measured by the conquest of civilization over 'savage nature' and equally 'savage peoples'. It is perhaps no coincidence that the lands that were chosen for the process of 'civilization' held rich natural resources that fuelled industrial growth in home nations.

Developing society devised ever more clever means for manipulating the world around it towards its own ends. And, by exploiting and converting natural resources into products, huge and unprecedented advances in human health, wealth creation and material 'quality of life' were made possible. Agriculture was mechanized to free up people to work in factories, as urbanization and industrialization boomed cheek by jowl with the demand for urban infrastructure. Profound changes were wrought throughout the Industrial Revolution, and the benefits to society generated through that process were enormous and unprecedented.

However, there was a downside. Benefits were assessed through the prevalent worldview, which was utilitarian rather than informed by the workings of the biosphere. The inevitable implications of over-extraction and the generation of waste were invisible to the predominant cultural mindset of the 19th century, which held that nature was both bountiful and boundless. It is only in recent decades that we have begun to wake up to aspects of our industrial past, and its implications for natural resources, supportive ecosystems, those with whom we share the world, and our collective future.

Today, despite our greater awareness of environmental mechanisms and implications, the legacy of the Industrial Revolution mindset persists in the structure of our economic system, assumptions about resource use patterns, and governance systems. It also persists in our language. We talk of flood defence, pitting civilization against the perils of nature, despite the fact that the inclusion of the word 'flood' in the term 'flood plain' should at least give us a clue about the way in which those riparian flatlands operate! We 'reclaim' land that supports natural processes, and not our own economic purposes. We 'improve' grassland through drainage and fertilization, entraining it into agricultural production while degrading its biological diversity and the important ecosystem processes it performs. Even the term 'environmental protection' reinforces a division between civilization and nature, protecting 'it' from 'us' (and vice versa) as if we were not indissoluble parts of each other.

More insidious still is the extent to which Industrial Revolution assumptions about the 'separateness' of us and nature are still embodied in economic systems and habits of resource use. To set this in context, we have to remember that the human population of planet Earth stood at only half a billion people at the outset of the Industrial Revolution, and much of the world lay undiscovered by Western nations. Nature appeared boundless, its capacity to supply resources and absorb waste unlimited. The limiting factor to economic growth was human labour to power the machines of industry. Now, two-and-a-half centuries of progress later, these two sets of potential limitations are turned on their head. Global human population boomed to 2 billion by the 1930s, exceeded 6 billion in 1999, and is projected to reach 9 or 10 billion by 2050. We are most definitely not limited by human numbers! And, as discussed elsewhere in this book, we now know the natural world to be far from boundless in all of its dimensions. Indeed, we are overexploiting virtually all of its resources to an extent that, if left unchecked, is surely catastrophic.

Rediscovering our nature

Today, we are not playing by the rules of nature. Consequently, we degrade its integrity every day. Since we humans are inextricably a part of nature, we therefore unavoidably also degrade our world's capacities to support social and economic progress. Even in our most technological activities, it is nature that pays the bills and takes away the waste, at least as far as it is capable of so doing. We need to learn again that this is so and that, as co-dependants upon the integrity and wellbeing of nature, we overlook it at our peril. We need a new pathway of development that aspires to the sustainable workings of the natural world, our host and provider.

Our evolved capacity for communication and our accumulated collective intelligence provide humanity with the capacity to 'see' ourselves and our home planet as one whole interdependent biosphere. Indeed, for many, that first published colour photograph of the Earth in space, taken during the American Apollo space programme during the late 1960s, is an icon of humanity's growing self-awareness in the latter half of the 20th century. Collective consciousness and learning denote humanity's evolutionary leading edge, our physical form having hardly changed for 1000 centuries while our brains collaborate to map the globe, the solar system, and the structure of our own DNA, and to invent machines capable of exploring and exploiting them all.

There is a stark division between our recent destructive path of development and that required for future survival. This transition is one that calls upon our uniqueness – our collective consciousness, will and creativity – to discover new ways of thinking and acting together.

Further reading

Capra, F. (1983) *The Turning Point: Science, Society and the Rising Culture*, Fontana Flamingo Series, London

Lovelock, J. (1991) *Gaia: The Practical Science of Planetary Medicine*, Gaia Books, London

Suzuki, D. (1997) *The Sacred Balance: Rediscovering our Place in Nature*, Greystone Books, Vancouver

Chapter 1.2

The State of the Global Environment

All things are linked

The biosphere of planet Earth is a system of almost infinite complexity and variability within which all things, both living and non-living, are intimately interconnected. Every patch of earth or drop of water is host to a complex network of microhabitats. Different organisms within ecosystems are adapted to differing regimes of temperature, nutrient concentration, light level and countless other variables, succeeding each other in activity, and often in dominance, throughout changing seasons, lunar phases and times of day. Yet, within this pattern of constant change, all parts of the global ecosystem interact to maintain the stability of the whole.

Humanity too is an integral component of this Earth system, affecting and affected by its changing state. It is to be expected that humans, like all other species, should influence the world of which they are part. However, the activities of a burgeoning global human population are placing great pressures upon the Earth ecosystem. This chapter explores aspects of pollution, physical destruction, resource limitation and over-harvesting, and their ecological, economic and social effects. The facts and figures relating to the state of the Earth come from a variety of sources, listed at the end of this chapter, though special thanks must go to Lester R. Brown, president of the Earth Policy Institute, Washington DC, from whose book *Eco-economy: Building an Economy for the Earth* a substantial proportion is sourced.

Material behaviour within nature's cycles

The basic mechanics of the global ecosystem, and the features that make it sustainable, have already been summarized in the preceding chapter. It is instructive to review the fates of four sets of substances – heavy metals, phosphorus, nitrogen and organic matter – to understand two things. First, how substances flow through the natural world. Second, since pollutants are in essence merely resources out of place, to inform us about the potential modes of impact of substances when present in excessive concentrations. Life is impossible without key substances, yet it is a matter of distribution and concentration that renders them medicine or poison.

Heavy metals

As noted in the preceding chapter, billions of years of natural meteorological and biological cycling have resulted in the locking away into the Earth's crust of large quantities of heavy metals that were once in free circulation. Some heavy metals, such as copper and chromium, remain essential to living organisms as components of some enzyme systems, yet are toxic beyond trace concentrations. Living organisms continue to cycle metals at trace concentrations, maintained by slow releases from weathering of rocks, vulcanism, and other natural phenomena but counterbalanced by slow redeposit back into rock. Precipitation and biomineralization (this is biological activity that converts metals and other substances into inert forms) have effectively acted as a one-way flow valve for heavy metals over evolutionary and geological time scales, locking them away from the biosphere into rock. Any reversal of this flow resulting in increasing concentrations, locally or by diffuse accumulation, immediately poses hazards to ecosystems since cellular mechanisms have not become adapted to cope with higher concentrations than exposure levels throughout evolutionary time scales.

Phosphorus

Phosphorus is also present in low concentrations in nature, largely due to the clean up effect of the same mechanisms of precipitation and biomineralization. However, as a constituent of cellular energy transfer systems and many other biologically important molecules, phosphorus is an essential micronutrient without which living cells cannot function. Indeed, for various ecosystems (many freshwater ecosystems across the world are examples), low levels of phosphorus limit the productivity of plants and thereby the rates at which ecosystems cycle resources. There are in essence two interlocking phosphorus cycles: one operating at a geological scale and the other at an ecosystem scale. Over geological time scales, there is a net movement of phosphorus from land to the seas and back again as rocks weather; phosphorus entering the oceans eventually accumulates during rock formation on the sea floor, and tectonic movements raise crustal plates forming new land. Ecosystem time scales operate at a range of temporal (seconds to decades or centuries) and spatial scales, though all are extremely fast compared to geological time scales. Plant uptake of phosphorus from soils and water is in turn utilized by herbivores, carnivores, shredders, decomposers and other functional components of ecosystems. If phosphorus enters natural systems at anything greater than the slow trickle of geological processes, it tends to accelerate productivity and perturb the structure, integrity and function of ecosystems.

Nitrogen

Nitrogen is also an essential micronutrient, a structural component of proteins and many other biologically fundamental molecules, flowing through complex cycles throughout the food web. However, it differs from phosphorus to the extent that it is predominantly sequestered in relatively inert forms in the air, and not within the crust of the Earth. The molecular form of nitrogen is a relatively inert gas comprising two bonded nitrogen atoms, N_2, which accounts for approximately 79 per cent of the volume of the air. Many links in the nitrogen cycle are mediated by the activities of micro-organisms, including the fixing of nitrogen from the air into organic molecules and other bioavailable forms. Though essential for life, more reactive forms of nitrogen (such as nitrate or ammonia) are problematic when present in excessive concentrations. As for all essential micronutrients, anthropogenic (human-induced) increases over and above low natural concentrations can trigger runaway growth of plants and often catastrophic disturbances in ecosystems, particularly in marine waters where nitrogen is frequently the principal growth-limiting nutrient.

Organic molecules

Organic molecules are those composed substantially of a skeleton of carbon atoms. In considering nature's capture of energy in carbon bonds through photosynthesis and its release through respiration, we have already touched upon a key aspect of the cycling of carbon. Most naturally occurring organic substances, to which biota has become adapted over evolutionary time scales, are broken down readily by efficient enzyme systems. However, some less common but nevertheless naturally occurring organic substances are highly persistent by virtue of the inability of enzyme systems to break them down and reintegrate their constituents. Dioxins, furans, and a range of other families of complex organic molecules are produced relatively rarely in nature (for example in forest fires), and living cells are therefore poorly adapted to handle anything above minimal concentrations. Analogously, many man made substances tend to be poorly broken down by cells, since nature has not evolved specific enzyme pathways for substances not encountered during evolution. Those organic substances that nature cannot break down tend to be able to penetrate cells where, since they are not then metabolized, they tend accumulate. This phenomenon is known as bioaccumulation. And, worse still, predators suffer the cumulative concentrating effects of all organisms in downstream food chains, a phenomenon known as biomagnification. Obviously for fully man made substances, as well as human production of substances rare in nature, the potential for both bioaccumulation and biomagnification is significant. Neither would it be safe to assume that all relatively common natural substances are automatically entirely benign. For example, plants have evolved elaborate chemical defences to deter or disadvantage their predators, and so a range of chemical substances found commonly in plants can be toxic, disruptive to DNA, or exert oestrogen-mimicking effects (phytoestrogens).

Pollutants within the Earth system

Industrialized society has used substances in a cavalier fashion throughout most of its history, generally with little or no understanding of environmental fate and consequences. Only as symptoms have appeared have we tended to develop techniques to manage acute effects and establish safe exposure levels for various chemicals in common use.

It is important to understand how different categories of substances move through ecosystems, in terms of net inputs, ultimate fate and effects while in transit, to fully appreciate their impacts upon ecosystem health and stability. Based on the behaviours of substances outlined above, it is possible to understand how different categories of pollutants exert their adverse effects:

- For heavy metals, concentrations occurring naturally are now relatively low. And anthropogenic – or more rarely natural – increases in environmental concentrations, locally or regionally, can therefore have direct toxic effects. Unrestricted mining and release post use of metals threaten the vitality of the global ecosystem.
- For phosphorus, human activities that result in concentrations in excess of those low levels commonly encountered in nature can disrupt ecosystem balances, function and health. Many of the adverse effects of this phenomenon of eutrophication are known. Uncontrolled mining and releases into natural systems, such as through various industrial processes and agricultural or domestic applications, can have wide scale and long term effects, the implications of which may not be fully foreseeable.
- Nitrogen is abundant in nature, forming 79 per cent of the air, yet human activities that change the form in which it occurs can also radically affect competitive success within ecosystems, threatening integrity and functioning. Again, some of the known adverse effects of eutrophication provide examples.
- Large amounts of carbon have been sequestered into the lithosphere (the non-living rocky parts of the Earth) throughout history, resulting in a carbon concentration in the atmosphere that is substantially lower than that during much of the Earth's history. Human activities that liberate excessive quantities of stored carbon into the atmosphere, such as the release of carbon dioxide through burning of fossil fuels, threaten the functioning of the biosphere. Climate change is just one example of adverse effects resulting from this.
- Allowing the uncontrolled release of potentially persistent organic substances may result in increasing concentrations of these materials, and/or their breakdown products, in living systems. The effects of this may be long known (some forms of direct toxicity), long suspected but only relatively recently demonstrated (contribution to mutations or some forms of cancer), or largely unforeseen but recently discovered (such as the phenomenon of endocrine disruption in which substances mimic or interact with hormones). The full ramifications of these effects are often not known. And clearly we have been surprised many times in the past by such unforeseen effects as mutations induced by thalidomide, endocrine disruption, and so on.

In recent decades, sophisticated methods for assessing human health risk as well as ecotoxicology (i.e. toxicity to species or natural systems) have been developed. However, these tend to lack adequate precaution for fully sustainable decision making if used alone, as all depend upon analysis of known effects. And, as we have seen, many effects observed from pollutants have been formerly unforeseen. Many more undoubtedly remain to be discovered.

It is for this reason that a sound understanding of the Earth as an integrated system is essential, as the behaviour of substances in natural systems (and specifically the capacity for accumulation locally or at a wider scale) can give a better indication of the potential for adverse effects. From that ecocentric, or Earth-centred, perspective, any disruption to natural concentrations is a threat to the system as a whole, and therefore inherently unsustainable. This approach is used by sustainable development charity The Natural Step, as outlined in the next chapter.

Physical degradation of natural systems

Over much of our industrial history, human valuation of nature has been vanishingly small. We have instead, as discussed previously, regarded natural assets and their functions as inexhaustible sources for resources, places to get rid of waste, or places best improved by industrial or urban development. Any deeper concept of the value of nature, and particularly of the value of nature in our own long term survival and protection of quality of life, is (as we'll review in the next chapter) a surprisingly recent innovation.

If we view nature as limitless, then we can afford to pour concrete over it forever, and to over-harvest from marine, aquifer, forest and other resources. We can afford also to transfer alien species from one geographical zone to another in which they have not evolved as interdependent functional components. We can also afford to be cavalier in our use of agricultural land, regardless of the upstream cost of lost soil through erosion or downstream damage from siltation.

However, as we have seen, humanity has started the process (recently and arguably far too slowly) of loosening its historic attachment to these anachronistic views. And, as environmental disasters and resource scarcities slowly conspire to embed that awareness of our connectedness to natural systems, a new respect for nature will have to be embraced as fundamental to a new paradigm of human development with long term viability (known as sustainable development).

We will need to ensure that the systematic loss of natural systems – aquifers, freshwater systems, forests, soil, and so on – is abated and ideally reversed. We need to value the fact that nature is not just a fixed asset of 'nice green things' to look at. Instead, natural functions such as purification of air and water, formation of soils, provision of food and fibre are the primary resources underwriting our long term health, wealth creation and quality of life. When we look at a natural resource such as land or river corridors, we have to recognize that we are seeing an irreplaceable and multipurpose functional unit. Degrade its capacity to purify air and water, detain floods and retain water resources, produce food, support diverse ecosystems, and provide economic and aesthetic potential, and we degrade our future in a direct way. The corollary is that if we protect or restore it, we do the same for our own collective potential.

We are all part of the same living biospheric system, and the protection of physical resources is an urgent priority. The converse of this is graphically illustrated by the many examples throughout the remainder of this chapter.

The human population

The human population of planet Earth stood at only half a billion people at the outset of the Industrial Revolution. In the past century, global human population boomed to 2 billion by the 1930s, exceeding 6 billion in 2000. Demographers expect a billion more people to be added to the world population between 2000 and 2030, almost all of this increase in cities in Africa, Asia, and Latin America. Global population is projected to reach 9 or 10 billion by 2050. Today's population growth has no precedent, and is a largely unstoppable consequence of current pressures.

Yet numbers alone do not tell the whole story. Each person has an individual potential of direct relevance to the achievement of a sustainable world. Disempowerment, loss of creativity or denial of opportunity wastes this human potential, and sows the seeds of social unrest and overexploitation of resources. Poverty can therefore be measured not only in economic terms but also through access to resources. There are numerous indicators of equity of access to resources. For example, only 12.2 per cent of the world's population can access the internet, while traffic jams in Brazil waste 200 billion litres of fuel a year (according to the Research Institute on Applied Economics). Today, 1.6 billion people have no access to electricity, and 2.4 billion rely on unprocessed biomass fuels – straw, wood, agricultural waste and dung – for cooking and heating. Worse still, it is projected that, in 30 years, 1.4 billion people will still have no electricity, and 2.6 billion will rely on these biomass fuels.

Hydrological poverty, lack of access to adequate safe water for basic needs and economic activities, is a local form of impoverishment that is difficult to escape. This is particularly pressing in arid areas of the world, and where there is competition for severely limited resources. For example, if the Nile basin countries do not quickly stabilize their populations, they risk becoming trapped in inescapable hydrological poverty with all of its attendant risks of disease, human misery, constraints on economic and social progress, and conflict.

Overburdening an interconnected world

A burgeoning population also places demands upon the productive capacities of nature. There are serious question marks over the capacities of our home planet to sustain the ever more populous and resource hungry mass of humanity indefinitely. The World Wide Fund for Nature (WWF, 2002) estimates that the Earth has about 11.4 billion hectares (about a quarter of its surface area) of productive land and sea space, after all unproductive areas of ice, desert and open ocean are discounted. Divided between a global population of 6 billion people, this total equates to just 1.9 hectares per person.

WWF calculations suggest that the environmental footprint (resource demands normalized to an area of productive land) of the average African or Asian consumer was less than 1.4 hectares per person in 1999. This compares with the average Western European's footprint of about 5.0 hectares and the average North American's of around 9.6 hectares.

Energy use accounted for the fastest-growing component of the global footprint between 1961 and 1999, increasing at an average rate of more than 2.3 per cent per year. For the total human population of our planet in 1999, the average consumer used 2.3 hectares; 20 per cent above the Earth's biological capacity of 1.9 hectares. In other words, humanity's demands now exceed the planet's capacity to sustain its consumption of renewable resources. The unbending laws of science tell us that we can maintain this global overdraft only on a temporary basis before inevitable catastrophe. And this is before we factor in runaway population growth.

The remainder of this chapter collates information on trends in resources, environmental media and social progress. But, in interpreting each trend, we have to hold in our minds their interdependence. Just as no man is an island, no unit of the biosphere is discrete, no symptom of change stands alone, and feedback between them is an integral feature of the complex world of which we are a part. As noted previously in this chapter, if we degrade physical habitat, we also degrade its capacity to purify air and water, detain floods and retain water resources, produce food, support diverse ecosystems, and provide economic and aesthetic potential. Through feedback loops in the biosphere, there are intimate links between climate change, ozone depletion, bioaccumulation of pollutants, depletion of natural resources and the loss of biodiversity. And these in turn impinge directly upon scarcity of food and fertility of croplands, land use patterns and population pressures, education, access to contraception and other attributes of healthcare, and population growth. By degrading the environment, we degrade human potential, which in turn places ever greater stresses on the environment; a fundamental tenet that distinguishes sustainable development from basic environmental protection measures.

Trends in water

Planet Earth looks blue from space, largely because water covers two thirds of its surface and pervades the atmosphere in the form of vapour. Of this apparent abundance, only 2.5 per cent of the 1.4 billion cubic km of water on Earth is fresh, all but 3 per cent of which is permanently buried or frozen (much of this locked up in polar ice caps). The Earth's hydrological cycle constantly replenishes this fresh water supply. Six billion people and much of the world's animal and plant life depend upon this renewable resource of just 0.075 per cent of the Earth's water. Since much of that is seasonally or geographically inaccessible, it is estimated that more than half of what is actually available is used by humanity. As an essential solvent for all living processes, a sink for the residues of polluting activities, and a key natural cycle, the state of the water environment is a prime indicator of the sustainability of the Earth.

Yet, remarkably, water is a resource we continue substantially to take for granted, despite the fact that it has long been acknowledged as a limiting factor to human wellbeing and development worldwide. As living standards rise along with material expectations, concerns about water quantity and quality are set to increase. In some areas, especially cities, rapidly growing populations are making demands on water far in excess of available supplies. Even when there is sufficient water, distribution infrastructure can be woefully inadequate leading to inequities in access. An estimated 26 countries with a combined population of more than 300 million people currently suffer from water scarcity. By the year 2050, projections suggest that 66 countries, comprising two thirds of the world population, will face moderate to severe water scarcity. Today, about 1.2 billion people, a fifth of the world's population, do not have access to clean drinking water, while 2.9 billion people lack access to adequate sanitation facilities.

These factors combine to drive them downwards in a spiral of increasing incidence of disease, lost productivity and potential, and higher costs entailed in obtaining water.

Some of the world's major rivers are being drained dry, failing to reach the sea, and not all of them are in remote corners of the globe. One example is the Colorado, one of the major rivers of the south western US. In China, the Yellow River, the northernmost of the country's two major rivers, no longer reaches the sea for part of each year. In Central Asia, the Amu Darya sometimes fails to reach the Aral Sea because it has been drained dry by upstream irrigation demands. The Aral Sea itself is shrinking beneath the relentless sun in this semi-arid region. Since 1960, the sea has dropped 12m, its area has shrunk by 40 per cent and its volume by 66 per cent. Towns that were once coastal are now 50km from the water. If recent trends continue, the sea will largely disappear within another decade or two, becoming a geographic memory existing only on old maps. At a wider geographical scale, there is a threat to the balance of water fluxes between continents and oceans.

Natural ecosystems, especially wetlands and forests, capture water and stabilize seasonal flows, while recharging groundwater and improving water quality. They are also hotspots for both biodiversity and natural productivity. Conserving wetland ecosystems is vital to maintaining the supply of renewable fresh water, yet half the world's wetlands were lost to development during the last century. And, as we over-harvest the scarce resource of groundwater, we also pollute it. UNESCO estimates that there is a US$5 billion market in remediating contaminated groundwater and land throughout Europe, reflecting greater hidden costs from issues 'out of sight and out of mind'. Pollution from agriculture, industrial and municipal sewage, and salinization from irrigation have also reduced the availability of clean fresh water.

The world is also running up a water deficit as rising development pressures across the world are leading to both surface waters and aquifers running dry. Irrigation problems are as old as irrigation itself, but the new threat that has evolved over the last half-century with the advent of powerful diesel and electrically driven pumps dwarfs yesterday's risks. The over-pumping of aquifers, now commonplace on every continent, has led to falling water tables as pumping exceeds natural recharge rates. Water reserves are being used up or polluted faster than they can be replenished. Around 1.5 billion people today are reliant upon groundwater for drinking, and 10 per cent of people's water consumption worldwide is from depleting groundwater. Falling water tables are occurring over large expanses of all key food-producing countries. Under the North China Plain, which accounts for 25 per cent of China's grain harvest, the water table is falling by roughly 1.5m per year; probably much faster in some places. The same thing is happening under much of India, particularly the Punjab, the country's breadbasket. In the US, water tables are falling under the grain-growing states of the southern Great Plains, shrinking the irrigated area. Today, 480 million of the world's 6.1 billion people are being fed with grain produced by over-pumping aquifers. Drop by drop, the long term implications for the sustainability of the aquifers, together with potential for food production, are ominous.

We live in a water challenged world, one that is becoming more so each year as 80 million additional people stake their claims to the Earth's water resources. The situation promises to become far more precarious, since most of the 3.2 billion people being added to world population by 2050 will be born in countries already facing water scarcity. With 40 per cent of the world food supply coming from irrigated land, water scarcity directly affects food security. If we are facing a future of water scarcity, we are also facing a future of food scarcity and one that is increasingly threatening for wildlife.

Urgent action is needed. In recent years, water issues have received higher prominence. These include, for example, the resolutions of the World Summit on Sustainable Development (WSSD) and the World Water Forum (Kyoto, 2003). One of the key agreements at the WSSD was a target to halve the number of people without access to adequate sanitation (now 2.4 billion people) by 2015. 2003 was designated by the United Nations as the International Year of Freshwater, the aim of which was to focus attention on protecting and respecting our water resources, as individuals, communities and countries. Although the UK does not face the severe water problems experienced in many other countries, there is no room for complacency. Pressures such as new development, climate change and excessive domestic consumption are substantial and increasing, particularly in the south east of the country where the water environment is already most significantly overstretched.

Biodiversity struggling on

If water is a key indicator of the effects of human development, and the space available for humanity and all species sharing this planet, then the biological diversity of the Earth is a direct 'read out' of society's impacts upon its home planet. The omens are not good.

With each update of its *Red List of Threatened Species*, the World Conservation Union (IUCN, 2000) charts an increase in all categories of critically endangered species. The 2000 IUCN assessment reveals one in eight of the world's bird species is in danger of extinction, about 70 per cent of bird species are declining in numbers, 10 (out of 17) species of penguins are threatened or endangered, and a quarter of the mammals and one third of fish species face extinction. The bushmeat trade together with progressive habitat loss exacerbates the situation for chimpanzee species, as for example in West and Central Africa where 97 per cent of bonobos (the species most closely related to humans) have disappeared in less than a human generation.

A major, yet commonly underestimated, threat to organisms of all types is the introduction of alien species, which can alter local habitats and communities, driving native species to extinction. Although this phenomenon is as old as human adventure, for example the impacts of introduced rats on island ecosystems or the deliberate introduction of European foxes to Australia, the pace of species transfers around the world seems to be quickening dramatically. One consequence of globalization, with its expanding international travel and commerce, is that more and more species are being accidentally or intentionally brought into new areas, where natural controls are absent, and are thriving to the detriment of established ecosystems. Thirty per cent and 15 per cent respectively of bird and plant species on the IUCN Red List are threatened by non-native species.

No one knows how many plant and animal species there are on Earth today, though current estimates range from 6 million to 20 million species with the best working estimates falling between 13 million and 14 million. It is impossible to fully quantify the biological effects of the most recent explosion in human economic activities, since we know even less about the number of species and their global and local distribution, that occurred a half-century ago. We can measure losses where we have something approaching a complete inventory of species, such as for birds. However, for the many groups of small organisms, whose species number in the millions (such as insects), only a fraction have been identified, described and catalogued. We understand far less about their roles within ecosystems, their potential as a source of pharmaceuticals or other resources, and the consequences of their loss. We know virtually nothing about microbial diversity and function, beyond the fact that it is precisely these 'bugs' that are the major players in the functioning of global cycles.

Best estimates place the current species extinction rate at least 1000 times higher than the background rate. Irreplaceable species and ecosystem services, the products of 3.85 billion years of evolutionary fine-tuning, are being expunged by the march of technological progress over infinitesimally small time scales. As its diversity diminishes, nature's capacity to support the growing needs of humanity shrinks. Nature's larder, pharmacy, supply cupboard and cleansing service are depleted, depriving future generations of new discoveries, potential for sustenance, economic opportunity, heritage and quality of life.

Shrinking earth, vanishing forests, barren oceans and empty food baskets

As a consequence of short term exploitation eroding long term interests, the loss of topsoil from wind and water erosion now exceeds the natural formation of new soil over large areas of the world, gradually draining the land of its fecundity. These trends are converging to form increasingly large dust storms, such as the huge dust plumes that now commonly shade out the sun in cities of north east china.

Once, the land masses of the world were dominated by 'climax vegetation', comprising substantial tree cover. Today, forests are disappearing under the chainsaw and intensive agricultural practices at manifestly unsustainable rates. Worldwide, forests are shrinking by over 9 million hectares (an area equal to Portugal) every year. Over-harvesting of forests is common in many regions, particularly south east Asia, west Africa, and the Brazilian Amazon. After losing 97 per cent of the Atlantic rainforest, Brazil is now destroying its Amazon rainforest. This huge forest, roughly the size of Europe, was largely intact until 1970. Yet, by 2000, 14 per cent had been lost, with 17,000 square km deforested in 1999 alone. The past decade has witnessed fires on an unprecedented scale in the tropical forests of Brazil and Indonesia.

Wood may be an economically valuable asset to harvest, yet deforestation can be costly. As reported in *China Daily* (1 September 1998) and reviewed in *Watersheds of the World* (Worldwatch Institute, 1998), unprecedented flooding in the Yangtze River basin during the summer of 1998 drove 120 million people from their homes. Although initially referred to as a 'natural disaster', the removal of 85 per cent of the original tree cover in the basin had left little vegetative cover to hold the heavy rainfall, and the surge of storm water, no longer slowed and stored by mature forests, carried with it huge quantities of topsoil, the core resource of agriculture. Today, these hidden environmental and social costs, referred to as externalities, are almost wholly excluded from commercial decision making. For example, a case study involving Madagascan rainforests revealed that conservation generated significant benefits over logging and agriculture locally and globally, yet logging continued, driven by greater incentives at the national scale. Such perverse economic signals continue to exacerbate tropical deforestation and wetland loss worldwide, even where we can already foresee the long term harm they may produce. The principle applies equally in catchment and coastal management, where most of the benefits of good practice accrue to a range of other users of catchments who may not pay for the actions that deliver them. More sophisticated economic tools are essential if sustainable management is to be realized.

It is commonly agreed that two thirds of oceanic fisheries are now being fished at their sustainable yield or beyond. Many are collapsing, or have already done so. The FAO (Food and Agriculture Organization of the UN) report *The State of World Fisheries and Aquaculture 2000* (FAO, 2000) reviews the doleful tale of the Newfoundland 'Grand Banks' cod fishery. This rich fishery had been supplying fish for centuries, yet in 1992 collapsed abruptly. This cost an estimated 40,000 Canadians their jobs. A decade later, the fishery has yet to recover despite a subsequent ban on fishing.

The addition of 80 million people a year to world population at a time when water tables are falling suggests that food supplies may be a vulnerable link between environment and economy. An estimated 70 per cent of the water consumed worldwide, including that diverted from rivers and pumped from underground, is used for irrigation. Of the remainder, 20 per cent is used by industry and 10 per cent for residential purposes. In the increasingly intense competition for water among these three sectors, the economics of water do not favour agriculture. Neither do they favour the continued existence of viable sources of water, the ecosystems that depend upon it, and long term human wellbeing dependent upon these ecosystems.

It is not just how much a growing population consumes that should concern us, but also what those people eat. A US diet, rich in livestock products, requires four times as much grain per person as a rice based diet in a country like India. Using four times as much grain means using four times as much water, greater demands for energy, fertilizers and other agrochemicals, and pressures upon the land with widespread consequences for wildlife and soil health. As overexploitation of water, ecosystems and soils compromises the viability and fertility of the land, so too these impacts affect the climate, and in turn the resilience of the land in the face of changing climate. We are literally planting the seeds of a vicious cycle, unravelling the very web of life upon which humanity depends.

Caught in the cross-winds

We've examined some aspects of the carbon cycle in the preceding chapter. Atmospheric carbon in the form of carbon dioxide (CO_2) plays an important role in making this planet habitable. The term 'greenhouse effect' was first coined by Swedish scientist Svante Arrhenius, yet the effect itself was first predicted in 1827 by French mathematician Joseph Fourier. This effect is a phenomenon of the Earth's atmosphere by which solar radiation, reaching the inner atmosphere and re-emitted from the Earth's surface, is prevented from escaping by various gases acting much like the glass in a greenhouse. The main naturally occurring 'greenhouse gases' are carbon dioxide, methane and water vapour. The result is a rise in the Earth's temperature above that which could be predicted from its distance from the sun alone. This warming effect enables the existence of water in its liquid form, itself supporting the genesis and proliferation of living things on this planet. Nature's cycles maintain greenhouse gases in balance, contributing to the stability of the atmosphere.

Today, the concentrations of many greenhouse gases are rising sharply. Fossil fuel consumption and forest fires are the main causes of carbon dioxide build up, with methane a byproduct of agriculture (predominantly from rice, cattle and sheep). Prior to the start of the Industrial Revolution in the 18th century, CO_2 emissions from the burning of fossil fuels were negligible, and the atmospheric CO_2 concentration was estimated at 280 parts per million (ppm). By 1950, global emissions of CO_2 from fossil fuel burning had reached 1.6 billion tonnes per year, a quantity that was already boosting the atmospheric CO_2 level. In 2000, CO_2 emissions totalled 6.3 billion tonnes, boosting mean atmospheric concentrations to 370 ppm, a rise of 32 per cent from pre-industrial levels, with the rate of increase now estimated at 0.5 per cent per year and rising. The build up of atmospheric CO_2 from 1960 to 2000 of 54 ppm far exceeded the 36 ppm rise from 1760 to 1960. Atmospheric CO_2 levels have risen each year since annual measurements began in 1959, making this one of the most predictable of all environmental trends. The concentrations of other greenhouse gases also give cause for concern. Chlorofluorocarbon levels are rising by 5 per cent a year, and nitrous oxide levels by 0.4 per cent a year.

The resulting rise in atmospheric CO_2 levels is widely believed by atmospheric scientists to account for the fact that, up to 2000, the 14 warmest years since record keeping began in 1866 had all occurred since 1980. While the geological record shows that climatic changes have taken place regularly, most notably during the ice age, modern climatic changes are occurring at an unprecedented rate and appear to be linked to increasing levels of pollution in the atmosphere. Over the last three decades, global average temperature has risen from 13.99°C in 1969 to 1971, to 14.43°C in 1998 to 2000; this represents a gain of 0.44°C. The United Nations Environment Programme estimates that, by 2025, average world temperatures will have risen by 1.5°C with a consequent rise of 20cm in sea level.

Rising temperatures lead to more extreme climatic events including, for example, record heat waves, the melting of ice, rising sea level and more destructive storms. Evidence of the effects of warming and climate change is everywhere. The July 1995 heat wave in Chicago, when temperatures reached 38 to 41°C on five consecutive days, claimed more than 500 lives and helped shrink the 1995 US corn harvest by some 15 per cent, or US$3 billion. There has been a recorded rise of about 1°C in the temperature of the world's oceans during the 1980s. Arctic ice was 6 to 7m thick in 1976 and had reduced to 4 to 5m by 1987. On 19 August 2000, the *New York Times* reported that an icebreaker cruise ship had reached the North Pole only to discover this famous frozen site was now open water. The Arctic sea ice has thinned from nearly 2m thick in 1960 to scarcely 1m in 2001. Some scientists predict that, within 50 years, the Arctic Ocean could be ice free during the summer. In Europe's Alps, the shrinkage of the glacial volume by more than half since 1850 is expected to continue, with these ancient glaciers largely disappearing over the next half-century.

All of this extra water has to go somewhere, and contributes substantially to the phenomenon of sea level rise. During the 20th century, sea level rose by 10 to 20cm, more than half as much as it had risen during the preceding 2000 years. If current estimates are correct, sea level could rise by as much as 1m during the 21st century, with the coastline retreating, on average, by 1500m and some smaller islands becoming uninhabitable.

A further consequence of higher temperatures is more energy driving storm systems. From 1920 until 1970, there were an estimated 40 major storms per year but, since 1985, the northern hemisphere has experienced close to 80 storms a year; a doubling in less than a generation. With rising frequency has also come increasing force and consequent economic damage, such as the three powerful and damaging winter storms in France in December 1999 or 1998's Hurricane Georges in Central America. As a consequence of higher-energy storms and other phenomena relating to climate change, natural disasters are on the increase. Munich Re, one of the world's largest reinsurance companies, reported that three times as many great natural catastrophes occurred during the 1990s as during the 1960s. Economic losses increased eightfold. Insured losses multiplied 15-fold. The CGMU Insurance Group (Britain's largest) reported in 'Environment News Service' (24 September 2000) that property damage worldwide is rising at roughly 10 per cent a year. We may only just be beginning to see the economic fallout from climate change. At this rate of growth, by 2065 the amount of damage would exceed the projected gross world product; well before then, the world would face bankruptcy. As Lester Brown, president of the Earth Policy Institute, suggests, 'Nature was levying a tax of its own on fossil fuel burning'.

An apparently small temperature rise in sea surface water of less than 1°C can lead to the effect of 'coral bleaching', the mass death of corals which has already devastated huge areas of reefs in the Caribbean, Indian, and Pacific Oceans. If the reefs continue to die, oceanic ecosystems will be altered, directly affecting the fisheries that depend on the coral reefs as nursery grounds. And, as fisheries fail, in both tropical and temperate waters, we travel further to exploit remaining grounds, increase the potential for conflict, drive the land ever harder to produce farmed crops to make up the shortfall in protein and other essential food groups, and all the while expend more energy which feeds back in turn to climatic instability.

At the 1992 Earth Summit, it was agreed that, by 2000, countries would stabilize carbon dioxide emissions at 1990 levels. However, to halt global warming, emissions would probably need to be cut by 60 per cent (with some authorities calling for an 85–90 per cent cut in developed countries to allow the developing world to catch up in economic and technological terms). We eagerly await substantive action to honour these commitments, while simultaneously counting the rising cost of our legacy.

The human cost

The conflict between the economy and Earth's natural systems can be seen in daily news reports of collapsing fisheries, shrinking forests, eroding soils, deteriorating rangelands, expanding deserts, rising carbon dioxide levels in the atmosphere, falling water tables, rising temperatures, more destructive storms, melting glaciers, rising sea level, dying coral reefs and disappearing species. For the first time since civilization began, sea level has begun to rise at a measurable rate, threatening habitation of low-lying islands and land (including many major cities). It also raises questions of intergenerational responsibility that humanity has never before faced, at least not consciously. These trends mark an increasingly stressed relationship between the economy and the Earth's ecosystem, and exact a growing economic and human toll.

At some point, these trends will, without radical overhaul of our economic and resource use habits, overwhelm the capacity for further human progress and economic prosperity worldwide. The window of opportunity is tight, if we wish to change our dangerous trajectory of development. To remind us that this is more than mere rhetoric, we can look back to many earlier civilizations, such as Easter Island, the Aztecs and Incas, that outstripped their resources only to subsequently implode due to resource starvation. The difference is that never before has this threat occurred at the present scale, affecting the total global ecosystem, and within the understanding of contemporary science. The evidence is that we are a long way overdrawn upon nature's capacity to underwrite our survival and prosperity.

Money makes the world go around

The global economy has expanded sevenfold since 1950, raising output from US$6 trillion of goods and services to US$43 trillion in 2000, and boosting living standards to levels not dreamed of before. Growth in the world economy during the year 2000 exceeded that during the entire 19th century. Yet what does the transfer of all this money actually mean?

As we have seen from the view of Earth as an internally interdependent system, there are at core only two types of capital resources underpinning the totality of production and trading: natural resources and human resources (both toil and creativity). Bales of hay, sacks of wheat, sand (silicon) chips in our computers, biologically derived oil, and all such resources are ultimately a manifestation of nature's productive and supportive cycles, put together into socially useful and economically valuable products by people. Economic systems evolved from the barter of skills, labour and produce, all with a biophysical basis underwritten by these fundamental capitals.

Today, the majority of global trade is in things that do not exist. Speculation on likely future market values creates profit out of thin air, largely divorced from the biophysical realities supporting the world. A sack of wheat degrades in quality over time, reflecting the inevitable effects of entropy upon natural resources. Conversely, a financial debt accrues interest in diametric opposition to the forces of nature upon the physical resources underpinning the economy. If I lend you US$3 to buy a bag of wheat, you will owe me US$6 by the time you have eaten it! And, to compound the situation still further, market values can place a figure on the value of exploitable timber but not upon the biodiversity, production of fresh air and water, climate and hydrological regulation, amenity and heritage value of old forests. Today, some US$2 trillion per day of trade flashes across computer screens worldwide, 97 per cent of which is speculation. We have a system geared to making the rich (lenders such as developed-world banks) richer as the poor (in inner cities or the developing world) toil to pay back interest on debt by producing and trading non-durable commodities, while all the while irreplaceable ecosystem services are liquidated for short term financial gain.

Our contemporary model of economic growth has lost its connection to the real world of natural and human productivity. It is also subsidized by the burning of vast quantities of artificially cheap fossil fuels, exploitative trade relationships and a host of other externalities (economic dependencies that are not reflected in market values). The market substantially fails to tell the ecological and human truth. Compare, for example, the cost of wind-generated electricity with that from a coal-fired power plant. The cost of the wind-generated electricity reflects the costs of manufacturing the turbine, installing it, maintaining it and delivering the electricity to consumers. The cost of the coal-fired electricity includes building the power plant, mining the coal, transporting it to the power plant and distributing the electricity to consumers. What it does not include is the cost of climate disruption (contribution to more destructive storms, melting ice caps, rising sea level, record heat waves, etc.) caused by carbon emissions from coal burning, nor damage to freshwater lakes and forests from acid rain, or the healthcare costs of treating respiratory illnesses caused by air pollution. Thus the market price of coal-fired electricity greatly understates its cost to society.

Without fundamental reform, the consequences of our current economic progress can only be more intense heat waves, more destructive storms, melting ice caps, a rising sea level, depletion of resources, shrinkage of productive land area, and growing social inequities. We need a wholesale shift in worldview, in how we think about the relationship between the Earth and the economy. Economists may, today, see the environment as a subset of the economy, to be paid for and protected on the back of profitable activities, but the realities apparent to ecologists reveal the economy as a fully dependent subset of the environment.

Our common destiny

We share one world, fragile yet endlessly renewable provided its natural limits are respected. We can choose collectively to allow it to support us indefinitely – or in other words sustainably – or else suffer together where we overrun its supportive capacity. Ensuring access to basic resources and improving the health and livelihoods of the world's poorest people cannot be tackled separately from maintaining the integrity of natural ecosystems. In the face of high and rising population, allied with resource hungry habits, this quest for sustainability is ever more pressing and ever more difficult.

Sensible long term policies seem elusive. For example, in 1994, the Chinese Government decided that the country would develop an automobile-centred transportation system. However, if Beijing's goal were to materialize, and the Chinese were to have one or two cars in every garage and consume oil at the US rate, China would need over 80 million barrels of oil a day; slightly more than the 74 million barrels per day the world now produces. We are learning that the Western industrial development model is not viable for China, simply because there are not enough resources for it to work. We seem to be learning, albeit at a slower pace, that it has no long term viability in the West either. The portents are ominous, and the responses of the educated world appear far from educated.

Immersion in too many scary facts and figures about our current plight and ongoing trends does run the risk of 'rabbit in the headlights' syndrome: a paralysis of action in the face of the insurmountable. But, in the face of the apparently impossible, human nature also seeks solutions, and the chinks of light in the darkness. Are there any crumbs of optimism? Maybe a few.

We have the resources to tackle at least some of the most pressing sustainability problems. For example, it would cost about US$200 billion to supply clean drinking water and sanitation for every village, town and city on the planet. This is roughly the same amount of money that is spent on advertising in the US every year. The resources are there, but maybe not yet the will to make the transition from short term self interest to collective survival.

To date, our collective response to the pressing challenge of sustainability has been slow, but it is evident and steady. Worldwide, renewable energy production and use is soaring as exemplified by the tenfold and sevenfold growth in wind and solar power respectively in the last decade. By comparison, in 1902, petroleum accounted for about 2 per cent of total supply, but was already expanding quickly in niche markets. Today, renewable energy also accounts for about 2 per cent of total generation, with wind and solar energy markets now doubling in size every three years. Its growth is on the scale of the internet or mobile phones, with manufacturers able to scale up production and drive down costs. We seem to be seeing the turning of the technological tide, concerns about some aspects of renewable energy production notwithstanding.

And in places we can also agree upon a common good. For example, if India, which shares the River Ganges with Bangladesh, were to use all the water that it wants, the Ganges might not even reach Bangladesh during the dry season. But fortunately, a treaty has been signed that allocates an agreed-upon amount of water to Bangladesh.

We have the capacities for agreement, scientific understanding and economic refor- mation to make a progressive transition to a sustainable path of development. It may be difficult, but then we have to reflect that it seemed impossible only 20 years ago, and 30 years ago we were barely aware of needing a new pathway at all! In the following chapter, we will review some of the positive movements of society towards sustain- ability, and the tools to help us move forwards.

References and further reading

Brown, Lester R. (2001) *Eco-economy: Building an Economy for the Earth*, W. W. Norton and Company Inc., New York

FAO (2000) *The State of World Fisheries and Aquaculture 2000*, Food and Agriculture Organization of the United Nations, Rome

Pretty, J. (2002) *Agri-culture*, Earthscan, London

IUCN (2000) *IUCN Red List of Threatened Species*, Species Survival Commission, Gland, Switzerland and Cambridge

Kyoto (2003) 'The 3rd Water Forum, Kyoto', www.worldwater-forum3.com

Worldwatch Institute (1998) 'Watersheds of the World', www.worldwatch.org

WSSD (2002) 'World Summit on Sustainable Development, Johannesburg', www. johannesburg

WWF (2002) 'Living Planet Report 2002', www.panda.org/downloads/general/ LPR_2002.pdf

Chapter 1.3

Sustainability and Sustainable Development

Sustainability is really quite a simple concept. Literally, it relates to the capacity to continue indefinitely. The Earth is a prime example of a sustainable system, its ecosystems having evolved over billions of years to maintain physical resources in perpetual cycles through the net capture of solar energy. The waste products of each link in its complex and intertwined food chains, which comprise the biosphere, form the food for subsequent links in those chains. Not only is the Earth an excellent example of a natural sustainable system, it is also highly pertinent to understanding what sustainability means for humanity.

Sustainable development is also quite a simple concept, and is distinct from the term sustainability despite their all-too-common usage as synonyms. While sustainability is a state, sustainable development is a process of development, from where we stand today towards that ideal state. As we have seen in previous chapters, our species is currently far from sustainable. And, as we become aware of the parlous state of global support systems and interactions between different parts of humanity, the need for sustainable development becomes ever more urgent.

There is nothing random about the workings of nature. Ecosystems may appear endlessly diverse and chaotic, but natural laws determine every interaction and its contribution to the stability of the whole. Of the wide diversity of living forms on Earth, it is today only humanity that threatens the integrity of this whole Earth system. Survival is an instinct hard-wired into humans, as indeed into all of nature. Yet, ultimately, the decision to embark upon sustainable development to protect human potential in the longer term is also a value judgement. Once decided, we have as our guide the scientific principles upon which the biosphere operates. The wrong decisions based on the right intentions are of little use; we need solid conceptual foundations from which to turn intent into appropriate and strategic decisions.

A track record of progress

The wetlands of this planet are remarkable habitats. Marking the transition (or ecotone) between fully aquatic and fully terrestrial systems, wetlands are habitats of extraordinary diversity. They are among the most productive of all habitats on Earth, supporting an extraordinarily large proportion of the world's biological richness. They are also important in performing ecological functions that purify air and water, detain floodwater and smooth river flows, recharge groundwater, and support the breeding and growth of many terrestrial and aquatic species. In many human cultures, they provide economic resources as diverse as food, building materials, products for crafts such as weaving, thatching and making musical instruments, medicines, and many more uses besides. In many regions, they have religious or cultural significance. Rivers, lakes, seas and major swamps divide land masses and cultures, yet at the same time support communication and transport between them. Along with their great diversity and productivity, wetlands are also highly vulnerable. Indeed, there is a global pandemic of overexploitation of wetlands, starving them of water supplies, polluting or overwhelming them, or draining them for 'productive uses' such as agricultural or urban development.

By the 1960s, it was well understood by many aquatic scientists around the world, and particularly by ornithologists aware of the importance of connected chains of wet environments for the flyways for migratory birds, that the world's wetlands were fast diminishing in quality and quantity. And, as the primary natural capital of many cultures for nourishment, economic resources and quality of life, real human hardship was as pressing a consequence as the sharp decline in ecological assets. One solution would have been to argue for more nature reserves, preserving the ecological quality of these dwindling resources by fencing them off from human interference. This was impractical on ethical as well as economic and political grounds and was, in any case, far from readily enforceable. A new approach was necessary.

Just as life appears to have evolved in and emerged from water, so, too, many trace the roots of modern thinking about sustainable development to wetland policy. This approach was embodied under the Convention on Wetlands of International Importance Especially as Waterfowl Habitat, established in 1971 at a global conference in the Iranian city of Ramsar. The 'Ramsar Convention', as it is better known, remains the only global convention on any specific habitat type. Today, it has in excess of 100 signatories worldwide. The Ramsar Convention had at its heart the integration of social with environmental and economic development, recognizing that to take humans out of wetlands was no panacea for their protection. One of the core concepts underpinning the convention is that of Wise Use, which determines that human exploitation is an essential aspect of wetlands but that patterns of development (frequently traditional low-impact management adapted to specific environments) should protect the natural character and ecosystem functions of wetlands.

Many wetlands around the world, of a great variety of types, are now designated under the Ramsar Convention. The degree to which the spirit of the convention has been embodied in practical action, and that the designation therefore affords real protection, is variable throughout the world. However, the Ramsar Convention established the important principle of identifying that the three attributes – social, economic and environmental – are inextricably linked, and need to be considered in parallel if development could truly be considered as sustainable. In the 1990s, after the term 'sustainable development' had entered common usage, the Ramsar Commission determined that this was synonymous with its definition of the term 'Wise Use'.

Various authors point to alternative roots to the 'green movement'. All have justifiable claims, and the very diversity of initiatives itself points to an evolving worldwide human consciousness of the need for a new and sustainable relationship with the Earth. As long ago as the 1940s, Aldo Leopold called for a new 'land ethic' if we were to protect land and river resources from the damage that he was observing in the Round River catchment in Sand County, US. As the far-sighted Leopold then stated, 'When land does well for its owner, and the owner does well by his land; when both end up better by reason of their partnership, we have conservation. When one or the other grows poorer, we do not.' Rachel Carson's seminal book *Silent Spring* (Carson, 1963) amassed evidence about the persistence and long term detrimental effects of pesticides, and presented it in a cogent and startling way. Indeed, the 1960s was a decade of unprecedented environmental and social awareness, a stage onto which the disastrous consequences of heavy metal pollution in Japan's Minimata Bay and the major tanker spill from the Torrey Canyon off the UK's Cornish coast were relayed directly into our homes by the new wonder of real-time global media coverage.

Notwithstanding these early shoots of environmental and sustainability consciousness, for many the green movement proper and the interest of global political leaders date back to the United Nations Conference on the Human Environment held in Stockholm in March 1972, better known as the Stockholm Conference. At this point in history, not one country in the world had a ministry of the environment, a staggering fact given the ubiquitous presence of such government departments today and the level of importance accorded to environmental issues. The Stockholm Conference brought environmental issues to the fore in government thinking, summarized in a seven-point proclamation supported by 26 principles. Set against the almost complete absence of such considerations on the national and intergovernmental agenda of the time, the proclamation of the Stockholm Conference, 'having considered the need for a common outlook and for common principles to inspire and guide the peoples of the world in the preservation and enhancement of the human environment' was, in summary, that:

- 'Man is both creature and moulder of his environment... Both aspects of man's environment, the natural and the man-made, are essential to his well-being and to the enjoyment of basic human rights – even the right to life itself.'
- 'The protection and improvement of the human environment is a major issue.'
- 'Man has constantly to sum up experience and go on discovering, inventing, creating and advancing... We see around us growing evidence of man-made harm in many regions of the earth.'
- 'In the developing countries most of the environmental problems are caused by under-development ... the industrialized countries should make efforts to reduce the gap between themselves and the developing countries.'
- 'growth of population continuously presents problems for the preservation of the environment... Along with social progress and the advance of production, science and technology, the capability of man to improve the environment increases with each passing day.'
- 'A point has been reached in history when we must shape our actions throughout the world with a more prudent care for their environmental consequences.'
- 'To achieve this environmental goal will demand the acceptance of responsibility by citizens and communities and by enterprises and institutions at every level; all sharing equitably in common efforts.'

The United Nations Environment Programme (UNEP) extended this agenda for action in the form of the World Conservation Strategy, which reported in 1980. This new strategy for human development built upon an emerging understanding about the integral linkages between the three strands – society, environment and economy – emphasizing aspects of the direct contribution of economic activities to potential environmental and human degradation.

'Our Common Future', best known as the 'Brundtland Report' (of the World Commission for Environment and Development or WCED), first brought the term and concept of sustainable development to mass media awareness in 1987. The report takes its name from the chair of the commission, Gro Harlem Brundtland, then a former minister of environment for Norway and subsequently its prime minister. Members of the commission came from 21 nations, more than half in the developing world. Although not the originator of the term 'sustainability', Brundtland succeeded significantly in pushing it onto the world political stage from when the United Nations General Assembly established the WCED in 1983. Among the report's findings were that:

> Over the course of this century, the relationship between the human world and the planet that sustains it has undergone a profound change. When the century began, neither human numbers or technology had the power radically to alter planetary systems. As the century closes, not only do vastly increased human numbers and their activities have that power, but major, unintended changes are occurring in the atmosphere, in soils, in water, among plants and animals, and in the relationships among all of these. The rate of change is outstripping the ability of scientific disciplines and our current capabilities to assess and advise.

In issuing a call for various actions, the report offered the now-famous definition of sustainable development, most commonly referred to as the Brundtland definition, 'A form of development that meets the needs of the present without compromising the ability of future generations to meet their own needs.'

The Brundtland Commission called for an international conference to be convened 'within an appropriate period' after the presentation of its report to review progress and create a follow up structure. That conference, the United Nations Conference on Environment and Development (UNCED or the Earth Summit) was held in Rio de Janeiro, Brazil, in 1992. The Earth Summit in Rio de Janeiro was unprecedented for a UN conference, in terms of both its size and the scope of its concerns. Twenty years after the first global environment conference, UNCED was tasked to help governments rethink economic development and find ways to halt the destruction of irreplaceable natural resources and pollution of the planet. Hundreds of thousands of people from all walks of life were drawn into the Rio process. They persuaded their leaders to go to Rio and join other nations in making the difficult decisions needed to ensure a healthy planet for generations to come.

The Earth Summit's message, that nothing less than a transformation of our attitudes and behaviour would bring about the necessary changes, was transmitted by almost 10,000 on site journalists and heard by millions around the world. The message reflected the complexity of the problems facing us: that poverty as well as excessive consumption by affluent populations placed damaging stresses on the environment. Governments recognized the need to redirect international and national plans and policies to ensure that all economic decisions fully took into account any environmental impact. And the message has produced results, making eco-efficiency a guiding principle for business and governments alike. At Rio, representatives of more than 170 nations agreed to work toward sustainable development of the planet. More specific agreements, most not legally binding, focused on topics of global significance such as climate change, loss of bio-diversity (the Convention on Biodiversity), management of the Earth's forests, and the responsibilities and rights of nations. A global plan of action titled 'Local Agenda 21' (referring to the 21st century) was aimed at local government, with the urgent and evocative message to 'Think Global, Act Local'. Local Agenda 21 has subsequently served to unlock creativity at the local scale in addressing specific sustainability challenges.

The Earth Summit influenced all subsequent UN conferences, which have examined the relationship between human rights, environmental trends and pressures, popu-lation, social development, women and human settlements. The World Conference on Human Rights, held in Vienna in 1993, for example, underscored the right of people to a healthy environment and to development; both controversial demands that had met with resistance from some member states until Rio.

The ten day World Summit on Sustainable Development (WSSD), held in September 2002 in Johannesburg, South Africa, was in effect a ten year follow up to the original Rio Earth Summit. The goals of the meeting were to strengthen global commitments on sustainable development. These included ratification of several international agree-ments such as the 1997 Kyoto Protocol that deals with global climate change, as well as integrating and setting specific time targets for plans to deal with issues such as health, children, water and poverty. As the summit's organizers said prior to WSSD:

> Sustainable development is a dynamic process, and it is one that will continue to evolve and grow as lessons are learnt and ideas re-examined. By reinvigorating the spirit of Rio we can begin to move to a deeper and broader level of sustainability.

The realities of the event in Johannesburg were reported commonly throughout the media to be far less visionary and far more concerned with protection of developed-world national interests. However, some of the actions emerging from the summit, particularly those relating to water, were impressive, and are summarized below:

- Governments agreed to halve the number of people lacking clean drinking water and basic sanitation by 2015. Such is the importance of water to the basic needs of the impoverished people of the world that this commitment to water services is symbolic of the need to address disparities in wealth and power across the world.
- Governments agreed to take action to help the poor gain access to affordable energy. The summit's action plan calls on countries to 'substantially increase' the global share of renewable energy, but governments failed to agree on specific targets to boost the share of global energy produced from renewable sources.
- The Kyoto Protocol on climate change gases got a new lease of life at the summit when Russia announced that it would ratify the treaty, the treaty having previously received a massive setback when the US said it would not ratify it.
- Governments agreed to cut significantly by 2010 the rate at which rare animals and plants were becoming extinct.
- With respect to global trade, negotiators ironed out a row over the wording of a key paragraph, which gave precedence to the World Trade Organization (WTO) over environmental regulations. The text was revised to say that nations will 'continue to

enhance the mutual supportiveness of trade, environment and development', omitting a clause which added, 'while ensuring WTO consistency'.
- The summit plan emphasizes human rights and governance, including commitments to fight corruption and promote democracy and the rule of law.
- The plan recognizes that access to healthcare should be consistent with basic human rights and 'cultural and religious values', a point that had been hotly debated.

Having taken this stroll through the history books of emerging 'green' awareness, and evolving, some would say far too slowly, definitions and decisiveness with respect to sustainable development, three key messages emerge:

- First, that society remains on a far from sustainable course; a dangerous trajectory that threatens its capacity to achieve its potential both internationally and into the future.
- Second, that the track record of summits and conventions demonstrates evolving, albeit sporadic, progress.
- Third, there is at least consensus on the three constituent elements of sustainability: economy, environment and society. These three elements are more widely known as the 'three-legged stool' and 'triple bottom line' (a term coined by John Elkington of sustainable development consultancy SustainAbility, www.sustainability.com). The three elements have elsewhere been referred to by a diversity of context relevant names – for example, 'people, planet, prosperity' – but the principle remains the same.

Oft-repeated these components may be. However, they are not always applied as a connected system. Frequently, there are trade-offs made between the elements, such as in the still-widespread planning decisions that favour industrial development upon valuable habitat on the spurious grounds that the economic and social aspects of development via new regional employment outweigh environmental concerns. Truly connected and sustainable decision making is not about trade-offs, but concerns itself with innovations that enable all aspects to benefit, or at the very least not to be degraded.

The funnel effect

We live in a world that is fast-changing and where, it seems, change is now the only constant. Sustainable development is not about imposing additional social and environmental burdens upon unchanging economic conditions. Rather, it is concerned with an appreciation that changing environmental pressures and social awareness are defining features of a changing future economic climate in which there will be a constant need for adaptation. In this changing future, natural selection will apply to ensure the 'survival of the most fit' – i.e. that increasingly sustainable enterprises will enjoy competitive success. The converse of this is that we can be assured of numerous extinctions en route to a different future, be they literal in the form of natural catastrophes or figurative in the form of corporate or policy failure. A true understanding of the importance of sustainable development, then, sees it not as a matter of costly altruism but of improved risk management for a future that will inevitably be shaped by the limits imposed by natural systems and social opinion.

A diverse range of pressures are accelerating the pace of change in the world, but many of the most important pressures stem from the squeeze between diminishing resources and a rising global population with increasing material expectations. Sustainable development charity The Natural Step uses the metaphor of a funnel to describe how these pressures are impinging increasingly on the 'licence to operate' granted to businesses and other organizations by society (see Figure 1.3.1), progressively squeezing them towards more sustainable practice.

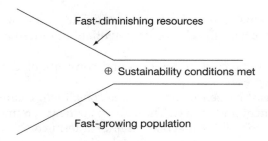

Source: Robèrt, 2002

Figure 1.3.1   The Natural Step funnel, illustrating the squeeze arising from diminishing resources and increasing population

Near the funnel's walls, sustainability related pressures are brought to bear in a number of ways. Consider, for example, materials use in the UK. These pressures include: economic factors such as the relatively recent aggregates and landfill taxes; reputation issues arising from media interest in business practices and materials with a pariah status; more stringent emission regulations; health and safety liabilities; shareholder concerns about risk management; and possibly the increasing difficulty of obtaining capital funding or planning permission.

Such pressures for sustainable development will, inevitably and increasingly, define the future business agenda. If these pressures are tackled proactively, sustainable development initiatives can not only steer companies clear of the 'walls of the funnel' but will also help to identify future business opportunities created by those sustainability pressures. The dramatic market penetration of low phosphorus detergents is an example from the early 1990s of a sustainability based market decision successfully and profitably pre-empting public concern and subsequent regulatory requirements.

Sustainability principles

In order to make progress with sustainable development, some fundamental principles of sustainability have first to be established to ensure we are moving in the right direction.

In addition to the importance of rooting our understanding about sustainability in natural laws, and understanding the importance and appropriate application of the 'three-legged stool', a number of other principles have become associated with sustainable development. Some key principles are outlined below:

The precautionary principle

The precautionary principle relates to management of unknown risk where scientific uncertainty combines with the potential for substantive harm characterized by the irreversibility of cumulative effects, or where the impacts may affect large areas or extend over long periods of time. These circumstances call for precautionary action that is either anticipatory or preventative. An example of this that is current at the time of writing is the establishment by the UK Government of an inquiry into nanotechnology, before the technology gathers its own momentum (and learning from the unanticipated backlash against the rapid commercialization of biotechnology).

The prevention principle

The prevention principle allows action to be taken to protect the environment at an early stage, preventing damage rather than repairing it when it has occurred. This principle is not as far-reaching as the precautionary principle, meaning that, in practical terms, it is better to prevent than repair. Applied as far upstream in industrial processes as possible, it obviously bears upon design and material choice decisions rather than retrospective management of risk from poor design or problematic materials.

The polluter pays principle

The polluter pays principle holds that all producers of waste should be legally and financially responsible for safe handling, environmentally sound disposal and creating an incentive to produce less waste. This principle has been applied from the late 1980s, but was widely discussed at the Rio de Janeiro Earth Summit in 1992 and endorsed by all attending national representatives. It underpins many approaches to pollution charging, and is a principle for slowly internalizing into organizational decision making those currently non-market costs borne by the environment and society.

The proximity principle

The proximity principle says that treatment and disposal of waste should take place as near as possible to the point of production as is technically and environmentally possible. It therefore represents prudent risk management, avoidance of excessive costs and risks entailed in transport, and embodies some aspects of social equity in terms of local responsibility for local waste arising.

Three further principles agreed within the Brundtland Report were that sustainable development should respect **intergenerational equity**, **public participation**, and that environmental protection should be **integral to economic development**. As we approach the second decade after Brundtland, this fully integrated thinking about sustainability as a central feature within all development decisions is clearly not ubiquitously applied, with consequences for future generations. However, tangible progress can be observed in some areas.

The reality that overarches each of these principles is that, unavoidably, we are part of the biosphere of planet Earth. There is nothing that we can do, personally or collectively, that is independent of this biospheric system, or which will not affect it and all those who share it. Throughout human history, few of our collective actions have been undertaken with that implication in mind. Take, for example, coal. At some indeterminate time, we found this mysterious black deposit, and discovered that we could exploit the energy released by burning it in air. All well and good as far as delivering immediate economic return and human utility were concerned but, in the absence of robust scientific understanding about the climatic and other contexts of that decision, wider consequences were not factored into decisions to commercialize that process. The net result is that environmental harm, health risk and trading inequities remain substantially external to the market price of coal based (or oil or gas based) energy, contributing to unsustainability and the threat it poses to our collective capacity to achieve our human potential in the future.

Seeking to retrofit technological fixes to isolated problems is no substitute for reconsidering technological advancement from the broader canvas of the supportive systems of the biosphere and human society. To find sustainable solutions, we have to think at wider scales than were applied in causing them. As Albert Einstein put it, 'The significant problems we face today cannot be solved at the same level of thinking we were at when we created them.'

We have to ask bigger questions about how local decisions will affect environmental and social systems. Sustainable development therefore represents the conscious imposition of a 'feedback loop from the future', which has never been a part of our development in history, establishing a new paradigm for setting human decisions within broader principles and contexts. I am indebted to my colleague Dr Rahman Khatibi for this illuminating insight into sustainable development as an evolutionary paradigm for human development.

Systems thinking

The development of science throughout history has provided for humanity a growing body of knowledge, and of methods for testing and extending that knowledge. Early scientific understanding was founded in a paradigm (framework of thinking) now referred to as reductive science, which entails reducing complex phenomena down to their component parts as a means of developing understanding. Throughout the Industrial Revolution, reductive science acted as a key to opening up new understandings about natural systems and our capacities to exploit them. Powerful though it has been, and remains, in developing understandings of mechanisms within nature, and exploiting them for economic and social gain, reductive science is based upon a narrow definition of problem and solution. For example, the internal combustion engine has revolutionized the global economy, healthcare, agriculture and industry. However, the pursuit of purely mechanical solutions also served as blinkers to the development of the technology, blinding its proponents to associated threats to the global climate and inequities along fossil fuels supply chains. Many in industry and national governments still fail to see these pressing threats as relevant to economic progress.

It is against this backdrop that the second paradigm of science evolved in the 1940s; that of holistic science. In this holistic paradigm, the connections between disciplines were highlighted, together with the need to think in multidisciplinary terms. For example, in urban flooding control, different perspectives – hydrological, physico-chemical, ecological, and so on – are drawn together to form a balanced view and a basis for more holistic and sustainable action. Recognition of different disciplines of science, and of their linkage in complex systems, was a major step forwards but, in practice, all too often led to trade-offs between competing disciplines. It did not address the fact that scientific and technical disciplines are in fact purely human inventions, with nature itself having no seams between its different attributes.

The third and current paradigm of science is systems thinking. Systems thinking is founded upon the fact that the behaviour and properties of complex systems – be that system a cell, a football team, a region, a person or a planet – are facets of the system as a whole. Some of these behaviours and properties are explainable in reductive science (the mechanisms of their component parts) but many are what is known as emergent properties, that arise from the system as a whole and the relationships between its components. The emphasis is upon patterns and relationships within complex systems, which cannot necessarily be deduced by analysis of constituent parts. Human person-ality arising from interactions of neurones in the brain is one instance of an emergent property, not predictable from reductive analysis of component parts. So too are the catalytic properties of enzymes, which are not predictable as additive properties of constituent amino acids. The life support functions of nature at ecosystem, catchment or global scale are another example of emergent properties, underlining the need to think at the systems scale for sustainable solutions.

This brief review of successive paradigms of science is of more than purely academic interest. If we seek solutions at a parochial scale, be that a local flood defence scheme or a resource use issue in an industrial process, we risk addressing a local problem yet simultaneously causing wider scale problems elsewhere in the system. In the former example, our history of water management is replete with examples of flood defence activities that merely increased flood risk downstream, possibly also damaging conser-vation and fishery interests together with landscape and other valuable attributes of catchment systems. In terms of material choice, we must be aware that every resource use decision has a range of social, economic and environmental implications which may be long term and affecting a wide geographical radius.

Many problems of material use today are a legacy of assumptions made during the Industrial Revolution that the supportive capacities and resources of the Earth were limitless, and that growth depended upon stimulating consumption among a relatively low human population. Both assumptions are reversed today, with human numbers far from limiting and the resources, critically including the resource of waste absorption, of the biosphere at or beyond their limits. However, in the face of this reversal of paradigm, our economic and governance systems remain predominantly rooted in the linear model of resource use – make, use once and dispose – established in the early days of industri-alization. This linear process is illustrated in Figure 1.3.2. Such linear use patterns differ from nature's cyclic and sustainable resource flows, within which wastes are reused as the resources for subsequent processes. Societal accumulation of pollutants, destruction of ecosystems, wastage, and reinforcement of the inequitable distribution of resources and impacts are consequences of continuing linear patterns of resource use.

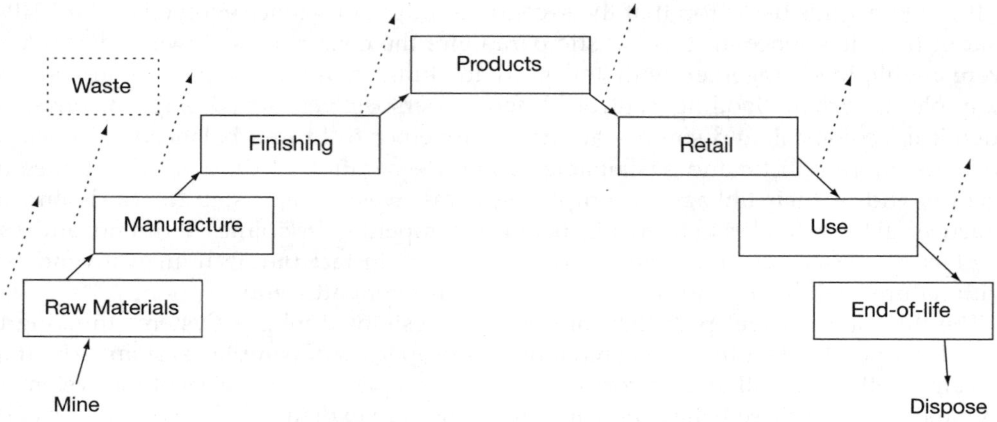

Figure 1.3.2 Linear resource use

Industrial environmental management systems are commonly based upon stewardship of products and materials from cradle to grave. This has significantly enhanced the environmental performance of many sectors of industry. The chemicals industry is a prime example of this, adopting and developing on a global scale the 'Responsible Care' initiative. Responsible Care is a voluntary initiative to make progress with a main stated aim of 'continual improvement in health, safety and environmental performance in the chemical industry'. It is a commitment to develop and produce chemicals that can be manufactured, transported, used, and disposed of safely. However, in common with many such initiatives, progress towards sustainability is hampered by the very defi-nition 'cradle to grave', which implies a linear process from source to waste. (Responsible Care defines this as between the two, largely arbitrary, points of 'raw material acquisition through ... [to] ... disposal'.) The obstacle arises simply because the natural supportive systems of this planet have no 'grave'; resources are constantly rein-tegrated and reused in new productive processes. The term 'cradle to cradle' would fit better with this cyclic concept of sustainability, and is a model that industry will have to emulate if it is ultimately to be truly sustainable.

Most current management approaches in organizations commonly fail to think of resources at the systems scale, and may therefore improve management control yet miss key issues relevant to sustainability. A local definition of waste just does not stack up at the ecosystem scale, so 'sustainable management of waste' is an oxymoron. As we have seen, decisions that are not informed by an adequately broad context can all too often result in problems elsewhere in the system. Helpful though it is in addressing environmental concerns within defined situations, even the widely accepted environ-mental management process of 'life cycle assessment' (LCA) can make only a limited contribution to sustainable development if applied on too parochial a basis. As we have discussed already, the type of life cycle illustrated in Figure 1.3.2 is not in fact a cycle at all, merely reflecting a short linear section of resource use. It potentially overlooks, for example, the fate of post end-of-life products and processes.

To maximize the strategic value of LCA, we have to set it within the context of the full life of resources within the life support cycles of this planet. Without this broader context, and targeted application of the tool, LCA may be helpful in addressing some of the environmental hotspots along a selected segment of a limited lifeline, but it may overlook broader scale sustainability issues. In effect, when used thus, it could lead to more eco-efficient unsustainability (i.e. making the linear use of resources more efficient) rather than true progress towards sustainability.

From the broader context of sustainable development, the life cycle must automatically incorporate fate beyond end-of-life or after disposal. After all, burying or burning does not make things disappear from the Earth's system, and the capacity for harmful effects upon life support systems is not inhibited over anything other than the most parochial of human time scales. Furthermore, linear use is wasteful and, where no further beneficial use of the resource occurs post disposal, may perpetuate existing economic distortions and inequities in the way that resources are shared across society. If one is genuinely concerned about sustainable development, setting a problem within the context of objective sustainability principles is essential. Primarily, this entails reframing the life cycle as comprising the cyclic life support systems of this planet, which make life and economic activities possible. This may in turn lead to a different view of requirements to deliver sustainable use of materials, and of the economic opportunities arising from the funnel effect on the future economy, as illustrated in Figure 1.3.3.

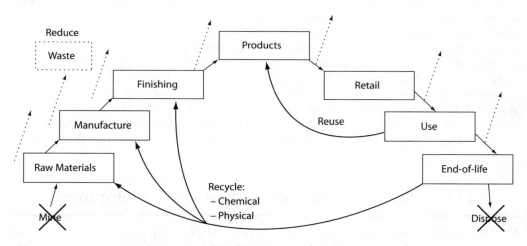

Figure 1.3.3   Closing the loop on material flows

Thinking of the Earth as a connected system is obviously highly germane to truly sustainable decision making. Addressing environmental, social or other issues with solutions conceived at any lesser scale can merely contribute to further unforeseen problems within the broader catchment, biosphere or social systems.

Backcasting

Another valuable approach to strategic planning of any type, and particularly to sustainable development, is that of backcasting. This differs diametrically from the more common approach of forecasting, which is generally based upon extrapolation of trends and predictable future events. Forecasting still underpins the majority of business and governance decisions. Backcasting instead takes as its reference point a clearly articulated end goal, and seeks to put in place plans to make a transition to that different, or preferred, future. Instead of perpetuating today into tomorrow (potentially sustaining unsustainable practices or products), backcasting seeks underpinning principles of sustainability upon which to identify a different type of tomorrow, and the innovations that will be necessary to make step changes towards it. Development without innovation and a clear long term outcome cannot, without overwhelming good fortune, lead to sustainable outcomes.

By starting from the end goal perspective, backcasting can also help make sustainable development tractable, enabling the breaking down of sustainable development actions into bite sized chunks that lead towards a far longer term result. This can comprise, for example, helping organizations make short term investment decisions which, though not delivering the end goal themselves (full sustainability is remote from where society is today), nevertheless constitute steps leading incrementally towards further future actions that lead to the desired goal of full sustainability.

If backcasting is used to tackle sustainable development proactively, we are far better positioned to avoid the walls of the funnel, to use The Natural Step's metaphor illustrated in Figure 1.3.1, and to identify the new opportunities available to businesses and other organizations in a more sustainable future world. If we continue to react to issues as we go on blundering into those walls, we will merely perpetuate the historic pattern of responding reactively, at substantial cost and disruption to business and society (not to mention risk of extinction), as issues hit us one after the other. Proactive and strategic decisions are, in the end, more intelligent and cost effective than merely reacting to sustainability issues as they inevitably arise. A true commitment to sustainable development is therefore about a great deal more than altruism, as it helps deal strategically with the unavoidable sustainable development pressures that will define the future.

The social dimension of sustainable development

Nothing on this Earth exists, or was evolved, in isolation. From prion to pachyderm, all are interdependent parts of and active agents within ecosystems at scales from the microscopic to the global. Humanity is inextricably part of both local and global ecosystems. Connectedness with nature is our natural state, the product of 3.85 billion years of evolution, and this includes relationships between other members of our own kin. A place and a belonging within community are equally central to human ecology, of which empathy, love and self affirmation are natural attributes. Many have worked on attributes of human need, including Manfred Max-Neef, Abraham Maslow, Robert Putnam and Ken Wilbur, and all concur that socialization is a core human need.

Today, much of developed society suffers the chronic disease of disconnection, both from nature and from community. Water comes from the tap or bottle with no questions asked, and goes away down the plughole or lavatory with equal alacrity. Food comes from supermarkets, and milk is delivered to the doorstep. Inner city children in particular, and developed culture and its political governors in general, remain utterly dependent upon nature for survival and wealth creation yet disconnected from it in practical terms.

Worryingly, surveys of school-age children in British inner cities have revealed that many think that milk comes 'from supermarkets', unaware that it is produced by cows.

Progress within today's industrialized nations often breaks the nourishing links between its constituent communities and individuals. Roads connect cities but bisect neighbourhoods, and cars take us to other places and organizations, sometimes in air-conditioned isolation. Commuting spreads the tentacles of cities into the countryside, populating villages with people too busy to play a part in rural communities while pushing property prices beyond the means of those that do. Extended families fragment as employment opportunities make us economic migrants from the places to which we may feel we belong, uprooting with us our children from the nourishing soil of their special places and people. Global media feed us a homogeneous multinational mix in place of the traditions and culture of our localities. At the wider scale, supply chains span regions and continents, spreading trade though often resulting in artificially cheap labour and resources feeding the economies of the already wealthy.

Refugees within internally fragmented enclaves of humanity substitute close family and community with soap operas, accrue possessions and wealth as an inadequate sop for status and self worth, and wear 'brands' to seek the acceptance of others as a market driven alternative to true kinship. Self affirmation and self worth are sought not from deed but through the drug of consumerism.

Development on a genuinely sustainable path must include healing that chronic disease of disconnection: environmentally; intellectually; emotionally; and economically. The social context, of which awareness of the environmental and economic contexts is an indissoluble part, is central to genuine sustainable development. In the sustainable world, the quality and practice of humanity would not be an academic concept or an Oscar-winning role, but an automatic instinct in all decision making.

Models of sustainability and sustainable development

Sound science based principles are essential as a foundation for robust policy and action but, no matter how elegant, they are of course no panacea without equally pragmatic methods for application on the ground. The challenge of sustainable development is to identify pragmatic commercial decisions, local actions and regional policies that enact the necessary principles for survival (biological and quality of life). This will necessarily vary contextually and culturally, but a basis in common sound principles is of fundamental importance.

The term 'Think Global, Act Local', first used in defining the local authority focused Local Agenda 21 process agreed at the Rio Earth Summit, is commonly applied to this principle of local relevance. Of course, global action and local thinking are also important! There are numerous models of sustainable development that are helpful in setting local decisions within greater contexts. A number of these are discussed below.

Circles, balls and circuses

The most widely known model of sustainability goes by various names, including the 'three circles', 'three balls' or 'three-ringed circus' model, as illustrated in Figure 1.3.4.

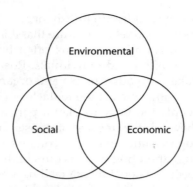

Figure 1.3.4   The three circles model of sustainability

It is simply a Venn Diagram (interlocking circles reflecting areas of overlap between different attributes) helping decision makers identify wherein their decisions lie. Using this model, sustainability conditions are met when decisions sit in the central zone where environmental, social and economic attributes are all addressed. This is a very simple communication tool, and helps convey simple messages in easily understood ways. However, in practice, it is very much a coarse filter and is poorly attuned to sophisticated decision making, subject as it is to considerable freedom of interpretation.

Russian doll

Closely akin to this is the 'Russian doll' model, in which the dependencies of these three attributes of sustainability are acknowledged and nested. In the Russian doll model, the primacy of the environment as the supportive medium of humanity and the totality of social activity places it as the largest circle. Within this, society sits and, acknowledging that the economy is a social construct and not an end or viable entity in itself, the third circle of economy sits within society, as illustrated in Figure 1.3.5. This model serves a valuable educational role, though at odds with prevalent views in a world often dominated by economic decisions to the detriment of social and environmental wellbeing.

Environmental footprinting

Another widely known model, which helps communicate readily understood and important messages about sustainability in a graphic way, is environmental footprinting. An environmental footprint is a calculation of the land area for the provision of resources and absorption of wastes required to support the total environmental resource demand of a region, individual or corporate activity. This is achieved by various methods that include land use requirements for crop production, absorption of carbon dioxide emissions, and so on. The normalization of resource demands to an area of productive land, a better comparator than money, provides a graphic demonstration of the input-intensity, and is very useful as an educational tool. Indeed, the WWF's environmental footprinting has been used in this context in the preceding chapter, illustrating as it does disparities in resource demand across the world and their implications

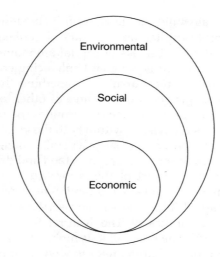

Figure 1.3.5   The Russian doll model of sustainability

for overspending global supportive capacities. Footprinting of this type clearly lacks sophisticated economic and social criteria, but serves a valuable communication and benchmarking role when applied in context.

Integrated catchment management systems

Since its inception, the concept of integrated catchment management systems (ICMS) has reflected the need to treat river catchments as whole systems comprising interdependent components. This, in theory, sets local decision making within a far wider context of the natural processes of catchments, and the processes and beneficial functions that take place within them. The natural boundaries of the catchment (albeit not always reflecting groundwater movement) thereby provide relevant units for integrated management for sustainable development purposes. In practice, implementation of ICMS has commonly failed to realize this ideal, with early efforts commonly seen as little more than an aggregation of poorly integrated plans with no strategic vision. However, in principle, ICMS is a powerful and geographically relevant method for integrated decision making reflecting local carrying capacity. The emerging discipline of ecohydrology also reflects the interconnected nature of all facets of the catchment, including the involvement of human society, representing both a scale at which sustainability is possible and focusing on the natural feedback mechanisms that may enhance self restoration of degraded catchments.

Five Capitals

The Five Capitals model of sustainability advanced by UK sustainable development charity Forum for the Future provides a cohesive model in a form analogous to existing methods of financial accounting. From an economic standpoint – and that's the standpoint which still dominates virtually all principal societal decision making processes in the developed world – sustainability can most usefully be described in terms of capital and income. The five types of capital are listed and described in outline in Box 1.3.1. Sustainability is only possible if *all* stocks of capital are maintained or increased over time. This reinforces the case for protecting and enhancing critical natural capital and avoiding knee-jerk trade-offs in the pursuit of something that is merely a little less unsustainable. Within any single geographical area or other local set of circumstances, the type and abundance of natural resources determines the range of possible options for land use, supporting decision making within both the global and local contexts. The processes by which natural resources – such as soil, water, biomass and air – are converted into key products and services – such as food and drink, energy and a leisure landscape – are what lie at the heart of this approach to integrated land use and management. For policymakers, planners and landowners, what really matters is how we convert this natural capital into products and services to create jobs, wealth and gainful livelihoods. Some attributes of The Natural Step's approach (see the next subsection) are included within the Five Capitals model. For more detail about the Five Capitals model and Forum for the Future, refer to www.forumforthefuture.org.uk.

Box 1.3.1 *The five capital types comprising the Five Capitals model*

- **Natural capital** encompasses any stock or flow of energy and matter that yields valuable goods and services. It includes natural resources, some of which are renewable (timber, grain, fish and water), while others are not (fossil fuels); resource sinks that absorb, neutralize or recycle wastes; and processes, such as climate regulation. Natural capital is the basis not only of production, but of life itself.
- **Human capital** comprises our health, knowledge, skills and motivation. Investing in human capital (for instance, in education) is vital to a flourishing economy. Failure to invest generates poverty, which is both morally indefensible and socially inefficient, since it prevents millions of people from fulfilling their potential and becoming engaged in the creation of wealth.
- **Social capital** means the value added to any activity by human relations and cooperation. It is found in social structures and institutions such as families, communities, businesses, trade unions, schools and voluntary organizations.
- **Manufactured capital** comprises material goods (tools, machines, buildings and other forms of infrastructure) that contribute to the production process, but are not used up in it.
- **Financial capital** reflects the productive power of the other types of capital and enables them to be owned and traded.

The Natural Step Framework

International sustainable development charity The Natural Step has developed a set of tools, collectively known as The Natural Step Framework (TNS Framework), based on a systems view of the sustainable natural cycles of this planet and presented within a methodology supporting practical sustainable development decision making. The funnel metaphor used by The Natural Step has already been illustrated in Figure 1.3.1 earlier in this chapter, and relates to pressures enforcing, and increasing the need to meet, sustainability criteria. These criteria are defined on the basis primarily of the laws of thermodynamics, as articulated within a systems model of the cycling of matter and energy within the biosphere of planet Earth. From this systems model are derived a set of four system conditions, or first-order principles, defining the basic conditions necessary for sustainability to be achieved (see Box 1.3.2). These system conditions not only support an objective analysis of how sustainable a product, process, organization or region is today, but can also be used to construct a vision of what would constitute a fully sustainable end point. Once we know where we are today and where we need to get to tomorrow, we are then in a position to backcast from this vision (as discussed earlier in this chapter), identifying the incremental steps necessary to reach that sustainable future. Some of the key strengths of The Natural Step's approach are that it is founded upon robust scientific principles, it serves as a readily comprehensible awareness-raising tool about what sustainability actually means, it covers all aspects of sustainability, and it supports backcasting and strategic planning within normal business planning cycles. For more information about The Natural Step and its approach to sustainability and sustainable development, refer to www.naturalstep.org.uk.

Box 1.3.2 *The four system conditions of The Natural Step Framework*

In the sustainable society, nature is not subject to systematically increasing:
… concentrations of substances extracted from the Earth's crust
… concentrations of substances produced by society
… degradation by physical means
and
…human needs are met worldwide

The six basic models to aid sustainable development decisions, summarized here, are only a subset of the wide range of tools available to those seeking to put sustainable development into practice. However, they do represent a useful suite of approaches relevant to different circumstances and communication needs.

Transformation

As we have seen, retrospective thinking and action about social and environmental issues, after commercial decisions have been taken in isolation from them, cannot constitute sustainable development. Backcasting is a better approach, reflecting the need for strategic planning and actions that internalize wider scale sustainability considerations, enabling local decisions to lead cumulatively towards a clearly articulated sustainable end point.

The costs and benefits of all three elements of sustainability have to be considered in an integrated manner at the outset of planning, and carried through to decision making and the continuing operational life of an investment. There are good business reasons why this should be so, including addressing a diversity of risks on a proactive basis as well as the obvious ethical and moral reasons.

For this to become common practice, rather than the stuff of an interesting test case peripheral to the main business, a revolution in understanding and commitment will be necessary. Learning to make sense of sustainable development for a mainstream business or governance audience is therefore of fundamental importance.

Making sense of sustainable development

In the mid-1980s, little was widely understood about the pressures necessitating a sustainable path of development. Indeed, there was a pervasive consensus that assumptions laid down in the past on matters of resource use, trade and governance were acceptable into the future.

The world has changed significantly since that time, with the notion of sustainable development becoming mainstream and awareness of the need for it, and some of its implications, penetrating at least some of society. The situation has moved from one of total ignorance to one of an excessive number of ideas confounding those seeking to make practical progress! This is of course evolution in action, with new ideas emerging, competing and subject to natural selection as part of a growing global consciousness about the need for a new paradigm of development that can continue into the long term future.

There are a number of simple concepts that can be helpful in making sustainable development seem more like informed common sense, rather than something wholly new. Some of these are that:

- Nothing comes from nowhere. The primary resources of economic activities, as indeed all societal activities, really just fall into two camps: natural resources and the creativity and sweat of humanity. We need to learn to live as if this were true, and to protect those resources for our own individual and collective wellbeing.
- We live in a world that is fast changing, and where change is the new norm. Sustainability pressures help us understand the roots of much of that change, to make guided rather than reactive responses, and to be better prepared to adapt to a fast-changing world.
- Sustainable development is not about altruism. It is about self interest or, more properly, enlightened self interest, as it will help us better pre-empt and innovate in a world shaped increasingly and inevitably by greater natural forces.
- Sustainability is not achievable immediately, and we needn't feel guilty about not achieving it immediately. But, if we know where we are headed, each decision can form a stepping stone towards it.

References and further reading

Calder, I. R. (1999) *The Blue Revolution: Land Use and Integrated Water Resources Management*, Earthscan, London

Carson, R (1963) *Silent Spring*, Hamilton, London

Robèrt, K.-H. (2002) *The Natural Step Story: Seeding a Quiet Revolution*, New Society Publishers, Gabriola Island, Canada

Roszak, T. et al (1995) *Ecopsychology: Restoring the Earth, Healing the Mind*, Sierra Book Club, San Francisco
Suzuki, D. (1997) *The Sacred Balance: Rediscovering our Place in Nature*, Greystone Books, Vancouver
Wilson, E. O. (1990) *Sociobiology*, Harvard University Press, Cambridge, Massachusetts
Wilson, E. O. (1999) *Consilience*, Abacus, London

Section 2

Policy and Legislation

Chapter 2.1

Overview of the Law and International Legislation

Introduction

This chapter introduces the concept of law in the context of environmental management. It defines law and explains how laws arise. It shows, through examples, the cascading nature of environmental law, starting out at a global level but then delivered at a national or local level. It outlines what happens when laws are breached, giving examples of decided cases. It also considers key aspects of international law and the relationship between international trade and the environment.

What is law?

Law is a body of principles or rules recognized and applied by a state or community in the administration of justice. It includes legal rules of conduct that may be enforced by the imposition of penalties. It can also encompass policy processes and guidance, which may provide advice on, rather than enforce or implement, the law. Principles tend to be very broad and general in style and often need to be translated into rules to have effect. Rules tend to apply to people or a specific class, rather than singling out individuals, and they are normative, in other words they set a standard of how things should or ought to be done. Law, as policy, process and guidance, offers ways of compliance with the regulatory system. It can also include other non-enforceable legal mechanisms that may only, in theory, be persuasive but are, nevertheless, effective. A key role of the law is to provide an operational system for securing values that society desires, for example security, freedom and the provision of sufficient material goods. Law is not only about resolving disputes; if a legal system works well, disputes may be avoided (Elliot and Quinn, 2001; Higgins, 1994; NODE, 1998; and Wilkinson, 2002).

In environmental management, the law in all its forms comes into play. General principles are found in international treaties such as the United Nations Declaration on Environment and Development 1992 (the Rio Declaration). Rules of conduct are found in regulatory compliance regimes such as integrated pollution prevention and control (IPPC). Process as law can be seen by the Eco-management and Audit Scheme (EMAS) and ISO 14001 management systems that were introduced by European Union (EU) regulation and the International Organization for Standardization (ISO) respectively. Policy and guidance may arise as guidance notes such as the English land use planning policy guidance (PPG) notes or as government circulars (e.g. waste circulars). Policy may also arise in strategic documents such as the UK Sustainable Development Strategy 1999 that reiterates the national commitment to cut carbon dioxide emissions to 20% below 1990 levels by 2010.

Types of law

In most Commonwealth countries and others, such as the US, the legal system is based upon the common law and there are two broad legal categories: private and public law. Private law covers the relationships, agreements and disputes between two or more persons (including corporate bodies). On occasion, private law is used to protect the environment, usually through court action based on nuisance, negligence – mainly personal injury claims – or trespass. Public law covers the administration and regulation of activities taken on behalf of, and for the benefit of, society. It includes the criminal justice system, which aims to protect society and punish those who act unlawfully. Environmental protection relies on both aspects of public law; in regulation and control of polluting activities, for example through the IPPC regime, and by imposing criminal sanctions for breach of regulations. However, the public/private dichotomy does not arise in all countries. For example, in France the legal system is based primarily on a body of rules or principles, the Code civil, enacted by the state, and supported by legislation that judges use to interpret the code.

How laws arise

In the environmental field, laws often start life as broad principles or objectives introduced at an international level that are designed to resolve a particular problem. They will have as much to do with politics, negotiation and general discussion as an intention to formally lay out a specific legal framework. After prolonged debate and revision of drafts, the principles will be settled in international treaties (or conventions) which countries, or regional communities will sign up to and then ratify. Box 2.1.1 outlines the typical steps in implementing international legislation by considering the global efforts over 25 years to protect the ozone layer, an example of international agreement for global benefit. International legislation is likely to be implemented in two ways. It can be by the signatory states complying with the laws themselves for the benefit of their own citizens and the global good, or by the signatory states enacting legislation with which its own citizens must comply.

For much of the international environmental legislation that is designed to regulate activities within countries rather than between them, the EU usually signs up on behalf of its member states and then itself promotes legislation that begins to put the principles into effect. The EU will usually use directives but can also issue regulations and decisions. Once enacted by the EU, member states are required to implement, or transpose, the directives into national law.

Box 2.1.1 *Development of international legislation: protecting the ozone layer*

The ozone layer absorbs all but a small fraction of the UVB radiation from the sun, shielding plants and animals from its harmful effects.

1974   Molina-Rowland hypothesis published in the journal *Nature* linking chlorofluorocarbons (CFCs) to ozone depletion.
1977   Agreement to initiate a world plan of action on the ozone layer following meeting of experts in Washington, DC.
US ban of CFC aerosol products.
1978   Second political conference held in Munich to consider harmonizing national laws on regulating CFC production and use.
1981   United Nations Environment Programme (UNEP) Governing Council sets up group to negotiate a Global Framework Convention for the Protection of the Ozone Layer.
1982   First draft convention submitted to UNEP Governing Council.
1985   Agreement reached to implement the Convention for the Protection of the Ozone Layer (the Vienna Convention).
Discovery of the Antarctic ozone hole.
1987   Agreement and signing of the Protocol on Substances that Deplete the Ozone Layer (the Montreal Protocol).
1990   The London Amendment to the Montreal Protocol designed to increase regulation of ozone-depleting chemicals.
1992   The Copenhagen Amendment to the protocol approved new non-compliance procedure.
1997   The Montreal Amendment provided for further strengthening of the protocol including trade between the parties
1999   The Beijing Amendment to the protocol including a freeze in production of hydrochlorofluorocarbons (HCFCs), trade restrictions and replenishment of the Multilateral Fund, which provided financial assistance for developing countries.

Source: Anderson and Sarma, 2002

Once national laws are enacted by the government, they continue to evolve. They will be subject of delegated legislation, which often sets out the detail (in the form of rules, guidelines etc.). As time passes, they are likely to be subject to judicial interpretation, administrative guidance, legislative amendment; even repeal. Using environmental impact assessment (EIA) as an example, Box 2.1.2 demonstrates how the law can shift from global principles to local legislation and how it is subject to review over time.

Box 2.1.2 *The evolution of EIA legislation*

Environmental impact assessment is a management tool designed to prevent rather than alleviate harm; it may be regarded as an emanation of the preventative, precautionary and polluter pays principles.

1969   Section 102 of the US National Environmental Policy Act 1969 introduced the requirement for EIA, thereby setting a precedent.
1972   Declaration of the United Nations Conference on the Human Environment (the Stockholm Convention) including the need for development planning and environmental protection (Principles 13, 14).
1977   Second EU Environmental Action Programme set EIA as a policy objective.
1980   Draft EIA Directive to the EU Council of Ministers (following at least 20 early drafts).

continued overleaf

Box 2.1.2 *continued*

1985   EU Directive 85/337/EEC on the assessment of the effects of certain public and private projects on the environment (the EIA Directive) approved with member states having to implement by 3 July 1988.
1988   UK transposed the EIA Directive by enacting secondary legislation: the Town and Country Planning (Assessment of Environmental Effects) Regulations 1988.
1997   The EU issued amending legislation to improve EIA process: Directive 97/11/EC (the EIA Amending Directive).
1999   The UK took account of the EIA Amending Directive by issuing further secondary legislation including the Town and Country Planning (Environmental Impact Assessment) (England and Wales) Regulations 1999. This revoked and superseded the 1988 regulations. Similar secondary legislation was required for Scotland and Northern Ireland. Government guidance is issued in Circular 02/99.
2000   In the case of Berkeley v Secretary of State for the Environment (2000), the House of Lords re-emphasized the importance of EIA in land use planning and clarified the role of the non-technical summary.
2002   In the UK, the Office of the Deputy Prime Minister issued updated guidance and notes to local planning authorities including the revision of Circular 02/99.
2003   The EU enacted Directive 2003/4/EC on public access to environmental information, further amending the EIA Directive (among others).

Environmental principles

There are a number of principles that lay at the heart of environmental law and practice. Some now form the basis of specific legislation but a comprehensive set has not been adopted globally although the legal expert group advising the Brundtland Report 1987 prepared a full set of principles as an annex to 'Our Common Future'. Indeed, the proposed principles included fundamental human rights such as the right to an environment adequate for health and wellbeing (Munro, 1987). Despite the fact that a comprehensive set was not adopted internationally, many key principles were incorporated into the Rio Declaration 1992 including: the prevention principle, the precautionary principle and the polluter pays principle.

The prevention principle

Principle 21 of the Stockholm Declaration 1972 provided that states have the right to exploit their own resources and 'the responsibility to ensure that activities within their own jurisdiction or control do not cause damage to the environment of other States or of areas beyond the limits of national jurisprudence'. This was affirmed in the Rio Declaration 1992 and has also been incorporated into international law, for example Article 1 of the International Convention for the Prevention of Pollution from Ships 1973 (the Marpol Convention). Article 174 of the EU Treaty provides that environmental policy should be based on the principle that preventative action should be taken. At a national level, Section 1 of the Pollution Prevention and Control Act 1999 states that the purpose of the act is to make provision for regulating or otherwise preventing or controlling emissions capable of causing pollution.

The precautionary principle

Article 15 of the Rio Declaration states that in order to protect the environment, the precautionary approach should be widely applied by states according to ability and that 'where there are threats of serous or irreversible damage, lack of full scientific certainty shall not be used as a reason for postponing cost effective measures to prevent environmental degradation'. In the recent case of Pfizer Animal Health SA v Council of the European Union (T13/99, 11 September 2002), the European Court of Justice re-affirmed that 'under the precautionary principle the Community institutions are entitled, in the interests of human health, to adopt, on the basis of as yet incomplete scientific knowledge, protective measures which may seriously harm legally protected provisions, and they enjoy a broad discretion in this respect'.

The polluter pays principle

Article 16 of the Rio Declaration provides that states 'should endeavour to promote the internalization of environmental costs and the use of economic instruments, taking into account the approach that the polluter should, in principle, bear the costs of pollution, with due regard to the public interest and without unduly distorting international trade and investment'. This again, can be found in more specific areas of international law, for instance the preamble to the Oil Pollution Response Convention 1990 describes it as a 'general principle of international environmental law'. What the polluter pays principle is not, is an opportunity for the rich to pay to pollute; it should be regarded as a deterrent and a response to pollution incidents not a polluter's charter. In the UK, the principle underpins many of the criminal sanctions in environmental law. In particular, that environmental offences are often based on strict liability and carry penalties by way of fines and prison sentences up to four times as high as comparable non-environ-mental crimes.

By way of an example of a comprehensive approach to these key principles, the EIA Amending Directive 97/11/EC provides in its principle that EU policy on the environment is based on 'the precautionary principle, and on the principle that preventive action should be taken, that environmental damage should as a priority be rectified at source and that the polluter should pay'.

When laws are breached

Perhaps the most easily recognizable aspects of the law are when matters resort to the courts in order to test or try a particular issue. This may relate to breaches of agreement, a claim for compensation for negligent acts or nuisance caused by a neighbour or to a breach of a regulatory regime resulting in criminal punishment. Further, international disputes may relate to trade and environmental concerns, something considered in more detail in the next section.

Private law court action begins when an injured party claims compensation for some act or omission that has caused harm to human health or property. A common type of environmental action relates to personal injury, for example in claims for harm relating to industrial diseases. However, the courts have shown some reluctance in expanding environmental litigation beyond personal injury. In the case of Hunter and Canary Wharf [1997] 2 WLR 684 over 500 residents living next to the Docklands development in London claimed damages and an injunction for dust and vibration nuisance and interference with television signals. In handing down judgement the House of Lords emphasized that it was for Parliament to legislate for increased environmental protection, not the courts.

Perhaps the most important aspect of breaches of law for the purpose of environmental management is the failure of organizations to comply with regulations put in place to protect the environment. The sanctions available to the courts range from financial penalties by way of fines and compensation orders to imprisonment for those deemed to be in control of the offending organization or business activity. In addition, not only will a defendant be punished but they will also be liable to pay the prosecution costs and contend with the related publicity. This can have a significant adverse effect on the image of an organization, something that is becoming increasingly relevant, as polluters are being named and shamed in the media. For instance, the Environment Agency for England and Wales publishes an annual report of the worst polluters while the environmental non-governmental organization (NGO) Friends of the Earth runs a Factory Watch internet programme highlighting the worst polluting factories in the UK. Outlined below are some case studies, which provide examples of sanctions for breaching both EU and UK laws. Recent trends are that both the prosecuting authorities and the courts are getting tough on environmental crime with the Magistrates' Association publishing detailed guidance for the judiciary in environmental sentencing (MA/ELF, 2003). Box 2.1.3 provides a few examples of recent environmental sentencing decisions.

Box 2.1.3 *Recent sentences for environmental crimes in the UK*

R v Milford Haven Port Authority (Sea Empress) [2000] JPL 943

Erroneous navigation by the pilot caused the oil tanker *Sea Empress* to run aground and spill around 70,000 tonnes of crude oil. Milford Haven Port Authority were responsible for the pilots and was prosecuted by the Environment Agency under Section 85(1) of the Water Resources Act 1991 (WRA) and under common law for the offence of causing a public nuisance. The port authority pleaded guilty to the WRA offence (the public nuisance offence being left on the file) and the judge ordered a fine of £4 million plus an agreed £825,000 towards the costs of the prosecution. The defendant appealed to the Court of Appeal who reduced the fine to £750,000.

R v Sissen [2000] AER (D) 2193 CA

The defendant was charged with the illegal import of a Lear's macaw, one of the most endangered bird species in the world (only around 150 remain in the wild). The defendant was imprisoned for 30 months. The judge stated that: 'the law is clear as to where the interests of conservation lie. These are serious offences. An immediate custodial sentence is usually appropriate to mark their gravity and the need for deterrence.'

R v Yorkshire Water Services Ltd [2001] EWCA 2635

Yorkshire Water Services (YWS) faced 33 counts of breaches of Section 70(1) of the Water Industry Act 1991 and pleaded guilty to 17 counts (the remainder being left on the file). YWS were fined a total of £119,000 plus prosecution costs of £125,599. YWS appealed against the fines and costs and the Court of Appeal reduced the fine to £80,000. It did not disturb the costs award.

continued

Box 2.1.3 *continued*

R v David Power [2002] *Environment Times*, **vol 8, no 1, p42**
The defendant, David Power, was found guilty of his workmen removing asbestos roof sheets from a building in Wimborne, Dorset. The defendant had failed to comply with the duty of care under the waste regime and had not completed the required consignment notes for the transfer and disposal of the special waste. The defendant was sentenced to a 100 hour community punishment order plus costs of £2000.

R v Anglian Water Services Ltd [2003] Crim 2243
Anglian Water pleaded guilty to an offence under Section 85(3) of the WRA of causing sewage effluent to be discharged into the River Crouch. The magistrates committed the case to the Crown Court for sentence on the basis that the maximum sentence they could impose (£20,000) was insufficient. Crown Court fined the defendant £200,000 plus costs of £9579.58. The Court of Appeal reduced this to £60,000.

Source: MA/ELF, 2003

Aspects of international law

Legislation arising from within individual countries remains the single most important source of law in protecting the environment. However, it should be recognized that international and regional law making is highly influential and is becoming increasingly so as international trade agreements are implemented; not least because many environmental and sustainability concerns are transnational, for example marine pollution and acid rain. And, although international agreements form the basis of regional and national law, most international law formulates and regulates relations between countries. Yet, international environmental law is not new. The Behring Fur Seals Arbitration (1898) involved a complaint by the US that Britain was overexploiting areas outside the 5km US territorial zone whereby the Arbitration Panel concluded that the US had no property rights in the seals.

International legislation is often divided into hard law and soft law. Hard law includes the formal conventions such as treaties and statutes, protocols and other express written agreements or obligations between states. The Framework Convention on Climate Change 1992 and the Convention on International Trade in Endangered Species of Wild Fauna and Flora (CITES) 1973 provide good examples. Soft law consists of statements, resolutions and declarations. They include the Rio Declaration and the Statement of Principles for a Global Consensus on the Management, Conservation and Sustainable Development of all Types of Forests 1992. Countries are more likely to agree to soft laws because, while often very persuasive, they are not legally binding. There is also what may be regarded as a third form of international law, namely custom. This requires both the practice of states in general and that the state allegedly breaking the law recognizes that the customary practice is binding upon them. It is potentially binding on all states regardless of whether they have signed or ratified any agreement.

There are a vast number of international environmental agreements and declarations and Box 2.1.4 sets out the key legislation relevant to environmental management. It can be seen that conventions often provide the overarching framework for environmental protection with protocols setting more defined and detailed requirements. See, for example, the link between the Convention on Biological Diversity 1992 and the Cartagena Protocol 2000.

Box 2.1.4 *Key international environmental legislation*

UN Convention on the Law of the Sea (UNCLOS) 1982. To establish a legal order for the seas and oceans that will facilitate international communication and promote the peaceful uses of the seas and oceans, the equitable and efficient utilization of their resources, the conservation of their living resources and the study, protection and preservation of the marine environment.

Convention for the Protection of the Ozone Layer 1985 (the Vienna Convention). Requires signatory parties to take measures, including the adoption of legislation and administrative controls, to protect human health and the environment against adverse effects resulting or likely to result from human activities that modify or are likely to modify the ozone layer.

Protocol on Substances that Deplete the Ozone Layer 1987 (the Montreal Protocol). Sets targets for reducing and eliminating the production and consumption of ozone-depleting substances, makes financial provision for developing countries in terms of alternatives to ozone-depleting chemicals and bans trade of ozone-depleting substances with non-signatory parties.

Convention on the Control of Transboundary Movements of Hazardous Wastes and their Disposal 1989 (the Basel Convention). To control the export of hazardous/toxic waste and dumping by industrial nations in developing countries, and to reduce the amount of hazardous waste generated.

Convention on Environmental Impact Assessment in a Transboundary Context 1991 (the Espoo Convention). To reduce and control significant adverse transboundary environmental impacts from proposed activities, for example crude oil refineries, thermal power stations and reprocessing plants.

Declaration of the UN Conference on Environment and Development 1992 (the Rio Declaration). Statement of 27 key principles for sustainable development and international law including the precautionary principle, the polluter pays principle, public participation, risk communication and support for environmental assessment. It updated and consolidated earlier law including the Stockholm Convention 1972.

Framework Convention on Climate Change 1992 (the Climate Change Convention). To stabilize atmospheric greenhouse gas concentrations at a level that would prevent dangerous anthropogenic interference with the climate system.

Convention on Biological Diversity 1992. To secure the conservation of biodiversity, the sustainable use of its components and the equitable sharing of the benefits of genetic resources.

Convention on the Transboundary Effects of Industrial Accidents 1992. Recognized the importance and urgency of preventing the serious adverse effects of industrial accidents on human beings and the environment, and of promoting all measures that stimulate the rational, economic and efficient use of preventative, preparedness and response measures.

Convention on the Protection and Use of Transboundary Watercourses and International Lakes 1993 (the Helsinki Convention). To strengthen national measures for the protection and ecologically sound management of transboundary surface waters and groundwaters.

Protocol to the Framework Convention on Climate Change 1997 (the Kyoto Protocol). Sets targets to deliver commitments under the Climate Change Convention, providing joint implementation, carbon trading and clean development mechanisms.

Convention on Access to Information, Public Participation in Decision Making and Access to Justice in Environmental Matters 1998 (the Aarhus Convention). To secure public rights of access to environmental information, public participation in decision making and the right of access to review environmental decision making (Europe-wide only).

continued

Box 2.1.4 *continued*

Convention on the Prior Informed Consent Procedure for Certain Hazardous Chemicals and Pesticides in International Trade 1998 (the Rotterdam Convention). To promote a shared responsibility between countries to protect human health and the environment from the harmful effects of pesticides and other toxic and hazardous chemicals.

Protocol on Biosafety 2000 (the Cartagena Protocol). To meet requirements under the Convention on Biological Diversity for the adoption of a protocol on international aspects of biotechnology that may adversely affect human health and conservation and sustainable use of biological diversity.

Convention on Persistent Organic Pollutants 2001 (the Stockholm Convention). To protect human health and the environment from persistent organic pollutants (POPs) by restricting and ultimately prohibiting their use and trade.

The enforcement of international law depends on its nature. As soft laws are non-binding, there are no real means of forcing state compliance, except through political pressure. In contrast, non-compliance of a state to a signed and ratified convention may be put before the dispute settlement mechanism of that convention, for example UNCLOS has its own dispute settlement mechanism. Alternatively, the parties in dispute may refer the matter to the International Court of Justice (ICJ) which is based in The Hague. Article 38 of the ICJ Statute 1945 provides that the court's function is to decide in accordance with international law such disputes as are submitted to it relating to, among other things, conventions, international custom accepted as law and the general principles of law recognized by civilized nations. The ICJ has no priority over other dispute settlement forums, such as the International Tribunal for the Law of the Sea, and requires the consent of all parties to the dispute to apply to the court for settlement. Further, as a general rule, the ICJ does not allow private citizens to bring proceedings against states or other international organizations.

The commentary may lead to the conclusion that international environmental law can, in some instances, be ineffective and unenforceable and to an extent that may be correct, and this is perhaps when politics comes into play. Nevertheless, it still has a vital role to play in environmental protection and management by providing regulation, boundaries and clarification for many of the activities carried out across the world.

International trade and the environment

International environmental law interrelates with international trade. Key trade laws acknowledge the environment and environmentally related laws introduce economic considerations into environmental protection through concepts such as best practical means and best available techniques. Yet, while environmental law has no overarching global framework for environmental protection, international trade is governed by the World Trade Organization (WTO) and its component parts. These include the General Agreement on Tariffs and Trade (GATT), the General Agreement on Trade and Services (GATS), the Agreement on Trade-related Aspects of Intellectual Property Rights (TRIPS), the Agreement on the Application of Sanitary and Phytosanitary (SPS) Measures (animal and plant health, and hygiene) as well as their associated dispute panels. Further, the panels report their decisions on disputes to the WTO Dispute Settlement Body and an appeal can be made to the Appellate Body on the panel decision.

The primary purpose of the WTO is to encourage economic growth through international trade and many environmental protection measures are defined in vague terms. Rao (Rao, 2002, p286; see also Birnie and Boyle, 2001) explains that some of the main provisions in WTO agreements dealing with environmental issues include Article XX of GATT and Article 14 of GATS which provide that policies affecting trade in goods and services for protecting human, animal or plant life or health are exempt from normal GATT/GATS disciplines under certain conditions. Also, that the technical barriers to trade (i.e. product and industrial standards) and SPS measures recognize some environmental objectives and that certain subsidies are allowed to firms adapting to new environmental laws. Further, the WTO recognizes that many international environmental regulations (referred to as multilateral environmental agreements) have implications for international trade, such as CITES, the Basel Convention and the Montreal Protocol.

In recent years it is litigation against the US that has provided judicial pronouncements on apparently environment based trade restrictions. In the tuna/dolphin dispute (1992), the GATT panel upheld a complaint by Mexico that US import restrictions on tuna fished in a way that harmed dolphins was unfair. By contrast, in the shrimp/turtle dispute (1999), the WTO Appellate Body found that, in principle, US requirements on shrimp importers to demonstrate that their harvesting methods did not endanger turtles was acceptable, although the US approach was found to be arbitrary and discriminatory among countries.

It is felt by many that, despite the proliferation of legislation in the past 30 years, environmental protection remains subservient to international trade. Rao (2002, p294 citing Nordstrom and Vaughan) suggests that the globalization of the world economy may have 'reduced the regulatory autonomy of countries, thereby making it more difficult to monitor environmental standards unless as part of a concerted effort among nations'. He comments that various trade measures contained in some international environmental agreements are either too weak in their specifications or in their implementation. Measures to ensure compliance with provisions do not normally attract sanctions or penalties, thereby perpetuating free-riders rather than responsible environmental partnerships.

References and further reading

Anderson, S. K. and Sarma, K. M. (2002) *Protecting the Ozone Layer: The United Nations History*, Earthscan, London

Birnie, P. and Boyle, A. (2001) *International Law and the Environment*, 2nd edn, Oxford University Press, Oxford

Elliot, C. and Quinn, F. (2001) *Law for AQA*, Pearson Education Ltd, Edinburgh

Higgins, R. (1994) *Problems and Process: International Law and How We Use it*, Clarendon Press, Oxford

MA/ELF (2003) *Costing the Earth, Environmental Sentencing Guidelines*, revised edn, Magistrates' Association and Environmental Law Foundation, London. For further information go to www.magistrates-association.org.uk

Munro, R. D. (1987) *Environmental Protection and Sustainable Development: Legal Principles and Recommendations*, (Experts Group on Environmental Law of the World Commission on Environment and Development, R. D. Munro, Chairman, J. G. Lammers, Rapporteur), Graham and Trotman, Martinus Nijoff: London, Dordrect, Boston

NODE (1998) *New Oxford Dictionary of English*, Oxford University Press, Oxford

Rao, P. K. (2002) *International Environmental Law and Economics*, Blackwell Publishers, Oxford

Wilkinson, D. (2002) *Environment and Law*, Routledge, London. This is an excellent introduction to environmental law. It explains how the law relates to the many areas of environmental protection, and is written for non-lawyers in a clear, concise and informative manner.

Chapter 2.2

European Union Environmental Policy and Legislation

Introduction

The treaties ratified by the member states since the early 1950s are the legal foundations of the European Union (EU). These treaties are multilateral international agreements that have been developed for differing reasons; but they all have the same underlying goal of achieving an ever-closer union among the member states and the citizens of the member states. The primary objective of this union is to ensure peace and prosperity within the geographical region occupied by the signatory states. The original treaty (the Treaty of the European Economic Community) did not contain a specific environmental chapter. Other articles, relating to trade, and the living and working conditions of the citizens, provided the legitimacy for the EU. The first explicit environmental articles were included in the Single European Act in 1987 (Table 2.2.1).

Europe's environment

The EU launched the first of six environmental action programmes (EAPs) in 1973. Five have now been completed with more than 200 major environmental directives, regulations and decisions being introduced. Directives are the most often used form of legislation for environmental policy as they provide national governments with flexibility in the way they are implemented. The objectives set out in the legislation have to be achieved in all the member states, but governments are left with choices as to how this is to be done. Regulations are used to ensure complete uniformity across the EU on a specific issue. Regulations are binding in their entirety and are directly applicable in all member states. This means that there is no requirement for intervening legislation by the national governments. Decisions are addressed to the member states, but perhaps only one or two states rather than all. Decisions are binding in their entirety. Decisions may also be directed towards private enterprises. This happens most often in the area of the EU's competition policy, where a company may be fined for a breach of competition law.

These directives, regulations and decisions have established environmental standards in relation to environmental quality, pollution emissions, product specifications, or set common approaches to various aspects of environmental management in the

Table 2.2.1   The treaties of the EU

Date	Title	Signatory states	Remarks
1951	European Coal and Steel Community (ECSC)	France, Germany, Italy, Belgium, the Netherlands, Luxemburg (the Six)	Free trade in coal and steel products. It became the model for the EEC and was absorbed into the TEU in 2000
1957	European Economic Community (EEC)	The Six	Economic and trade integration
1957	European Atomic Energy Community (EAEC), EURATOM	The Six	Civilian use of nuclear technology
1965	Treaty of the European Community (TEC)	The Six	Merger of the ECSC, EEC and EAEC treaties into one European Community (EC)
1987	Single European Act (SEA)	The Six with Eire, Denmark, the UK, Greece, Spain and Portugal (the Twelve)	First major revision of the TEC. Signed by an additional six member states which joined the EC during the 1970s and 1980s
1993	Treaty on European Union (TEU) (Maastricht)	The Twelve	Created the three pillars of the EU. The first pillar, the TEC, includes the environmental chapter, the second and third pillars (known together as the Treaty on European Union) include policies on justice and home affairs and common foreign and security policy
1999	Treaty of Amsterdam (ToA)	The Twelve with Austria, Finland, Sweden (the Fifteen)	Amendment to the TEU, statement that sustainable development is a primary commitment of the EU
2003	Treaty of Nice (ToN)	The Fifteen	Amendment to the TEU, institutional changes for the EU to enlarge to 25 member states
2003	Draft constitutional treaty	The Fifteen with observers from the accession states	Draft prepared for discussion by the governments of the EU states between summer 2003 and summer 2004. Maintaining the status quo for environmental issues

EU's member states. Notable progress has been achieved in improving the quality of water and air in the EU but severe problems remain in the areas of chemicals and their impact on human health, hazardous waste management and disposal, soil erosion and degradation and decline of biodiversity.

New issues are also gaining prominence on the EU's environmental policy agenda. Within the EU, increased commitment to the concept of sustainable development has linked environmental objectives to economic development and job creation. The EU increased in size from 15 member states to 25 in 2004. The new member states of Central and Eastern Europe (CEE) are Hungary, Poland, Slovakia, Latvia, Lithuania, the Czech Republic, Estonia and Slovenia. Cyprus and Malta also became members of the EU in

2004. Turkey is expected to join some time after Bulgaria and Romania accede in 2007. The CEE states are different in physical, economic and political terms to the current member states, and they have some severe problems of environmental degradation. The ability of the EU to introduce new policy measures and legislation may be undermined because of the compromises needed to accommodate these differences.

The use of directives, regulations and decisions will continue to be the predominant form of EU action for the future. Legally binding instruments are needed to ensure compliance from all member states, but a wide range of economic policy instruments is being developed to supplement the legislation. These include 'getting the price' of environmental degradation right by removing national government subsidies to polluting industries, encouraging the use of environmental taxes and incentives, the introduction of tradable permits, improved consumer knowledge, environmental management and procurement systems, and sustainable land use in urban, coastal and other environmentally sensitive regions.

Making policy

The EU is a unique organization of member states with a number of institutions to negotiate and decide on policy measures and legislation. Consensus building among the diverse national and sectoral interests in the EU is the main aim of the negotiating process. The environmental policy agenda is set by the heads of governments of the EU states in the summit meetings of the European Council. The European Commission develops proposals for legislation. They are amended and adopted as legal instruments by the Council of Ministers and the European Parliament (EP), and ultimately are enforced by the European Court of Justice (ECJ). In some areas of policy a more open approach is used, based on the voluntary coordination of the national environmental policies and shared policy learning.

Landmarks in the development of EU environmental policy are shown in Table 2.2.2. To enthusiastic environmentalists the EU's policy developments have been disappointing. It is believed that a lack of political will among the policymakers is the reason for policy failures, as governments and sectoral interests defend their positions. Increasing the number of actors to include the general public, local authorities and non-governmental organizations (NGOs) to develop and implement policy could lead to fragmentation of effort and undermine the improvements that have been made to the EU's environment. A more flexible and inclusive approach produces effective policy; but reliable and comparable information flows have to be established with stringent reporting and monitoring procedures.

Table 2.2.2   Landmarks in EU environmental policy

1967   First Environmental Directive, 67/548 on classification, packaging and labelling of dangerous substances. This directive was one of a small number of pieces of legislation adopted in the 1960s that had strong health and safety aspects. They were not part of an overall strategy to protect the environment.

1973   Launch of the First EAP 1973–1976
As living standards rose during the 1960s there was greater global awareness of the problems being caused to the environment and the ways in which they damaged human

Table 2.2.2   continued

health. The EU's response was the First Action Programme. It was based on limited remedial action for specific problems, but did establish the basic principles on which policy has been built. First, that the principle of subsidiarity should be applied in the decision making process. The objective of this principle is to ensure that the appropriate level of government is chosen, so that decisions are taken as closely as possible to the people who are affected by them. The EU therefore should take action 'only if, and in so far as the objectives … cannot be sufficiently achieved by the Member States and … [their] scale or effects will be better achieved by the Community' (Art 5, TEC). Second, responsibility should be shared – the EU establishing the action needed and the national governments ensuring that it is carried out. Third, prevention of pollution is better than trying to cure the problem after it has emerged. Fourth, the polluter should pay for pollution control and clean up. Fifth, the problems should be remedied at the source of the pollution.

1987   The Environment Chapter to the SEA
Environmentalists raised concerns about the impact of market liberalization measures in the transport and energy sectors on the environment. The outcome was pressure, led by the Danish Government, to ensure that a chapter on the environment was included in the SEA in July 1987. As it provided a legal basis for action on environmental protection to be taken by the EU this was arguably the most important of the early stages in the development of the EU's environmental policy.

1992   The Fifth EAP (1992–2000), Towards Sustainability
The Fifth EAP was the first attempt to develop policy that would contribute to sustainable development. Five sectors of economically important activity that had the greatest potential for environmental damage were targeted – agriculture, energy, manufacturing industry, transport and tourism. A range of instruments was proposed in addition to legislation including: voluntary agreements, environmental management and auditing and eco-labelling schemes, and tradable permits and environmental taxes.

Three networks were established to support the participation of interested groups in the development of policy. These were the European Consultative Forum on the Environment and Sustainable Development (the 'Green Forum'), the Network for the Implementation and Enforcement of Environmental Law (IMPEL) and the Environment Policy Review Group. Measures were also identified so that information could be made more accessible to the public and the policymakers to help their participation in environmental policy making.

1993   TEU (Maastricht)
Article 6 TEC – all EU policies and activities must integrate environmental protection objectives.

1998   Cardiff process launched
To develop strategies to integrate environmental objectives into nine policy areas – strategies for transport, energy and agriculture have been completed.

1999   ToA
Clear commitment to sustainable development in Article 2 TEC and Article 2 TEU. Protection of the environment on the same basis as economic development within the EU and now a primary objective of the union.

2000   Launch of the Sixth EAP and its seven thematic strategies (e.g. strategy for future chemicals policy, July 2001, strategy on waste prevention and recycling, May 2003).

2002   EU and the member states ratified the Kyoto Protocol.

2003   Draft constitutional treaty maintained the status quo of legal support for EU environmental policy and legislation.

The Sixth EAP, 'Our Future, Our Choice', 2001–2010

The Sixth EAP was adopted at the end of 2000 to cover the period from 1 January 2001 to 31 December 2010. Its main priorities are to find solutions for the continuing failings in implementation and enforcement of policy and to target issues where existing policy appears to have failed. These include climate change, biodiversity loss, efficient use and management of natural resources, waste management, reduction of risks to the environment and human health from chemicals and genetically modified organisms, soil degradation and desertification.

The EAP supports a strategy of combining a mix of policy instruments, such as voluntary agreements, the use of eco-taxes and tradable permits, and increased funding opportunities, with legislation. The primary objective is to create a more flexible policy that will contribute to the EU's sustainable development strategy. The Brundtland definition of sustainable development was included in the Fifth EAP in 1992 but it was not stated in the 1993 Maastricht Treaty. Instead the treaty contained a much weaker statement of support for actions leading to sustainable growth respecting the environment. However, the 1999 ToA did contain an unambiguous reference to sustainable development. Sustainable development is now a central principle of the EU.

The EU adopted its sustainable development strategy in Gothenburg in June 2001. The strategy recognizes the importance of balancing economic growth, social cohesion and environmental protection in future policy and legislative developments within the EU. The strategy is an integral part of the EU's ambition to become 'the most competitive and dynamic knowledge-based economy in the world capable of sustainable economic growth with more and better jobs and greater social cohesion' (European Council, 2000). One of the first steps towards fulfilling the strategy's commitments was the action plan to encourage investment in environmental technology that was launched in March 2003. Other objectives from the Sixth EAP include overcoming persistent environmental problems, facilitating the full integration of environmental protection requirements into other EU policies, and building measures based on extensive dialogue and sound science.

The Sixth EAP is also the EU's strategic programme for dealing with international environmental issues. The environmental challenges associated with the 2004 enlargement are the immediate short term priorities. The EU is making significant contributions to the search for effective solutions to global environmental problems. The EU was the driving force in ensuring that environmental issues were included on the World Trade Organization's (WTO's) agenda in Doha, Qatar that launched a new round of trade negotiations. The EU has ratified a number of other international treaties, including: the Rotterdam Convention on prior informed consent, which strengthens the rights of poorer states to be protected from hazards; the Basel Convention to protect poorer states from dumping of toxic wastes by the developed states; the Bonn Convention on the conservation of migratory species; and the Biosafety Protocol of the Biodiversity Convention.

Implementation and enforcement of legislation

As the number of environmental issues covered by EU's policy has grown, so have concerns about the effectiveness of their implementation and enforcement. Treaties give the primary responsibility to the national governments to ensure that they take all appropriate measures needed to fulfil the obligations contained in the legislation. Firstly, national governments must ensure that there is an appropriate national law to transfer or transpose EU directives. Secondly, national governments must put the appropriate infrastructure into place to introduce the measures and procedures needed for practical compliance with EU derived legislation. For example, in the case of the EU's Eco-labelling Regulation this means ensuring that the appropriate agency is put into place to enable companies to register to use the scheme. Enforcement by the national authorities includes the process of monitoring, imposition of national sanctions and 'on the spot' investigations and controls.

The commission is the competent authority with responsibility to ensure that member states implement and enforce EU legislation to agreed deadlines. Since 1996 the European Commission has conducted annual surveys on this aspect of the responsibilities. One purpose of these surveys is to 'name and shame' governments into action. In 2002, a total of 555 new complaints about breaches of environmental law were received by the commission. A number of other complaints were raised in written questions and petitions to the EP.

The commission is responsible for referring cases of infringements of legislation to the ECJ. It brought 65 new cases forward to the ECJ in 2002. There are several procedures and penalties that the commission may recommend to the ECJ. In most cases, procedures are used that carry lesser penalties or identify practical measures for the national governments. This approach has the advantage of being flexible, less consuming of the ECJ's time and more efficient, as the specific member state is identified and subject to targeted action. Initially the member state will be notified that they are in breach of the law and asked for their own observations. If the national government fails to respond within a reasonable period of time then the commission prepares a reasoned opinion that identifies the grounds for a complaint to be taken before the court. In 2002, 137 reasoned opinions were issued by the commission. By far the largest number of cases will be resolved at this stage with perhaps one third proceeding to a judgement by the ECJ.

In cases of blatant continued inaction by a national government more stringent penalties are available under the terms of Article 228 TEC. This article carries the ultimate sanction of a fine against a member state that has continued in its failure to implement legislation. Up to August 2003 only the Greek Government had been fined, in 2000, because of continued failures to implement two directives on water quality in Crete. However, the threat of the sanction has been used to great effect against other member states that have continually failed to implement legislation, including the UK, Belgium, Italy, Germany and France.

Some EU member states find it easier to deal with environmental issues than others. There is no single all-encompassing problem leading to implementation failure by the national governments, but three issues are more prominent than others: first, delays in notifying national implementing measures and communicating them to the commission within the deadlines given in the legislation; second, doubts about conformity with the legislation; third, bad application of the measures that provide the infrastructure for operation of the legislation. Other concerns include poor drafting of the legislation and failures to take account of the diversity of national conditions when setting standards in the legislation. In 2002 the UK came bottom of the league (Table 2.2.3) primarily because of failures to notify implementation measures on time.

Table 2.2.3   Naming and shaming – the environmental scoreboard

Member state	Number of directives for which the implementing measures have been notified to the European Commission	% of directives that have been implemented by member state*
Austria	167	95.98
Belgium	169	94.41
Denmark	174	98.86
Finland	169	96.02
France	163	93.14
Germany	169	95.48
Greece	163	93.68
Ireland	168	95.45
Italy	166	94.32
Luxemburg	170	96.59
Netherlands	169	96.57
Portugal	169	97.13
Spain	169	96.02
Sweden	173	98.86
UK	149	84.66

Note: *Based on a total of 183 directives having been adopted
Source: European Commission, 2003

The annual reports on the implementation of environmental legislation presented by the commission have simplified the information gathering process for all interested parties. Creating the opportunity for open debate about proposals is a vital element in enabling the public to participate in all stages of the policy process, from policy making to implementation. It is an essential element of any strategy to involve all the stakeholders in the development of future legislation to increase their commitment to implementation. General Directive 90/313/EEC on the freedom of access to information on the environment contains a requirement for the national authorities to respond to requests for environmental information from the public. This directive is one that several member states, including Germany, a state with good environmental credentials at the national level, have not correctly transposed, yet it is a vital element of the information flow.

A number of other mechanisms are in place to assist the information gathering and dissemination process. For example, the European Environment Agency (EEA) was established in 1990. It has no direct role in the policy making process, but provides information and alternative scenarios for the policymakers. Since the mid-1990s it has produced three wide ranging assessments of the state of the environment in Europe plus numerous briefing papers on specific aspects of environmental issues.

The informal EU network of implementing authorities (IMPEL) was established in 1992. Its primary objective was to create the impetus at the national level to ensure that large industrial processes complied with the relevant legislation. Its work has expanded since 1992 to include the promotion of improved standards of permitting, inspection, monitoring and enforcement by the member states and exchange of information on the best practice for implementation. Since 1998 the environmental inspectorates and authorities in the accession states have participated in a number of IMPEL projects.

Other practical measures include guidelines and interpretative texts published by the commission to assist the national authorities, for example for Directive 96/61/EC on integrated pollution and prevention control and Directive 200/60/EC, the Water Framework Directive. The EU's 'Europa' web site has become a vehicle for disseminating information and also a portal for email access to commission officials. Consultation on policy has been increased through the use of the internet.

Climate change

Climate change was identified in the sustainable development strategy as one of the most pressing problems for the EU. The causes of climate change are complex and cut across many areas of policy. This highlights the necessity for holistic solutions if the EU is to make an effective contribution to global action. The EU and all the accession states have now ratified the Kyoto Protocol to cut the emissions of the dominant greenhouse gases.

When the US Government announced its withdrawal from the Kyoto Protocol in 2001, the EU took the lead in encouraging the other states to support its objectives by continuing with a package of measures to curb emissions. Somewhat disappointingly, not all EU states have been able to cut their emissions and at current levels emissions will only have fallen by 4.7 per cent not the 8 per cent Kyoto target by 2008.

The EU is in the process of introducing new measures and reinforcing existing measures in the three main contributory sectors of transport, energy (including heating in commercial and residential areas) and industry. If all these proposals are adopted than a reduction of 12.4 per cent could be achieved (Table 2.2.4).

Table 2.2.4   Packages of measures to meet the EU's Kyoto commitments (2002–2003)

Cross-cutting measures	Status of implementation
Directive on emission trading	Proposal in March 2003
Effective implementation of integrated pollution prevention and control (IPPC) directive	Work is continuing on: i) IPPC reference document on generic energy efficiency techniques ii) Sector specific BAT reference documents iii) Revision of already published BAT reference documents
Linking project based mechanisms to emissions trading	Proposal in July 2003
Review of Commission monitoring procedures	Proposal in February 2003

continued overleaf

Table 2.2.4   continued

Cross-cutting measures	Status of implementation
Energy	
Directive on taxation of energy products	Adopted
Directive on energy performance of buildings	Before the Council and the European Parliament
Directive on energy efficiency requirements for end use products	Proposal from Commission
Directive on combined heat and power	Adopted by Commission
Directive on the promotion of electricity from renewable energy sources	Adopted by Council and the European Parliament
Initiatives on increased energy efficient public procurement	In preparation
Public awareness and Campaign for Take-Off	Launched in 2003
Transport related	
ACEA/JAMA/KAMA voluntary agreement between EU, Japanese and Korean car manufacturers to reduce fleet carbon dioxide emissions by 140g/km by 2008/2009	Yearly monitoring reports
White Paper on Common Transport Policy	Package of measures to encourage a shift in the balances between the modes of transport
Proposal for improvements in infrastructure use and charging	In preparation
Promotion of biofuels for transport	Proposals for a directive
Communication on taxation of passenger cars	Adopted by Commission
Proposals for tax regime for diesel fuel used for commercial purposes and alignment of excise duties	Adopted by Commission
Proposal for funding to help improve the environmental performance of freight transport	Adopted by Commission
Industry	
Directive on fluorinated gases	Proposals to the EP in September 2003

Source: European Commission, 2004a

The European Climate Change Programme (ECCP) was launched in June 2000 with the aim of establishing a framework of support for EU action. Some policy measures may be more appropriately applied at the national level and others require action by all the member states together. It is intended that the ECCP should provide an opportunity for the commission to work with all the major stakeholders to identify the most effective combinations of measures to use and provide coordination between national and EU levels. Seven technical working groups – including energy, transport, agriculture and industry – have been established and more than 40 measures identified, some of which are already being put into place (e.g. the 2003 directive on an EU scheme for greenhouse gas emissions trading). Others will focus on strengthening research on climate change and 22 measures relate to longer term support for environmental technology developments.

The EU scheme for greenhouse emissions trading will come into operation by 2005. It is intended to limit carbon dioxide emissions from 4000–5000 large scale producers such as power generation stations. The national authorities will provide the regulatory framework for the scheme. Allowances will be allocated to the large emitters on an annual basis outlined in agreed national allocation plans. If emissions are reduced below the level of the allowance, the excess may be sold to another polluter or saved for future use. Companies that exceed their limits may invest in pollution abatement technology or buy allowances on the market. In July 2003 the commission introduced a proposed directive to allow EU companies to carry out emissions-curbing projects around the world and convert the credits they gain in this way into emissions allowances under the trading scheme. Emissions trading will only work if accurate data is available. In February 2003 a revised monitoring mechanism for greenhouse gas emission was introduced to provide that support.

Fluorinated gases have a more potent impact at smaller volumes than carbon dioxide. A proposal for legislation to cut emissions of fluorinated gases by 25 per cent was made in 2003. This will have a significant effect on a range of products from vehicle tyres, non-refillable containers, fire extinguishers, footwear, double-glazing, industrial refrigerators, and car air-conditioning systems, in addition to innovations such as a self cooling drink can.

Strategy for chemicals

The chemical industry is the EU's third largest manufacturing sector. It employs 1.7 million people directly and supports up to 3 million jobs. There are a small number of large scale multinational companies in the industry but there are also 36,000 smaller businesses that account for 28 per cent of total production. In 1998 global production of chemicals was in excess of 400 million tonnes with a value of €1244 billion. Of that global total the EU produced 31 per cent, generating a trade surplus of €421 billion, more than the US with 28 per cent of production and a trade surplus value of €12 billion. 100,000 different chemical substances are registered in the EU, 10,000 being marketed in volumes of more than 10 tonnes and 20,000 substances in the range 1 to 10 tonnes.

The chemical industry performs a major role in the economic prosperity of the EU but some chemicals have been shown to have serious impacts on human health and the environment. Many of these effects were not obvious in the early history of their development and usage, but have come to light over time. Serious gaps exist in knowledge and understanding of these impacts and a major review of the EU's chemicals strategy began in 1998 to identify the gaps and find mechanisms to overcome them. This review led to the development of the EU's 2001 Strategy on Future Chemicals Policy.

The 2001 strategy was built on a commitment to introduce a regime that would lead to sustainable development. The legislative framework will not be replaced but there will be revisions to ensure that there is comparability of treatment between those substances that have been on the market for a long time and new products. A key element of the new strategy is the development of a single system for the testing of chemicals and determination of risk and identification of risk reduction measures. The scheme known as REACH (Registration, Evaluation, Authorization of Chemicals) was open to an eight week online consultation in July 2003 that stimulated 7000 responses.

The chemicals strategy demonstrates many of the features common to the development of environmental legislation and policy in the EU since the 1970s. An approach based on separate pieces of legislation to deal with very specific problems has been replaced by a broad ranging strategy to ensure a high level of protection for human health and the environment without undermining economic growth. Participation of the relevant stakeholders is considered to be an important part of this strategy as is wider dissemination of information in a format that the general public is able to readily access.

The challenge of enlargement

Enormous problems have been left in the accession states of CEE as a legacy of practices during the communist period. Increasing the size of the EU to 25 member states multiplies the number of concerns that have to be taken into account by policymakers. These include the physical conditions in the new states, their levels of administrative capacity to provide the government departments and appropriate environmental authorities, the levels of pollution which have to be dealt with and the economic capacity of the new states to deal with problems of clean up. In addition, environmental policy was not ignored during the period of communist rule, but it was often not implemented effectively. Against this background the incidences of implementation failures are likely to increase, certainly in the short term in the enlarged EU.

Candidate states for membership of the EU are required to accept all the existing EU legislation. The enlargement strategies agreed by the accession states and the commission have focused on identifying a number of key objectives, including transposition of environmental legislation into national legislation as the prerequisite for EU accession. Derogations have been agreed for the introduction of some legislation while for others such as wastewater treatment there are long transitional periods. This was because of the problems for the accession states in finding the finance to introduce the measures. It has been estimated that the new states will face immediate costs in the region of €120–140 billion for the environmental measures needed for enlargement. In addition, the new member states will have to spend around 2–3 per cent of their total gross domestic product (GDP) over the next 15–20 years on environmental improvements.

The 15 existing member states are reluctant to fund measures in the accession states, but some financial support has been given through the Instrument for Structural Policies for Pre-accession (ISPA). €500 million have been allocated annually to support investment in environmental infrastructure during the preparations for enlargement. It is apparent that a lot of financial support in the CEE states must be found from the private sector and foreign investment.

Limited funding is available within the EU to promote sustainable development and following enlargement the accession states will have access to these resources. Funding from the Structural Funds will be available in the next programming period that begins in 2007. The Structural Funds are designed to help promote a more balanced socio-economic development across the member states and include funding for environmental improvement projects, for example clean up of coastal areas and harbours, to stimulate new economic activity. Other sources of funding come from research programmes and agri-environmental resources. The LIFE programme (Financial Instrument for the Environment) was established in 1992. Three strands are identified for projects – LIFE-nature, LIFE-environment and LIFE-third countries. In addition the European Investment Bank provides long term loans for projects designed to safeguard the environment. These loans made to the national governments may cover up to 50 per cent of the investment costs for schemes such as waste management, waste treatment and urban renewal.

The future of EU environmental policy

From an early history of command and control regulatory measures to remedy specific problems, the EU has developed an environmental policy which is wide ranging and focused on the complexity of designing policy measures and legislation that will lead to sustainable development. The policy is now formally established around three main axes – subsidiarity and the sharing of responsibility between the national governments and local authorities, and the EU; more open consultation and greater involvement of all the stakeholders; and the goal of long term and sustainable development.

Among its recent achievements the EU has:

- made a contribution to sustainable development and global environmental issues;
- adopted a more targeted approach to policy development;
- introduced a wider variety of policy instruments;
- introduced more assessment and review of the effectiveness of policy measures; and
- initiated strategies to take environmental requirements into account in the EU's sectoral policies.

As a result, the policy has achieved the goal of greater flexibility, but a number of problems do remain for action. These include:

- improving the effectiveness of the design of new policy instruments;
- ensuring the implementation of current policies in the existing member states and in the new CEE states;
- effective application of the integrative strategies to include environmental objectives in all sectoral policies; and
- fulfilling the commitments of the sustainable development strategy.

References and further reading

Barnes, P. M. and Barnes, I. G. (2000) *Environmental Policy in the European Union*, Edward Elgar Publishing, Cheltenham

Bomberg, E. and Stubb, A. (2003) *The EU: How Does it Work?*, Oxford University Press, Oxford

European Commission (2001a) 'A Sustainable Europe for a Better World – EU Strategy for Sustainable Development', COM (2001) 264 final, Brussels

European Commission (2001b) 'Environment 2010 – Our Future, Our Choice, the Sixth Environment Action Programme of the European Community 2001–2010', COM (2001) 31 final, Brussels

European Commission (2001c) 'White Paper – Strategy for a Future Chemicals Policy', COM (2001) 88 final, Brussels

European Commission (2002) *Choices for a Greener Future – the EU and the Environment*, Office for Official Publications of the European Communities, Luxemburg

European Commission (2003) 'Fourth Annual Survey of the Implementation and Enforcement of Community Environmental Law – 2002', SEC (2003) 804, Brussels

European Commission (2004a) The web site of the Directorate-General for the Environment is at www.europa.eu.int/comm/environment

European Commission (2004b) The web site of the UK representatives is at www.cec.org.uk

European Council (2000) Conclusions of Lisbon Summit 23/24 March 2000, Conclusions of the Gothenburg Summit 16/17 June 2001

European Eco-label (2004) The web site is at www.eu.int/ecolabel

European Environment Agency (2003) *Europe's Environment – The Third Assessment*, Office for Official Publications of the European Communities, Luxemburg

EEA (2004) The European Environment Agency's web site is at www.eea.eu.int

European Environmental Bureau (2004) The web site is at www.eeb.org

EP Office (2004) The European Parliament Office web site is at www.europarl.eu.int

EU (2004) The European Union web site is at http://europa.eu.int

Gower, J. (ed) (2002) *The European Union Handbook*, 2nd edn, Fitzroy Dearborn, London

McCormick, J. (2002) *Understanding the EU*, 2nd edn, Macmillan, Basingstoke and London

UN (2004) The United Nations Framework Convention on Climate Change web site is at http://unfccc.int/

Chapter 2.3

The UK Legislative Context

Introduction

Since the devolution of law-making powers to Scotland, Wales and Northern Ireland, aspects of environmental legislation have become specific to those countries even if the differences in substance are not necessarily that significant. For example, there may be many differences in the administrative structures in place to implement and enforce regulations and procedures.

The main reason for the continuing similarity in the nature of environmental laws found in the various parts of the UK is the fact that a significant proportion of new environmental legislation is passed in order to secure compliance with European and international legislation. And although the compliance mechanisms may differ within the UK, the main goal of compliance with European and international obligations is the same. Practical examples of these differences can be seen in the following list:

- The contaminated land regime under Part IIA of the Environmental Protection Act 1990 (EPA; UK Parliament, 1990) was brought into force in different parts of the UK at different times, with Wales being almost two years after England. Part of the reason for this was the failure of the Welsh Assembly to approve the necessary regulations (UK Parliament, 2001a).
- The Scottish Executive introduced amendments to the waste management licensing regime in order to change the rules on the land spreading of certain types of waste after a political outcry (UK Parliament, 2003).
- The waste management licensing system in Northern Ireland is governed by legislation passed in 1978, and even then the legislation is not comprehensive. It only applies to disposal and not across the chain of waste management. A framework of more modern waste management laws exists – it was passed in 1997 – but it was only in June 2003 that proposals were issued to implement the new laws.

What does this lack of unity in UK environmental law mean in practice? First, never make the assumption that the English position in any area of environmental law is reflected elsewhere. Second, never assume that the legal positions in Wales, Scotland and Northern Ireland are a subset of English law. In particular Scotland has laws that do not exist in England. Third, always remember that in addition to different and separate law making powers, Scotland and Northern Ireland have different legal systems, and although they are similar to the systems in England and Wales, certain classes of potential environmental liability, such as nuisance, may be dealt with in a different manner. Finally, there are certain fundamental differences in procedures that have a significant impact. For example, in Scotland, criminal prosecutions are all brought by the Procurator Fiscal. This adds an extra tier of decision making in comparison to England and Wales where such prosecutions are brought directly by the Environment Agency (EA).

Even in England, with which this chapter is primarily concerned, there is no single codified system of environmental laws. Instead, there are distinct legal regimes governing different aspects of the environment and activities that impact in different ways on the environment. In places these systems overlap and in others they exist in parallel and are generally fairly uncoordinated, but taken as a whole they provide a relatively comprehensive tapestry of laws to protect the environment.

These laws reflect their disparate historic evolution. For example, the public sanitation legislation derived from 19th century initiatives to protect public health in the increasingly squalid and plague-ridden conditions that were developing in the growing urban areas in the industrial revolution. More visionary and forward-looking laws, such as the town planning system and the integrated pollution control (IPC)/integrated pollution prevention and control (IPPC) regimes, are later developments in the legal evolutionary cycle and are aimed at strategically avoiding harm to the environment, rather than primarily focusing on cleaning it up or penalizing those who have caused it.

This chapter provides a broad picture of this vast legal tapestry without focusing too closely on the technical legal details. Inevitably, there is a need to simplify and be selective in the topics discussed and to omit material, which in the daily practice of business activities or legal practice will be fundamentally important in determining liabilities and rights. For that reason, it is appropriate to emphasize from the outset that this chapter is not intended as a legal reference work and should not be used as a basis for legal advice on the matters that it covers.

This chapter will examine the different mechanisms deployed by the law in England to protect different aspects of the environment from harm and to penalize or obtain compensation from those who are responsible for causing environmental damage. These mechanisms include:

- spatial strategies to avoid or reduce environmental harm;
- benchmarking or standards setting;
- regulation and enforcement by licensing and consent procedures;
- criminal sanctions;
- compensation for harm caused;
- remediation of environmental harm by compulsory or other means;
- enhancement of the environment; and
- public education, scrutiny and involvement.

These mechanisms are examined by reference to two legal regimes. Firstly, holistic approaches to environmental protection: this includes the planning system, and IPC and IPPC. Secondly, specific environmental protection regimes: this includes air and atmospheric pollution controls; protection of water resources – marine and surface waters; the statutory framework relating to contaminated land; the waste management licensing regime; and laws relating to statutory nuisance.

The planning system

The planning system provides a legal mechanism for reducing the environmental impacts of development and is increasingly being used for the purpose of remedying past environmental harm or providing environmental enhancements. The planning system is a statutory code that, as a national system, was first codified in 1947. The current statutory code is mainly comprised of the Town and Country Planning Act 1990 (TCPA, 1990, etc).

Very important environmental provisions are contained in the Town and Country Planning (Hazardous Substances Control) Act 1990 and regulations made under that act. There is a parallel and closely related statutory framework for the protection of historic and architectural heritage in the Town and Country Planning (Listed Buildings and Conservation Areas) Act 1990.

The need for planning permission

At the heart of the planning regime is the requirement under Section 57 of the 1990 Act, which provides that planning permission is required for the development of land. Planning permission is generally obtained by making an application to a local planning authority, which will usually be a unitary authority such as a London borough or a metropolitan district council. In areas with a county council this will be the district council for most purposes but will be the county council for certain types of development, including mineral extraction and waste applications.

The First Secretary of State (FSOS) and the Office of the Deputy Prime Minister are the minister and central government department with central control over the planning system. The FSOS or a minister in his department or an inspector appointed by the Planning Inspectorate will make planning decisions where the development is subject to an appeal under Section 78 of the 1990 Act or has been called in by the FSOS under powers in Section 77 of the act. Over the past ten years or so, environmental considerations have featured with increasing frequency in planning decisions.

The statutory duty in determining planning applications or appeals

The fundamental duties of local planning authorities in determining a planning application are contained in Sections 54A and 70 of the 1990 Act. These provide as follows:

- Section 54A: where, in making any determination under the planning acts, regard is to be had to the development plan, the determination shall be made in accordance with the plan unless material considerations indicate otherwise.
- Section 70(2): in dealing with such an application the authority shall have regard to the provisions of the development plan, so far as material to the application, and to any other material considerations.

The importance of these statutory duties in the context of English environmental law is that development plans and material considerations have environmental protection and enhancement as essential elements.

Development plans

Development plans may be called unitary development plans in the areas of unitary authorities or they may be made up of structure plans and local plans in county areas. There will also be special minerals local plans and waste local plans to govern those specific activities within county areas.

The regulations governing the preparation, adoption and review of development plans (the Town and Country Planning (Development Plan) Regulations 1991 – Regulation 9) require the local planning authorities preparing them to have regard to 'environmental considerations'. Government guidance as to the meaning of this requirement is contained in Planning Policy Guidance Note 12 (Defra, 1999a, particularly at Section 4). Section 4 encourages a holistic approach in formulating development plans in a manner that will achieve social and economic growth that is sustainable. In paragraph 4.4 the guidance states that:

> Development plans should be drawn up in such a way as to take environmental considerations comprehensively and consistently into account (either as policies/proposals or as part of the explanatory memorandum/reasoned justification of plans).

The guidance then sets out an extensive list of environmental matters that need to be incorporated into plan policies including: global atmosphere, climate change and greenhouse gases; air quality and atmospheric pollution; biodiversity; noise and light pollution; contamination of ground and groundwater; heritage protection; and conservation of finite resources.

Thus, by making the development plan a primary consideration in the determination of planning applications (and other decisions in development control and enforcement decisions) the legislation is making environmental protection and enhancement an integral objective of the process. This is reinforced by the application of the concept of 'material considerations'.

Material considerations

Apart from the obligation to include environmental policies in development plans, the concept of material consideration, which makes environmental protection and enhancement a relevant consideration in all planning decisions where such issues are germane to the land use aspects of the matter being decided, opens up an almost infinite range of possible environmental dimensions that may be taken into account in deciding whether development is acceptable.

The following examples indicate the enormous potential for deciding planning applications by reference to the environmental impacts of a proposal:

- Under Section 71A of the 1990 Act and the Town and Country Planning (Environmental Impact Assessment) (England and Wales) Regulations 1999, the decision maker must take account of the environmental information emerging from an environmental impact assessment (EIA) in relation to EIA applications.
- Even where the application is not an EIA application (i.e. an application in which an environmental statement is by law required to be submitted or is otherwise

submitted), the environmental effects of a development will be a material consideration irrespective of whether the development plan contains policies dealing with the specific environmental issues in question. Essentially the whole range of environmental and sustainability issues is made a material consideration by planning policy guidance notes and regional planning guidance, which are themselves material considerations where they apply to the matter in question.

- Under the Conservation (Natural Habitats) Regulations (UK Parliament, 1994), Regulation 48, a local planning authority is required, where a planning application is likely to have a significant effect on a European site protected under the Habitats Directive, to carry out an 'appropriate assessment' and shall only grant permission if that assessment shows that there are not likely to be adverse effects on the integrity of the European site. There are provisions in Regulation 49 that allow an authority to grant permission despite the development having adverse effects on a European site but only if there are 'considerations of overriding public importance', as narrowly defined in the regulations.

- Finally, Regulation 50 requires an authority to review permissions granted before the site became a European site (or before the regulations came into force) and to carry out an appropriate assessment where it is likely to have a significant effect and unless that assessment suggests that the permission is unlikely to adversely affect the integrity of the European site it shall revoke or modify the permission accordingly – provided that this cannot affect anything already done pursuant to the permission. This power under Regulation 50 could therefore prevent the further implementation of permissions that are either wholly or partially unimplemented at the time of the assessment. To the extent that these provisions constrain the planning balance that the planning decision maker is required to carry out in the planning process (and severely limit its discretion) this legislation is a unique fetter on the planning judgement of planning decision makers.

Future trends

The growth in importance of the environment and sustainable development principles in the planning process is likely to continue. The government is intending to impose a statutory duty (currently under Clause 38 of the Planning and Compulsory Purchase Bill) on local and regional authorities to exercise their functions in relation to local development documents and regional spatial strategies 'with a view to contributing to the achievement of sustainable development'. To this can be added the obligation of the UK Government to transpose into domestic law the provisions of the Strategic Environmental Assessment Directive.

IPC and IPPC

This section describes regimes of control that are intended to reduce or avoid environmental harm caused by emissions and waste products affecting the full range of environmental media (land, water and air) from specified processes and activities that may already have been permitted under the planning regime.

There are two principal statutory codes of IPP that apply at the present time, and they will continue to operate in parallel for some period to come. They both have to be taken into account in dealing with IPC regimes. They are:

- Integrated Pollution Control (IPC) under Part I of the Environmental Protection Act (UK Parliament, 1990) and the Environmental Protection (Prescribed Processes and Substances) Regulations 1991 (as amended) (IPC Regulations). The EPA and the IPC Regulations also introduced the system of local authority air pollution control (LAAPC).
- Integrated Pollution Prevention and Control (IPPC), under the Pollution Prevention and Control Act (UK Parliament, 1999b) and the Pollution Prevention and Control (England and Wales) Regulations (UK Parliament, 2000). Under the IPPC Act and IPPC Regulations, the local air pollution prevention and control (LAPPC) regime is a continuation of the LAAPC regime under the new IPPC framework.
- IPC and IPPC are the responsibility of the EA. LAAPC is the responsibility of the local authority (district council).

These regimes are mutually exclusive, in the sense that where a process that has hitherto been covered by IPC is included by designation within the IPPC regime it no longer falls within IPC. In the case of sites where multiple processes are carried on, of which some are within IPC and some are covered by LAAPC, there are rules to determine which regime covers them according to the relative level of activities associated with the respective regimes.

IPC and LAAPC under the EPA and the IPC Regulations

Prescribed processes: Schedule 1 to the IPC Regulations contains a long list of industrial processes divided (for each industry) into two parts: Part A and Part B. The list of industries in Schedule 1 includes:

- Chapter 1: fuel production and combustion processes;
- Chapter 2: metal production and processing;
- Chapter 3: cement and lime manufacture and associated processes;
- Chapter 4: the chemical industry;
- Chapter 5: waste disposal and recycling; and
- Chapter 6: other industries, including paper and pulp manufacture and so on.

IPC applies to those processes that are prescribed by the Secretary of State under Schedule 1 to the IPC Regulations as Part A processes. These include generally more complex processes, which are liable to give rise to greater risks of pollution. Close examination of Schedule 1 is required in order to identify whether or not a particular process is Part A or Part B within any particular industry type. This list of processes (Part A and Part B) is subject to review from time to time by the Secretary of State.

Prescribed substances: IPC controls on the emission of prescribed substances from Part A processes into all environmental media is the responsibility of the EA. LAAPC, as the name implies, is operated by the local authority for the area in which the relevant Part B process is carried out and this regime controls the release of the prescribed substances to air only. The EA is responsible for dealing with emissions of prescribed substances to land and water under separate regimes of control.

'Prescribed substances' means substances which the Secretary of State has prescribed under Section 2(5) of the 1990 Act. Schedule 4 to the IPC Regulations contains a list of prescribed substances whose release is to air. These are prescribed substances for the purposes of both IPC and LAAPC depending upon whether the process that produces them is a Part A or a Part B process. Schedule 5 prescribes substances for the control of releases to water and Schedule 6 is for releases into land.

The need for IPC or LAAPC authorization: Under Section 6 of the 1990 Act, no person may carry on a prescribed process except under an authorization granted by the relevant enforcement authority. For an application to be made, processed and authorized, in accordance with Schedule 1 to the 1990 Act and the Environmental Protection (Applications, Appeals and Registers) Regulations 1991 ('the IPC Applications etc. Regulations'), it must be made to and determined by the relevant enforcement authority. The application must be accompanied by the prescribed fee. The Secretary of State has a call-in power to enable the application to be referred to him or her for determination.

IPC applications regulations specify the information that must be contained in an IPC or LAAPC application. This includes: the address of the premises where the prescribed process is to be carried out and a location map; details of the prescribed processes and the prescribed substances involved; techniques to be used to prevent or minimize the release of prescribed substances and for rendering harmless any substances that are released; details of any proposed release into any environmental medium; and an assessment of the consequences and monitoring proposals. In addition, the application has to show how BATNEEC (see below for an explanation) will be achieved.

Authorizations under the IPC and LAAPC regimes will include such conditions as are specified by the Secretary of State together with such other conditions as the relevant enforcing authority considers appropriate, and an obligation to achieve BATNEEC and, in the case of IPC only, to achieve BPEO (see below for an explanation).

BATNEEC: Section 7 of the IPC Act requires authorizations under the IPC and LAAPC regimes to include a condition which, in the case of an IPC authorization, requires the person authorized by the relevant authorization to use **best available techniques not entailing excessive cost**. This is to prevent the release of substances, prescribed for any environmental medium, in that medium. Where this is not practicable, such releases should be reduced to a minimum and rendered harmless along with any other substances that might cause harm if released into an environmental medium. In the case of an LAAPC authorization, this applies only to releases to air. Guidance on the meaning of BATNEEC is published by the Department of the Environment (DoE, 1997).

In the licensing context, it requires a rigorous and holistic examination of each and every process involved with a view to finding the optimum solution for the environment as a whole so as to prevent pollution at source.

BPEO: This means **best practicable environmental option** and Section 7(7) of the 1990 Act requires BATNEEC to be used to minimize pollution caused to the environment as a whole by reference to BPEO where IPC authorizations are sought. There is no statutory definition of BPEO but the term has been defined by the EA (1997). This defines BPEO as 'the option which in the context of releases from a prescribed process, provides the most benefit or the least damage to the environment as a whole, at acceptable cost, in the long term as well as the short term'.

Court decisions on questions arising out of decisions on BATNEEC and BPEO have established that the EA does not have to carry out an exhaustive examination of every practical option and technique if, in the circumstances, such a review is not justified. In each case it will be a matter of fact and degree. However, where the guidance establishes maximum levels for emissions of particular prescribed substances, it will not be acceptable for authorizations to simply specify such levels as the relevant maxima without properly examining whether the circumstances of the case (including technological advancements) make it appropriate to specify lower levels in the interests of achieving BPEO.

Revocation and enforcement powers and appeals: Sections 12–15 of the 1990 Act deal with enforcement powers and appeals. Section 12 is expressed in general terms but specifically states that (without limitation) the power may be exercised where the authorizing authority has reason to believe that the relevant prescribed process has not been carried on for 12 months.

Section 13 empowers the enforcing authority to serve an enforcement notice if it has reason to believe that the conditions on which an authorization was granted have been breached or are going to be breached. The notice must specify the breach, the measures taken to avoid it or make good or avoid the breach or impending breach, and the time within which such measures must be taken.

A prohibition notice may be served, on a person carrying on a prescribed process, under Section 14 where the authority is of the opinion that there is an imminent danger of serious pollution of the environment from the continuation of the prescribed process. The prohibition notice must state the authority's opinion, the risk involved, the steps that must be taken and direct that until the notice is lifted the authorization shall, to the extent specified, cease to authorize the specified process.

A right of appeal may be brought under Section 15 against: refusal of an authorization; conditions imposed in an authorization; revocation of an authorization; an enforcement notice; or a prohibition notice. Any appeal lies with the Secretary of State, unless the action complained of was the result of a direction of his/hers. A public inquiry may be held if the Secretary of State thinks fit.

Offences, penalties and High Court proceedings: Under Section 23 of the 1990 Act it is an offence to:

- carry on a prescribed process without an authorization or in breach of a condition attached to an authorization;
- fail to comply with an enforcement notice or a prohibition notice;
- fail without reasonable excuse to provide information when required by a Section 19 notice to provide it;
- wilfully or recklessly provide false or misleading information in circumstances specified in the section; and
- falsify records.

Penalties include fines and possibly imprisonment: Under Section 24 an enforcing authority can apply to the High Court if it is of the opinion that criminal proceedings for breach of an enforcement or prohibition notice would be an ineffectual remedy.

The IPPC Regulations

The IPPC Regulations, which implement the IPPC Directive 1996, came into force on 1 August 2000. They introduce a more extensive and integrated approach to the prevention and control of pollution caused by industrial activities. From that date new applications for authorizations must be made under the IPPC regime rather than the IPC regime, although existing IPC authorizations will continue in force until replaced in accordance with phased transitional arrangements contained in Annex IV of the IPPC Regulations. The transitional arrangements should be complete by 2007. Helpful guidance on the new system is provided by Defra (2002), which explains the new procedures in detail.

The IPPC regime will apply to an extended range of activities covered by the IPPC Directive as well as to the rump of activities that are currently covered by the IPC regime and which are outside the scope of the directive. It is estimated that the new IPPC regime will apply to about 8000 installations, compared to the 2000 that were subject to the IPC regime.

The need for a permit: Regulation 9 makes it an offence to operate an installation or mobile plant without a permit granted by the regulator. 'Installation' and 'mobile plant' are defined in Regulation 2(1) by reference to activities listed in Schedule 1 (Part 1) to the regulations. These activities are grouped under six chapters in that schedule as follows:

- Chapter 1: energy industries;
- Chapter 2: production and processing of metals;
- Chapter 3: mineral industries;
- Chapter 4: the chemical industry;
- Chapter 5: waste management; and
- Chapter 6: other activities including paper, pulp and board manufacturing; carbon; tar and bitumen; coating, printing and textile treatments; manufacture of dyestuffs, printing ink and coating materials; timber; rubber; animal and vegetable matter and food industries; intensive farming.

The activities within each chapter are further divided into Parts A (1) and A (2) and B. Part A contains the activities in the industrial sector that are subject to IPPC and Part B lists those subject to LAPPC. The IPPC activities in Part A (1) are regulated centrally by the EA, those in Part A (2) are regulated by local authorities.

Control under the regulations only applies if an activity may lead to the release of certain prescribed substances. These are indicated in Part 2 of Schedule 1, and different substances are prescribed for releases to air, water and land. In Part 2 of Schedule 1 there are exceptions for activities that are unlikely to involve harm to the environment such as activities carried out in schools, museums or private dwellings.

An application for a permit must be made in a prescribed form and accompanied by the relevant fee. The regulator has four months (or such longer period as may be agreed) to determine the application, and in the event of failure to do so within that period the applicant can appeal to the Secretary of State against deemed refusal. The regulator may grant or refuse the permit. If granted it will be subject to conditions.

Conditions in a permit: In granting a permit, the regulator must include such conditions as it considers appropriate having regard to the general principles set out in Regulation 11. These principles include the following:

- Waste production is minimized, and where waste is produced it is recovered or, where that is technically and economically impossible, disposed of while avoiding or reducing any impact on the environment.
- Energy is used efficiently.
- The necessary measures are taken to prevent accidents and limit their consequences.
- Upon the definitive cessation of activities, the necessary measures should be taken to avoid any pollution risk and to return the site of the installation or mobile plant to a satisfactory state.

Apart from conditions specifically designed to achieve these objectives, Regulation 12(10) suggests that in operating the installation or mobile plant, the operator shall use the best available techniques for preventing or, where that is not practicable, reducing emissions from the installation or mobile plant – except in relation to any aspect of the operation that is covered by a specific condition (Regulation 12(11)).

The practical guide (Defra, 2002), paragraph 9.1, explains the basis for setting conditions as follows:

> The essence of IPPC is that operators should choose the best option available to achieve a high level of protection of the environment taken as a whole. IPPC achieves this by requiring operators to use the best available techniques (BATs).

Best available techniques (BATs): Regulation 3 defines this central term. BAT means:

> the most effective and advanced stage in the development of activities and their methods of operation which indicates the practical suitability of particular techniques for providing in principle the basis for emission limit values designed to prevent and, where that is not practicable, generally to reduce emissions and the impact on the environment as a whole.

For the purpose of this definition:

- 'Available techniques' means those techniques that have been developed on a scale that allows implementation in the relevant industrial sector, under economically and technically viable conditions, taking into consideration the cost and advantages, whether or not the techniques are used or produced inside the UK, as long as they are reasonably accessible to the operator.
- 'Best' means, in relation to techniques, the most effective in achieving a high general level of protection of the environment as a whole.
- 'Techniques' includes both the technology used and the way in which the installation is designed, built, maintained, operated and decommissioned.

This definition sets a generally higher standard than the BATNEEC test under the IPC regime. Guidance as to what constitutes BAT is provided at the European level by the European IPPC Bureau in the form of BAT reference documents (BREFs). Sector specific guidance notes are also available from the EA.

Review and variation of conditions: Regulation 15 requires periodic reviews of conditions – in the case of activities not formerly covered by IPC or waste management licensing within four years and thereafter every six years and in the case of activities formerly covered by IPC every six years. However, the regulator can review permit conditions at any time.

An operator is required by Regulation 16 to give not less than 14 days' written notice to the regulator of any proposed change in the operation of the installation, giving details of the proposed change.

Regulation 17 empowers the regulator to vary the conditions of a permit. This must occur if it appears to the regulator in a review or after notification of a proposed change of operation of the installation that different conditions should be applied from the existing conditions. The regulator must have regard to the principles in Regulations 11 and 12 in deciding whether and how to vary the conditions.

Transfer, surrender and revocation of permits: The regulator will need to be satisfied that the transfer will be held by the person having control of the installation or mobile plant both in the initial grant and in subsequent sales or dispositions of the operation. If control of an installation changes hands the permit must be transferred and in that case or in any other case the permit may be transferred upon the application of the transferor (Regulation 18).

Regulations 19 and 20 deal with the surrender of permits where the activities cease to be carried out. An application for a Part A installation or mobile plant must be made in the prescribed form with the appropriate fee. The regulator will need to be satisfied that the operator has taken such steps as may be required to avoid pollution risk from the installation or mobile plant and to return the site to a satisfactory state. The surrender of a Part B permit does not require the regulator to determine the application – the operator merely specifies the date when the permit shall cease to exist.

A permit may be revoked in whole or in part by the regulator by means of a revocation notice in circumstances specified in Regulation 21.

Enforcement: Regulations 23–26 contain provisions relating to the enforcement of IPPC control by means of enforcement notices, suspension notices and direct action by the regulator to prevent or remedy pollution and to recover the cost from the operator.

Appeals: Regulation 27 deals with appeals to the Secretary of State against a variety of decisions and notices in relation to permits, including refusal of a permit, conditions imposed, variations of conditions and enforcement action. A public inquiry may be held and the Secretary of State has various powers and discretions in determining the appeal.

Information and publicity: Part V of the regulations provides for publicity and public access to information relating to processes and determinations under the IPPC Regulations, including extensive rights to see the information on which the decisions are made. There is limited protection for commercially confidential information and information that should be protected for reasons of national security. The regulator is required to set up a register of information prescribed under Regulation 29 and Schedule 9.

Offences: Regulation 32 specifies offences under the regulations, and Regulations 33–35 enable the regulator to apply to the High Court for a remedy if prosecution is not considered to be an effective remedy.

Main differences from the IPC regime: Hughes et al (1999) list the key differences between the IPPC regime and the IPC regime; these include the following:

- IPC is concerned with the control of pollution from processes; IPPC is concerned with the control of activities.

- IPPC thus applies to installations rather than just processes.
- IPPC seeks to prevent or reduce emissions whereas IPC is concerned with preventing harm to the environment from releases.
- IPPC defines 'pollution' more widely than IPC – it includes vibrations and noise.
- BATs will reflect issues not relevant to BATNEEC – such as use of less hazardous substances, furthering waste recovery and recycling, consumption of raw materials and water, energy efficiency and the need to prevent accidents. IPPC will look at the pollution impact of plants and will strive for the best environmental way of doing a job.
- In determining BAT, costs have a wider meaning than under BATNEEC.
- IPPC will impose obligations to minimize waste production, to use energy efficiently, to restore sites on closure; IPC does none of these.
- IPPC will take account of an EIA undertaken at the planning permission stage, whereas this was not a requirement under IPC.
- IPPC sets fixed emission limit values or other equivalents for certain listed pollutants; IPC makes a distinction between prescribed substances and non-prescribed substances.
- Emission monitoring requirements are an essential part of IPPC permits; in IPC they did not have to be included (although they often were).

In summary, the IPPC regime is likely to be a far more stringent and coordinated system of controlling the pollution effects of industrial and other activities than the system that it replaces.

The control of air pollution

The control of air pollution is heavily regulated both at national and EU level and is one of the most significant areas in which environmental improvements are sought. Air pollution issues were the subject of international discussion at the Earth Summit in Brazil in 1992 and in Kyoto in 1997.

Air pollution in England

The main statutory provision is the Clean Air Act 1993. The act controls emissions of smoke, dust and grit from certain buildings. It also prohibits the emission of 'dark smoke' from the chimney of any building. The provisions of the act are backed up by criminal sanctions. The act regulates the height of chimneys by requiring chimney heights to be approved by the local authority so as to avoid local pollution. It is also likely that planning permission will be required for chimneys.

Future developments in air pollution control

The former system of local air pollution control is in the process of being replaced by IPPC. Installations will continue to have emissions to air regulated by local authorities or in more environmentally sensitive installations by the EA.

Air quality standards

The government periodically develops national strategies for air quality by publishing air quality standards and objectives for controlling atmospheric pollutants. The use of these strategies and objectives is implemented by regulations that require local authorities to review and assess air quality in their region.

Water pollution and water quality

As with many other areas of UK environmental regulation, the control of water quality and water pollution is remarkably complex. It is made all the more complicated by the fact that the central aim of this collection of laws is not simply preventing the entry of substances into water. Water quality regulation is concerned with the control of discharge of substances that are not inherently toxic or harmful, but which may have negative impacts depending on: how much is discharged; where such substances are discharged; and to what use the water is put.

The position throughout the UK

Water quality control and the administrative arrangements differ throughout the UK. In Scotland the water supply and sewerage system is still in public ownership with a small number of publicly owned combined water and sewerage authorities undertaking the water and sewerage functions. The Scottish Environment Protection Agency (SEPA) mirrors the EA in England and Wales and brings together all water pollution functions in one body, although SEPA does not have the EA's broad range of other water related functions. In Northern Ireland, the Environment and Heritage Service of the Department of the Environment (Northern Ireland) has responsibility for water pollution control.

These differences mean that any comprehensive coverage of UK water pollution control law would have to be extensive. Therefore what appears below reflects the position in England and Wales only. Although there are broad similarities in the substance of the law across the UK, specific checks should be made to verify the position in any individual country.

In England and Wales the EA takes overall responsibility for water quality under powers found in the Water Resources Act 1991 (WRA). The focus of the regulatory system for the control of water pollution is the system of discharge consents. These arrangements embody the flexible idea of individualized consents based on such things as existing water quality and the location of sensitive receptors in the vicinity. That is not to say that such consents are entirely flexible. Water quality standards for particular uses have been set, for example in relation to drinking waters and bathing waters, and these will have a significant impact upon the nature of individual discharges to water. It should be noted, however, that there is no requirement to seek permission to discharge substances to water. The purpose of a discharge consent to water under the WRA is merely to act as a defence to any criminal charge of polluting water.

It isn't only point discharges that prove a threat to the water environment. Other sources of water pollution are subject to regulatory control – for example diffuse sources such as agricultural runoff, and pollution from urban development and vehicle emissions. These have brought in legislative schemes such as the Groundwater Regulations 1998, The Nitrate Sensitive Areas Regulations 2002, and the Control of Pollution (Oil Storage) (England) Regulations 2001 which combine such things as construction based standards for oil storage with a risk based approach to the prevention of groundwater pollution. Such non-point sources of water pollution cannot really be controlled by consents, and instead need an imaginative mix of policy and legal mechanisms.

The discharge consent system

The discharge consent system and water pollution offences apply to 'controlled waters', which cover most inland and coastal waters, and groundwaters. The only inland waters that are excluded are land-locked waters that do not drain into other controlled waters. This could include such things as distillation lagoons. The system for acquiring a consent is set out in the WRA, Schedule 10, and the Control of Pollution (Applications, Appeals and Registers) Regulations 1996. Unlike other areas of pollution control, the consent applies to each discharge point as opposed to a single installation or process. A consent is personal to the operator but can be transferred (see WRA, Schedule 10, paragraph 11).

In granting a consent, the EA has complete discretion over the conditions that may be attached but typically they cover such things as biochemical oxygen demand, levels of toxic or dangerous substances and suspended solids. Other matters commonly covered include: the quality, quantity, nature, composition and temperature of the discharge; the siting and design of the outlet; the provision of meters for measuring these matters; the taking and recording of samples by the discharger; and the provision of information to the regulator (see WRA, Schedule 10, paragraph 2). For industrial discharges it is normal to attach absolute numerical limits for the various parameters covered in the consent, with the result that any excess amounts to a breach of the consent.

Conditions requiring a specified treatment process are legal, but are not generally imposed, since in the past it has been government policy to require compliance with environmental standards while giving the discharger a choice of methods to achieve the standard. For some discharges, however, the effect of the Urban Waste Water Treatment Directive (EC, 1991) has been such that specific treatment methods are often required (e.g. biological treatment), although generally the directive requires quality standards to be met.

Offences

There is a general offence under WRA, Schedule 85(1) of causing or knowingly permitting any poisonous, noxious or polluting matter or any solid waste to enter controlled waters. In addition, there are more specific offences including discharging trade or sewage effluent without consent (WRA, Schedule 85(3)) and discharging substances not in accordance with the conditions of a discharge consent (WRA, Schedule 85(6)). For all Schedule 85 offences the potential penalties are the same. On conviction in the Magistrates' Court there is a maximum fine of £20,000 and/or a three month prison sentence. On conviction in the Crown Court, there can be an unlimited fine and/or a two year prison sentence.

A number of defences are available (see WRA, Schedule 88). For example, a discharge or entry made in accordance with an existing pollution control consent (e.g. discharge consent, waste management licence or IPPC permit) is a defence. There is a further defence if the entry or discharge was made in an emergency in order to avoid danger to life or health: in such a case the discharger must inform the EA as soon as reasonably practicable and take reasonable steps to minimize any pollution. Under WRA, Schedule 87(2) sewerage undertakers have a defence where a contravention of Schedule 85 is attributable to an unconsented discharge into the sewerage system by a third party which the sewerage undertaker could not reasonably have been expected to prevent.

Groundwater protection

The protection of groundwater is not always covered by discharge consents, particularly in the case of indirect discharges where there is seepage of pollutants through the ground via leaking containers. The Groundwater Regulations 1998 control such discharges (as well as direct discharges to groundwater via specific discharge points) by requiring the prevention of the entry of the most polluting substances and seeking to minimize the polluting nature of certain less polluting substances. Thus the regulations use authorizations to regulate indirect discharges such as might arise from the disposal and tipping of certain listed substances, at least where these are not regulated by waste management provisions. The regulations also provide for a 'notice' provision where pollution might arise (Regulation 19). The EA has discretion over whether to serve such a notice, and must take account of any code of practice issued – codes of practice exist in areas such as the disposal of spent sheep dip and the storage of petrol in underground tanks.

Remedial powers

Powers to clean up water pollution are available under the works notice provisions found in WRA, Schedule 161 and the powers to issue enforcement notices under WRA, Schedule 90B. In the latter case, where there has been or is likely to be a breach of a discharge consent condition, the EA may serve an enforcement notice which must identify the breach (or likely breach), the steps required to remedy the breach, and the time within which these must be carried out. Failure to comply with an enforcement notice is an offence.

Under the works notice provisions in Schedule 161, the EA can serve a works notice on the appropriate responsible person requiring them to prevent or clean up pollution, unless it is necessary to carry out works 'forthwith' or the polluter cannot be found. Failure to comply with a works notice is an offence (UK Parliament, 1999a).

Preventative controls

Although discharge controls form the backbone of water pollution legislation, there are other preventative powers. Under WRA, Schedule 92, the Secretary of State is able to make regulations setting out precautions to be taken in order to prevent water pollution. There are two sets of regulations in force, the Control of Pollution (Silage, Slurry and Agricultural Fuel Oil) Regulations 1991 and Control of Pollution (Oil Storage) (England)

Regulations 2001. The latter cover a large range of businesses and operations. They require that oil is stored in a container and that the container has a secondary containment system, as defined in the regulations. There are exemptions including underground storage, small tanks and waste oil storage. It is an offence for anyone to contravene the regulations and there is a backstop date of September 2005 for full compliance.

There are powers to create water protection zones under WRA, Schedule 93. These orders can restrict certain activities that pose a risk to controlled waters within the zone. The first water protection zone covers most of the River Dee catchment. In practice, the order provides for a specialist consent regime within the zone to regulate the storage and use of certain controlled substances by industrial and other processes, although construction sites, retail premises, farms and sites covered by IPPC permits are excluded. Consents are determined following a risk assessment, and BATNEEC principles apply where there is an appreciable risk of pollution, see the Water Protection Zone (River Dee Catchment) (Procedural and Other Provisions) Regulations 1999.

There are similar powers in WRA, Schedule 94, but these are substance and activity specific, in that an area may be designated a nitrate sensitive area by order with a view to preventing or controlling the entry of nitrates into controlled waters as a result of agricultural activities. The controls can be found in the Nitrate Sensitive Areas Regulations 1994. There are two types of order that may be made, respectively imposing voluntary and mandatory controls. Voluntary controls are available where any nitrate sensitive area has been designated. In such areas agreements may be reached between the government and landowner as to restrictions on certain activities and compensation paid by the government. A mandatory order may require positive obligations, such as the construction of containment walls around agricultural stores, as well as prohibitions and restrictions on activities. Compensation can be granted to anyone affected by the order (including tenant farmers) although no levels of compensation are set in the act.

In addition to the 1994 Regulations, there are further controls over nitrates found in the Protection of Water against Agricultural and Nitrate Pollution (England and Wales) Regulations 1996. These regulations designate nitrate vulnerable zones (NVZs) in specific areas where there are excessive levels of nitrate pollution from agricultural sources. Two crucial differences between nitrate sensitive areas and NVZs are that the latter are always mandatory, and there is no prospect of compensation payments for farmers in NVZs.

Other powers to control water pollution

The powers found in the WRA are not the only powers that are used to control water pollution. In practice many other controls are used. For example, IPPC permits cover discharges to water (and accordingly act as a defence to the general water pollution offence) and there are additional controls that apply under the contaminated land regime and statutory nuisances. Perhaps the most common of these alternative controls is found in the trade effluent discharge system regulated by the privatized water and sewerage undertakers and found in the Water Industry Act 1991 (WIA) (UK Parliament, 1991d). Under that system it is a criminal offence to discharge any trade effluent from trade premises into sewers unless a trade effluent consent is obtained from the sewerage undertaker (WIA, Schedule 118). 'Trade effluent' and 'trade premises' are defined widely in WIA, Schedule 141, to include all liquid discharges from industry, shops, research establishments, launderettes and agriculture, except for domestic sewage. It is also an offence to breach the terms of a consent. The most confusing aspect of the system is that regulation can be effected either under a trade effluent consent or it is fairly common for an operator to reach an agreement formalized in the shape of a trade effluent agreement which, in all important respects, mirrors the consent.

Contaminated land regime

Contaminated land is most commonly remediated by means of redevelopment, and the planning regime includes specific guidance to ensure that necessary investigations are carried out and to standards that ensure that it is carried out in a satisfactory manner (see Defra, 1999b – especially Section 4). Sometimes, schemes involving the redevelopment of contaminated land will require an EIA under the EIA Regulations 1999. This section is, however, not concerned with voluntary remediation in the context of redevelopment, but the remediation and enforcement framework that is available to compel landowners and other parties to take steps to remedy contaminated land in circumstances where risk is considered to exist.

The primary statutory provisions relating to contaminated land regime are contained within Part IIA of the Environmental Protection Act 1990 and the Department of the Environment, Transport and Regions (DETR) Circular 02/2000. The regime was brought into force in England on 1 April 2000 and essentially requires local authorities to identify land that is contaminated in their area and then identify those persons responsible for its clean up. The regime imposes strict liability and applies retroactively so that historical contamination is also covered.

What is contaminated land?

Under the regime, land is contaminated if: significant harm is being caused by reasons of substances in, on or under the land; there is a significant possibility of significant harm being caused by reasons of substances in, on or under the land; or it is causing or is likely to cause significant pollution of controlled waters by reasons of substances in, on or under the land.

It can be seen from this definition that cause and effect are important. For land to be contaminated land under the regime, a full pollutant linkage must be in existence: i.e. a **source** being the contaminant present in the ground, a **target** such as human health, an ecological system or controlled waters, and a **pathway** along which the contamination may reach the target. This means that it is possible for there to be contaminants present in the ground, without the land being designated contaminated land, as the contaminants are not causing harm to a target.

Who is responsible for clean up?

Once land has been designated as contaminated land, it is for the regulators (usually the local authority, but in the case of so-called special sites the EA) to determine responsibility for remediation. That party is known as the appropriate person.

If land is contaminated, then the regime operates on the polluter pays principle. The person primarily liable for clean up costs is the Class A person – this being the person who caused or knowingly permitted the contaminants to be present in the soil so as to have an effect on a target. If no Class A person can be found (which includes the liquidation of a Class A company) then regulators may look at the current owner or occupier of the site to foot the remediation bill. This is called Class B liability.

It is possible for liability under the regime to be transferred between parties by way of contract. For example, the parties may agree to the apportionment of liabilities or the vendor may make a payment to the purchaser in respect of the costs of remediation, which effectively absolves it of any further liability.

Other issues

Under general legal principles, polluters and owners of contaminated land may also have potential liability to owners of land adjoining the contaminated site by way of civil action. An owner may also be liable under other statutory provisions including the WRA.

Even where a property is held on an occupational lease, contamination may still be an issue for a tenant. The costs of dealing with contamination could impact on the service charge of a multi-tenanted building or the maintenance costs of a standalone building. A tenant could also inherit clean up costs for pre-existing conditions via the covenants requiring repair and compliance with statutory notices.

What is a statutory nuisance?

A statutory nuisance is something that is prejudicial to health or a nuisance as defined under Part III of the Environmental Protection Act 1990. It is the duty of the local authority to inspect for and take steps to deal with statutory nuisance complaints made to it, within its area. A statutory nuisance would include that which is injurious to health or likely to cause ill health. These may be, for example, in the form of smoke, fumes, gases, dust, steam, odours, deposits or noise pollution.

Other relevant legislation

Since the introduction of the new contaminated land regime, the statutory nuisance provisions are disapplied in respect of issues arising under the contaminated land regime. This would be the case where the nuisance in question consists of or is caused by land being in a 'contaminated state' pursuant to the terms of the Environmental Protection Act 1990.

For specific types of nuisance which arise from smoke, dust, steam, smells etc. from industrial premises, accumulation or deposits, the local authority may not issue proceedings under the statutory nuisance provisions without the Secretary of State's approval if proceedings may be brought under Part I of the Environmental Protection Act 1990 instead. Part I currently governs the granting of authorizations for prescribed processes, setting standards to prevent pollution of the environment and harm to living organizations. This legislation may therefore be relevant for certain nuisance cases.

What action can be taken against statutory nisance?

If the local authority is satisfied that a statutory nuisance exists, or is likely to occur or recur, they have a duty to serve an abatement notice on the person responsible for the nuisance or, if the nuisance source cannot be found on the owner/occupier of the premises where it is occurring. The notice can impose various conditions on the person concerned, requiring the ceasing of the nuisance or, for example, requiring works to be carried out to restrict the occurrence/recurrence of the nuisance. The notice will also set a time scale for compliance with its terms.

What are the consequences of failure to comply with an abatement notice?

In the event that a person fails to comply with a notice on industrial, trade or business premises, fines of up to £20,000 can be incurred. For statutory nuisance not occurring on such business premises, a person who commits an offence shall be liable on summary conviction to a fine of up to £5000, together with the possibility of daily fines if the offence continues after conviction.

References and further reading

Defra (1999a) 'Planning Policy Guidance Note 2', Department for Environment, Food and Rural Affairs, London

Defra (1999b) 'Planning Policy Guidance Note 3', Department for Environment, Food and Rural Affairs, London

Defra (2002) *Integrated Pollution Prevention and Control: A Practical Guide*, 2nd edn, Department for Environment, Food and Rural Affairs, London

DoE (1997) *Integrated Pollution Control: A Practical Guide*, Department of the Environment, London

EA (1997) 'Best Practicable Environmental Option for Integrated Pollution Control, Non-statutory Technical Guidance Note E', Environment Agency, Bristol

EC (1991) 'Council Directive 91/271/EEC 1991 Concerning Urban Waste Water Treatment Amended by Commission Directive 98/15/EC', European Commission, Brussels

EC (1992) 'Council Directive 92/43/EEC on the Conservation of Natural Habitats and of Wild Fauna and Flora', European Commission, Brussels

Hughes et al (1999) *Environmental Law*, LexisNexis Butterworths, London

TCPA (1990) 'The Town and Country Planning Act', 'The Town and Country Planning (Listed Buildings and Conservation Areas) Act', 'The Town and Country Planning (Hazardous Substances Control) Act', 'The Town and Country Planning (Development Plan) Regulations 1991' and 'The Town and Country Planning (Environmental Impact Assessment) (England and Wales) Regulations 1999', The Stationery Office, London

UK Parliament (1990) 'The Environment Protection Act', The Stationery Office, London

UK Parliament (1991a) 'Environmental Protection (Applications, Appeals and Registers) Regulations' and 'Environmental Protection (Prescribed Processes and Substances) Regulations', The Stationery Office, London

UK Parliament (1991b) 'The Control of Pollution (Silage, Slurry and Agricultural Fuel Oil) Regulations', The Stationery Office, London

UK Parliament (1991c) 'The Environmental Protection (Prescribed Processes and Substances) Regulations (as amended)', The Stationery Office, London

UK Parliament (1991d) 'The Water Industry Act', The Stationery Office, London

UK Parliament (1991e) 'The Water Resources Act', The Stationery Office, London

UK Parliament (1993) 'The Clean Air Act', The Stationery Office, London

UK Parliament (1994) 'The Conservation (Natural Habitats) Regulations', The Stationery Office, London

UK Parliament (1998) 'Groundwater Regulations', The Stationery Office, London

UK Parliament (1999a) 'Anti-pollution Works Regulations', The Stationery Office, London

UK Parliament (1999b) 'The Pollution Prevention and Control Act', The Stationery Office, London

UK Parliament (2000) 'The Pollution Prevention and Control (England and Wales) Regulations', The Stationery Office, London

UK Parliament (2001a) 'The Contaminated Land (Wales) Regulations', The Stationery Office, London

UK Parliament (2001b) 'The Control of Pollution (Oil Storage) (England) Regulations', The Stationery Office, London

UK Parliament (2002) 'The Nitrate Sensitive Areas Regulations', The Stationery Office, London

UK Parliament (2003) 'The Waste Management Licensing (Amendment) (Scotland) Regulations', The Stationery Office, London

Section 3

Managing Environmental Performance

Chapter 3.1

The Response of Organizations

This chapter looks at environmental issues from the perspective of the organization. It aims to help the environmental professional understand how the concern in society about environmental issues is changing the context in which organizations operate, and forcing them to respond. It considers the tools needed to help an organization understand its position in relation to environmental issues, and the range of responses that needs to be considered.

Environmental issues from the perspective of the organization

There is a sizeable literature on the impacts of organizations on the natural environment – on resources used, pollution caused, waste created and habitats and biodiversity destroyed. Organizations are encouraged to reduce their impacts, and tools such as ISO 14001 and environmental impact assessment (EIA) are designed to help them do so. However, other tools are also needed.

When working within organizations, individual environmental professionals have to understand and manage their organization's impacts on the environment, but also have to consider the same issues from the perspective of the organization: the impact of environmental issues on the organization itself. Therefore one has to be clear about what one means by the term 'environmental impact'. The primary responsibility of the environmental professional is to protect the interests of their organization; in doing so, many are trying to juggle a personal interest in protecting the environment with their professional role.

The two goals of protecting the environment and protecting the organization do not always require the same set of actions, although hopefully there will be some overlap; in other words there will be a good business case for improving environmental performance. In the best case, an organization that gains a full understanding of the nature of the environmental pressures upon it, and develops appropriate response strategies, may obviate any potential disadvantages and even gain advantages. For example, energy taxes may prompt organizations to reduce energy use and overall costs. However, in spite of policies based on the polluter pays principle, organizations are still not forced to bear the full costs of the impacts they have on the environment, and therefore on the rest of society and future generations. Full liability would impose considerable costs. Attempts to make polluters pay can be financially and operationally painful for them, and generate a certain amount of resistance.

Environmental issues are now affecting most organizations in some way. At a minimum they will be subject to regulations on how waste is handled. The extent and nature of the way organizations are affected depend on the function of those organizations. A large supermarket chain is affected in one set of ways, a small engineering firm in another and a large public sector organization such as the National Health Service (NHS) in another. The details of responses that are appropriate are therefore specific to the nature of the organization affected, but there is a general approach that can help an organization reach the right solution for its own situation.

An environmental manager needs to:

- understand the pressures, risks and opportunities that environmental issues pose to the organization, and how these may develop over time;
- understand the nature of the impact the issues might have on the organization, depending on the response strategy that is adopted;
- work with directors and managers to develop response strategies that are appropriate to the potential impacts, the financial and operational constraints and the strategic direction of the organization; and
- drive, direct or assist with the implementation, maintenance and development of these strategies over time.

The impacts of environmental issues on organizations

The impacts of environmental issues on organizations fall into two categories:

- The direct impacts of changes to the environment such as climatic extremes, loss of fish stocks or the pollution of drinking water sources.
- The impacts on organizations of society's responses to environmental issues such as the imposition of regulations and environmental taxes, changes in the purchasing behaviour of consumers and investment decisions by investors.

Changes in the natural environment are already directly affecting the operations of some organizations, and others are likely to be affected in the future. Some examples of negative and positive effects are:

- An increase in flooding can affect organizations with premises in flood prone areas.
- Drought may affect agricultural yields and therefore farming companies and their customers.
- Warmer summers may enhance the wine growing season in the UK, with benefits for this industry.
- Less snow in Scotland is already reducing the viability of the ski industry.
- More frequent, stronger storms may damage property.
- Sea level rise may put properties at risk.
- Pollution of water supplies may raise costs for water companies in providing clean drinking water.
- Decline in fish stocks may affect the availability and cost of fish for supermarkets.

- Tourism companies may be affected if the destinations they are sending their clients to become damaged by environmental change.
- Weather extremes are impacting the emergency services and local councils.

In many cases the primary impact on one organization has a secondary impact on others. For example, the customers of water companies will have to pay more for their water, and supermarket customers have to pay higher prices or find some products are no longer available. Thus many more organizations may be affected indirectly by environmental change if their suppliers are affected directly.

Direct impacts of changes to the natural environment, as described here, are very important to some organizations such as those with vulnerable properties, water companies and others directly exploiting natural resources. However, most organizations are currently affected more by the actions being taken by governments and civil society in response to concerns about primary changes to the natural environment than by those primary changes themselves. The actions of civil society being referred to here are the actions taken by individuals and groups through means other than government action, such as individual purchasing decisions, demonstrations and action through pressure groups.

As certainty and concern about environmental changes increase in society, so measures are taken to try and prevent further change and ameliorate changes that have already taken place, or cannot now be prevented from happening. These measures are aimed at changing the behaviour of organizations and individuals, where that behaviour is thought to be detrimental to the common good. Examples of such measures include consumer boycotts of certain products, such as those made from mahogany in response to information circulated by non-governmental organizations (NGOs), and legislation introduced by governments. Each environmental issue that emerges is initially highlighted by NGOs. Ultimately, when there is enough evidence to support the assertions being made and enough support among the electorate, government takes action in terms of legislation, fiscal measures or encouraging voluntary action.

There is now a wide range of pressures that organizations may experience as a result of society's concerns about environmental issues:

Legal restrictions: All organizations are now subject to at least some environmental regulations; all have to comply with waste management regulations for example. Early environmental regulations were focused on end-of-pipe sources of pollution. More recently, the introduction of regulations, following the precautionary principle and producer responsibility principles, means that a much wider range of organizations is affected by environmental regulations. Furthermore, environmental regulations have moved from being in the domain of facilities and operations managers only, to become the concern of commercial and financial managers, meaning they have come closer to the strategic and risk management heart of the organization.

Financial drivers: These can come from a variety of sources. There are direct environmental taxes, such as the energy tax, fuel tax and aggregates tax, which give financial signals to organizations to change their behaviour. The Packaging Regulations and other producer responsibility regulations work in the same way – creating a financial incentive to reduce environmental impacts.

The costs of compliance with environmental regulations can be substantial for some organizations. For example, the requirement to change materials, such as removing lead from PVC water pipes, can result in development and material costs. The requirement to upgrade incinerators to meet new emissions limits has led to the closure of many hospital incinerators because they could not afford to upgrade them, and an increase in waste disposal costs for NHS trusts. The new integrated pollution prevention and control (IPPC) regime has cost regulated industries significant amounts in time, capital equipment costs and operational costs. These costs create a drive for organizations to reduce their impacts on the environment to a point where their regulatory burden is reduced. For example, reducing effluent content can reduce the costs of a discharge consent; reducing solvent emissions may reduce the need for expensive scrubbing equipment.

There is also a financial drive to ensure compliance: where non-compliance occurs, legal sanctions can be accompanied by fines and costs. The level of fines is still relatively low in the UK, but costs relating to repairing damage and paying compensation can be substantial, and there may be incidental losses such as loss of customer and employee confidence for organizations that are seen to be polluters.

The impact of regulations on some organizations can also affect costs for others in their supply chain. For example, costs of water and sewerage services are affected by the regulatory requirements on water companies to clean up effluent from sewage treatment plants; and the cost of waste disposal is affected by the landfill tax payable by waste contractors.

Finally, insurance premiums are increasing, as organizations are increasingly held to account for environmental damage caused in the past, and for current incidents.

Customer preferences: Supply chain pressure from major customers has been one of the most powerful forces for driving the improvement of environmental performance in a large number of organizations, large and small. A growing number of major corporations, government departments, public bodies and NGOs are using their purchasing power to encourage, or in some cases demand, improved environmental performance by their suppliers. Examples of organizations with supply chain environmental initiatives include the UK Government Department for Environment, Food and Rural Affairs (Defra), the NHS, Sainsbury's, BT, and the Co-operative Group. In some cases the pressure goes beyond the first-tier suppliers, further up the supply chain. In some cases the customer is protecting its own reputation from association with poor environmental practices, and in others it is simply attempting to encourage better environmental practices. The requirements of suppliers range from proof of compliance with environmental laws and demonstration of good environmental practice, through to the provision of data, cooperation in the design of products and components, and provision of assurance on the source of materials.

Investor concerns: In the UK the size of the ethical investment market is still tiny compared with the total investment funds available. However, it has considerable influence, and companies are concerned about their ranking in ethical indexes such as FTSE4Good because it affects their reputation with customers, shareholders and others. Anticipated changes to company law in the UK are likely to make it a requirement for major economic entities to report on the environmental and social risks they face as part of their audited annual report. This is likely to increase the focus of all investors on these issues, particularly where they have implications for future profits.

NGO campaigns: There are some very high profile examples of NGO campaigns against certain companies, such as those against Shell, BP and Esso. The purpose is to embarrass the company, and persuade customers to boycott it, hurting it financially. Campaigns can be about operational practices, such as the disposal of an oil rig, or about material used, such as PVC, or about supplier practices, such as hardwood timber logging.

Government and peer pressure: The UK Government has been putting pressure on businesses and other organizations to address environmental and social issues. Energy and waste have been key areas of focus. As an increasing number of organizations develop approaches to environmental issues, so peer pressure develops on similar organizations. This is formalized where trade associations such as the Society of Motor Manufacturers and Traders, the Engineering Employers Federation and the Chemical Industry Association encourage good environmental practice by their members.

Employee concerns: There has been increasing coverage of environmental issues in schools, in the media and in society in general, and most young employees are aware of the issues. A significant proportion of new graduates reports that the ethics of a company would affect their choice of employer. Employers cannot afford not to take advantage of opportunities to attract the best employees and motivate their workforce.

This list of the sources of potential pressures on organizations indicates that all organizations, regardless of their size and function, should take some action to understand and respond to the pressures upon them. Not doing so risks consequences such as prosecution for legal non-compliance with accompanying loss of reputation and possible costs; increased costs associated with environmental taxes and insurance premiums; loss of access to investment funds where screening on environmental issues is used; and a reduction in employee morale, or at least a missed opportunity to enhance it. On the other hand, making sure the organization has a good understanding of the pressures upon it opens up opportunities to reduce costs, build reputation and, where relevant, increase competitiveness.

The aim therefore of a response strategy for an organization is to reduce the potentially negative impacts of environmental issues and policies upon it, and to realize whatever benefits are available. The next section suggests what is required to ensure the organization does understand the pressures and the options and effectively implements an appropriate response strategy.

Understanding the pressures on organizations

There are three essentials that an organization needs in order to ensure it understands the pressures effectively:

- Access to expertise on environmental pressures on business and how they are manifested; this may be in-house expertise, or gained from external consultants. In some cases corporate customers or business partners with an interest in the environmental performance of the organization may offer guidance.
- A safe mechanism of talking to interested stakeholders in the environmental performance of the organization: safe in terms of gaining insight into stakeholder views without risking public criticism that could harm the organization.
- Integration of the identification and analysis of the impact of environmental issues into the core strategic and risk management function of the organization.

Access to expertise

There is still a widespread lack of appreciation and understanding of environmental issues among managers and directors. The issues are relatively new; few MBA courses have any significant content on these issues, or treat them as core subjects, and the issues have not been considered part of mainstream business. The risks that environmental issues pose to the organization can therefore be missed by senior management.

In-house expertise: There are now some very experienced and knowledgeable environmental professionals working within large organizations, many with considerable influence on the way in which an organization handles environmental issues at all levels. However, many organizations still have no one in-house who appreciates the nature of the environmental issues that they face, and how these may impact on the organization. Even where there is such expertise available, the environmental professional does not always have the necessary influence with senior management to be able to adequately protect the organization.

The position of an environmental professional within an organization significantly affects their effectiveness. Environmental issues can impinge on all aspects of an organization's operations from the core operational activities, through to purchasing, finance, insurance, investment and business development, so it is difficult to know where in the management structure someone with environmental expertise should be placed. This often leads to them being somewhat out on a limb, without direct line management control, having to use influence to persuade managers in other parts of the organization that environmental issues are relevant. The best solution is where the environmental manager reports directly to a very senior manager or director in the organization. This needs to be someone with the vision to appreciate how the issues affect the business as a whole, and the influence and drive to encourage others in the organization to address them.

External help: Government, insurers, some investors and organizations such as the Advisory Committee on Business and the Environment and some trade associations such as the Engineering Employers Federation have done a great deal to flag up to businesses and other organizations that they need to consider environmental issues as part of their core risk management and operational management processes. Smaller organizations can get advice from organizations such as Business Link, Groundwork, regional development authorities, local authorities, and Envirowise.

Talking to stakeholders

One of the most important tools for understanding the potential impacts of environmental issues on the organization is to ask interested stakeholders for their views. These may be biased or un-sifted, but they are a useful source of raw data that can then be analysed internally, or with the help of more objective professionals. There are many people who are interested in the environmental performance of businesses and other organizations, who are willing to engage in dialogue. Every organization will have a large range of stakeholders, and since each of these will have different interests, the organization will need to talk to a good proportion of them. Stakeholders and their concerns include the following:

- Employees and potential recruits – may be concerned about the reputation of the organization they work for, on a range of environmental and social issues.

- Unions – are becoming increasingly interested in environmental issues in general, and social issues that align with their core interests.
- Environmental pressure groups – will generally have a good overview of the range of issues, although will not necessarily be able to help the organization put this into its own context.
- Environmental NGOs/consultancies – there are a number of organizations, such as Forum for the Future, that have a strong environmental agenda and can therefore be very helpful in understanding the issues, but also understand them from the perspective of the organization.
- Local environmental groups – may have particular interests in a piece of land that has a good wildlife habitat.
- Local communities, neighbours, schools and so on – may be concerned about traffic generated by the organization and its operations, whether it is a warehouse or a hospital.
- Local government – will be concerned about traffic and planning issues, as well as any local environmental plans and objectives they may be trying to implement.
- Central government – could be interested in the environmental and social credentials of large organizations.
- Trade associations – in some cases are trying to encourage good environmental practice among their members, perhaps in order to respond to government pressure to do so.
- Customers – trade customers and consumers may be interested in the credentials of products they are buying and the organization they are buying them from.
- The Environment Agency (EA) and other regulators – have a strong interest in the legal compliance and good performance of organizations.
- Suppliers – will be interested in any future requirements of them to provide raw materials, products, and services with any particular environmental and social credentials.
- Joint venture partners – may wish to avoid association with poor environmental performance.
- Investors and financiers – could be concerned not to be associated with poor practices that their investors may not like. Ethical investors in particular will look for reassurance.
- Insurers – will want to be sure that the organization is managing its insured risks such as flood damage, and third party liabilities.

Often, organizations do not feel safe talking externally on issues about which they feel vulnerable. In these cases dialogue can be mediated by organizations such as the Environment Council, one of the most experienced organizations helping companies and others to create effective dialogue with their stakeholders over environmental and related topics. The Environment Council has written a number of guides and articles aimed at helping organizations understand where dialogue may fit into their management toolbox.

Integrating environmental issues into core strategic and risk management processes

One of the factors that determine how effectively organizations address environmental issues to the benefit of the organization is how well consideration of these issues is integrated into the mainstream risk management and strategic planning of the organization.

It is notable now that some of the larger, more high profile organizations are including reviews of environmental and social issues within their core risk management processes. This is a logical approach, but it is often not followed because such issues have not been understood by the managers and directors responsible for business risk identification. The anticipated changes to UK company law should encourage a wider application of risk and strategic management to include environmental issues.

Risk identification and evaluation is an exercise that must be updated regularly in order to ensure the organization keeps its information up to date. However, organizations must also remember to review environmental risks, alongside other business risks, in times of change such as sale, merger or acquisition. Organizations can often be particularly vulnerable to environmental issues at this time, and the issues may delay a transaction, or affect the value of a business.

Taking action

As well as understanding the pressures on the organization, the environmental professional must know the range of possible actions an organization might take. This section outlines the key areas of environmental activity to be considered by an organization, as part of its strategy for dealing with environmental pressures. The emphasis for any one organization depends on the particular pressures and opportunities it faces.

Responses to direct impacts of environmental change: Organizations need to assess the risks to their property and operations, and review their contingency plans and their insurance arrangements. The likely direction and rate of environmental change should be taken into account. There is advice available: for example, local authorities and the EA provide advice on how to protect premises and operations from the effects of flooding. Increasingly, insurers themselves can give advice on likely future risks.

Legal compliance: No organization can afford to do nothing. A review of legal compliance with the help of an in-house expert, external consultant or the regulator is a sensible step for any organization. Fines are not substantial, but costs can be, and repeatedly breaking environmental laws is frowned upon by society and reputations can be damaged. For small organizations, legal compliance may be a simple review of waste disposal procedures. For a larger one such as an international oil company, compliance with all national and international environmental legislation is a major undertaking.

Operational improvements to minimize costs: There is a substantial literature on approaches to reducing costs associated with energy, water, and raw materials from organizations such as Envirowise and Action Energy in the UK. To implement any of these approaches the managers in control of the relevant operations need to commit the necessary time, budget and resources.

Integrated environmental management procedures: In order to maintain legal compliance and operational improvements, environmental management procedures will be required. ISO 14001 provides a good template for an environmental management system; however, to be most effective for the organization, management procedures that are geared towards environmental performance should be integrated into mainstream management procedures. For example, the environmental requirements for part of a manufacturing operation should be part of the core operating protocol for the operation, rather than a separate instruction. Similarly, environmental audit should be part of the wider operational audit, and training should be part of core staff induction and training.

An important aspect of integrating environmental management into an organization is encouraging a culture of good environmental practice among employees. Developing such a culture is a long term project requiring considerable commitment and skill.

Communication: Internal communication is an important aspect of building a strong culture for good environmental practice and innovation. Regular external communication with key stakeholders is very important for maintaining the trust of these stakeholders.

Products and services: As well as addressing waste, pollution, energy consumption and other operational aspects, an organization needs to consider the environmental impacts of the products it produces. There is increasing pressure on businesses to reduce the life cycle impacts of products, from the raw materials used, to the energy consumed by the product in use, to the impacts of final recycling and disposal. To encourage 'eco-design' there are labelling schemes for various product types that indicate the environmental credentials of the product to the consumer, such as the mandatory energy label for fridges and washing machines, and the EU eco-label.

Suppliers: A great deal has been written about how to manage environmental issues in the supply chain. The key point to make is that with an inevitably vast number of suppliers, particularly beyond direct suppliers, an organization needs to be very clear about what it is trying to achieve with environmental supply chain management, and be realistic about what is possible within available resources. It needs to have a clear plan about where it is focusing its efforts, and a long term commitment to the project.

Summary

Any type of organization operating in today's society needs to be aware of the potential impact of environmental issues upon its current and future operations. In order to ensure it fully understands these impacts it needs to ensure it has access to appropriate expertise, talks to relevant stakeholders and integrates consideration of environmental issues into its mainstream risk assessment and strategic management. Organizations need to ensure they understand environmental issues in relation to their specific situation and use this knowledge to develop an appropriate response strategy that will protect and enhance it over time. The actions they should consider include compliance with legislation, reducing costs and environmental impacts of operations, reviewing product designs, and addressing environmental issues in supply and distribution chains. Professional environmental managers have a key role in steering their organizations towards the right solutions and driving implementation. It is important for their organizations, and for the environment, that they have the knowledge and the influencing skills to ensure they achieve this.

Chapter 3.2

Environmental Management Systems

Introduction

An environmental management system (EMS) is a structured framework for managing an organization's significant environmental impacts. Some organizations have adopted the approach specified in national or international standards which set out the requirements of an EMS and have had their systems externally assessed and certified against these; others have developed their EMS in a more informal way. Whatever approach has been adopted, the elements of the EMS will largely be the same.

This chapter provides background information on the development of EMS standards and their application by organizations. It describes the different elements of an EMS, how they interrelate and how they can be implemented.

EMS background

Most organizations adopt a systematic approach to the management of their day to day operations. Over the years, the different elements of such systems have become more defined, and standardized approaches have been developed to help organizations to manage certain functions, for example quality. In the early 1990s, work was initiated by the British Standards Institution (BSI) to develop an EMS specification, which was first published as BS 7750 (BSI, 1992). National EMS standards were also published in Spain and Ireland.

At around the same time, the European Commission (EC) was developing the Eco-management and Audit Scheme (EMAS), which was similar to BS 7750, but included some additional requirements. The requirements of EMAS were published as Council Regulation 1836/93 in 1993 (EC, 1993). Following publication of BS 7750, the International Organization for Standardization (ISO) developed ISO 14001 – Environmental Management Systems – Specification and Guidance for Use (ISO, 2004). Its adoption as a European Standard by the European Committee for Standardization (CEN) meant that in Europe, all similar national standards were required to be withdrawn.

More recently, a new British Standard, BS 8555 – for the phased implementation of Environmental Management Systems – has been published (BSI, 2003). It provides a staged way for organizations to implement an EMS and achieve accredited certification to ISO 14001 and registration to EMAS; it is primarily (but not exclusively) aimed at small and medium sized enterprises.

Although the development of different standards, at the national, European and then international level, was potentially confusing, all of the EMS standards followed the Denning Cycle of: plan what you're going to do, do what you planned to do, check to ensure that you did what you planned to do, and act to make improvements – see Figure 3.2.1.

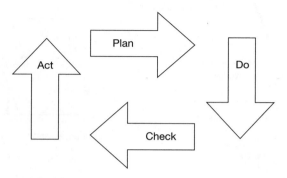

Figure 3.2.1   The Denning Cycle

ISO 14001 – EMS specification

ISO 14001 specifies the requirements of an EMS. It follows the plan–do–check–act model and at its core is the process of continual improvement. The ISO 14001 continual improvement process is shown in Figure 3.2.2.

ISO 14001 is the most widely used EMS standard, and is one of a broad range of environmental management standards in the ISO 14000 series – the series is listed in full at the end of this chapter. ISO 14001 is currently being revised. The purpose of the revision is to provide clarification of the original text and to ensure, as far as possible, compatibility with the ISO 9000:2000 quality management systems standards.

A revised edition of ISO 14001 has been published. An EMS is defined in the revision to the standard (ISO, 2004) as: 'Part of an organization's management system used to develop and implement its environmental policy and manage its environmental aspects'. Note 1 to the definition states, 'A management system is a set of interrelated elements used to establish policy and objectives and to achieve those objectives'. Note 2 states 'A management system includes organizational structure, planning activities, responsibilities, practices, procedures, processes and resources'.

ISO 14001 provides an organization's management with a structured framework for identifying, evaluating, managing and improving its environmental performance. The 14000 family of EMS standards uses the term 'organization' to describe the entity that falls within the scope of an EMS. 'Organization' is defined as 'company, corporation, firm, enterprise, authority or institution, or part or combination thereof, whether incorporated or not, public or private, that has its own functions and administration'. This gives a great deal of flexibility over where the boundaries of the EMS can be set.

The EMS helps to ensure that the organization's overall environmental objectives, as set out in its environmental policy, are implemented throughout the organization and

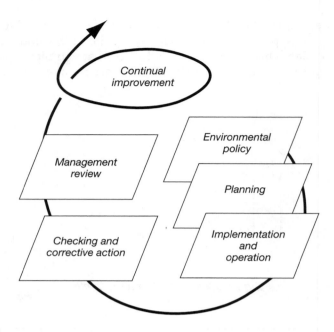

Source: ISO, 1996

Figure 3.2.2   The continual improvement process

that employees, contractors and suppliers know their roles and responsibilities in helping the organization to achieve them. Regular measurements, monitoring and auditing of the organization's environmental performance, and the system that is put in place to improve it, provide management with a basis for evaluating the effectiveness of the EMS and making changes as appropriate. A core principle in an EMS is that of continual improvement, thereby leading to better environmental performance by the organization on a sustained basis.

The following subheadings set out the different elements of an EMS defined in ISO 14001.

Environmental policy

Central to an EMS is the environmental policy. The environmental policy is a declaration of the organization's overall aims and principles with respect to the environment, as defined by its senior management. It must include a commitment to the continual improvement of environmental performance and to compliance with environmental, legal and other requirements. The policy must also be publicly available.

All organizations have, to some extent, an effect on the environment. The policy should recognize this, giving emphasis to those effects that are the most significant. The policy should also be used to communicate aims and objectives to employees and other interested parties including shareholders, customers and suppliers. In the case of a multi-site operation there may be a number of group or divisional operating statements which, when combined, represent the view of the company as a whole. The organization's environmental policy may be integrated with its other policies (e.g. health and safety, quality) or it can be a standalone document. In order to demonstrate the commitment of senior management to the environmental policy, it is often signed by the organization's chairman or chief executive.

Identifying and evaluating your environmental impacts

A key element of an EMS is the process of identifying and evaluating the organization's impacts on the environment, and its activities, products and services that cause them – environmental impacts may be positive or negative, beneficial or adverse. They are referred to as 'environmental aspects' in ISO 14001. The evaluation is important as it ensures that the EMS is focused on the environmental issues that really matter (those that are most significant) and that resources and management time are concentrated on controlling and improving them.

The identification of significant environmental aspects needs to take account of the legislative, regulatory and other environmental requirements that affect the organization. These may be pollution control permits, laws and regulations relating to the disposal of waste, or contractual requirements that specify environmental criteria required by customers of the organization. For each of these significant environmental aspects, it is important that the EMS is set up to provide assurance to management and others who might have an interest (e.g. environmental regulators and customers) that these are being properly managed and the organization is able to comply with the requirements. It is good practice to consult with key stakeholders to identify what their expectations are for your environmental performance. They might have useful information and the consultation process might help to prioritize the most important issues to address in your EMS.

When establishing an EMS, many organizations undertake an environmental review. The environmental review is a systematic process to:

- determine the impacts the organization has on the environment, and which of them are significant;
- understand which of its activities, products and services cause the significant impacts;
- know which of its activities, products and services are covered by environmental legislation and regulations, whether it is complying with them and whether this can be sustained on an ongoing basis;
- know the extent to which it is controlling its significant environmental aspects and whether effective controls are already in place; and
- be in a position to develop objectives and targets for environmental improvement and implement additional operational controls where they are necessary.

An easy way to get started on the environmental review is to map out the boundaries of the EMS and highlight areas where there are environmental considerations. These could include internal and external drainage plans, chemical storage points, location of waste skips, chimney stacks from boilers and the nearest neighbours. Alternatively, if the EMS doesn't lend itself to being identified on a map (this is particularly the case for service organizations), a process flow diagram highlighting inputs and outputs might be more appropriate.

Your EMS should address your direct and indirect environmental aspects. Direct aspects are those caused as a direct result of the organization's operations, whereas indirect aspects are those over which the organization has influence, but no direct control. Examples of environmental aspects include:

- emissions to air;
- releases to water;
- disposal of waste and contamination of land;
- use of energy, raw materials and natural resources;
- land use and habitat loss;
- disposal of the organization's products by customers; and
- environmental performance of contractors and suppliers.

Consideration should be given to impacts caused during normal and abnormal operating conditions and periods of maintenance and shutdown, and to significant environmental impacts that could occur during emergencies. Once impacts have been identified, their significance should be evaluated.

Assessing significance

Assessing the significance of an environmental impact is one of the most difficult parts of environmental management. There are many different tools and techniques and, frequently, more than one approach can be used for a given situation. In many circumstances, professional judgement will play an important role in determining how to address significance and this can be helped through consultation with appropriate stakeholders. The significance of an environmental impact can be assessed through consideration of:

- size, nature, frequency, likelihood and duration of the environmental impact;
- the sensitivity of the receiving environment and the extent to which the impact is reversible;
- the extent to which the impact (or the activity, product or service which causes it) is covered by environmental laws and regulations, or contractual requirements; and
- the importance of the impact to interested parties – for example employees, neighbours, regulators.

It is important that the criteria for evaluating significance are clearly defined and that the procedure and outcome are capable of being replicated by someone else. Some organizations develop risk matrices to help them evaluate the significance of an environmental impact and to prioritize its relative importance; however, care should be taken to ensure that all significant impacts are identified and that there is a robust means of allocating the scores.

Operational control, targets and objectives

The results of the environmental review and the evaluation of the significance of the environmental impacts are used to identify operational control measures and to set objectives and targets for environmental improvement. Objectives and targets need to relate to the organization's environmental policy and its environmental aspects. All significant environmental aspects will require operational controls to ensure that actions are carried out as planned and some of them will require objectives and targets for improvement, within the EMS.

Objectives are broad based environmental goals that the organization sets itself for environmental management and improvement. They may relate to a specific environmental issue, for example:

- to reduce the overall amount of solid waste produced over the next five years by 25 per cent; or
- to manage issues that will help to deliver the policy – for example to ensure that all employees receive appropriate environmental training by the end of the financial year.

Targets are detailed performance requirements that need to be met in order to achieve the objectives. A number of targets might be required to achieve a particular objective. In some cases, objectives and targets might relate to the need for further research and analysis on how to achieve improvements. Where possible, objectives and targets should be SMART – specific, measurable, achievable, relevant and time related. This will help to track progress and ensure that achievements are being realized.

Environmental programme

The environmental programme turns the environmental objectives and targets into practical actions that can be taken to improve the organization's environmental performance. The programme should identify individual responsibilities and the means to achieve the defined objectives and targets within the specified time scales. It should translate the commitment to continual environmental improvement set out in the environmental policy into practical actions.

Structure and responsibilities

The organization's management will need to assign tasks to people so that everyone knows what has to be done. It is vital, if the system is to operate effectively, to know who does what, how, when and with what authority.

Whatever the size of the organization, the activities of all employees will have an impact on the environment. Directly or indirectly, significant or small, everyone can contribute positively by innovating with new ideas, changing behaviour and involving other people. This will require information, training and the development of new skills. Different people in the organization will need different types and levels of training: some will require general environmental awareness training; others training as auditors; the design team might need training on how to integrate environmental considerations into new product designs. The key is to make sure that people are given the knowledge and skills to fulfil their roles in the EMS and to be able to achieve the environmental targets and objectives they have been assigned responsibility for.

Communication

An EMS relies on good communications for it to be effective. Internal communication needs to ensure that people are kept up to date with how progress is being made against environmental objectives and targets, and that they are able to influence the development of the EMS and environmental improvement programmes. External communications help to ensure that stakeholders are kept informed of the organization's progress and can be engaged in the improvement process.

Procedures and documentation

The EMS must be documented and procedures need to be established to ensure that everyone knows how the system operates and what is required. Documents should be kept up to date and controlled so that only the most recent versions are available for use. Procedures should be established to ensure that activities are carried out in the appropriate manner.

Contrary to popular belief, ISO 14001 doesn't require extensive documentation. Long narrative procedures may be required in some circumstances, but a flow diagram might be equally effective in ensuring that a task is carried out properly. Wherever possible, organizations should build on existing systems and integrate environmental issues into them, rather than developing them separately.

Monitoring and audit

Information on the environmental performance of the organization is essential if it is to track progress against its environmental objectives and targets. Without reliable and robust data, it cannot be sure that it is in control of its environmental performance, or that performance is improving as intended. In many cases the organization will already be carrying out measuring and monitoring activities, for example as a requirement of a pollution control licence, and should build on these in its EMS.

One of the important requirements in ISO 14001 is for organizations to carry out a periodic evaluation of legal compliance. This is a key task, which will help to inform the organization on its performance against environmental laws and regulations and provide information on whether it is adhering to its environmental policy. The frequency with which the organization carries out the periodic evaluation should depend on the potential environmental impacts of the activity, with the most significant being checked more often than those of lesser importance. However, it is advisable to ensure that compliance checks are carried out at least on an annual basis.

Auditing helps to determine whether the planned elements of the EMS are being implemented as intended and that the EMS is functioning as planned. It also provides information to management on the overall performance of the system.

Management review

The EMS operates as a cyclical process of identifying, improving and checking. Periodic reviews by management ensure that the EMS is achieving the desired outcomes and that the environmental policy is being implemented. It will also provide a means for management to review the organization's environmental performance trends to ensure that performance is being improved.

EMS certification and accreditation

Organizations may decide to have an external body confirm that their EMS meets the requirements of ISO 14001; this is known as certification. Certification is not mandatory – ISO 14001 does allow organizations to self declare that they have met all of the requirements of the standard. However, there are a number of benefits that can be gained by an organization having its EMS externally certified, including:

- confidence that the EMS meets recognized requirements and standards;
- a means of maintaining momentum and helping to keep the EMS 'alive' and dynamic and driving forward the process of continual improvement;
- a fresh pair of eyes to review the EMS and the way that it functions; and
- the potential for recognition for their achievements from third parties, such as customers and environmental regulators.

While organizations use ISO 14001 as the specification for the EMS, certification bodies use ISO Guide 66 (ISO, 2003) as the specification for how they should operate. ISO Guide 66 is being revised and is scheduled to be published as ISO 17021, General Requirements for Bodies Providing Assessment and Certification of Management Systems, in 2006.

In order to ensure that certification bodies undertake their EMS assessments in a similar and comparable way and that certificates issued by different certification bodies are equivalent, a process of accreditation has been established. National accreditation bodies undertake assessments to ensure that certification bodies carry out their assessments appropriately and use competent people. In the UK, the United Kingdom Accreditation Service (UKAS, 2004) is the national accreditation body.

An International Accreditation Forum (IAF) has been established to ensure consistent standards between accreditation bodies, which is achieved through a process of peer review. The IAF has published guidance to help participating accreditation bodies undertake their work (IAF, 2001). Accredited certification to ISO 14001 is usually the only form of recognition that is given by customers and regulators, so you should check that your certification body is accredited through the IAF process.

Eco-management and Audit Scheme (EMAS)

The Eco-management and Audit Scheme (EMAS) is a voluntary initiative designed to improve organizations' environmental performance. It was initially established by European Regulation 1836/93 (EC, 1993) although this has been replaced by Council Regulation 761/01 (EU, 2001). The scheme is open to any type of organization from any economic sector. EMAS uses the same definition of 'organization' as ISO 14001. The scheme applies in the European Union (EU); but at the time of writing, the EC is considering allowing organizations from anywhere in the world to participate. Participation in EMAS is voluntary.

The overall aim of EMAS is to recognize and reward those organizations that go beyond minimum legal compliance and continually improve their environmental performance. In addition, it is a requirement of the scheme that participating organizations regularly produce a public environmental statement that reports on their environmental performance. It is this voluntary publication of environmental information, whose accuracy and reliability has been independently checked by an environmental verifier, that gives EMAS and participating organizations enhanced credibility and recognition.

Participating organizations are required to implement an EMS that meets the requirements of ISO 14001. In addition, they are required to ensure that:

- they comply with legal requirements as a minimum and demonstrate the ability to do so on an ongoing basis;
- the organization's environmental performance improves over time;
- dialogue takes place with interested parties over their environmental performance, and they publish a publicly available environmental statement; and
- employees are involved in the process of continual improvement of environmental performance.

To ensure that the scheme's requirements have been met, organizations are required to have their EMS verified, by an independently accredited environmental verifier. The verifier is required to validate the reliability, credibility and correctness of the data and information in the environmental statement, and the environmental statement must include the following (EU, 2001, Annex III 3.2):

- A clear and unambiguous description of the organization registering under EMAS and a summary of its activities, products and services, and its relationship to any parent organizations as appropriate.
- The environmental policy and a brief description of the EMS of the organization.
- A description of all the significant direct and indirect environmental aspects that result in significant environmental impacts of the organization and an explanation of the nature of the impacts as related to these aspects (Annex VI).
- A description of the environmental objectives and targets in relation to the significant environmental aspects and impacts.
- A summary of the data available on the performance of the organization against its environmental objectives and targets with respect to its significant environmental impacts. The summary may include figures on pollutant emissions, waste generation, consumption of raw material, energy and water, and noise as well as other aspects indicated in Annex VI. The data should allow for year by year comparison to assess the development of the environmental performance of the organization.
- Other factors regarding environmental performance including performance against legal provisions with respect to their significant environmental impacts.
- The name and accreditation number of the environmental verifier and the date of validation.

The organization is then required to apply for registration. The application must be made to the organization that deals with EMAS registrations in their particular member state, known as the competent body. In the UK, the competent body is the Institute of Environmental Management and Assessment (IEMA, 2004). The competent body will check that the application is complete and consult with the environmental regulators to ensure that the organization is complying with relevant laws and regulations. Provided that these checks are satisfactory, the organization will be added onto the register. The EU EMAS register can be found at http://europa.eu.int/comm/environment/emas/index_en.htm.

Registered organizations may use EMAS logos to promote their achievements and their participation in the scheme. The two versions of the logo are shown in Figure 3.2.3. Version 1 indicates that the organization is registered whereas version 2 indicates that the information associated with the logo has been independently validated.

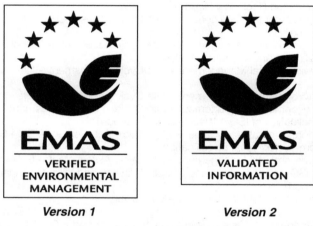

Version 1   **Version 2**

Figure 3.2.3   The EMAS logos

The EC has published a number of guidance documents to assist organizations implementing the scheme's requirements (EC, 2004). The registration process, checks made with the environmental regulators and the requirement to publish validated environmental performance data give EMAS added credibility over ISO 14001.

The ISO 14000 environmental management series

The ISO 14000 series of standards provides a comprehensive set of tools available to companies to manage and improve their environmental performance. A full list of current ISO standards can be found at www.iso.ch. Table 3.2.1 lists the standards that have been published to date and identifies others that are under development.

Table 3.2.1　The ISO 14000 series of standards

14001: 2004	Environmental Management Systems – Specification with Guidance for Use
14004: 2004	EMS – General Guidelines on Principles, Systems and Supporting Techniques
19011: 2002*	Guidelines for Quality and/or Environmental Management Systems Auditing
14015: 2001	Environmental Management – Environmental Assessment of Sites and Organisations
14020: 2000	Environmental Labels and Declarations – General Principles
14021: 1999	Environmental Labels and Declarations – Self-declared Environmental Claims (Type II Environmental Labelling)
14024: 1999	Environmental Labels and Declarations – Type I Environmental Labelling – Principles and Procedures
14025: 2000	Environmental Labels and Declarations – Type III Environmental Declarations (Technical Report)
14031: 1999	Environmental Management – Environmental Performance Evaluation – Guidelines
14032: 1999	Environmental Management – Examples of Environmental Performance Evaluation (Technical Report)
14040: 1997	Environmental Management – Life Cycle Assessment – Principles and Framework
14041: 1998	Environmental Management – Life Cycle Assessment – Goal and Scope Definition and Inventory Analysis
14042: 2000	Environmental Management – Life Cycle Assessment – Life Cycle Impact Assessment
14043: 2000	Environmental Management – Life Cycle Assessment – Life Cycle Interpretation
14047: 2003	Environmental Management – Life Cycle Impact Assessment – Examples of Application of ISO 14042 (Technical Report)
14048: 2002	Environmental Management – Life Cycle Assessment – Data Documentation Format (Technical Specification)
14049: 2000	Environmental Management – Life Cycle Assessment – Examples of Application of ISO 14041 to Goal and Scope Definition and Inventory Analysis (Technical Report)
14050: 2002	Environmental Management – Vocabulary
14061: 1998	Information to Assist Forestry Organizations in the Use of Environmental Management System Standards ISO 14001 and ISO 14004 (Technical Report)
14062: 2002	Environmental Management – Integrating Environmental Aspects into Product Design and Development
Guide 64: 1997	Guide for the Inclusion of Environmental Aspects in Product Standards

Standards Under Development:

14063	Environmental Communication – Guidelines and Examples
14064–1	Greenhouse Gases – Part 1: Specification for the Quantification, Monitoring and Reporting of Organization Emissions and Removals
14064–2	Greenhouse Gases – Part 2: Specification for the Quantification, Monitoring and Reporting of Project Emissions and Removals
14064–3	Greenhouse Gases – Part 3: Specification and Guidance for Validation and Verification
14065	Greenhouse Gases – Specifications for Bodies Providing Validation or Verification Assessments

Note: *ISO 19011: 2002 replaced the following standards in the ISO 14000 series: (i) ISO 14010 Guidelines for Environmental Auditing – General Principles of Environmental Auditing; (ii) ISO 14011 Guidelines for Environmental Auditing – Audit Procedures – Part 1: Auditing of Environmental Management Systems; (iii) ISO 14012 Guidelines for Environmental Auditing – Qualification Criteria for Environmental Auditors

References

BSI (1992) 'BSI 7750, Specification for Environmental Management Systems', British Standards Institution, London

BSI (2003) 'BS 8555, Guide to the Phased Implementation of an Environmental Management System including the Use of Environmental Performance Evaluation', British Standards Institution, London

EC (1993) 'Council Regulation (EEC) 1836/1993 of 29 June 1993 Allowing Voluntary Participation by Industrial Companies in the Industrial Sector in a Community Eco-management and Audit Scheme', *Official Journal of the European Community*, L168 10/7/93, Brussels

EC (2004) Guidance is available at http://europa.eu.int/comm/environment/emas/index_en.htm on: the entities suitable for registration; verification, validation and audit frequency; the use of the EMAS logo; the EMAS environmental statement; employee participation; the identification of environmental aspects and assessment of their significance; the verification of small and medium sized enterprises, particularly small and micro businesses; and environmental performance indicators

EU (2001) 'European Parliament and the Council of the European Union Regulation 761/2001 Allowing Voluntary Participation by Organisations in a Community Eco-management and Audit Scheme (EMAS)', *Official Journal of the European Community*, L114/1 24/4/2001, Brussels

IAF (2001) 'Guidelines on the Accreditation of Certification Bodies for EMS', International Accreditation Forum, www.iaf.nu

IEMA (2004) Further information on the Institute of Environmental Management and Assessment as the UK EMAS Competent Body is available at www.iema.net and www.emas.org.uk. ISO environmental standards can be purchased from www.iema.net/shop

ISO (1996) 'ISO 14001, Environmental Management Systems – Specification with Guidance for Use', International Organization for Standardization, Geneva

ISO (2003) 'ISO Guide 66, General Requirements for Bodies Operating Assessment and Certification/Registration of Environmental Management Systems', International Organization for Standardization, Geneva

ISO (2004) 'ISO 14001, Environmental Management Systems – Requirements with Guidance for Use', International Organization for Standardization, Geneva

UKAS (2004) Further information on the United Kingdom Accreditation Service is available at www.ukas.com

Chapter 3.3

Towards Sustainable Procurement

Introduction

Organizations use a wide range of products, from basic items such as paper to composite materials such as plastics and electrical components, and bulk materials such as iron and aggregates. The bought-in element of an organization's activities can be the source of its highest environmental impacts; however, environment is only part of the picture. People make products and provide services and the way they are treated and their terms and conditions of employment are equally important. Then of course organizations have to cover their costs or make a return on shareholders' funds otherwise they are not economically viable.

In the past, items were purchased and savings delivered with little regard to their impact on the environment and society at large. More recently, the term 'procurement' has been introduced to mark the change of emphasis from the traditional approach to one that incorporates both risk and value management. Organizations that are now beginning to engage with sustainable procurement need to broaden this approach to take account of environmental, social and economic impacts. The key elements of sustainable procurement are shown in Figure 3.3.1.

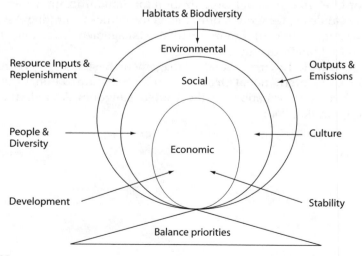

Source: EA, 2003a

Figure 3.3.1   The key elements of sustainable procurement

The first step towards sustainable procurement is a sustainable procurement strategy. Without a strategy, procurement professionals cannot set priorities and levels of resource input for their activities. An organization's strategy may be to minimize environmental impacts but only where there is no financial impact. Alternatively, an organization may decide it will focus on risk and consider incurring additional costs if the risks can be managed. The requirement here is a strategy that:

- takes account of the organization's vision and mission;
- is acceptable to those managing the organization; and
- provides some boundaries for those charged with its implementation.

Developing a sustainable procurement strategy

Procurement activities can make a significant contribution to an organization's sustainability policy goals by ensuring that suppliers, contractors and the goods and services bought achieve optimum environmental and ethical performance. Furthermore, procurement has an additional role to play in minimizing any risk to reputation from environmental despoliation or social exploitation in the supply chain. Procurement can also make a significant contribution to promoting environmental and social awareness in the market place through its supply community.

Figure 3.3.2 shows a sustainable procurement strategy model developed by the Environment Agency (EA). It defines the key areas of activity, the boundaries

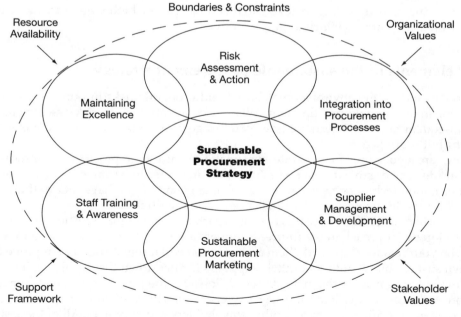

Source: EA, 2003b

Figure 3.3.2   Sustainable procurement strategy model

(the dashed circle) and the constraints impacting on procurement that must be considered to ensure that the strategy can co-exist within the organization's culture and systems.

Each element in the model needs to be addressed in a systematic manner. All the elements are interlinked and at the centre of the chain is the strategy, which should underpin the procurement philosophy of the organization. The outer circle shows the boundary and constraints that impact upon the strategy. These need to be adequately analysed to ensure that approaches to procurement take account of wider organizational and stakeholder values. This will help to ensure that any strategy is deliverable in both organizational and practical terms. To develop a sustainable procurement strategy the following issues need to be considered:

Boundaries and constraints

- What are my organization's true values on the subject of sustainability? Is sustainability a core belief or is it a public relations exercise?
- What are my stakeholders' values on the subject of sustainability? First of all identify your stakeholders and rank them in importance, for example shareholders, customers, general public, suppliers, pressure groups, government and so on. Then consider what you believe their views are and how far they would want your organization to go.
- What support framework is available to deliver a sustainable procurement strategy? Consider accessibility to expert information, managers' expectations, performance measures other than financial, use of the internet and other research tools.
- What resources are available to deliver sustainable procurement? Consider how much time you are willing to devote to this subject and whether there are likely to be any financial impacts which require approval.

Key elements of the sustainable procurement strategy

- Understanding the environmental, social and economic risks in purchases is a key factor in sustainable procurement. What is your approach to risk assessment and subsequent action? Determine how you are going to assess risk and the extent to which it is applied.
- How are you going to integrate sustainability into your procurement processes? Consider any organizational procedures that may need to be amended, whether any information technology systems need enhancing and, if you have ISO 9001 and ISO 14001 accreditation, do any manuals need to be rewritten?
- How will you communicate this new approach to your suppliers? And how will you develop the approach in the future? Suppliers are a key factor so you need to reflect upon your relationships with them and how you will motivate them to improve their own sustainability and that of their suppliers further down the supply chain.
- How will you market this new strategy? Consider the type of marketing campaign you will need to motivate the key players. You will need to engage with senior managers, specifiers, users, and other stakeholders and suppliers. All of these stakeholders require subtly different messages.

- How are you going to train staff and raise awareness? People will need to change working practices and challenge specifiers and suppliers on their recommendations. A support framework will be required during the transitional phase. The marketing campaign should help to raise awareness.
- How are you going to maintain excellence? Consider your approach to continual improvement and the measurement of progress. Do you need a development programme with measures to demonstrate success?

Determine your sustainable procurement strategy

On the basis of the boundaries and constraints and the key elements, referred to earlier, define your sustainable procurement strategy. The strategy is a vision of how sustainable your organization wants your procurement contracts to be. For example:

> Our sustainable procurement strategy is to procure the goods and services we need while balancing environmental, social and economic impacts to ensure that we meet the needs of stakeholders and the requirements of our customers. We will take a risk based approach to decisions and where risks are unacceptable we will invest to manage them.

A strategy statement such as this provides a succinct message to staff and demonstrates the organization's commitment to sustainable procurement. The detailed strategy that then follows covers all the key elements described previously, such as the approach to risk assessment. This integrated approach will then give procurement staff the framework within which they can deliver sustainable procurement on the ground, ensuring they are in step with the beliefs and values of the organization.

Towards sustainable procurement – risk assessment

Risk assessment is a vital step in understanding and prioritizing the issues involved in the contract and then determining what can be done to manage them. The risk assessment, if properly conducted, identifies the most significant sustainability impacts. For example, if you work for a chemical manufacturer the biggest impacts are likely to be associated with the procurement of raw chemicals, not paper and other items of stationery.

Risk assessment determines not only where effort is placed, but also how far an organization should go to manage the risk. If an item is being procured that is very high risk the organization may be willing to pay a premium to manage the risk. However, if the item is low risk then the focus should be on driving down cost and switching suppliers to get the best possible terms. This basic philosophy should underpin an organization's approach to procurement, saving money where it can and managing risk where it is necessary to protect against corporate risk, sustainability impacts and potential damage to reputation.

The approach to risk assessment needs to be tailored to an individual organization's circumstance. The example shown below has been developed by the EA. Some issues such as biodiversity impacts are missing from the example. The assessment could be much more detailed to incorporate many more issues; however, it is best to make a start and then develop it over time. The example below is not simple, it has evolved over the last five years and it will evolve further in the future. The approach is illustrated in four steps as follows and uses adhesives as an example commodity.

Step 1 – determine the key life cycle inputs and outputs

Using the key life cycle stages of raw material, manufacture, use and disposal, consider the main issues, inputs and outputs, as shown in Table 3.3.1. This table and the subsequent analysis are based on publicly available information and provide an overview of the impacts associated with adhesives generally. It contains a description of the most commonly used raw materials, and the possible environmental impacts and potential byproducts. It should be noted that there might be some other commodity types and manufacturing processes not covered in this example where the impacts are managed more effectively.

Table 3.3.1   Issues at each stage of the life cycle for adhesives

Raw material	Use
● Oils;	● VOCs (volatile organic compounds);
● Rubber;	● Health and safety dangers;
● Solvent;	● Energy if used in a glue gun;
● Plastics, metals, paper, card (packaging);	● Packaging waste (paper, card, metals, plastics).
● Energy and water;	
● Plant, materials, people.	

Manufacture	Disposal
● The main components of the manufacturing process are formulation, coating, drying, curing and packaging.	● VOC emissions to the atmosphere;
	● Unused glue, tins, plastic, cartons, packaging;
● Material is highly processed using significant amounts of energy and water.	● Typically non-biodegradable waste;
● Heavy machinery, plant and people.	● Possible chemical leachates in landfill;
	● Possible toxic emissions if incinerated.

Source: EA, 2003b

Step 2 – key life cycle impacts at each stage

Based on the life cycle inputs and outputs identified in Step 1, the next step is to identify the key aspects for each stage. This will be a subjective judgement. These aspects are shown in the left hand column of Table 3.3.2 (overleaf) and are determined at an organizational level reflecting values and areas of concern. The symbols used are a world for an environmental impact, a person for a social impact and a plus or minus to indicate the contribution the commodity (in this case adhesives) makes to society and the economy in the UK. The 'dashed rings' indicate initial priority areas; the aspects are marked with a 'dashed ring' where there are at least four impacts. This gives an initial focus for effort.

Strategic sustainability risk information can be gathered from the following sources:

- Information on existing and forthcoming legislation is available from the EA web site, see www.environment-agency.gov.uk/business/.
- A list of industries subject to IPPC Regulation is available at www.environment-agency.gov.uk/netregs/.

Unfortunately there isn't one web site that holds data on commodities linked to a 'green' or 'ethical' pressure group campaign. The best course of action is to monitor the main pressure group web sites such as Greenpeace, Friends of the Earth, Oxfam and Amnesty International.

Is there the likelihood of a developing-world supply chain? The answer to this should be evident from the materials inputs you have identified and whether they typically originate from the developing world. Generally, bulk raw materials have a high likelihood of coming from the developing world as do textiles and electronics.

The overall risk rating does not come from a score, it is a qualitative judgement based on the findings of the life cycle inputs and outputs, the mapping to key impacts and the sustainability risks identified in the table. In this example, as there are so many impacts coupled with specific environmental legislation and a developing-world supply chain risk, adhesives are judged as being of high risk.

Step 3 – procurement actions and control measures

One of the main attractions of the life cycle approach is that it is possible to link procurement actions directly to the different life cycle stages. This then gives some direction to the buyer as to how to proceed in managing risks within the contract. This point is illustrated in Table 3.3.3 (on page 126).

Table 3.3.2 Key aspects for each stage in the life cycle for adhesives

Aspect/Impact	Raw materials/pre-manufacture — Extraction of base material	Primary processing	Manufacture of components	Manufacture and assembly of finished article	Use	Disposal	Reason for impacts	Actions to take
Non-renewable or natural resource use	●	●	●	●		Disposal blocked out as it will always be an impact	Principal ingredients, oils, solvents, chemicals, applicators (plastic/metal based) and energy	Specification and 1st-tier suppliers, supplier management and their own EMS
							Oils and solvents are principal ingredients, are non-renewable with considerable processing	Focus on suppliers, supplier management and specify water based
Energy	Energy blocked out as it will normally be ticked in these stages and is usually a key impact			●	●	●	High degree of processing of materials to arrive at product. Energy use is only applicable if adhesive is being heated in a glue gun etc.	Check supplier EMS and look for energy management systems
Water use and pollution	●	●	●	●	●	●	Considerable water use in key raw materials (oil and solvent manufacture). Waste water from washing out of containers and applicators in use.	Focus on suppliers, supplier, management, check EMS and water mgt protocols/targets
Air/emissions/VOC	●	●	●	●	●	●	Solvent ingredient has significant air emission impacts and can be a VOC	If possible specify water based adhesives, minimize usage
Solid waste		●	●	●	●	●	Oil and solvent based raw materials have high degrees of waste in the manufacturing process	As above
Hazardous substances	●	●	●	●	●	●	Oil, solvent and the eventual adhesive are all hazardous substances	As above
Packaging						Disposal blocked out as it will always be an impact	Drums/containers for oils and solvents. Then eventual drums/containers for finished adhesive.	Check supplier packaging control system, use of recycled materials
Social impact noise	●	●	●				Noise impacts through raw materials, oils extraction/processing and manufacture	If possible specify water based/ask 1st-tier supplier about supply management

	👤	👤👤	👤👤👤	👤👤👤👤	N/A	Notes	
Social impact: developing-world supply chain	−	+	+	+/−		Oil and solvent ingredient may come from developing-world oil fields/refineries. Adhesives are manufactured worldwide.	Focus on 1st-tier supplier, ethical supply chain policy
Social impact: UK contribution	−	+	+	−	−	Raw material inputs are key employers (oil sector) and major economic contributors to local society. Adhesives less so, but still a key employer. Both industries can have health impact, solvent abuse issues.	No action, for information only
Economic impact: UK contribution	+	+	+	+	−	Oil industry is a major contributor to UK economy. Adhesives while not a major sector in itself is a key component for many others.	No action, for information only

STRATEGIC SUSTAINABILITY RISK	Scoring	Notes
(1) Existing or forthcoming legislation or national strategy concerning product/service?	Yes	Some adhesives are classified as special wastes. Adhesives are affected by a number of European directives.
(2) Is the industry subject to IPPC Regulations?	No	
(3) Commodity linked to or subject of 'green' or 'ethical' pressure group campaign.	No	Not adhesives directly, but be aware of issues further down the supply chain through the oil extractors and refiners.
(4) Is there a likelihood of a developing-world supply chain?	Yes	Raw material inputs and manufacture of adhesives has a high potential of being in the developing world.
Risk Rating	**HIGH**	Priority to supplier's own supply chain management policy/system and management of the manufacturing process/EMS. Consider disposal options.

Note: For examples of 35 commodities go to www.environment-agency.gov.uk/business

Source: EA, 2003a

Table 3.3.3 Procurement actions linked to life cycle stages

Life cycle stage	Procurement action
Raw materials	Enhance specification/invitation to tender. Examine suppliers' systems and approach to supply management focusing on their supply chain management principles and techniques. How are they ensuring their suppliers are managing their own sustainability impacts?
Manufacture	Manage through supplier selection/appraisal. Look for EMS/management systems, ethical policies and how they actually manage sustainability issues in their manufacturing process.
Use/provision of service/ maintenance	Enhance specification/contract terms/contract monitoring and educate end user as to their role in minimizing impacts, e.g. through proper use of equipment to minimize energy use.
Waste management/ end-of-life	Enhance specification/tender requirement/contract terms/contract monitoring, consider options for supplier take back, ensure end user is aware of any disposal legacy issues and that this is built into any cost analysis.

Note: This list is a guideline and is not intended to be definitive; there may be occasions when a procurement action may be appropriate in more than one stage of the life cycle
Source: EA, 2003c

Based on the example of adhesives the control measures shown in Table 3.3.4 have been identified. These control measures should again flow from the issues identified in Steps 1 and 2.

Table 3.3.4 Control measures for adhesives

Raw materials/ processing/ manufacturing stage	Ensure suppliers are complying with specific regulations on solvent use and also have solvent management plans.
	Where feasible, select products from suppliers who have minimized (1) the content of toxic or harmful substances, (2) the release of VOCs into the environment, (3) the energy required to manufacture and transport products, (4) the creation of toxic wastes during production.
	Ensure analysis and identification of the environmental impacts of raw materials used in the product, such as solvents, chemicals and other hazardous substances.
	If possible, devote resources to develop a priority list of environmentally safer adhesives that are less toxic and more biodegradable.
Procurement stage	Specify, where possible, low-solvent water-based adhesives. An alternative to solvent based adhesives is natural adhesives, for example starch or dextrin based adhesives in paper board packaging.
	Also where possible use white glues, glue sticks, library pastes and yellow glues. These glues effectively adhere to most porous surfaces including cloth, wood, fabric and pottery and are the least hazardous and safest glues on the market. Operating costs for water based adhesives are approximately one third lower than for solvent based adhesives.

Table 3.3.3   continued

Procurement stage *continued*	Identify suppliers that are able to provide more detailed information in relation to (1) the specific raw materials that they use, and (2) guidance on safe use and disposal (particularly of packaging).
	Encourage suppliers to develop environmentally safer products, in particular to minimize the use of solvents and other chemicals.
Use and disposal stage	Avoid wasteful use of adhesives by ensuring the purchase of the specific amount required for the job.
	Categorize adhesive related waste as hazardous waste and manage it accordingly.
	Train staff in the safe storage, handling and disposal (particularly related to packaging) of adhesive products. (This will ensure staff implement safety and environment guidelines and wear the appropriate protective equipment.)

Source: EA, 2003c

Step 4 – the overall approach

This final stage considers some general actions that could be taken in the future, for any commodity being purchased. These are shown in Table 3.3.5 (overleaf). They have been subdivided into environmental and social/ethical actions.

Benefits of risk assessment

By linking the risk assessment directly to the values of the organization, procurement staff can demonstrate their commitment and contribution to the wider aims of the organization.

All actions should flow from risk assessment; the risk governs not only how much effort to place on a contract or commodity, but it also highlights, to the organization, the issues involved so that informed decisions can be made on how best to manage the risk. This can be achieved by eliminating or minimizing the purchases, sourcing alternate supplies, motivating suppliers to improve products or possibly incurring additional cost to manage the risk and secure supply.

Costs will always be an important factor, but they are not the only factor that has to be managed. It is through risk assessment that procurement professionals can really demonstrate the value they bring to an organization. It shows that the process is more than just about saving money; it's about managing risk, and safeguarding the organization's reputation.

Selection of the most sustainable suppliers

A key procurement decision is the selection of suppliers. Often it is the suppliers who will directly manage the key sustainability impacts either through their own business activities or through their own suppliers along the supply chain. Following risk assessment, if the significant impacts are in the raw materials phase the focus should be on the supplier's own sustainable supply chain management policies. If the significant

Table 3.3.5   General actions to consider

Environmental actions

High environmental risk	• reduce consumption (rethink the purchase); • seek alternatives (based on cost benefit analysis); • incorporate environmental credentials into supplier selection processes; • incorporate environmental design issues into specifications; • specify eco-labelled products, if feasible; • develop environmental improvement plans and environmental performance measures, if appropriate; • include environmental issues in supplier auditing; • include environmental clauses in conditions of contract; • exercise caution regarding 'green' marketing from suppliers; • investigate possibilities for collaboration on joint R&D, if appropriate.
Medium environmental risk	• reduce consumption; • seek alternatives (based on cost benefit analysis); • incorporate environmental credentials into supplier selection processes; • incorporate environmental design issues into specifications; • specify eco-labelled products, if feasible; • provide suppliers with training material; • exercise caution regarding 'green' marketing from suppliers.
Low environmental risk	• reduce consumption; • increase supplier awareness of issues; • provide supplier with training material.

Social/ethical actions

High social/ ethical risk (e.g. risk in three life cycle stages)	• undertake more detailed research of the supply chain, map the social impacts; • incorporate social credentials into supplier selection processes; • specification of Social Accountability 8000. SA8000 is a set of guiding principles for proactive ethical management of a business. It is designed to link into ISO 14001; • develop social improvement plans and social performance measures, if appropriate; • include social issues in supplier auditing; • include social clauses in conditions of contract (SA8000); • exercise caution regarding 'ethical' marketing from suppliers; • investigate how suppliers are managing the disposal of their equipment at the end of its life in the developing world; • investigate possibilities for collaboration on joint R&D, if appropriate.
Medium social/ ethical risk (e.g. risk in two life cycle stages)	• undertake more detailed research of the supply chain, map the social impacts; • specification of SA8000; • incorporate social credentials into supplier selection processes; • incorporate social issues into specifications; • include social clauses in conditions of contract (SA8000); • exercise caution regarding 'ethical' marketing from suppliers.
Low social/ ethical risk (e.g. risk in one life cycle stage)	• investigate with first-tier suppliers their supply chain and how they manage their social impacts; • specification of SA8000; • incorporate social credentials into supplier selection processes; • increase supplier awareness of issues.

Note: For organizations in the public sector see 'OGC–Defra Joint Note on Environmental Issues in Purchasing' at www.ogc.gov.uk
Source: EA, 2003c

impacts are in the manufacturing stage then the focus may be on the supplier's own EMS and personnel management for their business.

One way of gathering information from suppliers is through a questionnaire. This is also sometimes augmented with interviews and presentations. The questionnaire can provide a consistent approach to all suppliers and should allow the buyer to compare one supplier with another.

It is of particular importance that the supplier's environmental and social policies actually address the key impacts of their business. For example, an environmental policy from a chemical manufacturer needs to deal with the environmental issues of making chemicals rather than looking at its paper consumption and car policy, which while valid are not the main impacts. An example of a questionnaire is shown in Table 3.3.6.

The continents underlined (Questions 9 and 12) show where there is potential for a high social/ethical risk. Care needs to be taken where organizations are operating in or buying from the developing world. Continents have been used in this questionnaire because it is easier for suppliers to answer from this broader perspective, rather than naming each individual country. However, there are of course countries within the continents underlined that are developed and world leading economies, such as Japan. However, this initial assessment is designed to flag potential risk. Once flagged, buyers can then go into more detail with individual suppliers.

Table 3.3.6   An example of a questionnaire

Environmental policy and practice

No	Question	Answer
1.	Does your company have an environmental policy statement committing it to a programme of environmental improvement?	YES/NO (If yes, please provide a copy.)
1a.	Does the policy statement extend to all the products and services supplied?	YES/NO (If yes, please indicate how. If no, please indicate which products and/or services are included.)
2.	In your company, who has overall responsibility for environmental performance of the organization?	Please name and give job title.
2a.	Is there a director or member of the board accountable?	YES/NO (Please name and give job title.)
3.	Has your company undertaken a review of its environmental impact?	YES/NO (If yes, please detail the top five environmental impacts of your company.)
4.	Does your company have an environmental management system?	YES/NO (If yes, please provide details, plus any evidence of accreditation.)
5.	Does your company communicate environmental objectives to employees, suppliers and other interested parties?	YES/NO (If yes, please provide details.)

continued overleaf

Table 3.3.6   continued

Environmental policy and practice

No	Question	Answer
6.	Does your company set environmental performance targets and objectives against which performance is audited?	YES/NO (If yes, please give examples that directly relate to the five environmental impacts identified in Question 3.)
7.	Does your company formally report on progress towards meeting these objectives?	YES/NO (If yes, please indicate how and to whom, and provide examples: if possible provide your Annual Environmental Report.)
8.	Has your company been successfully prosecuted for an infringement of environmental legislation in the past three years?	YES/NO (If yes, please give details, date and outcome of the prosecution.)

Social/ethical policy and practice

No	Question	Answer
9.	Do you have overseas operations?	YES/NO (If yes, in which continent?) Europe Asia Africa North America South America Australasia
10.	How do you comply with the local legal minimum age for employment?	
11.	Do you have an ethical policy for managing your overseas operations?	YES/NO (If yes, what does it cover?) Working conditions Age of employees Pay Trade union membership for staff Equality of employment opportunities Use of natural resources Emissions and waste Other
12.	Do you purchase goods or materials from overseas?	YES/NO (If yes, from which continent?) Europe Asia Africa North America South America Australasia

Table 3.3.6   continued

Social/ethical policy and practice

No	Question	Answer
13.	How do you ensure that your suppliers comply with the local legal minimum age for employment?	
14.	Do you have an ethical policy for overseas purchasing?	YES/NO (If yes, what does it cover?) Working conditions Age of employees Pay Trade union membership for staff Equality of employment opportunities Use of natural resources Emissions and waste Other
15.	How do you assess the effectiveness of your policy for overseas sourcing?	Don't assess Internal assessment Comply with SA8000 Other independent assessment

Source: EA, 2003b

Assessing the completed questionnaire

To assess the responses, an assessment methodology and scoring matrix are required. These are described below:

Assessment matrix: The assessment matrix has been designed to link directly to the questions in the questionnaire. The supplier can be sent a pack containing the matrix, which they can use to assess their capability. The buyer, together with the contract client and any environmental specialist as appropriate, will then assess the evidence provided, together with the statements made in support of the self assessment. The result of the assessment should be a score for each element, which can then be transferred to a simple profile chart.

Categorizing of suppliers: The buyer can use the profile to determine where each supplier fits to the requirements of the contract as influenced by the risk assessment. Additionally, buyers can use this to target effort on environmental and social improvements in the supply chain.

Sustainably 'unaware': A supplier who is assessed predominately at Level 1 will generally be seen as being 'unaware'. This will usually mean that the company has made no real effort to consider the environmental impacts of supplying the products or services. It is likely to be primarily price focused or cost focused in those areas that offer a direct financial return to the business (for example, energy consumption).

Any environmental or ethical benefits will only arise as a byproduct of the cost or production changes implemented by the business to maintain its market competitiveness.

Sustainability 'settler': A supplier who is assessed predominately at Level 2 or 3 will be seen as a 'settler'. The supplier will be generally aware of environmental and ethical issues associated with any product or service provided and will be looking to incorporate their impacts into production and purchasing activities.

The extent to which they are included will depend directly on the environmental manager's and/or procurement manager's individual commitment to and influence over the organization's policies. The basis of any consideration is likely to be either risk avoidance, in the case of pollution and potential prosecutions, or cost reduction, in the case of energy consumption and waste minimization.

A reactive rather than proactive approach is likely and there will be wide variations in practice across the organization. The level of personal commitment to environmental and ethical issues is the key driver in determining the extent to which the organization incorporates environmental and ethical issues into its everyday operations. People will probably give personal views on what is being done rather than referring to an organizational strategy. Initiatives will be specific to functions and their benefits will be uncoordinated.

Sustainable 'pioneer': A supplier who is assessed predominately at Level 4 or 5 will clearly be seen as a 'pioneer'. This supplier will be fully familiar with all the concepts discussed earlier and will always include appropriate environmental considerations in their own purchasing decisions. They will have a formal method of evaluating performance, possibly using an EMS, and the company will be either ISO 14001 registered, be working towards registration, or, in the case of a European organization, be registered to the Eco-management and Audit Scheme. Furthermore, when considering products sourced overseas, particularly from developing countries, the supplier will consider the ethical impacts that this purchasing will have, for example the exploitation of under-age labour, the working conditions, use of natural resources and so on.

Each department will have its own internally developed targets aligned to an overall organizational target with clearly defined links to the business objectives. There will be a formal audit of performance, either internally or externally based, and a good system of communication of achievements and reporting methodology.

Assessment matrix – steps to best practice

The assessment matrix is shown in Table 3.3.7. It is designed to:

- provide a structured and consistent approach to the assessment of suppliers' environmental and ethical management of their businesses; and
- demonstrate to suppliers the steps needed to reach environmental best practice.

Suppliers can use the matrix to score themselves and observe the gap to best practice. The matrix then gives suppliers the steps they need to take in order to become a pioneer in this field.

Table 3.3.7 *Sustainability scoring matrix*

	Level 1	Level 2	Level 3	Level 4	Level 5	Score
Environmental policy (1)	No policy	An unwritten set of guidelines	Un-adopted environmental policy set by departmental manager	Formal policy but no active commitment from top management	Environmental action plan and regular review with commitment from top management	
Organization (2)	No environmental management or any formal delegation of responsibility for environmental impact	Environmental responsibility is the part time function of someone with limited authority or influence and no reporting requirement	Environmental responsibility post reporting to ad hoc committee, line management and authority unclear	Environmental manager accountable to environment committee chaired by a board member	Environmental management fully integrated into management structure with clear delegated authority	
Review of impacts (3)	No review of impacts undertaken	Informal review of impacts in limited areas of the company	Review of organizational impacts undertaken, no follow up actions taken	Formal review of all company operations, key impacts identified and actions plans agreed and supported by management	Formal review of key impacts undertaken on behalf of board, action plans signed off by board as part of integrated management plan	
Environmental Management System (EMS) (4)	No EMS in place	Processes in place for individual impact areas; no coordinated systems	EMS available to all parts of company, but no requirement to implement, or report on specific areas	EMS in place across company, reporting, regular review of performance by top management	EMS fully integrated into business, regular review of performance by top management and supplier evaluation programme	
Communication programme (5)	No communications plan in place	Informal plan in place for company	Formal plan in place for company	Formal plan in place for company with ad hoc communications with support	Comprehensive plan in place covering staff and suppliers	

continued overleaf

Table 3.3.7   *continued*

	Level 1	Level 2	Level 3	Level 4	Level 5	Score
Audit programme (6)	No audit programme	Informal review of processes as part of other audit regime	Formal audit of all compliance issues and general audit of other processes	Formal audit of EMS against policy and performance targets	Externally verified audit of EMS against policy and performance targets	
Reporting (7)	No external reporting	Annual report and accounts includes the company environmental policy statement	Annual report and accounts includes a review of environmental activity	Annual environmental report published as part of company external reporting	Annual environmental report published as part of company external reporting including external verification	
Successful prosecution for legal infringement of environmental legislation (8)		Yes or No; if yes obtain details and assess degree of risk with the supplier				Y/N
Overseas operations (9)	Yes or No; if yes obtain details, reflect upon continents with a high number of developing-world countries and assess degree of risk with the supplier; explore how the supplier is managing this risk					Y/N
Operations' compliance with local minimum age for employment (10)	No compliance	An unwritten set of guidelines	Awareness of legal age laws; however, process informal and un-adopted	Formal policy but no active commitment from top management	Local legal age for employment fully complied with	
Operations' ethical policy (11)	No policy	An unwritten set of guidelines	Un-adopted ethical policy set by departmental manager	Formal policy but no active commitment from top management	Ethical policy covering all aspects of personnel and natural resource ethics. Regular review with commitment from top management	

					Y/N
Overseas purchasing (12)	Yes or No; if yes obtain details, reflect upon continents with a high number of developing-world countries and assess degree of risk with the supplier; explore how the supplier is managing this risk				
Overseas purchasing compliance with local minimum age for employment (13)	No compliance	An unwritten set of guidelines	Awareness of legal age laws; however, process informal and un-adopted	Formal policy but no active commitment from top management	Local legal age for employment fully complied with
Overseas purchasing ethical policy (14)	No policy	An unwritten set of guidelines	Un-adopted ethical policy set by departmental manager	Formal policy but no active commitment from top management	Ethical policy covering all aspects of personnel and natural resource ethics. Regular review with commitment from top management
Policy assessment (15)	No assessment	Informal review of policy as part of other assessment regime	Formal assessment of policy	Formal assessment of policy against performance targets	Externally verified assessment of policy against performance targets

Source: EA, 2003b

Developing suppliers and improving their approach to sustainability

The questionnaire and assessment matrix are a good basis for assessing a supplier's current performance and for identifying areas for improvement. Suppliers need to be given clear and consistent messages about sustainability, otherwise they will think your organization isn't really serious about this subject and they won't put the effort in to improve.

A key to the improvement process is the relationship you have with your suppliers. It is important to reflect upon this before making demands of them. If you have a strong relationship, where the supplier views you as an important customer, it should be possible to drive the sustainability agenda. If the supplier wants to develop business with you it should also be possible to drive the sustainability agenda. However, if the relationship is not strong or you are a small customer, or the supplier is in a monopoly situation, it might be difficult to develop the sustainability agenda.

This relationship needs to be considered at three key stages. Firstly, in the risk assessment stage, as it will influence the risks that can be transferred to the supplier; secondly, at the contract strategy development stage. When the buyer develops a strategy for the contract detailing how risk is managed, how value is ensured and so on, the relationship with the supplier is often a determining factor. Finally, in supplier development, the relationship will determine to a considerable extent how much you can expect the supplier to improve over the course of the contract. If the relationship is poor then it is likely that performance problems may occur and further enhancements are unlikely. For more information on techniques to assess this relationship see www.environment-agency.gov.uk/business/.

Many suppliers and buyers will be unfamiliar with the concepts of sustainability and what they can do to manage the associated risk. Suppliers and buyers therefore need assistance to develop. Recently a new training package for suppliers and buyers has become available, called Greenmatters (EA, 2003c). It explores in a fun, interactive way the issues of sustainability in an organization. It focuses on procurement, finance, law and marketing. The training package is a useful mechanism to develop both suppliers and buyers and raise awareness of the issues involved.

It is through effective supplier development that sustainability issues will begin to be addressed and improved year on year which should be a key objective within any sustainable procurement strategy.

Conclusions

The subject of sustainable procurement is potentially complex and controversial, as was the case with environmental procurement in the early 1990s. However, sustainability is widely accepted as an important principle by the UK Government and organizations in the public and private sectors. The problem is that nobody seems to agree on what it means or how to achieve it. There is then a danger of inaction as everyone waits to see what everyone else does first.

The techniques and tools detailed in this handbook are not exhaustive, but they offer a way in to a wide range of issues. It is important for people to recognize that we all have a part to play in sustainability and by making a start we can learn from experience and begin to make a difference. The approaches described in this chapter should help to bring sustainable procurement one step closer to reality.

References and further reading

For approaches to environmental and sustainable procurement, and commodity guidance, see (all available in English): United Nations Sustainable Procurement Group, www.un.org/esa/sustdev/sdissues/consumption/cpppr01.htm; United Nations General Sustainable Procurement, www.uneptie.org/pc; Danish Environmental Protection Agency, www.mst.dk/homepage/; Environment Canada, www.ec.gc.ca/envhome.html; Environmental Protection Agency USA, www.epa.gov/; European Union, ICLEI, www.iclei.org/europe/ecoprocura/index.htm; Greening Purchasing (GRIP) Norway, www.grip.no/Felles/english.htm; Green Purchasing Network of Japan, http://eco.goo.ne.jp/gpn/files/gpne/

Behrendt, S. et al (2001) *Eco-service Development: Reinventing Supply Demand in the European Union*, Greenleaf Publishing, Sheffield

Chartered Institute of Purchasing and Supply, www.cips.org

EA (2003a) *Risk Assessment Methodology, Research and Development Project E2055*, Environment Agency, Bristol

EA (2003b) Strategy development and supplier questionnaire and assessment from *Sustainable Procurement Guide*, Environment Agency, Bristol

EA (2003c) 'Greenmatters' CD-ROM training package developed in conjunction with EcoTraining Ltd, Environment Agency, Bristol, www.greenmatters.org.uk

Environment Agency, www.environment-agency.gov.uk/business for business risk assessment for items such as steel, IT, electronics, and further web links to other studies on environmental/sustainable procurement

Envirowise, www.envirowise.gov.uk for free consultancy, help and advice on environmental issues in commodities and business

Erdmenger, C. (ed) (2003) *Buying into the Environment*, Greenleaf Publishing, Sheffield

IEMA (2002) *Environmental Purchasing in Practice*, vol 2, Practitioner Series, Institute of Environmental Management and Assessment, Lincoln, www.iema.net/shop

Social Accountability 8000, for further information on social and ethical business management go to www.sa8000.com

UK Government, for the procurement section of sustainable development in government, see www.sustainable-development.gov.uk/sdig/improving/contextf.htm

Chapter 3.4

Environmental Product Development

Introduction

Twenty years ago, the focus of environmental legislation was on end-of-pipe measures, and while emissions were considered as unavoidable, they could no longer just enter the environment via a stack or pipe. The aim was to reduce emissions via the use of so-called environmental technologies such as stack filters and water treatment plants.

Such measures are still very much in use today (for example car catalysers), but during the 1980s attention started to shift towards the improvement of production processes and the development of new and more efficient techniques. This led, in part, to concepts such as 'cleaner production' and 'waste minimization' and later to the development of environmental management systems (EMS).

In the early 1990s, it was generally acknowledged that, while these measures had been fairly successful, the focus was still very much on inside-the-factory-gate efforts and important environmental impacts such as product related energy use or waste were not being addressed. As a result, legislative attention shifted towards other parts of the product life cycle shown in Figure 3.4.1. For example, under the heading of extended producer responsibility, waste legislation, such as the 1994 EU Packaging and Packaging Waste Directive, was introduced.

Accompanying this shift, was the development of a range of approaches and tools to help companies address the environmental impacts of their products after leaving the factory gate. Eco-design and life cycle analysis (LCA) are perhaps the two most important, and have helped companies take environmental considerations into account during product development processes.

At the same time, policymakers realized that other instruments could be used to encourage companies to design and produce products with a reduced environmental impact. While legislation was used to push companies towards product take back and recycling, information tools were seen as the main way to establish pressure in the market by helping consumers choose 'greener' products. Key examples of such instruments are the various eco-labels (e.g. the EU Eco-label, the Blue Angel, the Nordic Swan), mandatory labels (e.g. the EU Energy Label), self declared environmental claims and, more recently, environmental product declarations (e.g. the Swedish EPD system).

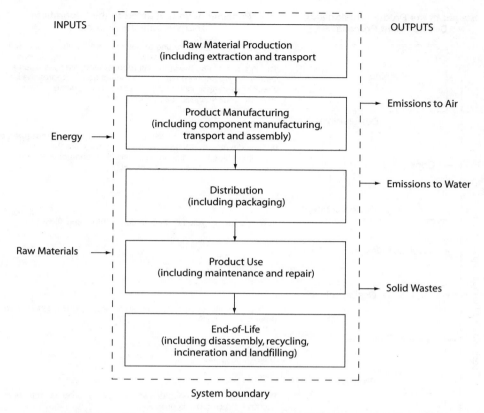

Figure 3.4.1   The product life cycle from an environmental perspective

Environmental product development

With the realization that the environmental impact of products is largely determined during the design phase, researchers, companies and others went in search of useful tools and processes, firstly to understand the impacts of products on the environment and subsequently to reduce these impacts. Environmental product development or eco-design can thus be seen as the overall process for understanding and improving the environmental impact of products. It is often defined as the integration of environmental considerations into the existing product development and design processes. Figure 3.4.2 gives an example of a generic model for integrating environmental aspects into the product design and development process.

One of the first attempts to implement the concept of environmental product development in practice was the Dutch Ecodesign 1 programme. It started in 1990 with sponsorship from the Dutch Ministries for Environment and Economic Affairs. This programme, in which eight companies took part, aimed specifically at the integration of environmental considerations into product development and provided important experience with the practicalities of eco-design. The importance of this project was

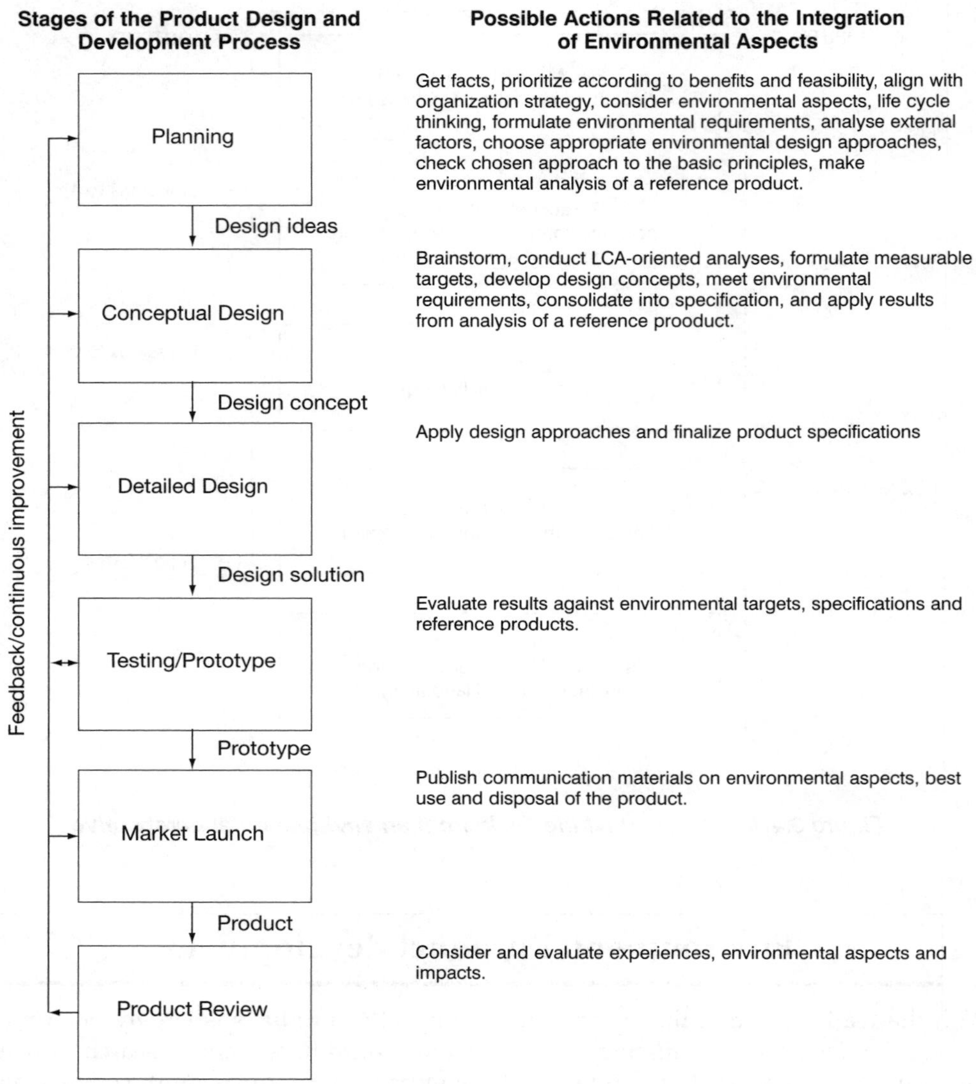

Stages of the Product Design and Development Process	Possible Actions Related to the Integration of Environmental Aspects
Planning	Get facts, prioritize according to benefits and feasibility, align with organization strategy, consider environmental aspects, life cycle thinking, formulate environmental requirements, analyse external factors, choose appropriate environmental design approaches, check chosen approach to the basic principles, make environmental analysis of a reference product.
Design ideas	
Conceptual Design	Brainstorm, conduct LCA-oriented analyses, formulate measurable targets, develop design concepts, meet environmental requirements, consolidate into specification, and apply results from analysis of a reference prooduct.
Design concept	
Detailed Design	Apply design approaches and finalize product specifications
Design solution	
Testing/Prototype	Evaluate results against environmental targets, specifications and reference products.
Prototype	
Market Launch	Publish communication materials on environmental aspects, best use and disposal of the product.
Product	
Product Review	Consider and evaluate experiences, environmental aspects and impacts.

(Left-side vertical axis label: Feedback/continuous improvement)

Source: ISO/TR 14062, 2002

Figure 3.4.2   *Integrating environmental aspects into the product design and development process*

recognized by the United Nations Environment Programme (UNEP), which supported the development of the so-called PROMISE manual (Brezet and van Hemel, 1997). This practical guideline describes the steps for conducting a successful eco-design pilot programme and provides background information on key tools and concepts.

During the 1990s others followed the Dutch example, leading to the development of more robust methodologies and tools. Several companies, notably in the electronics and automotive sectors, quickly added their own experiences and today a wealth of information regarding eco-design is available.

It is important to introduce environmental considerations as early as possible into the product development process. At the beginning there is still a lot of freedom; product concepts and technologies might still be up for discussion, materials are not yet chosen and production processes have still to be developed. Once such choices are made, design freedom is significantly reduced and the environmental impact is mostly determined.

The potential for environmental improvement is at its greatest during the formative stages of design. The decision to design, for example, a mains-powered versus a hand-powered radio can only be made at the start of the product development process, since key product characteristics depend on such a choice. Once this decision is taken the key environmental impact (i.e. energy consumption during the use phase) is largely fixed and subsequent choices (e.g. which materials to use) will only have a minor influence on the overall environmental impacts of the product.

It is also important to understand that the key to unlocking these significant opportunities usually does not lie within the product development process itself, but higher up in corporate decision making. It is when business strategies are determined and environmental policies are written that real commitment to environmental improvement or excellence needs to be expressed. For example, the decision by an oil company to start investing in renewable energy sources is entirely strategic and will have a much larger impact on the (future) environmental performance of that company and its products than the choice between the development of oilfield X or Y.

Understanding the environmental impacts of products

Before any effort can be made to improve a product, one first has to figure out what the main environmental impacts of that product are. This is necessary to guide product development and to prioritize possible improvement options so that limited resources can be allocated wisely.

The first attempts at assessing the environmental impacts of products were made in the 1970s. These so-called resource and environmental profile analyses focused mainly on energy and resource consumption, and waste generation. Knowledge of process emissions or hazardous substances was virtually non-existent. During the 1980s, interest in product assessments grew on the back of discussions about the environmental impacts of different types of packaging. A start was made with defining a more consistent methodological basis. These efforts resulted during the 1990s in the development of a number of International Organization for Standardization (ISO) standards for LCA (the ISO 14040 series) which today form the basis for environmental impact assessment of products (see Wenzel et al, 1997).

While LCA is the scientific response to the need to understand the environmental impacts of products, it became clear that conducting a proper and useful LCA was a very costly and time consuming exercise. Despite the development of software tools and generic databases, doing an LCA requires expert knowledge and significant amounts of product specific data, which makes it a methodology not always particularly suited to the needs of product design. This realization has led to the development of a number of specific tools aimed at 'translating' the knowledge gained by LCA into a more practical format.

MET matrix: One of the earliest aids for assessing the environmental impact of a product is the so-called material–energy–toxicity (MET) matrix. This qualitative, simple tool was developed on the basis of three environmental elements of sustainable development, namely:

- careful use and minimization of materials (M);
- minimizing the use of energy (E); and
- avoiding the use and release of hazardous and toxic substances (T).

The principle of the method is to fill in the matrix shown in Figure 3.4.3. The matrix consists of rows for the four main stages of the product life cycle and columns for the three environmental elements described above. The aim is to identify those product characteristics that constitute a relatively major impact on the environment. The matrix is simple, but it still needs to be filled in by one or more people with a good understanding of environmental product development and LCA, and basic information about the product under study (e.g. material composition, likely production processes, energy use) needs to be available. Nevertheless, this tool allows for a first prioritization of environmentally significant issues and provides a good start for further product improvements.

MET matrix	Materials input/output	Energy input/output	Toxicity input/output
Extraction and production of materials			
Product manufacturing			
Use			
End-of-life			

Figure 3.4.3   The material–energy–toxicity matrix

Checklists: Specific knowledge about the environmental impact of materials and processes gained through LCA has led to the development of checklists for identifying key product impacts. Sometimes this takes the form of so-called red flag lists, indicating that the use of a certain material or process gives rise to significant environmental concerns and should be avoided. More often such lists are mere rankings of how, for example, materials score on a specific environmental aspect such as scarcity or energy use for the production of a unit weight of material.

Eco-indicators: A more sophisticated use of LCA knowledge has been achieved through the development of one-point or eco-indicators. Such indicators are a response to the problem that multiple environmental impacts from one material or process need to be judged against each other in order to come to a balanced view. For example, if the choice is between the use of copper or aluminium for a certain application, a judgement has to be made on how to weigh the relative scarcity of copper versus the relative energy intensity of aluminium. To ask designers to make such complex choices is not realistic. Eco-indicators deal with this issue by making the choice for the designer and presenting it in a one-point indicator, which can easily be compared with that of others (see Table 3.4.1). While care needs to be taken with the application of such indicators and some understanding of their background is advisable, they are a good way of supporting product developers' use of eco-design concepts. An example of a company making extensive use of eco-indicators for product design is Philips, which has been instrumental in the development of specific design software called EcoScan, and has also developed indicators for frequently used components.

Table 3.4.1 Eco-indicators for the production of plastic granulate

Production of plastic granulate (in millipoints per kg)		
	Indicator	Description
ABS	400	
HDPE	330	
LDPE	360	
PA 6.6	630	
PC	510	
PET	380	
PET bottle grade	390	used for bottles
PP	330	
PS (GPPS)	370	general purposes
PS (HIPS)	360	high impact
PS (EPS)	360	expandable
PUR energy absorbing	490	
PUR flexible block foam	480	for furniture, bedding, clothing
PUR hardfoam	420	used in white goods, insulation, construction material
PUR semi rigid foam	480	
PVC high impact	280	Without metal stabilizer (Pb or Ba) and without plasticizer
PVC (rigid)	270	rigid PVC with 10% plasticizers (crude estimate)
PVC (flexible)	240	Flexible PVC with 50% plasticizers (crude estimate)
PVDC	440	for thin coatings

Source: Goedkoop et al, 2000

Improving the environmental performance of products

Once the environmental impacts of a product are identified and before the actual redesign process can start, priorities for improvement have to be established. While it might be possible to do this simply on the basis of the main impacts, in practice other considerations will play an important role as well. Existing or upcoming legislation, costs, technical feasibility and other criteria will have an influence on whether certain environmental impacts can be addressed. Such a prioritization can be done in a number of ways, but one of the most elaborate methodologies is the environmental effect analysis (EEA), which is described briefly next.

Environmental effect analysis

Environmental effect analysis is a methodology based on the more widely used failure mode effect analysis (FMEA). The objective of EEA is to identify and evaluate significant environmental impacts of a product at an early stage of a development project. While the identification part is based on the traditional concepts for LCA, the evaluation phase introduces a systematic, semi-quantitative protocol for identifying improvement priorities. There are several methods in use today, but the one most commonly applied is the so-called SIO 1–3 method, in which the evaluation is achieved by grading the following criteria between 1 and 3:

- controlling documents, for example laws, internal policies or other requirements (S);
- public image, related to the reputation of the company (I); and
- environmental consequences, for example the extent and severity of possible damage to the environment (O).

A fourth criterion is the improvement possibility (F) with incorporates the technical, financial and timing feasibility. The grading is carried out by a multifunctional team within the company to ensure the widest possible input and subsequent acceptance of the outcome. Information on the methodology and its application can be found in Lindahl et al (2001).

Once priorities have been identified, the eco-design process can commence and the product can be redesigned with enhanced environmental performance. One of the earliest efforts at providing designers with advice on eco-design occurred in Germany where the Verein Deutscher Ingenieure (VDI) published its first guideline on design for recycling (VDI, 1991). During the 1990s this was followed by an explosion of guidelines, manuals and checklists on eco-design and today every self respecting company has its own eco-design reference book.

Eco-design strategies

There are numerous strategies for reducing the environmental impacts of a product depending on the impact itself, the material or process that causes the impact and the influence that companies have on minimizing it. One of the better attempts at providing a systematic overview of these strategies is the so-called LiDS wheel, an acronym for life cycle design strategies (van Hemel, 1998). This is shown in Figure 3.4.4.

Any decision on when and how to use any of these improvement strategies depends on priorities and the type of product under study. However, since seven of the eight macro-strategies are linked to a particular phase in the product's life cycle, most of them can be applied simultaneously, although care has to be taken that improvements in one phase do not lead to higher impacts in another.

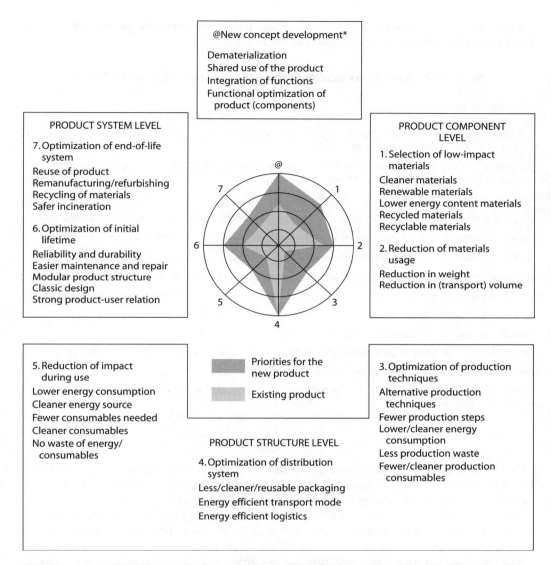

Note: *New concept development has been given the symbol '@' because it is much more innovative than the other seven strategies.

Figure 3.4.4   The life cycle design strategies wheel

Eco-design checklists

To some extent, eco-design checklists are complementary to the strategies described earlier, in that they tend to be more detailed and often focus on environmental issues related to the product life cycle. This is also known as 'design for X', where the X stands for a wide range of issues including dematerialization, recycling, reuse, disassembly, remanufacturing, recovery, chemical content, and so on. These checklists mostly contain rules and guidelines for improving the environmental performance of a product in that specific area, as shown in Table 3.4.2.

Table 3.4.2   Example of design for disassembly and disposal guidelines

Disassembly and disposal

Drawing up disassembly and disposal instructions to include details on the type and distribution of materials in accordance with SN 36350–2.

Designing product components containing materials cited in SN 36350–2 in such a way that they can be removed easily and without their destruction.

Minimizing the number and variety of connections.

Designing all connections in such a way that they can be dismantled easily and non-destructively.

Designing all connections that require dismantling to be readily identifiable and easily accessible.

Minimizing the number of steps necessary for disassembly.

Enabling disassembly using a small number of standard tools and with few changes of position.

Enabling the reuse or further use of products or components, for example through standardization.

Employing recyclable materials.

Marking plastic components suitable for recycling.

Taking account of compatibility between materials with respect to recycling (SN 36350–3,4).

Avoiding non-recyclable composites and coatings.

Using company logos and labels made from the same material as the body of the products or a compatible material.

Source: Siemens, 2000

Other examples of possible checklists of use to designers are black and grey lists for hazardous chemicals, ecological rucksack values for materials, material scarcity indicators, energy contents and global warming potentials for substances.

As with the identification of the key environmental impacts, improvement options need to be prioritized in order to select those with most benefits at least cost. Since the development process is usually not linear but tends to go through different 'improvement' iterations, this selection can be done throughout the process and not just at one fixed point in time. Again, several methods can be used but most will focus at least on the likely environmental improvement and the associated cost (or return on investment). An example of such a prioritization tool is given in Table 3.4.3.

Table 3.4.3   *Example of a prioritization tool for environmental improvement options*

Green Options	Environmental Benefit	Business Benefit	Customer Benefit	Societal Benefit	Feasibility Technical	Financial
First option						
Second option						
Third option						
………						
Nth option						

Source: Stevels, 2000

In addition to environmental benefits the matrix in Table 3.4.3 also weighs business, customer and societal benefits. These benefits are considered in following categories:

- tangibles: cost of ownership, reduction of resources;
- intangibles: simpler to produce, easier to operate, fun, quality of life, better compliance; and
- perceptions and emotions: better image, feel good, 'we make progress on green'.

Under technical feasibility, the physical and chemical aspects as well as the amount of research and development needed to realize the green option are analysed. Also, industrial aspects such as changes in supplier base and different organizations of production are investigated. Once this prioritization is done and product design changes are justified, one or more improvement options can be implemented.

Today, a large number of tools and processes are available to assist product designers in their efforts to improve the environmental performance of products. Many companies practice eco-design and often report significant benefits in terms of product quality and cost. Also, policymakers are now addressing these issues and this suggests that environmental product development is something businesses can only ignore at their peril.

Communicating the environmental performance of products

The drive to improve the environmental performance of products has led to a desire to communicate this performance. Businesses hoped that by giving such information to their customers, they would be able to increase their market share and improve brand image. Policymakers hoped that by providing product related environmental information to consumers, they could be persuaded to buy those products, thus driving the market towards 'greener' consumption. Governments have also started to use their own purchasing power (approximately 10 to 15 per cent of gross domestic product in the EU) to drive environmental product improvements via their procurement programmes. These factors resulted in the development of a multitude of information instruments including energy labels, eco-labels, product declarations, environmental claims, single issue labels and combinations of them.

In an attempt to define specific requirements for the most common labelling types, the ISO established, in the 1990s, a number of standards for environmental labelling, now known as Type I, II and III labels and declarations (see Table 3.4.4).

Table 3.4.4   ISO standards in the field of environmental labelling

ISO 14020	Environmental labels and declarations – general principles
ISO 14024	Environmental labels and declarations – Type I environmental labelling – principles and procedures
ISO 14021	Environmental labels and declarations – Type II environmental labelling – self declared environmental claims
ISO/TR 14025	Environmental labels and declarations – Type III environmental declarations

Type I eco-labels

One of the first environmental policy tools related to product information was the so-called Type I eco-label. In 1978, the Blue Angel scheme was started in Germany and since then governments around the world have put a lot of effort into establishing similar labelling schemes. Examples are: the EU Eco-label, the Nordic Swan, the Dutch Milieukeur, the US Green Seal, and the Japanese Eco Mark – see Figure 3.4.5 for some examples.

EU Eco-label   Nordic Swan   Blue Angel (Germany)   Eco Mark (Japan)   Green Seal (US)

Figure 3.4.5   Five examples of eco-labels

Eco-labelling schemes are voluntary, multiple criteria based, third party programmes that award a licence, authorizing the use of a label on products. Such a label or logo indicates overall environmental preferability of a product within a particular product category based on life cycle considerations.

Companies wanting to use the logo on their products have to comply with a set of established criteria before being awarded the label. Since compliance is checked by a third party, people buying the labelled product can be ensured that the environmental information provided is credible and not just a self declared statement by the company itself.

Type II environmental claims

Self declared environmental claims are probably the most widespread form of environmental information given to consumers. Typically they are some kind of statement (or symbol or graphic) made by a manufacturer or retailer itself about an environmental aspect of its products or services. There are numerous examples of such claims such as 'made from 50 per cent recycled material', 'contains no PVC', or 'uses 20 per cent less energy than our previous model'.

While most of these statements tend to be accurate reflections of the environmental performance of the product, several surveys have found that claims can easily be misleading or vague and are sometimes simply untrue. This has been a serious problem in the past, with companies being accused of so-called 'greenwash' and consumers distrusting almost every type of environmental information provided to them.

The ISO 14021 standard has tried to address these issues by establishing strict guidelines as to what companies should and shouldn't do when making environmental claims. This includes avoiding vague claims such as 'environmentally safe', 'nature's friend' or 'non-polluting', and making sure that their claims can be substantiated and verified by retaining relevant information such as test results or other documentary evidence.

Type III environmental declarations

One of the most extensive forms of product related environmental information is the so-called environmental declaration. These declarations consist of quantified product data based on an LCA, although other information, such as the use of an EMS by an organization, is also allowed. A relatively late addition to the labelling family, they have so far been used mainly in the building sector – for more information and examples of this form of declaration go to www.environdec.com.

Since the reported environmental information is in the form of unprocessed elementary inventory flow data, such as weights of oxides of sulphur (SO_x), oxides of nitrogen (NO_x) and carbon dioxide, valid product and process information could be passed along the product supply chain thus allowing, at least in theory, a comprehensive overview of the environmental performance of a product across its entire life cycle. By adding up the different declarations, final products could be compared on the basis of life cycle data and in this way encourage the demand for and supply of products and services with an improved environmental performance. For this final comparison to work, declarations for products within the same product group or product chain need to be based on the same rules regarding functional unit, system boundaries, data requirements and so on. These rules are usually agreed beforehand and laid down in product specific requirements.

Given the relative complexity of environmental declarations, they are still seen as too sophisticated for final consumers and so far have been used mainly in a business-to-business context.

Mandatory labels

Since the beginning of environmental policy, companies have been obliged to provide environmental or health information about their products to customers and final consumers. This was initially focused on the hazardousness of certain products (e.g.

chemical preparations and paints) but it has recently been widened to other issues such as energy (e.g. the EU Energy label) and fuel consumption – for examples of this type of information go to www.saveenergy.co.uk/appliances/whatis/label.cfm or www.defra.gov.uk/environment/consumerprod/energylabels/index.htm.

However, labels and warnings are not the only types of mandatory information that companies need to provide. Legislation has compelled companies to become increasingly open about the environmental characteristics of their products. For example, under the packaging and packaging waste, end-of-life vehicles and waste electrical and electronic equipment (WEEE) directives, businesses are obliged to give information about a variety of issues including the material and substance contents of their products, dismantling and recycling guidance, and data on the amount of recycled materials and components.

Single issue labels

Labelling programmes focusing on a single environmental issue have often been set up by non-governmental organizations (NGOs) in an attempt to draw attention to a specific environmental problem. Examples of such labels are the Forest Stewardship Council (FSC) for sustainable forest management and the Marine Stewardship Council (MSC) which identifies products from well-managed and sustainable fisheries (see Figure 3.4.6; www.msc.org). Fair Trade schemes and organic labels also come within this category. Such programmes almost always use multiple criteria (within the context of the single issue) and often involve extensive verification and chain of custody procedures to ensure credibility of the label. As such, they resemble Type I eco-labels, although they typically have stricter criteria as a result of strong NGO participation.

Environmental reporting

A more recent development is the use of environmental reports to convey product related information to stakeholders. Traditionally, they have reported on the environmental performance of production processes only, but are now being used more and more to give information about specific product characteristics such as the use of recycled materials, reduction or elimination of hazardous substances, energy consumption during the use phase, improvements in logistics and end-of-life characteristics. Also, environmental research and development and eco-design efforts often feature in these reports.

Figure 3.4.6   Single issue environmental labels

Since it is the companies themselves that are collecting and communicating such information, product related data in environmental reports are essentially self claims. They are sometimes criticized for their (perceived) lack of credibility. This problem has led to the idea of using EMS for the verification of product related information. Since most EMSs are certified by external auditors, there is the possibility that during the certification process the management procedures are verified and a check is made of any product related information the company might want to use in its external communications. While this has not yet been put into practice, it would be a cost effective way to improve the credibility and quality of the information given by companies to the outside world.

The wide range of product information instruments described above and the importance that policymakers and other interested parties attach to them indicate that product related environmental information is an important element in today's business environment. The time that companies could simply 'greenwash' their communication efforts is long gone and, if they care about their reputation, they need to make every effort to inform their stakeholders in a transparent and accurate way.

References

Brezet, J. and Hemel, C. van (1997) *Eco Design: A Promising Approach to Sustainable Production and Consumption*, United Nations Environment Programme, Paris

Goedkoop, M. et al (2000) *The Eco-indicator 99. A Damage Oriented Method for Life Cycle Impact Assessment, Manual for Designers*, 2nd edn, Pré Consultants BV, Amersfoort

Hemel, C. van (1998) 'Eco Design Empirically Explored', PhD thesis, Delft University of Technology, Delft

ISO/TR 14062 (2002) 'Environmental Management – Integrating Environmental Aspects into Product Design and Development', International Organization for Standardization, Geneva

Lindahl, M. et al (2001) *A Small Textbook on Environmental Effect Analysis*, Department of Technology, University of Kalmar, Kalmar

Siemens (2000) 'Environmentally Compatible Products Part 1: Product Development Guidelines', SIEMENS NORM SN 36350–1, Siemens, Munich

Stevels, A.L.N. (2000), *Application of Eco Design, Ten Years of Dynamic Development*, Delft University of Technology, Delft

VDI (1991) 'Design of Technical Products for Ease of Recycling', Guideline VDI 2243, Verein Deutscher Ingenieure, Düsseldorf

Wenzel, H. et al (1997) *Environmental Assessment of Products, Volume 1, Methodology, Tools and Case Studies in Product Development*, Chapman & Hall, London

Chapter 3.5

Waste Management and Packaging

Environmental impacts caused by waste

Landfill is the predominant disposal route for waste in the UK. Figures in the UK Government's 2000 waste strategy (Defra, 2000) show that around 60 per cent of controlled waste (excluding sewage sludge and dredged spoils) is currently landfilled. Recycling and reuse account for 26 per cent. In 1990 approximately 435 million tonnes of waste were produced annually in the UK, of which 245 million tonnes were controlled wastes. Industrial waste (other than construction and demolition waste) accounted for 70 million tonnes and commercial waste 15 million tonnes.

Waste management and disposal give rise to a number of environmental risks and related issues, most notably:

Landfill pollution risks: While landfills are operational, they cause noise and nuisance impacts such as odour, airborne dust/litter and vermin. There are also impacts associated with the transporting of waste to landfill. Operational and closed-off landfill sites have the risk of toxic substances and leachate (polluting liquid) seeping out and potentially contaminating soil and groundwater. There are concerns about a possible correlation between health problems and proximity to landfill, for example reproductive toxicity and congenital malformations (DoH, 1999). There is also the risk of methane gas being emitted, following the path of least resistance to the side of the landfill or its surface. This presents an explosion risk as well as being an important global warming gas.

Incineration pollution risks: The burning of waste for disposal and/or heat generates emissions to air in the form of dusts, toxics such as dioxins and heavy metals and acid gases. These have implications in terms of risk to public health, air quality and acid deposition.

Insufficient disposal sites: Landfill disposal sites are a finite resource and space in the UK is running out.

Strategy and policy background

The UK Government's waste strategy for England and Wales was published in 2000. In the strategy it defines the UK's broad waste strategy objectives as: to reduce the amount of waste society produces; to make the best use of any waste; and to choose waste management practices that minimize the risks of immediate and future environmental pollution and harm to human health. The main targets in the strategy are:

- by 2005, to reduce the amount of industrial and commercial waste landfilled to 85 per cent of the 1998 levels and to reduce the proportion of controlled waste going to landfill to 60 per cent of 1998 levels; and
- to recover 45 per cent of municipal waste by 2010 and to recycle or compost 30 per cent of household waste by the same date.

The government is increasingly using measures besides legislation to deliver its environmental goals. In the waste strategy, it pledges to: use market based measures such as the landfill tax; encourage producer responsibility initiatives, such as the packaging waste regulations; use planning considerations; and promote best practice in waste minimization and alternative waste management options, including information on best practicable environmental options (BPEOs) for specific waste streams.

A central principle in the strategy is the waste hierarchy. This is:

increasing
desirability

- Reduction;
- Reuse;
- Recovery (Recycling, Composting, Energy Recovery);
- Disposal.

The hierarchy provides a framework for policy within which waste management decisions can be taken to help meet the government's objectives. It is intended to act as a checklist for an initial assessment of the most appropriate waste management option for a particular waste stream. Under the hierarchy the first priority is to reduce the amount of waste produced, especially waste with hazardous constituents. Disposal is considered as the least attractive option in general terms. The government's overall policy aim is to increase the proportion of waste managed by the options towards the top of the hierarchy – see Table 3.5.1.

Table 3.5.1   The waste hierarchy

Reduction	Avoidance of the production of waste, e.g. avoiding the production of faulty materials or products, improving yield/reducing scrap.
Reuse	Using products or materials, again without their reprocessing, e.g. packaging, reusing bottles and coathangers.
Recycling	Processing of waste materials to produce a usable material or product, e.g. pulping of waste paper, melting of scrap metal or glass items.
Composting	Processing of organic waste to produce a soil improving material, e.g. composting of catering waste.

Classification of wastes

The UK operates with several definitions of waste – derived from EU legislation, which must be implemented nationally, and from its own statute book:

- 'Directive waste' is the basis of the legal definition of waste in the UK – the other legal categories of wastes (i.e. controlled and special) are subsets within this definition.

Under it, waste is defined as: 'any substance or object ... which the producer or the person in possession of it discards or intends or is required to discard'. The concept of 'discarding' is the key element of the definition.

- 'Controlled waste' is a UK term covering wastes subject to the duty of care under the Environmental Protection Act 1990. It is broadly equivalent to the EU term 'directive waste'.
- 'Hazardous waste' is an EU term for waste with various toxic or harmful properties as defined by the EC Hazardous Waste Directive (94/31/EC) and the EC Hazardous Waste List (Decision 94/904/EC).
- 'Special waste' is the UK term for waste that has certain hazardous properties as defined by the Special Waste Regulations 1996. The definition incorporates the EC definition of hazardous waste. Special waste is also controlled waste, but subject to extra controls.

Managing waste at industrial sites – the duty of care

Section 34 of the Environmental Protection Act 1990 introduced a duty of care on anyone who is the holder of controlled waste. A holder is any person who produces, imports, keeps, treats, carries, disposes of, or is a waste broker of, controlled waste. Householders are exempt from the duty of care for their own household waste.

The duty represents good business practice and places a duty on anyone who in any way has a responsibility for controlled waste to ensure that it is managed properly and that it is recovered or disposed of safely. The duty is set out in a code of practice (DoE, 1996). The code recommends a series of steps, which should be taken to meet the duty of care. The legal obligation is to comply with the duty itself rather than with the code. It is, however, admissible as evidence in any legal proceedings. The key requirements of the duty are for holders of waste to:

- contain it securely to avoid escape;
- transfer it only to someone with authority to take it (e.g. a registered carrier or licensed waste manager), or be allowed to actually take the waste if receiving it;
- keep appropriate records using transfer notes (including descriptions and information on any potential problems), making sure the documentation is properly completed; and
- be alert to the non-compliance of others.

Documentation

The Duty of Care Regulations 1991 set out the documentary requirements. Transfers of waste must be accompanied by a transfer note containing certain information. There is no compulsory form for keeping waste transfer records; however, an example is given in the code of practice. Details on the note must include:

- a description of the waste;
- details concerning the person transferring the waste (transferor);

- details about the person receiving the waste (transferee); and
- details about the place and time of transfer.

The transfer note must be kept for at least two years and copies must be provided to the Environment Agency (EA) or Scottish Environment Protection Agency (SEPA) if requested. Where there are a series of transfers of the same waste between the same parties within a 12 month period, one transfer note can cover that series of transfers. This is referred to as a 'season ticket'. The consignment note used for special waste shipments fulfils requirements of transfer documentation and therefore can also act as the transfer note under the duty of care.

Special waste

Special wastes are those that are hazardous – that is, they are considered to be capable of causing the greatest environmental damage or are dangerous to human life if not properly handled.

Such wastes are controlled by the Special Waste Regulations 1996 (as amended) which have replaced earlier regulations made in 1980. These implement the EC Hazardous Waste Directive (94/31/EC), and incorporate the EC Hazardous Waste List (Decision 94/904/EC). The range of hazardous items that is included in the list has recently been greatly increased by EU Decision 2000/532/EC, which has been partially implemented in the UK by the Landfill (England and Wales) Regulations 2002. For example, items of electrical equipment and discarded cars have become classed as hazardous waste.

The regulations define what constitutes special waste (based on the EC legislation), and set out the controls on handling such wastes (in addition to the duty of care). Guidance is provided in DoE Circular 6/96 and various special waste explanatory notes produced by the EA. The key requirements of the Special Waste Regulations are:

- pre-notification of movements of special waste to regulators (e.g. the EA or SEPA);
- movements of waste to be documented by a system of consignment notes;
- the consignment note advising of the movement of special waste to be submitted to the regulator at least three working days before the movement occurs;
- consignors (those despatching the waste), and carriers (those moving the waste), must keep documents for three years, and consignees (those receiving the waste for treatment or disposal) until they surrender their waste management licence; and
- fees are charged for most consignments.

Hazardous properties

The definition of special waste is linked to the CHIP 3 Regulations (Chemical Hazard Information Packaging for Supply Regulations 2002). CHIP should be used to establish whether or not a waste contains a hazardous substance.

Waste management on site

There are various basic good practice techniques that a company can employ to ensure that it is compliant with the waste legislation requirements and minimizes potential environmental impacts of waste.

Segregation of waste

Waste should be separated as far as reasonably practicable to ensure that the maximum potential for reuse and recycling is achieved. Mixed wastes may be more problematic to dispose of and liquid wastes may cost the company money for analysis. Segregation can assist with:

- preventing mixing of hazardous wastes that could react together;
- saving money through identifying opportunities for waste minimization, and the landfill tax;
- helping to ensure that the duty of care is fully complied with; and
- gaining maximum potential from waste minimization and from selling scrap/waste.

Operational control and good housekeeping

A clean, tidy and organized site engenders a more positive attitude in those who work there. Mess and waste result in the feeling that it doesn't matter, so individuals may be less careful. 'Rubbish attracts rubbish' – encouraging people to clean up their own work areas can help remove the attitude that waste doesn't matter. It can also improve the attitude to product quality, getting it right first time – so reducing waste.

Responsibilities

Waste should be controlled on site as well as off site. Depending on the size and complexity of the organization, one or more individuals should be given responsibility for waste management. All waste on site must be traceable and controllable. This helps with management or minimization measures.

The duty of care is a major piece of waste legislation. It is designed to ensure the correct storage, handling, transfer and disposal of waste throughout its life cycle. Responsibility for site waste will therefore not end at the site gates.

Waste on site must be kept safely. It should be stored in suitable containers that are labelled and secure. Skips should be covered to prevent the wind-blow of waste and ingress of rainwater. Inadequate storage can lead to waste being discharged via surface waters or foul sewers, with compliance implications.

Transfer should only occur to an authorized person, normally a waste carrier registered with the local waste regulation authority. Transfers should be accompanied by a transfer note and written description detailing the type, quantity, producer and receiver. Proper training and education of staff is vital. Employees must understand what they are doing, and the implications of their actions.

Waste minimization

Waste minimization is another name for process efficiency. It involves reduction or prevention of waste before it is generated, by reducing raw materials, energy and water consumption – see Table 3.5.2. It brings about both environmental and financial benefits. Many companies only consider the cost of waste to be that of having their waste taken away. However, there are many other hidden costs, including wasted raw materials, packaging, waste treatment, lost production and rework.

Overall efficiency can be improved by prevention at source – by reducing spills and leaks, better material use, redesigning processes and products, closing internal material loops and examining supplier and customer links.

Table 3.5.2   Advice on waste minimization

Activity sector	Advice
Product design	• Design products to minimize waste and assembly costs.
Raw material selection	• Discuss with suppliers how to select materials that will minimize waste or facilitate the reuse or recycling of waste. • Check to make sure that materials are not over-specified; could a lighter grade be used? • Use recycled materials if practicable.
Packaging	• Avoid unnecessary packaging. • Where possible, use packaging that can be returned to the supplier for reuse. • Switch to recyclable void fill material for packaging, e.g. shredded waste paper.
Energy	• Measure energy consumption on a routine basis. • Identify the parts of the process that consume the most energy. • Check efficiency of the heating system (boiler, pipe insulation and control system for temperature). • Check insulation (walls, roof, windows, doors). • Check lighting systems for cleanliness, lights being left on unnecessarily, age and condition of lamps, controls. • Investigate the advantages of recycling heat where possible. • Switch off when not in use.
Water	• Evaluate water charges, sewerage and effluent disposal costs to determine weekly or monthly figures. • Monitor water usage: monitor use of hot water and water use as a whole. If water is being 'lost' not only is it a waste of resource but it is a waste of energy and other materials. • Fit occupancy controls if you have urinals flushing round the clock. • Avoid overconsumption of water during wash downs and use manual spray guns to control use. • Reuse water for wash downs, which can have numerous benefits including reduced water charges. • Locate and cure any leaks. • Can effluent be economically treated on site to reduce disposal charges? Is there scope for sharing treatment facilities with adjacent businesses?
Transport	• Share vehicles. • Investigate liquefied petroleum gas (LPG) schemes for company cars. • Limit engine size of company vehicles. • Optimize vehicle routing.

Source: The EA, www.environment-agency.gov.uk and the Scottish Environment Protection Agency (SEPA), www.sepa.org.uk

Managing packaging waste obligations

Producer responsibility is an important element of the UK Government's waste strategy. It aims to ensure the productive use of products and materials that have served their original purpose (i.e. 'end-of-life' products or materials). Provisions in the Environment Act 1995 allow regulations to be issued to introduce statutory obligations for producers to reuse, recover or recycle specified levels of any end-of-life product or material.

In the packaging waste regulations (UK Parliament, 1997), 'obligated businesses' are required to recover and recycle specific tonnages of packaging waste, based on calculations incorporating national targets. The waste packaging materials are glass, paper and cardboard, metal, plastics and wood. The targets are in line with the EC Directive on Packaging and Packaging Waste (94/62/EC). Unless obligated businesses are in a compliance scheme, they are required to register with the EA in England and Wales, with SEPA in Scotland and with the Environment and Heritage Service in Northern Ireland. The compliance schemes exempt member businesses from individual requirements, but the scheme must meet their aggregate obligations.

Obligated businesses: In outline, these are businesses that either manufacture packaging materials, convert materials into packaging, pack and fill packaging with product, or sell products with packaging. In addition, to be obligated the business would need to own the packaging involved, and supply to another stage in the packaging chain or the final user. An obligated business would also handle more than 50 tonnes of packaging or packaging materials a year and initially have an annual turnover of £2 million or more – the tonnage of packaging would include imports but exclude exports, process waste and any packaging that is being reused.

Recovery obligation: This is established by the formula:

$$\text{recovery obligation} = \text{obligated packaging handled (tonnes)} \times \text{activity obligation (\%)} \times \text{UK recovery target (\%)}$$

where:

Obligated packaging handled is:	Activity obligation is:	UK recovery target is:
the tonnage of packaging handled in a calendar year (less exclusions)	6 per cent for manufacturing 9 per cent for converting 37 per cent for packing/filling 48 per cent for selling product	63 per cent for 2004, increasing to 70 per cent in 2008

Recycling obligation: This forms part of the total recovery figure. The recycling obligation is established by the formula:

$$\text{recycling obligation} = \text{obligated packaging handled (tonnes)} \times \text{activity obligation (\%)} \times \text{UK recycling target (\%)}$$

where:

Obligated packaging handled is:	Activity obligation is:	UK recycling target (per material) is:
Tonnage of packaging handled in calendar year (less exclusions)	6 per cent for manufacturing 9 per cent for converting 37 per cent for packing/filling 48 per cent for selling product	94 per cent for 2004, up to 95 per cent in 2007

Organizations can demonstrate compliance by proving that the relevant tonnages of packaging material have been recovered and recycled. This is undertaken by reprocessors, who must be accredited by their regulator. Reprocessors produce packaging waste recovery notes (PRNs) to demonstrate that a certain tonnage of packaging material has been recovered or recycled. PRNs have a market value and can be sold to anyone who will pay the market price. The reprocessors must use money gained from selling PRNs to invest in improving the recycling infrastructure.

Obligated companies can choose to join a compliance scheme or 'go it alone'. A compliance scheme charges its members a fee based on the level of their obligation. It then takes the sum of all members' obligations and bulk buys enough PRNs to meet the amalgamated obligations and prove compliance to the agencies. Companies going it alone send packaging waste, including on site material or 'back door waste', to reprocessors and purchase PRNs to reflect this amount.

Obligated companies should have a system in place to measure and track the amount of obligated packaging waste they handle. At any time, the company could be subject to an audit by the regulator to check the data they have put forward (through either a compliance scheme or going it alone). These audits can be extremely detailed. They can require a company to explain how its amounts were calculated, to justify packaging weights associated with detailed product lines, to demonstrate weighing equipment calibration and to show sources of information for imports and exports. It is therefore most beneficial to set up a database to record this information. Another key aspect is to ensure that the relevant staff are properly trained to manage the packaging compliance activity, and that procedures are in place to ensure this knowledge and skill is passed on when staff leave.

Future trends: the EU framework

Major changes are to be introduced into the management of waste in the UK and the rest of Europe, and many of these changes are due to the EU Directive on the Landfill of Waste (1999/31/EC). This aims to standardize landfill procedures across Europe and to minimize methane emissions. The key measures of the directive are:

- to reduce biodegradable municipal waste to landfill to 35 per cent of that produced in 1995, by 2016 – intermediate targets of 75 per cent by 2006, and 50 per cent by 2009 have also been agreed;
- to ban co-disposal of hazardous and non-hazardous wastes, and require separate landfills for hazardous, non-hazardous and inert wastes from July 2004;

- to ban landfilling of tyres by 2003 for whole tyres and by 2006 for shredded tyres;
- to ban landfilling of liquid wastes, infectious clinical waste and certain types of hazardous waste (e.g. explosive and highly flammable wastes), all by 2001; and
- to establish acceptance criteria for different types of waste at landfill sites across the UK by 2005.

Under the directive, the practice of co-disposal – placing hazardous and non-hazardous waste in a landfill together – will be banned. Landfill operators have already had to choose whether they will, after July 2004, accept one kind of waste or the other. As a result of this, the number of landfills accepting hazardous waste has dramatically reduced – from around 200 to 12. After July 2004, hazardous waste must be pre-treated to meet the waste acceptance criteria (WAC), or otherwise be sent to a different source of disposal.

The Landfill (England and Wales) Regulations 2002

The regulations set out a pollution control regime for landfills for the purpose of implementing Council Directive 1999/31/EC on the landfill of waste in England and Wales. The regulations set out a range of controls that will be applied to both new and existing landfill sites. For example, the regulations will be used to establish WAC, which landfill operators will use to determine which types of waste will be committed to landfill at a particular site. While many of the directive's requirements reflect practices already in place in the UK under the Waste Management Licensing Regime, it will nevertheless introduce some key changes, as listed earlier.

Landfill tax

This landfill tax was introduced from 1 October 1996 for waste going to landfill. It is charged by the landfill operator at two rates – a standard rate of £14 per tonne for 2003/2004 and a lower rate of £2 per tonne for inactive waste. The government has announced that in 2004/2005 the landfill tax rate will be £15 per tonne. Thereafter, the standard rate will increase by at least £3 per tonne a year until the tax reaches £35 per tonne. It will also revise how the funds from the increased landfill tax will be spent. Currently favoured options are those that improve the UK waste management infrastructure and assist companies to change their behaviour with regard to reducing waste.

Waste Electrical and Electronic Equipment (WEEE) Directive

A directive on waste electrical and electronic equipment (WEEE) and a sister directive on restriction of hazardous substances (RoHS) in such equipment were adopted by the EU in 2003 (DTI, 2004). This legislation has an impact on manufacturers of a wide range of equipment, ranging from mobile telephones to computers, fridges, lighting, monitoring equipment and toys. The WEEE Directive makes producers responsible for take back and recovery of these products when they reach the end of their life. By making producers responsible in this way, the aim is that producers will improve product design to facilitate recovery and recycling (e.g. better ability to dismantle, better labelling, use of recycled materials, less use of hazardous substances).

Recovery and treatment systems

By September 2005, producers (or third parties acting on their behalf) must set up systems to provide for the recovery, treatment and recycling of WEEE using best available techniques. Priority must be given to the reuse of the whole appliances. The last owner will have the right to return unwanted equipment to producers, retailers or civic amenity sites free of charge.

The WEEE Directive seeks to promote the separate collection, reuse or recycling of electronic waste. The WEEE Directive requires producers to recover 75 per cent of goods taken back for disposal and to reuse 70 per cent of those goods by 2006.

A collection target of 4kg of WEEE per inhabitant per year has been set by the UK Government for 2006. It is expected that targets for medical devices, once established, will apply from 31 December 2008.

Historic waste or waste produced before the directive comes into force must be paid for collectively by all producers according to their market share. Waste generated after the directive is in force must be paid for by producers, principally on an individual basis. Individual producer responsibility places a legal and financial burden on individual producers to manage end-of-life equipment in the best way and improve design to facilitate these activities and reduce waste management costs.

If companies go out of business, management of their waste products will have to be funded by financial guarantees provided by the producer. Commercial producers will also have to ensure that they offer services for the management of discarded products when they sell new products.

In order to monitor whether the targets are being met, producers or third parties acting on their behalf must keep records on the mass of WEEE, and their components, materials or substances, when entering and leaving the treatment facility and/or when entering the recovery or recycling facility. To assist these recovery and treatment systems, producers will be required to appropriately mark products put on the market from September 2005 with their name.

Hazardous materials including mercury, lead, cadmium, hexavalent chromium and certain brominated flame retardants will be banned from use in electronic equipment by July 2006.

End-of-Life Vehicles Directive

This EU directive is now in force, having been adopted in summer 2000. It requires transposition into national legislation. The directive aims to improve the reuse, recycling and other forms of recovery of end-of-life vehicles and their components, with a view to reducing waste disposal. Under the directive, the last holder and/or owner of a vehicle will have the right to deliver it to treatment facilities, without having to bear any cost. Manufacturers must meet all or a significant part of the take-back costs and the timing of this responsibility is as follows:

- from 1 January 2001 for vehicles put on the market as from this date; and
- from 1 January 2007 for vehicles put on the market before 1 January 2001.

Prohibition of the use of lead, mercury, cadmium or hexavalent chromium in materials and components of vehicles was fixed at 1 January 2003. By 1 January 2006, reuse and recycling of end-of-life vehicles will be increased to a minimum of 80 per cent (by average weight per vehicle and year). For vehicles produced before the year 1980, member states may have targets of at least 70 per cent.

References and further reading

Defra (2000) 'Waste Strategy 2000, England and Wales', Department for Environment, Food and Rural Affairs, London. The report can be downloaded from the following web sites: www.defra.gov.uk/environment/waste/index.htm; www.doh.gov.uk/land1.htm

DoE (1996) 'Waste Management: The Duty of Care, A Code of Practice', The Stationery Office, London

DoH (1999) 'Health Effects in Relation to Landfill Sites', Department of Health, Environmental Chemicals Unit, London. The report can be downloaded from the following web site: www.defra.gov.uk/environment/waste/management/ doc/ pdf/waste_man_duty_code.pdf

DTI (2004) Details of the WEEE Directive can be found on the Department for Trade and Industry's web site at www.dti.gov.uk/sustainability/weee/

IEMA (2003) *Producer Responsibility and the Packaging Regulations: Five Years On*, vol 3, Practitioner Series, Institute of Environmental Management and Assessment, Lincoln

SEPA (2004) Scottish Environment Protection Agency's waste minimization programme can be found on their web site at www.sepa.org.uk/wastemin/programme/

UK Parliament (1997) 'The Producer Responsibility Obligations (Packaging Waste) Regulations', The Stationery Office, London

Chapter 3.6

Contaminated Land

What is meant by contaminated land?

The term 'contaminated land' is often used in a general sense to mean any form of contamination of soil or ground. In the main, this contamination is caused by releases from industrial processes (such as leakages, spillages or airborne emissions which have been deposited back on the ground) or by deliberate or accidental deposits of material on the ground (such as waste disposal, mine workings or other application of materials to land). However, it is important to bear in mind that the contamination does not always have to be man made for a problem to be identified (such as the risk from natural radon) and the nature of the contamination may not be just chemical (for example biological substances can contaminate soil).

Changes in industrial processes and increasing environmental controls over the last 10 to 20 years have meant that most industrial processes do not produce the same types of land contamination as before. UK policy has been to encourage prevention of land contamination. Controls on waste disposal, the former integrated pollution control (IPC) and the current pollution prevention and control (PPC) regimes, continue to enforce this approach. The statutory regimes have penalties and restoration requirements that are specifically related to breaching these controls on new contamination.

Although this does not always mean that all new land contamination will be prevented, in recent years there has been an increased focus on the other side of the coin, i.e. managing land that was contaminated by past practices where the current preventative regimes do not apply (DETR, 2000).

Partly as a result of this new focus, there are some legal and technical aspects to be aware of in using the term 'contaminated land'. In UK law, the term has a very specific meaning, given in Part IIA of the Environmental Protection Act 1990. There is another specific legal term of 'land in a contaminated state' that is used, for example, in Schedule 22 of the Finance Act 2001 in connection with tax credits for remediation. To avoid confusion with the specific terms, the more general terms of 'land contamination' and 'land affected by contamination' can be used. To add to the need for precision in using terms, it is also important to remember that 'land' can mean much more than just soil or ground – it can include water beneath the ground and buildings and structures above it. At a European level it is also worth noting that the terms 'soil' and 'land' can also be interchangeable (CLARINET, 2003).

The issue of land contamination arises in a number of circumstances, ranging from assessments of land condition as part of environmental audit and risk assessment, to consideration of land contamination in deciding whether and how to change the use of the land for planning and regeneration processes. The issues may emerge on many different types of sites, ranging from large, complex sites used by former major industries such as steel works and gasworks, to sites of less than one hectare but which, for example, had oil storage tanks on the site. Sites may be partially in use for industrial processes, or derelict, or may have been redeveloped for a new use but with contamination still potentially present on the site (DoE, 1995).

A number of landowning organizations and individuals will therefore be interested in assessing land contamination on land that they currently own, or owned in the past, or are proposing to acquire. Owners and prospective purchasers may also want to assess the potential for land contamination and resulting problems from land adjacent to the site under consideration. Those who occupy or lease land may have similar interests. The process of managing land contamination also involves a number of regulatory bodies, and other public sector organizations such as UK Government policy departments and development agencies. Development of sites that may be affected by contamination can be a particularly complex process (CIRIA, 2002).

Why it can be a problem

The presence of contamination in land does not necessarily mean that there is any form of environmental problem; however, the contamination could be considered a deterioration in land quality. It could also become accessible or mobile through air, or water or other pathways and come into contact with people, crops, other ecosystems, buildings, other structures and materials, surface waters such as rivers, lakes and ponds, groundwaters or the marine environment. Not all of these receptors would necessarily be affected – the nature of the contaminant, the amount reaching the receptor, the duration of contact or other exposure and the particular vulnerability or type of response of the receptor will all be relevant to assessing the extent and possibility of adverse consequences (Defra/EA, 2002).

Two basic situations arise, which can lead to differences in the particular technical approach to identifying and dealing with the problem:

Breach of legislative controls

Should the contamination have been prevented? Is there a breach of legislative controls that requires remedies?

This requires knowledge of any specific regulatory permits and other controls which could apply to the land and set restrictions on release of contaminants (e.g. PPC permits) and also knowledge of all the regimes that may make it an offence to carry out the activities that have led to the contamination being there (e.g. controls on disposal of waste). There may also be circumstances where there are other legal requirements (e.g. under leases or other contracts in relation to the land) for contamination to be prevented or specific controls on the presence of certain substances on land (e.g. asbestos).

In these situations, the presence of the contamination as such is a problem. The technical assessment to decide whether or not the circumstances apply will depend on the particular detail of the legal requirements, but in general will include an assessment of the extent and type of contamination and the nature and timing of the activity that could have led to the contamination being in the ground. If there has been a breach, it is likely that restoration of the quality of the land will be required and that this will involve removal or treatment of the contamination, and dealing with any damage it has caused.

Risk of harm or pollution

Could the presence of contamination cause damage, for example by causing, or presenting a risk of, harm or pollution?

This requires more detailed consideration of the contamination, the pathways by which it might come into contact with a receptor, and the receptors themselves, leading to an assessment of the risk to the receptors. The starting point for this is the development of a conceptual model, which presents a simplified picture of relationships between contaminants, pathways and receptors (see Defra/EA/IEH, 2000; BSI, 2000; EA, 2004). These relationships are then assessed in progressively more detail to establish the level of risk and its significance. The particular methods and extent of the assessment will depend on the context for carrying out the assessment.

Actual or possible damage could mean that a regulatory regime which is aimed at protecting a particular part of the environment might apply – such as health and safety legislation and legislation which protects ground and surface water. It might also mean that the damage could lead to a civil liability claim. The planning regime will require contamination and the possible effects of its remediation to be considered if a change of use is proposed (ODPM, 2004b). If building works are to be carried out then there may also be a requirement to deal with contamination under the Building Regulations (ODPM, 2004a). To satisfy these regimes it will be necessary to identify the presence of any contamination, the circumstances in which it could lead to harm or pollution or other damage, and the extent of the damage.

But the main statutory regime aimed at proactive identification of land contamination that is currently presenting an unacceptable risk to human health and the environment, and ensuring its remediation, is Part IIA of the Environmental Protection Act 1990. This sets out a framework for local authorities (in England, Wales and Scotland) to identify land in their area that meets particular criteria for the degree and extent of harm to people, to specific ecosystems, to property and to controlled waters.

The different regimes each have a slightly different formal approach to deciding what needs to be done to prevent, reduce or restore the damage if it happens. For example, under Part IIA, the technical approach to deciding the standard of remediation, which will also determine the techniques to be used, has to correspond with the particular requirements of the primary legislation and statutory guidance (DETR, 2000; Scottish Executive, 2000; National Assembly for Wales, 2001; LGA, 2001; Welsh LGA, 2002).

The main process of managing land contamination

Although there will be different detailed technical approaches depending on the nature of the contamination and the context in which assessment and remediation are carried out, the basic technical process for dealing with past contamination follows the basic steps of a risk management procedure (Defra/EA/IEH, 2000). A set of model procedures specifically for managing the risk from land contamination has recently been finalized by the Environment Agency (EA) and the Department for Environment, Food and Rural Affairs (Defra) (EA, 2004). This outlines the stages in an overall technical framework, and provides links to the more detailed technical documents that may be relevant at different stages. An information map is included in the package to provide details of the currently available technical documents from key sources such as government departments, the environment agencies, standards organizations and other organizations that produce guidance and best practice documents.

The model procedures emphasize the need to set the context of the risk management process at the outset. This enables the formulation of the particular problem to be addressed, starting with the development of an initial conceptual model. The overall process is then divided into three main stages:

- risk assessment;
- options appraisal; and
- implementation of remediation options.

Each of the main stages contains a number of more detailed processes, with clear decision points and outputs. Appropriate information is needed to underpin each stage. This includes information about: the extent and nature of the contamination and the characteristics of the land and its surroundings, as well as about the behaviour of contaminants and their effects; methods for removing or treating or otherwise managing the contamination; and detailed practical requirements for achieving remediation. The model procedures provide a list of the inputs and outputs for each process stage, together with examples of these inputs and outputs and of the technical tools that can support the process and of the criteria needed to make key decisions.

The emphasis through the document is on identifying and following best practice, and maintaining a quality approach to the overall process. Maintaining records of decisions and assumptions, and formalizing outputs is a key part of this. In parallel with the quality assurance for the process, the document also emphasizes the need to complete any process of remediation with appropriate verification and if necessary further monitoring and maintenance.

The aim of the guidance on model procedures is to provide a basis for those involved in managing land contamination to follow a consistent process. Organizations with particular requirements for managing land, or with particular types of land, could use the model procedures to develop specific guides relevant to their circumstances. Some of these guides are already available, for example the guidance produced by the Institute of Petroleum, the National House-building Council and the Welsh Development Agency (IoP, 1998; EA/NHBC, 2000; WDA, 2003).

Land condition record

One of the key issues to emerge in discussions on developing confidence about land condition is the need for standardized documentation describing the condition of the land. This was a key recommendation of the Urban Task Force (UTF, 1999) and has led to the development of the land condition record (LCR) by a group consisting of representatives from organizations with interests in land management and regeneration (LCR Working Group, 2000).

The LCR is a structured presentation and summary of available information relevant to land contamination for a particular land or property. The LCR sets the context of the land, identifying possible receptors at the outset. It provides a summary of former uses of the land or other factors that may have led to the presence of contamination. Detailed summaries of site investigations can be used to indicate the presence of contamination and possible pathways. The last section in the main LCR is a record of any remediation, including references to any verification carried out. Detailed annexes provide further detail on regulatory issues and methods and quality assurance for the reports providing the site investigation and other data.

The main role of the LCR is to bring together data from different reports, often collected over time and with different levels of quality – the LCR emphasizes the need for provenance of data. It can be updated as new information emerges, and can be transferred with the land to new owners. It can be used, for example, as a basis for preliminary assessment of the risks from land, or as a formal document summarizing the history of site investigations and remediation reports.

Dealing with other issues

The technical process of risk management described above is aimed at identifying and mitigating the impacts of land contamination on people and the environment. However, there are other activities related to land contamination that may fall within the remit of environmental management. They can include:

- reviewing the outputs of the risk management process to confirm that they meet the **objectives of a particular organization** or circumstances;
- providing a detailed analysis of the nature and history of the contamination to support **apportionment of liabilities**, for example if the land is identified as contaminated land under Part IIA of the Environmental Protection Act 1990;
- providing information on the **environmental impacts** of remediation of land contamination, for example as part of a permitting process for a new remediation technology or to support an environmental assessment;
- providing information on the possible risks and nature of remediation required to assist in **valuation of land**;
- assessing the implications of contamination on the overall **costs and benefits of regeneration** of brownfield sites;
- explaining the nature of contamination, the risks and the wider implications to a wide **range of stakeholders**, from regulatory bodies to the public, and from different professions or backgrounds; and
- presenting and **negotiating agreement** on technical and other management solutions to land contamination problems.

These will require specialist knowledge of particular legislation or techniques, and most will involve dialogue and interaction with other professional disciplines.

Skills and professional development

This range of activities gives an indication of the complexity of land contamination issues, over and above the complexity of the contamination and the heterogeneity of land itself. Management of land contamination issues involves a number of different scientific and technical disciplines, as well as a wider knowledge of professional and other issues related to land. In recognition of this, and to provide greater confidence in both information on land condition and the assessment of that information, a number of key professional institutions – see Box 3.6.1 – have supported the creation of a registration scheme for specialists in land condition (SiLCs):

Box 3.6.1 *Professional bodies supporting the SiLC registration scheme*

- Association of Geotechnical Specialists;
- Chartered Institution of Environmental Health;
- Chartered Institution of Water and Environmental Management;
- Geological Society;
- Institute of Environmental Management and Assessment (IEMA);
- Institution of Civil Engineers;
- Royal Institution of Chartered Surveyors;
- Royal Society of Chemistry.

A SiLC is expected to have at least eight years' suitable experience, together with membership at an appropriate level of one of the professional institutions supporting the scheme, or their equivalent. To become registered, a candidate must pass a written assessment and peer interview. In the process they must demonstrate that they meet specific criteria related to being a specialist in land condition, ranging from the objective management of information and a thorough knowledge of their field to awareness and some understanding of other relevant fields and connected professions and the ability to provide advice and manage effective interaction between clients and other interested parties. SiLCs are also expected to adhere to a specific code of practice relevant to professional integrity and impartial and informed advice on land condition.

The IEMA provides the secretariat for the panel and administers the scheme. It provides a dedicated web site for the scheme, runs training courses, and coordinates publicity about the scheme (www.silc.org.uk).

A checklist for environmental management of land contamination

Good environmental management of land contamination will:

- be clear about the context and the particular nature of the problem;
- identify the objectives for the risk management process and the criteria that may apply for specific decisions;

- ensure that data are fit for purpose, and any uncertainties are identified;
- establish available best practice and use relevant approaches and techniques;
- develop robust but flexible solutions that satisfy any legal requirements and, if necessary, balance the different stakeholder needs; and
- consider short and long term implications for the land and the community, environment and other resources it may affect – so that sustainable solutions are found.

References

BSI (2000) 'BS 10175 Code of Practice: Investigation of Potentially Contaminated Sites', British Standards Institution, London

CIRIA (2002) *C578 – Brownfields – Managing the Development of Previously Developed Land. A Client's Guide*, CIRIA, London

CLARINET (2003) *Sustainable Management of Contaminated Land: An Overview. Report from the Contaminated Land Rehabilitation Network for Environmental Technologies*, Austrian Environment Agency, Vienna

Defra/EA (2002) *Potential Contaminants for the Assessment of Land*, R&D Publication CLR 8, Department for Environment, Food and Rural Affairs/Environment Agency, London

Defra/EA/IEH (2000) 'Guidelines for Environmental Risk Assessment and Management', Department for Environment, Food and Rural Affairs/Environment Agency/Institute for Environment and Health, The Stationery Office, London

DETR (2000) 'Environmental Protection Act 1990: Part IIA Contaminated Land, Circular 02/2000', Department of the Environment, Transport and the Regions, The Stationery Office, London

DoE (1995) Industry profiles (various titles), Department of the Environment, London

EA (2004) *Model Procedures for the Management of Land Contamination*, R&D Report CLR 11, Environment Agency, Bristol

EA/NHBC (2000) *Guidance for the Safe Development of Housing on Land Affected by Contamination*, R&D Publication 66, Environment Agency/National House-building Council, Bristol

IoP (1998) *Guidelines for Investigation and Remediation of Petroleum Retail Sites*, Institute of Petroleum, London

LCR Working Group (2000) 'A Standard Land Condition Record', Land Condition Record Working Group, available from www.silc.org.uk

LGA (2001) 'Local Authority Guide to the Application of Part IIA of the Environmental Protection Act 1990', Local Government Association/Chartered Institute of Environmental Health/Department for Environment, Food and Rural Affairs/Environment Agency, available at www.cieh.org

National Assembly for Wales (2001) 'Remediation of Contaminated Land', National Assembly for Wales, Cardiff

ODPM (2004a) 'Building Regulations: Approved Document C', Office of the Deputy Prime Minister, London

ODPM (2004b) 'Development of Land Affected by Contamination', Planning Policy Statement 23, Office of the Deputy Prime Minister, London

Scottish Executive (2000) 'Environmental Protection Act 1990 Part IIA Contaminated Land', Scottish Executive, Edinburgh

UTF (1999) *Towards an Urban Renaissance*, final report, Urban Task Force, London

WDA (2003) *A Manual on the Management of Land Contamination*, Welsh Development Agency, Cardiff

Welsh LGA (2002) 'Welsh Local Authority Guide to the Application of Part IIA of the Environmental Protection Act 1990', Welsh Local Government Association/Welsh Assembly Government/Environment Agency Wales, www.wales.gov.uk

Chapter 3.7

Engaging with People in Your Organization

Introduction

In today's world of changing business circumstances, organizations need people who are motivated, responsive to change and fully trained. Nothing much ever happens unless people are motivated and responsive, and helping people to understand the benefits of a particular course of action is very important. People will only give of their best if they fully understand the decisions that affect them, how and why these decisions arose, and how their contributions can make a difference. Training and communication failures can lead to costly errors and breaches of environmental regulations. Failure can be measured not only in terms of hours lost or fines, but also by the loss of cooperation between staff and managers, and stakeholder perceptions. A sound understanding of responsibilities is crucially important for all staff with a role to play in the implementation of an environmental initiative. Training and communication are key to this. They allow skills to be transferred to staff. They induce motivation, change attitudes and allow people to acquire a deeper understanding of the issues. In summary, training and communication can help to:

- equip all employees with the skills to perform their jobs more effectively;
- provide and maintain knowledge to enable staff to understand why their actions matter;
- increase employee commitment and motivation, and promote identification within the organization; and
- avoid failures and facilitate change.

Without staff engagement in an environmental issue – from the shop floor to senior management – a positive outcome is extremely unlikely. Staff involvement is vital, and a sustainable change in individual behaviours can only be achieved through effective training and communication. Good training has always been important. No individual can learn all they need to know before they commence employment. There will always be a skills gap between pre-work education and the knowledge and skills actually required in the workplace. Training bridges this gap. Table 3.7.1 illustrates why training is so valuable.

Table 3.7.1   The benefits of training

Who	Untrained	Trained
The individual	Likely to be stuck in a badly paid, low level job	Improved promotional prospects and better health
The organization	Risk of going out of business. Poor productivity. Poor staff motivation	Gives a competitive edge. Staff work more effectively with fewer errors. Better motivation
Society	Stagnating population	Training and education are the growing tips of a healthy economy. Well trained people improve environmental performance

Preparing the ground

There are seven areas to consider when preparing the ground for a training intervention. These are set out in the context of environmental management in Table 3.7.2.

Table 3.7.2   Preparing for a training intervention

Area	What to think about	Environmental issues
Outcomes	What is to be achieved: • for the trainees? • for yourself? • for the organization? What does the training needs analysis say?	An initial environmental review (IER) will point up those areas needing attention – e.g. the 'must do' legal areas and the 'will do' cost benefit areas such as energy and waste management.
The trainees	What is known about them? Do they know each other? What is their level of expertise? What are their expectations?	Think about the organization's significant environmental aspects – how are the trainees involved in improving management of these and what changes are desired?
The training space	Where will the training take place? How is the space to be used to maximize learning? What equipment and materials are required and how are they to be used?	Develop a good mix of classroom and site based activities to provide first hand experience of environmental issues. Use your resources to reinforce the desired outcomes. Practice with the technology so it works smoothly for you.
Design and structure	What knowledge, skills and attitudes need to be imparted? How will you increase the learning and how will this be achieved in an engaging way? How will the training be structured (trainer input, exercises, role play, use of case histories etc.)?	Map training needs analysis against the 'must do' and the 'will do' areas identified in the IER. This will reveal required knowledge, skills and attitudes. Think about the mix of activities and trainer input to keep trainees engaged and tuned into the relevant environmental issues for the organization.

Table 3.7.2   continued

Presentation skills	How will you present the training? Remember that most impact and perceived truth comes from body language (55 per cent) closely followed by voice quality (38 per cent) and the actual words come a poor third (7 per cent). Most adults have difficulty following the sense of a spoken sentence with more than 18 words.	Maximize the environmental impact of your training by making good use of case histories and practical examples including those the trainees already have or can easily relate to. Use colour pictures and diagrams as much as you can. Change the dynamics regularly and make use of working groups, breaks and the working space.
Beliefs and values	What are your own environmental beliefs and values? Beliefs are the generalizations we make about ourselves, other people and the world around us. Values are those things that are important to the individual.	People care about the environment, although how this is expressed varies hugely from person to person. Your environmental beliefs and values may not be shared by others.
Self management	Good training flows from a good emotional state.	Get yourself in the right frame of mind before training.

Change management

Change can only be introduced effectively with the support and agreement of the organization's management team. Any members of the team who are not convinced of the need to implement an environmental initiative will need to be convinced lest they undermine its realization. This commitment needs to be followed up by senior management. For change management, there are seven areas to reflect on, namely:

1 **Consider your own motives and integrity:** This is an important consideration. For example, do you have the respect and understanding of your colleagues? Are you concerned about environmental issues or are you doing it simply to boost your position in the organization? And do you practise what you propose to preach?
2 **Understand the people you are going to be working with:** List the criteria against which you would justify the initiative to your colleagues in the organization. The criteria could be expressed in terms of: human resources benefits; increased sales; an improved image for the organization; more reliable operation of plant and equipment; cost savings or cost neutrality; improved safety; legislative compliance; and the individual aspirations of employees and other stakeholders.
3 **Underpin decisions rigorously:** Plan environmental measures thoroughly and in time; match strategy with existing in-house mechanisms; emphasize and promote the positive at every opportunity; make sure collective decisions are followed through; and always acknowledge positive individual and team actions.
4 **Establish priorities** for the medium and long term, establish a realistic strategy for the organization and the people in it, and set a realistic progression of environmental implementation – don't try and do it all at once.

5 **Actions and legal requirements:** Produce a schedule of 'must do' requirements to implement environmental legislation; and seek to obtain unanimous support from management for these 'must do' actions by illustrating that:
   – contravening environmental regulation is not a choice;
   – breaking the law costs money in fines and lost business; and
   – management is personally responsible and may be fined or imprisoned.
   Ensure that the senior management is aware that: environment should always be on the agenda at the highest level in the organization; environmental issues are unavoidable, they are not a choice; and environmental legislation must be implemented, and is not negotiable.

6 **Benefits to the organization:** Set out an inventory of environmental actions that will benefit the organization; present the measures in ways that reinforce their positive aspects; make sure these actions are implemented; illustrate that environmental actions are essential and can bring cost benefits; and report on success stories once there is hard data to back them up.

7 **Investment:** Where no capital investment is required: draw up a programme of environmental measures – they might not have short term benefits so consider any longer term benefits to the organization; think carefully about how these ideas are introduced; publicize any positive benefits which occur as a result; and encourage the organization to publicize the successes. Where investment is required think carefully about whether the organization has the will or means to implement them; think about lobbying senior management, particularly by building on past successes; and consider funding investment from profits generated from previous actions.

The training cycle: analysis and design

The training cycle in Figure 3.7.1 shows the five areas to be addressed in the development of a training intervention. Successful training must change how people behave. From the environmental perspective environmental objectives provide the focus for identifying training needs.

For the analysis and design stages of the training cycle, the strategic, functional and individual components need to be considered. These are illustrated in Table 3.7.3.

Strategic training needs

The most important first step in any analysis of training needs is the strategic review of needs as a whole, and the starting point should be the organization's business plan. Human resource implications might not be explicitly stated in the business plan, but they will exist. For example, the introduction of a new production process will need staff with new skills to manage and operate the process and to manage the environmental implications. The new process may produce less waste, but the waste may need to be dealt with by new on site storage facilities and a specialist contractor. The organization can choose to recruit new staff with the required skills or it could retrain existing staff.

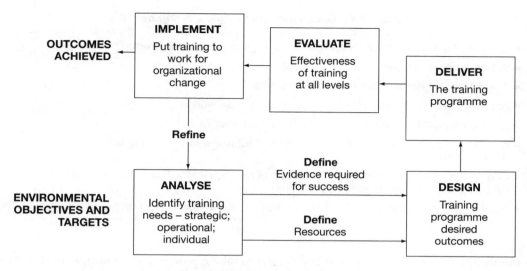

Figure 3.7.1   The training cycle

Table 3.7.3   Strategic, functional and individual training

Area	What is needed?	Where is the evidence?
Strategic	An examination of the overall picture for the organization. Short and long term organizational needs	The organization's business plan. Discussions with senior management. Environmental recommendations emerging from an initial environmental review
Functional	An examination and identification of functional training needs	Notes and reports from the information gathering stages of an initial environmental review. Supplementary interviews with managers, staff and customers in identified functional areas
Individual	Identification of individual training needs to deliver your environmental strategy	An initial environmental review. A more detailed analysis which may use existing personnel and management systems

A rigorous examination of the business plan, coupled with knowledge gained during any environmental review should uncover the environmental training needs. As these issues are addressed, it is worth keeping in mind the questions listed in Table 3.7.4.

Functional training needs

The second stage in the analysis is to identify functional and departmental issues. An initial environmental review should have revealed training issues for some of the staff. This knowledge now needs to be supplemented by interviews with a wider range of

Table 3.7.4   Questions on strategic training needs

- What are the environmental implications of the organization's business plan?
- What is being done well?
- Where is the commercial risk now and in the future?
- Are staff aware of the environmental implications of their work?
- Are any new skills required and how will they be obtained?
- Is the organization working well enough with respect to environmental requirements? If not, where is it not and why?
- Does the business plan indicate future functional changes that will have environmental implications and require training interventions?
- Does the business plan imply a culture shift that will require training interventions?

managers, staff and customers. It is essential to take a representative sample of staff in each functional area of the organization to ensure that the findings give an unbiased picture of needs. For example, not all machine operators will have had the same experiences before joining the organization. Some may be experienced 'old hands' while others may be relatively new to the organization. Questions to keep in mind when examining functional environmental training needs include:

- Which functions and departments contain the greatest environmental risks and what are the risks?
- Are staff meeting established standards? If not, why not?
- What training is already provided? Is it sufficient to meet functional needs?
- Are staffing levels sufficient for the job? Is staff turnover high? What are the training implications?
- What changes are proposed in operational practices? What will they mean for the operators and for environmental management?
- Where are the skills and knowledge gaps and can training effectiveness be measured?

Box 3.7.1 *Mountstevens*

Mountstevens Ltd, a manufacturing and retail baker, introduced staff awareness training and initiated an extensive waste programme. They saved over £6000 and reduced waste by 26 tonnes. 'We would have to sell a lot of extra doughnuts to make that sort of impact on our profitability' said the managing director.

Source: IFC, 2000

Individual training needs

This is the final step in the analysis. While the first two steps are mostly concerned with core and planned business functions, this step looks at the role of individuals. Staff need to be aware of the environmental issues that the organization is addressing and how their actions can influence its environmental performance. Within the organization, a number of procedures will already exist which directly or indirectly identify training needs. These include: appraisal and performance management; tests and examinations – for example arising out of competence based training such as National Vocational Qualifications (NVQs); assessments of prior learning; mentoring; individual career planning; and career counselling.

Before embarking on a training programme – be it for an individual, operating unit or a whole department – you will need to consider the position of your learners now and where you want them to be at the end of the training intervention. Think carefully about any barriers to change, what is realistically achievable in the time frame you have set or has been imposed on you and the resources that are available for the journey from one – or several – starting points to the destination. Your training objectives will need to take account of the following:

- The knowledge that will be needed to underpin your training programme – knowledge about environmental legislation, the organization's position and demands on employees.
- The skills staff will need to effect change. Some skills will already exist in the organization but others will need to be introduced among staff if they are to be active participants in the change process.

Active participation is an essential part of the learning process and good learning takes place when the adrenaline flows. Passive training activities – for example watching a video and then being asked to talk about the relevant issues – are a poor substitute for a dynamic training process that engages participants in an active way. And the training outcomes must ensure individual satisfaction and success.

Box 3.7.2 *Imperial Home Décor Group*

Building onto an existing quality management system and involving staff at an individual and team level, from investigation of the existing situation to developing new process improvements, saved Imperial Home Décor Group (UK) Ltd £750,000. The lessons have now been applied to other operating units and new product development.

Source: OU, 1999

One of the outcomes of this work will be an informal mapping exercise which links training needs with environmental objectives and targets. This is illustrated in Table 3.7.5.

Table 3.7.5   Linking training to environmental objectives and targets

Area under consideration – waste management

Objective/target: reduce waste by 15 per cent over the next two years

Who needs to know?	Training – what do they need to know about?	Example performance measures
Production manager	Analysis of volumes of waste being produced and the associated costs. Recommendations for modifying aspects of the production process to reduce waste. The benefits of changing practices – estimated and actual	*Management performance indicators:* • Number trained and those needing training • Compliance with relevant legislation • Product design for recycling • Cost measures
Site manager	Impact on the site management of introducing skips for waste segregation. Responsibilities for managing any new arrangements including relationships with waste contractors and regulators	*Operational performance indicators:* • Waste produced per unit of production • Packaging reductions • Raw material usage and reusage
Purchasing manager	Changes in purchasing patterns. Suppliers' attitudes and involvement.	*Environmental condition indicators:* • Contribution to local landfill • Ecosystem damage/rehabilitation due to waste burden
Operatives	How to record waste management data under duty of care regulations. Understanding the data	
Staff who interface externally	Dealing with external stakeholders such as insurers, financiers, suppliers, contractors and the local community	

The training cycle: delivery

However well an organization's environmental training needs have been identified, the training interventions will only be effective if suitable training methods are selected. For example, the practicalities of waste segregation must be demonstrated by practical activity, whereas management training on new environmental legislation might best be carried out by a combination of lectures and workshop sessions. The required outcomes can be categorized as changes in a combination of knowledge, skills and attitudes. The training methods employed will depend on what these required outcomes are. Training methods can be considered under two headings – group training and individual training. The methods are described in Table 3.7.6.

Table 3.7.6 **Comparison of training interventions**

Group training methods	Cost	Observations
Lectures	Low cost	One of the least effective training methods with only a 20 per cent retention of information. Trainees' attention spans are often much shorter than the duration of lecture. Lectures are often best suited to a general overview and introduction of new ideas.
Group discussions	Low cost	Trainees are much more actively involved than in lectures. Syndicate groups can ensure full participation of all and reporting back is an excellent way to test understanding of new knowledge and attitudes.
Role playing	Medium cost, and requires higher trainer to trainee ratios	Because role playing requires trainees or actors to simulate real work behaviours it is a powerful technique to develop interpersonal skills. It can help bridge the gap between theory and practice. It might exclude some trainees because of their reluctance to participate.
Audio visual	Medium/high cost	A well produced audio visual presentation should maintain trainees' attention. However, a commercial production may not reflect the organization's precise requirements and may be perceived as irrelevant. Too often, a video can be used as a light break in a training session rather than as an integral part.
Case studies	Medium cost	This training intervention can stand alone or be integrated with role play. It is an effective method to engage trainees in an activity which specifically relates to the organization's needs.
Games, board and computer based	Medium cost	Can be an effective training tool if well integrated with the overall training strategy.
Outdoor training	High cost	Primarily to develop team cohesion and skills. Ideally they should combine several of the training techniques noted, alongside outdoor programmes.
Individual training methods		
Structured reading	Low cost	Can be a useful technique alongside other activities but might not be appropriate for all trainees.
Open/distance learning	Medium cost	Requires strong self motivation from the learners. The best programmes combine knowledge based activities with work based practical activity.
IT based learning	Medium/high cost	One of the most quickly expanding training areas, often using CD-ROM. The best materials can fully engage the trainee at their own pace and provide feedback for the trainer.
Coaching and mentoring	Medium cost	These methods provide support and first hand interaction with more experienced staff and can reinforce other training interventions.
On the job training	Medium cost	Can be an effective technique for activities that combine knowledge, skills and techniques. Very dependent on the abilities of the instructor.

The training cycle: evaluation

Learning from experience and applying this learning in the workplace is a vital part of an effective environmental training programme. To ensure it is effective requires that:

- staff in the organization know and understand that any new and changed responsibilities are part of a continuous process and are not just important at the time of training; and
- regular evaluation takes place – through monitoring and measuring – of the wider environmental performance of the organization.

Three useful questions about training interventions are: did the training programme achieve its objectives? Did the training programme improve performance? Was the training worth doing?

Measurement and monitoring are words with specific meanings in the environmental context. These meanings are explained next.

Measurement and monitoring

An unblemished record on environmental issues, such as compliance with regulations or a zero accident rate, is not a guarantee that risks are being controlled. An accident at a particular site might be highly unlikely but the consequences of a single accident may be catastrophic. Effective implementation of environmental practices demands effective measurement of performance. Having control of the data is the key task. The data will signal the areas where potential environmental risks exist and the likelihood of these risks becoming hazards. They provide the baseline against which environmental progress can be measured. Environmental performance can be measured in two ways:

- Negative performance indicators such as accidents, incidents, staff absence due to environmental issues, damaged equipment, down time, and lost production while having to take remedial action. These can all be quantified.
- Auditing and sampling which provide a continuing analysis of the effectiveness of good environmental practice.

Like measuring, monitoring signals a commitment to good practice. To be effective, monitoring needs to reflect the realities of management in an organization. Two types of monitoring – active and reactive – ensure that the day to day activities are addressed.

- Active monitoring is the essential feedback on performance against environmental objectives. It involves checking compliance with performance standards and the achievement of specific objectives. Its key purpose is to demonstrate success.
- Reactive monitoring manages deficient environmental performance, for example accidents to people and the environment, incidents, hazards and direct non-compliance with regulations.

Measurement and monitoring of environmental performance can be encouraged and promoted by training and communication. The aim is to create an organizational culture that has a diligent approach to its environmental practices and allows management to take corrective actions in a timely manner.

Box 3.7.3 *Performance measurement*

If you can't measure it then you can't manage it.
You get what you inspect, not what you expect.
If you want to know whether what someone thinks is really important, you should look and see what he or she spends his or her time on.

Source: RSA, 1995

Evaluation

Too often training is simply an act of faith, which it is hoped will achieve some good. What is actually required is a rigorous evaluation of training outcomes. These must provide data on which to base management decisions in much the same way as we expect data to be available on the non-human resource aspects of environmental management. Evaluation is the assessment of the total value of a training programme in both social and financial terms.

Box 3.7.4 *Evaluation of training outcomes*

Compare the following statements:
We knew we needed to do something about training when we were prosecuted for the second time for the same problem.
Our training strategy is based on ensuring that, at the very least, we comply with all environmental legislation – present and planned.

Linking training needs to environmental objectives and targets produces a programme with clear, outcome based training objectives. It then becomes possible to measure the effectiveness of training programmes. An evaluation model can be constructed using the following four stages:

1 **The response of the trainees to the training:** Ask trainees questions about the training programme; this should provide valuable feedback both short and long term.
2 **The learning achieved:** Test knowledge, skills and attitudes before and after the training; this should measure the effect of the training. Having clear objectives before training commences is important – hence the importance of a training needs analysis and mapping this against environmental requirements for the organization.
3 **Changes in trainees' behaviours:** It does not follow that new knowledge and skills will transfer to the workplace. Many barriers exist, including the opposition of colleagues to change, and the trainees themselves being unsure of how to apply the learning. To apply objectivity here requires planned observation of the trainees' real job performance.

4 **Organizational effects:** It is important to relate training to the functional and strategic changes identified to achieve effective environmental practice in the organization. You will need to attempt to evaluate the effectiveness of training at the organizational level.

The four stage evaluation model above provides an overview of how training can be evaluated and the rationale for doing so. The actual measurements can be carried out with regard to the short term, the long term and cost effectiveness.

Short and long term effectiveness

Most environmental training interventions seek to produce changes in staff behaviour. This can be measured before and after training. For example the introduction of a new machine or process will mean operators need some form of training. The associated production process may be complex, involving hazardous materials, dangerous machinery and the potential for an environmental hazard. The technical process can be broken down into its component parts and each part analysed, so revealing the information and procedures operators need to know about and how this information is to be conveyed to them. Performance can be measured before and after a training intervention. Measurement can be made more useful and instructive by introducing precise objectives.

Box 3.7.5 *Measuring training effectiveness*

Compare:
We wish all our operatives to become effective in the use of new machinery and processes.

With:
For an operator to be deemed effective in the use of new machinery and processes means:

- waste metal should not exceed 7 per cent of raw material;
- machine electricity use should be less than 8kw per hour;
- solvent use should not exceed 25l per week;
- scrap metals should be segregated into the bins provided; and
- job sheets must be completed as specified.

If not practised and supported, new skills and behaviours will be abandoned and old, established ways of behaving will become the norm again. Ineffective training, with only partly developed skills and behaviours, does not transfer ownership for them to the trainees, it fails to integrate learning with the learners, and produces trainees who lack confidence. These are all good reasons for reevaluating the training for its long term effectiveness.

Cost effectiveness

Training for its own sake, because it is a good thing to be doing, is no basis on which to commit resources. Such an approach reinforces a negative attitude to training and the demands of environmental management preclude such a hit and miss approach.

Managing training means developing an understanding of how much is being invested, what the return is on this investment, and demonstrating this understanding in the implementation of an environmental training strategy. Measuring cost effectiveness assumes that short and long term effectiveness can be and is being measured in ways that generate monetary value. These include:

- reductions in breaches of environmental regulations, which in turn reduce costs;
- reductions in wastes produced and energy consumption;
- reduced rework of products and services;
- new contracts based on improved customer relations; and
- improved productivity and new products.

In addition, the actual cost of training needs to be determined. This is a straightforward budgeting operation, with budget lines for each element of the training activity. A training budget should include lines for: the training centre; trainers, trainees and the supporting administration; and equipment and materials. For each line you will need to identify whether the costs are: fixed, i.e. independent of the level of training activity; variable, i.e. dependent on the number of trainees; and marginal, i.e. the additional costs of one more unit of training.

The cost effectiveness of training can then be derived from these two sets of data – how much the training cost and how much profit was generated as an outcome of the training process. For many organizations, the effectiveness of training means more than monetary gains. Training can provide a competitive edge and improve staff motivation and retention. Organizations that don't train their staff risk stagnation.

Summary

Employees should not be regarded as an expendable commodity; they are a precious resource and environmental initiatives are an opportunity to build social capital within an organization. Employees need to be trained in an effective and efficient manner. To mean anything, training must be put to use. Those organizations that train people in environmental management report measurable benefits, and improving the proficiency of employees will go beyond many other single improvements that an organization can make.

Box 3.7.6 *RHP Bearings*

RHP Bearings made cost savings of £82,000 by integrating environmental matters into existing management systems including Investors in People (IIP). Training and awareness raising among all staff, focusing particularly on waste awareness, were key to this success.

Source: Envirowise, 2003

References and further reading

Business in the Environment (2003) Business in the Environment inspires businesses to work towards sustainable development as a strategic, mainstream business issue. For further information go to www.bitc.org.uk/programmes/programme_directory

Ellis, A. (2000) 'Getting the Best from Environmental Training', *Industrial Environmental Management*, vol 11, p22

Envirowise (2003) For practical environmental help and advice for business go to www.envirowise.gov.uk/envirowisev3.nsf

Hopkinson, P. and Dixon, F. (1998) 'Environmental Training for Business', University of Bradford, www.bradford.ac.uk/acad/envsci/Research/SB/Train.pdf

IEMA (2003) 'Training Programmes', Institute of Environmental Management and Assessment, Lincoln, www.iema.net/

IFC (2000) *Success Stories: Business Profiting from an EMS*, International Finance Corporation, Washington, DC

Machin, S. and Vignoles, A. (2001) *The Economic Benefits of Training*, Centre for the Economics of Education, London School of Economics, London

OU (1999) *Managing Waste, a Business Guide*, The Open University, Milton Keynes

RSA (1995) 'Tomorrow's Company', lecture by Sir Anthony Cleaver, The Royal Society for the encouragement of Arts, Manufactures & Commerce, London

Sheldon, C. and Yoxon, M. (2002) *Installing Environmental Management Systems – A Step by Step Guide*, Earthscan, London

Wehrmeyer, W. (1996) *Greening People*, Greenleaf Publishing, Sheffield

Woodward, J (2000) 'Training is the Key to Environmental Performance Improvement', Envirospace Training, www.envirospace.com

Woolfrey, C. (2001) 'Selecting a Training Style', *IFI Environment Business Magazine*, June

Yoxon, M. (1996) 'T835 Integrated Safety, Health and Environmental Management', Block V, Part 2 Managing Human Resources – Training, The Open University, Milton Keynes

Yoxon, M. (1998) *The Green Training Pack – 22 Activities for Better Environmental Management*, Fenman, Ely, Cambridgeshire

Section 4

Evaluation Tools

Chapter 4.1

Environmental Impact Assessment

Introduction

The rationale and purpose underpinning environmental impact assessment (EIA) are simple. One should only choose whether to move forward with a proposal or action based on an understanding of the environmental consequences of its implementation. The simplicity of this concept has lead to EIA being one of the most widely adopted environmental tools by governments and development institutions around the world.

The underlying purpose of EIA is therefore to contribute to environmental protection by enabling decisions to be taken that minimize environmental effects while meeting the objectives of the proposal, or preventing actions for which the cost to the environment is considered unacceptable. Set in this context, EIA can be regarded as an important tool to contribute to sustainability by providing the information on which more sustainable decisions can be based.

Thus far, EIA has been referred to as being applied to actions or proposals. These terms cover a wide range of applications, but in practice it has primarily been applied to development projects. We will see in the following sections of this chapter that the principles of EIA can be applied to other levels of decision making, specifically policy and plan proposals. This chapter is focused on the application of EIA to projects.

What is EIA?

A distinguishing feature of EIA, when compared to other environmental management tools, is that it is anticipatory. An EIA attempts to predict the likely environmental effects of a proposal and provide a basis for the developer and other decision makers to respond to this information.

The term 'predict' suggests that there may be some uncertainty or some 'guess work' associated with EIA. This is certainly true, but experience with EIA and knowledge of environmental systems are usually sufficient to make reasoned estimates of the likely significant effects of proposals. Alternatively, the knowledge that there is likely to be an impact of uncertain magnitude may be sufficient to indicate that some aspect of the proposal needs to change or that the precautionary principle should be applied and the proposal should not be developed any further.

The anticipatory nature of EIA provides a means of ensuring that projects conform with required levels of environmental performance. EIA can highlight when a project:

- is likely to result in irreversible environmental changes;
- causes adverse effects on valued ecosystems, landscapes and other environmental features;
- could result in adverse health effects on a community; and
- provides an opportunity for environmental or social improvements.

The anticipatory nature of EIA provides an opportunity for the developer to use the information to improve the environmental performance of a project and, in doing so, improve the sustainability of the proposals and enhance the probability of gaining consent.

EIA as a design tool

EIA is designed to inform decisions relating to project proposals and there are many decision points during the planning and execution of a project. One of the areas in which EIA can be most effective is in influencing the design of a project during the planning stages. The early identification of environmental problems provides an opportunity for these to be reduced or eliminated by the redesign of the project, whereas retrofitting 'end-of-pipe' solutions could prove to be expensive. Taking an environmental perspective on the design of a project may produce unexpected creative solutions that could eliminate the need for the project while meeting the objectives of the development – see Box 4.1.1.

Box 4.1.1 *EIA for Billund Airport*

A new runway was proposed for Billund Airport in order to reduce the number of homes exposed to noise above the recommended thresholds. As a result of the work undertaken as part of the EIA for the new runway, it became clear that the same reduction in noise levels could be obtained by changes in the take-off procedure. All aeroplanes that take off from east to west could leave the runway as quickly as possible and turn 30 degrees to the right (away from Billund) when they are at 150m height. As a result, the construction of a new runway is not necessary.
   The benefits of this solution included:

- a reduction of 1000 homes exposed to noise above the recommended thresholds;
- a doubling of the flying capacity;
- a saving of 350ha of farmland;
- the preservation of an old Danish forest;
- a saving of 300 million Kroner (€40.4 million) in the cost of construction;
- less environmental impact from the airport's operations; and
- environmental approval of the airport – without complaints.

Source: Based on a case study from EC web site: http://europa.eu.int/comm/environment/eia/eia-billund-airport.htm

---

Using EIA to improve certainty in decision making

Projects that are subject to an EIA required by regulations will be subject to a formal consent system. Using EIA as one of the tools to contribute to the design of a project can be a means of improving the prospects of gaining consent. If the environmental issues that are likely to be an obstacle are identified early and eliminated by changes to the design or reduced to acceptable levels, then the environmental reasons for refusing consent are also eliminated or reduced. Alternatively, the EIA may identify at an early stage that the environmental constraints are such that consent would be unlikely to be obtained and a significant investment in fruitless project planning and design can be avoided.

EIA can also be a powerful tool for gathering information on the affected community's environmental concerns and enabling the design of a project to respond to this. The ability to demonstrate a positive response to public concerns can increase the confidence of the public in the project and the developer. Again, this may help to remove some of the obstacles to consent for the project.

EIA as an information provision tool

A key purpose of EIA is to provide information to the key decision makers that will determine whether a project should be given consent. The environmental information will be just one of many factors that the decision maker will take into account, and it may or may not have a significant influence on the final decision.

Among the other information considered will be comments from the public, many of them generated by the EIA process. EIA is an important democratic instrument that ensures that communities are informed of developments that may affect their environment prior to a decision being made. It also provides for them to be involved in the decision making process by creating opportunities for them to communicate their opinions on the proposals and the environmental effects.

Background to EIA

EIA was first conceived in the US. It was a reaction to project planning and decision making based on economic efficiency and engineering feasibility often at the expense of the environment. The National Environmental Policy Act (1969) set a requirement for the environmental effects of federal actions to be assessed prior to a decision being taken.

There was close to a five year gap before Australia, Canada and New Zealand followed suit. Since then a steady stream of countries have identified EIA as an appropriate mechanism to assist in the control of the environmental effects of major project developments. Implementation in Europe arrived relatively late with a directive passed by the European Economic Community (EEC) in 1985. Nevertheless, this was significant as it added a large number of countries to those that were formally applying EIA.

By 1996 it was estimated that over 100 countries had national EIA systems (Sadler, 1996) covering most industrialized nations as well as a significant number of developing countries. Of the latter category, those without a formal EIA requirement would still be affected by one as by this time most development institutions had their own EIA requirements that had to be fulfilled before they would provide aid or loans to fund projects or programmes. In 1992 the role of EIA in contributing to sustainability was identified by the Rio Summit which, among other things, identified EIA as an implementing mechanism for the Conventions on Biological Diversity and Climate Change.

Legal context

EIA has a clear purpose in terms of environmental protection. From the point of view of a developer, the application of EIA to new project proposals can be seen to be a good management practice in terms of minimizing environmental risks to the project and the decision making process. Nevertheless, most EIAs are undertaken as a result of regulatory requirements.

EIA Directive

In the UK, EIA requirements result from the implementation of a European directive on EIA. This was originally adopted in 1985 (EC, 1985), with member states required to implement it by 3 July 1988. The directive was subsequently amended in 1997 (EC, 1997) with member states required to implement the amendments by 14 March 1999. Another revision to the directive was adopted in 2003 with member states required to implement the provisions by 25 June 2005.

The directives have been implemented in the UK through a series of statutory instruments that implement the requirements for the different consent systems. For example, there are separate regulations that make provisions for EIA, for the town and country planning systems, highways, land drainage projects, pipelines and offshore oil and gas development. In addition, there are separate regulations that relate to the part of the country in which the project is located. So, while England and Wales operate under the same regulations, there are separate ones for Scotland and Northern Ireland. Most of the regulations add little to the requirements that are set out in the directive. The following provides a brief summary of the main provisions. A more exhaustive legal discussion can be found elsewhere – see for example Tromans and Fuller (2003).

The purpose of a directive is to set the framework for the domestic regulations including setting the minimum requirements that are to be included in the regulations. The main features of the directive include:

- two lists of projects to which EIA is applied;
- a definition of the environment to indicate the range of issues that should be considered by EIA;
- establishing the minimum information requirements to be provided by an environmental statement (the report resulting from an EIA); and
- establishing the minimum procedural requirements.

When to apply EIA

EIA, under the terms of the directive, is triggered by the type of project proposed. The directive provides two lists of projects. Annex 1 projects will always require an EIA and include: oil refineries, large waste and waste water disposal and treatment facilities, pipelines over 40km long, large intensive agricultural units, and industrial facilities of various defined uses (e.g. chemicals, paper pulp production, metal smelting).

The list of projects in Annex 2 of the directive is much longer. These are projects that may require an EIA, if they are likely to have significant effects on the environment. These projects include: afforestation and deforestation, extractive industry projects (not included in Annex 1), wind farms, food industry projects, coastal defence works, and various tourism and leisure projects.

How the decision is taken as to whether an EIA is required or not is one that is left for the member states to decide, but some further advice is contained within the directive. Annex 3 sets out broadbrush criteria on which the decision should be based. The criteria are split into three categories relating to: the characteristics of the project, the location of the project and the characteristics of the potential impact.

What should an EIA cover?

The directive defines the issues to be covered in two ways. First, it defines the aspects of the environment that are considered to be the receptors of the environmental impact. These are: human beings, fauna and flora; soil, water, air, climate and the landscape; material assets and the cultural heritage; and the interaction between them. Human beings are considered to be part of the environment and therefore impacts upon them are issues that should be considered within an EIA.

The second way in which the directive defines the issues to be covered by an EIA is by setting out the minimum information requirements to be provided by the process. These include:

- a description of the project comprising information on the site, design and size of the project;
- a description of the measures envisaged in order to avoid, reduce and, if possible, remedy significant adverse effects;
- the data required to identify and assess the main effects which the project is likely to have on the environment;
- an outline of the main alternatives studied by the developer and an indication of the main reasons for his/her choice, taking into account the environmental effects; and
- a non-technical summary of the information mentioned in the previous four points.

There is scope for the information requirements to be more extensive, either as a result of national regulations or on a case by case basis. Annex 4 of the directive sets out more detailed information that can be required if the member state considers that it is relevant to the consent procedure. In the UK the regulations allow for this decision to be taken by the determining authority. So for example, while there is not a requirement for the impacts from the use of natural resources to be addressed by all EIAs it is within the powers of the determining authority to require this information for a particular proposal.

The directive has other requirements for the EIA process, mainly relating to the involvement of the public. It requires that they are consulted prior to a decision being taken on whether the project should proceed or not. There are also requirements for the determining authority to publish the reasons for the decision and, if consent is given, the main mitigation measures that are to form part of the development. This provides the public with the information to check that the developer is complying with the consent conditions. Enhancing the role of the public in the process is the main feature of the amendment to the directive passed in 2003.

The final major provision of the directive is of limited relevance to the UK, but requires a member state to consult with another state in the event that there is a project that could affect them.

Importance of ensuring legal compliance in the UK

Compliance with the directive and the relevant regulations in the UK has become a critical issue. EIA has become a common means of challenging major development if permission is granted. There is now a significant track record of major proposals being delayed or aborted as a result of legal challenges related to technical compliance with the regulations. Even if the non-compliance is the fault of the determining authority rather than the developer, this can still cause the consent to be quashed.

The EIA process

EIA is described as being an iterative process. This is because, while it can be illustrated as a linear set of steps – see Figure 4.1.1 – it contains a number of feedback loops that are designed to revise the proposal and reconsider the environmental effects of any changes that have taken place.

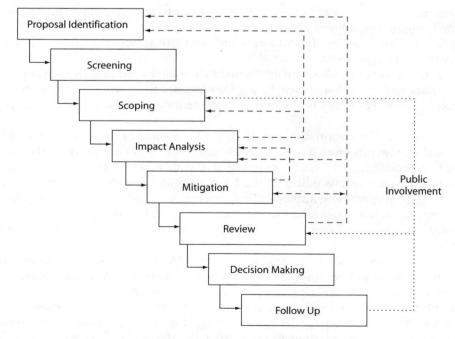

Figure 4.1.1   The EIA process

Who is involved in an EIA?

An EIA will involve a number of different stakeholders and successful EIAs are characterized by a clear effort being made to actively involve them. The following groups will typically be involved:

- Developers are responsible for undertaking the EIA but will usually employ a consultant to take full or partial responsibility for it.
- Consultants are usually employed to undertake the EIA. This is likely to involve a large multidisciplinary team or an EIA coordinator with a number of subconsultants.
- The determining authority will be required to evaluate the environmental statement and make a decision on the project, but they also have responsiblities to: determine the requirements for an EIA, advise on the issues to be addressed by the EIA and consult with other government departments and agencies.
- Government agencies provide specialist inputs into the EIA and decision making process.
- Non-governmental organizations (NGOs) provide inputs to the EIA and decision making processes.
- Affected and interested members of the public provide inputs to the EIA and decision making processes.

The interdisciplinary nature of EIA

EIA is a team event! It is usually undertaken by a group of people from a range of environmental and social science backgrounds relevant to the potential environmental impacts of the proposal. For large or complex projects this could cover up to 15 different disciplines. In successful EIAs the team of consultants is led and coordinated by an EIA project manager whose responsibilities include:

- ensuring that the EIA stays on schedule and on budget;
- providing quality control for the work provided by other members of the team;
- coordinating consultation with other stakeholders;
- working with the project design team to resolve environmental problems; and
- making sure that the report resulting from the EIA is coherent and defensible.

What is involved in an EIA?

The simplified diagram of the EIA process in Figure 4.1.1 illustrates the major steps in the process together with some of the feedback loops that will generate changes to the project and a reevaluation of the environmental effects.

Considering alternatives

EIA should start early by providing an environmental input on the decisions on what is to be constructed and where it is to be located. This provides the best opportunity to avoid significant environmental effects by steering clear of environmentally sensitive locations and selecting designs and processes that have a reduced environmental impact. For infrastructure projects there may also be an opportunity to have an input into strategic options in order to reduce the environmental impact, for example forms of transport; means of energy production; or location and technology for waste disposal.

Once the form and location for the development have been determined the more formal elements of the EIA process are followed.

Screening

Screening refers to the decision as to whether an EIA is required or not. In the UK, this is a decision that can be taken by the developer and often will be if the project is of a type or size where an EIA is clearly required or if they wish to be seen to be addressing the environmental effects of their development.

For most projects, particularly those covered by Annex 2 of the directive, the determining authority is likely to be asked to give a screening opinion. Their decision will be based on the type of criteria included in Annex 3 of the directive, more detailed guidance issued by the European Commission and the government and the opinions of government agencies (e.g. English Nature and the Environment Agency) and relevant local authority personnel (e.g. environmental health officers).

Scoping

The purpose of EIA is to focus on the significant environmental effects of a development, not on all of the environmental effects that can be thought of. The purpose of scoping is to identify the effects that are most likely to be significant in order to focus the time and resources devoted to the EIA on the important issues. The identification of the key effects is usually undertaken using a combination of professional judgement and gathering the opinions of others, particularly the determining authority and other government agencies.

Scoping is usually undertaken by those responsible for the EIA. However, there is provision in the EIA Directive for the developer to request a 'scoping opinion' from the determining authority. When this is requested it is usually accompanied by a report that outlines what the developer and consultants consider to be the most important issues. The determining authority will consult with other government agencies (statutory consultees) and amend or add to the developer's report accordingly.

The advantage of seeking a scoping opinion is that the developer will have some assurance that the issues being addressed by the EIA will be those that are considered to be important by the determining authority when a decision is to be made on the project.

To a degree, the scoping stage of an EIA continues throughout the process. For example, the identification of an unacceptable environmental effect may lead to a redesign of the project, which in turn could lead to the main environmental effects of the project changing, hence the scope of the EIA will also change.

Assessing impacts

One of the main purposes of an EIA is to predict the environmental effects of a proposal. The assessment of the environmental effects consists of three elements:

Understanding the baseline conditions: In order to understand the effect of the proposal it is important to know what the environment would be like in its absence. This will often be the current conditions on and around the proposed site, but in some cases may require the prediction of environmental conditions into the future. For example, if the project has a long lead time then account may need to taken of the changing environment within the vicinity of the proposed site.

The baseline conditions will normally be established by consulting existing publications and published data and undertaking surveys on the site and the surrounding area. The scope of the surveys should have been determined during the scoping stage of the EIA.

Predicting the magnitude of the impact: The change in environmental conditions generated by the project is predicted using a range of techniques. Where possible the changes should be expressed in quantitative terms – for example, changes in the ground level concentrations of particular air pollutants or noise levels. These predictions will often be made using models of varying sophistication. For some issues a more qualitative approach is required for which the changes will be described or illustrated (landscape and visual impacts) and the techniques used may rely on professional judgement and consultation with appropriate stakeholders. Not all environmental impacts can be predicted accurately and some account may need to be taken of the uncertainties associated with the predictions.

Assessing the significance of impacts: Having gained an understanding of the likely impact it is then important to know whether this change matters, i.e. whether it is considered to be a significant environmental effect. This assessment will usually be based on criteria relating to the change in environmental conditions (e.g. noise limits based on the increase over the background noise) or the quality of the environment (e.g. air quality limits or designated sites). Scales of classification of the significance of impacts are often used to communicate whether the impact is of minor, moderate or major significance.

Mitigation

In the event that significant environmental effects are identified, the developer and consultants may conclude that they are only likely to achieve a consent for the project if the effects are eliminated or reduced. The means of mitigating the environmental effects should follow a systematic process of attempting to avoid, reduce or compensate for them. There may also be opportunities to enhance the environmental condition of the site as part of the project and achieve an environmental gain.

While mitigation is routinely illustrated as being part of this stage of the process, in reality it is considered from the earliest stages of a project's inception.

Review and decision making

The findings of an EIA are written up in an environmental statement which is submitted to the determining authority together with the application for consent for the project. Up to this point the EIA process has primarily been in the control of the developer and the consultant. In order to have some assurance that the information that will be used as part of the basis for decision making is adequate, the information needs to be evaluated. This helps to ensure that the information is: relevant to the decision to be made; reliable in terms of the information provided and the interpretation of the data; and sufficient to form a sound basis for a decision.

The public also have an opportunity to review the document and provide their comments to the determining authority who has an obligation to take them into account when making a decision, together with the environmental statement and the views provided by other consultees.

Follow up

In order to ensure that the EIA results in improved environmental protection on the ground it is often necessary to implement follow up activities. These may consist of management or monitoring measures that ensure that mitigation is implemented and impacts do not exceed a certain level or identifying unanticipated changes to valued components of the environment. These follow up activities will often be implemented during the construction phase of a project.

Links to other environmental management tools

In order to place EIA in a context that provides a more integrated approach to the management of the environmental effects of new projects, it is important to understand the relationship to other environmental management tools.

Figure 4.1.2 illustrates the relationships between a range of tools and activities. Some provide a strategic framework within which the EIA takes place; these include strategic environmental assessment and best practicable environmental option studies. Some

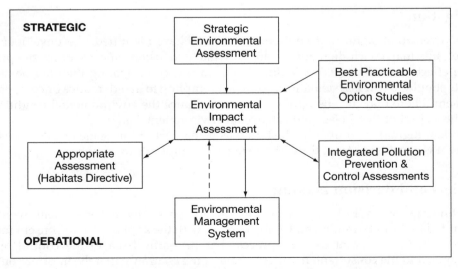

Figure 4.1.2   A framework of environmental management tools for new projects

would be undertaken at similar times to the EIA, and have some common data requirements and approaches; these include 'appropriate assessments' and integrated pollution prevention and control (IPPC) applications. Other tools can be developed on the basis of the work initiated by the EIA – this could include environmental management systems (EMSs). For example, a good starting point for the identification of the significant aspects of an operation for an EMS would be the key issues addressed by the EIA in relation to the operation of the facility.

Keys to success

EIA can make a significant contribution to reducing the environmental effects of new projects and, from the point of view of the developer, to improving the potential for gaining consent for a project. However, experience has shown that there are key lessons to be learned to improve the potential for achieving these benefits.

Start early

In the preamble to the 1985 directive it was stated that 'the best environmental policy consists in preventing the creation of pollution or nuisances at source, rather than subsequently trying to counteract their effects' (EC, 1985). In order to achieve this it is important that environmental expertise is incorporated into the project planning process at a point at which it can influence the fundamental decisions about what is built, why and where. This provides the best opportunity of being able to avoid significant impacts through the design and location of a project.

Involve stakeholders early

Traditionally, project developers have kept their plans secret until they feel they are sufficiently well developed to 'defend' them (known as the decide–announce–defend approach). Unsurprisingly, communities that would experience the impact of these proposals feel they have little control or influence over the development and in response mount vociferous opposition.

Many successful EIAs include early and effective consultation that takes account of the concerns of affected communities, ensures that they are addressed by the EIA and allows for some redesign of the project in order to remove or address their concerns. Such an approach has other advantages for the developer:

- There should be few surprises at later stages in the EIA or application for consent leading to the development of expensive last minute solutions.
- Some objections to the project may be removed as stakeholders learn more about the project.
- The affected communities may have information relevant to the EIA that the consultant would otherwise be unable to access or would not think to ask for.

Given the increased awareness of the EIA regulations among the public and their potential for being used as a tool to delay or to prevent development, compliance with the terms of the regulations is essential. Those responsible for the EIA should be satisfied that they are in compliance, but they may also want to ensure that other parties, especially the determining authority, have fulfilled their obligations appropriately. Many EIA teams now include an environmental lawyer to provide some assurance that all legal implications have been addressed.

To simply aim to comply with the regulations may not be satisfactory to achieve an efficient decision making process. The regulations set the minimum requirements and are often an insufficient framework to encourage the provision of adequate information to satisfy the determining authority, consultees or the public.

Apply good practice

Compliance with good practice in EIA is likely to enhance the potential for a favourable decision in a timely manner. A project has never been turned down because the EIA was too good, but many have been turned down because of insufficient environmental information or because the environment had not been considered sufficiently in the conception of the project. A good practice EIA gives confidence to all stakeholders in the process that the environmental effects will be well managed in practice.

Compliance with good practice is more expensive. It may mean carrying out additional surveys or delaying the project to ensure that the surveys are undertaken at an appropriate time of year. However, the cost of an EIA is usually a small proportion of the total capital cost of the project and is likely to be a fraction of the cost of a public inquiry.

Recognize the importance of scoping

Research has shown that EIAs often fail because insuffient attention was given to ensuring that the right issues were being addressed in the right way. The root of this problem is usually that insufficient time and resources have been given to the scoping stage of the EIA. Consultation with the determining authority, other consultees and the public will provide information to enable the EIA to address the issues that they consider to be important. It is also an opportunity to make the EIA more cost efficient by focusing on the key issues and 'scoping out' those that can be identified as being less important.

Scoping is an opportunity to gain the agreement of other stakeholders on the methods to be used to gather baseline information and predict the impacts, and the criteria to be used to assess the significance of impacts. These will reduce the scope for disagreement on the findings of the EIA when the application for consent for the development is submitted with the environmental statement.

Conclusions

EIA is widely regarded as an important environmental management tool which can be used to reduce the adverse environmental effects of major development projects. The establishment of formal requirements in laws and regulations means that it is difficult to avoid undertaking such a study for significant development proposals. Compliance with the regulations is likely to avoid legal challenges that could delay or prevent proposals from moving forward. However, only compliance with a good practice approach is likely to contribute to an efficient decision making process and to the developer gaining the trust of the determining authority, other consultees and the affected community.

While EIA is an important environmental management tool it does have its limitations. In particular:

- It cannot reverse higher level decisions that set a framework for the development proposal and in doing so have predetermined some of the environmental effects.
- While the regulations make provision for addressing the cumulative effects of development, they are generally inadequately considered.
- EIA tends to only address the direct effects of the construction and operation of the development, but does not address issues that may arise from the sourcing of resources for a process that forms part of the development.
- EIA is an information-providing tool and does not set a standard of environmental performance that proposals have to achieve.

References

EC (1985) 'Council Directive 85/337/EEC on the Assessment of the Effects of Certain Public and Private Projects on the Environment', *Official Journal of the European Community*, L175

EC (1997) 'Council Directive 97/11/EC Amending Directive 85/337/EEC on the Assessment of the Effects of Certain Public and Private Projects on the Environment', *Official Journal of the European Community*, L073

Sadler, B. (1996) *International Study of the Effectiveness of Environmental Assessment, Environmental Assessment in a Changing World, Evaluating Practice to Improve Performance*, International Association for Impact Assessment and Canadian Environmental Assessment Agency, Ministry of Supply and Services, Ottawa

Tromans, S. and Fuller, K. (2003) *Environmental Impact Assessment Law and Practice*, Butterworths LexisNexis, London

Chapter 4.2

Strategic Environmental Assessment

What is SEA?

An examination of the key environmental challenges facing the world can identify some common themes, for example:

- Adverse effects often result from many different activities that on their own may not be considered to be significant.
- The effects are influenced by several different policy agendas – industry, agriculture, transport, and so on.
- Institutions responsible for the development of these policy areas are driven by economic and social imperatives and often have little or no direct environmental responsibilities.
- Institutions driven by environmental imperatives often have little or no influence over these policy areas.

Strategic environmental assessment (SEA) is a tool aimed at ensuring that the environmental implications of strategic policies and programmes are taken into account and adaptions are made before decisions are taken to adopt them. SEA has a close association with environmental impact assessment (EIA) and to some degree was born out of the limitations of assessing the effects of development projects (see Table 4.2.1)

Decisions that lead to some of the most important environmental effects are taken at a more strategic level. EIA practitioners and others have called for a mechanism by which the environmental effects of policy and planning decisions could be considered prior to their adoption.

The increasing profile of sustainability and the commitment to integrate it into plan and policy making is another driver for the adoption of SEA. It provides a mechanism to not only manage the negative effects of plan and policy proposals, but to proactively identify the best environmental solution. One of the approaches to SEA is to identify environmental objectives that can provide an additional benchmark to the success of a policy or plan. SEA is particularly well positioned to address the management of cumulative effects, but can also provide an early warning of those that may occur in the future and thus enable the policymaker or planmaker to avoid or reduce them.

Traditionally, EIA has been undertaken by environmental specialists. SEA, on the other hand, is increasingly promoted as a tool that should be applied by those responsible for policy and plan development. SEA forces policymakers and planmakers to systematically consider the environmental implications of their decisions and enables them to make appropriate changes to their proposals. In the longer term it is hoped that it will have the benefit of mainstreaming the environment in the strategic decision making culture. The objective is to reach a point where the environmental implications of proposals are not something that is considered retrospectively or because it has been imposed by an SEA, but is built in to the formulation of new policy and plan proposals.

Table 4.2.1   The limitations of project EIA

EIA Limitations	Example
EIA takes place relatively late in the decision making process when many of the major alternatives have been foreclosed and strategic choices have been made.	An EIA for a gas-fired power station takes place too late to determine whether the energy requirements could be addressed by a renewable energy project or by energy efficiency measures.
EIA focuses on how best to include the environment in a project rather than whether development should occur and, if so, in what form.	An EIA for a new housing development does not have the opportunity to address whether the project provides an adequate solution to a perceived housing shortage.
Only a few projects are subjected to a full EIA whereas significant cumulative effects can result from many smaller projects.	Multiple small housing developments are potentially more significant in terms of their effect on biodiversity and their potential for adding to carbon dioxide emissions than one large housing development requiring EIA.
Despite the widespread adoption of EIA its effect in addressing significant global effects has been demonstrably limited.	The emission of greenhouse gases and the destruction of biodiversity have continued to grow despite the widespread adoption of EIA around the world.

Some elements of SEA have been in existence in the UK since the early 1990s, and their origins can be tracked back to the first EIA legislation in the US. However, it is still a relatively new environmental management tool and is developing rapidly. This progress is unlikely to slow in the foreseeable future. A European Union (EU) directive on SEA will institute the practice across Europe (EC, 2003), leading to the development of new techniques and approaches and, probably more importantly, the increasing acceptance of environmental and sustainability considerations being integrated with plan and policy making processes.

Policies, plans and programmes

Policies and plans are part of a hierarchy of decision making leading from the strategic to the specific at the project level. This is illustrated in Figure 4.2.1, which shows that strategic decisions will influence the environmental outcomes of levels of decision making that are lower down the hierarchy.

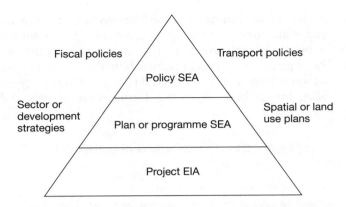

Figure 4.2.1 The hierarchy of decision making

It is often difficult to understand the difference between a policy, plan or programme. Different countries or even different institutions have their own interpretation of the terms. In many countries the terms 'plan' and 'programme' are used interchangeably. A broad generic definition that has been proposed (Sadler and Fuller, 2002) is:

- Policy – guiding intent, defined goals, objectives and priorities, actual or proposed direction.
- Plan – strategy or design to carry out a general or particular course of action, incorporating policy ends, options and ways and means to implement them.
- Programme – schedule of proposed commitments, activities or instruments to be implemented within or by a particular sector or area of policy.

Applications of SEA

The range of contexts to which SEA is applied means that it is not possible to identify a single generic process that adequately represents the reality of most SEA systems. An understanding of SEA is best gained by examining the types of plan and policy making activities to which it is applied, the types of information used, and the outcomes of the process. Potentially, SEA can be applied to the development of any policy or plan. In practice, its application is more limited and generally comprises of the following:

- sectoral specific policies or plans;
- spatial plans, particularly local or regional land use plans;
- regional plans for economic development;
- proposed legislative bills; and
- investment or lending activities particularly associated with international aid and structural adjustment funding.

Notable omissions from the above list are national fiscal and budget plans. While these are likely to have a fairly structured development to which SEA could be applied there is little experience of exposing a budget to an assessment of its likely environmental effects. The list of the types of policy or plan to which SEA is applied can be further reduced to one of three types of SEA: namely sectoral SEA, spatial SEA and policy SEA.

A survey of the status of SEA among Organisation for Economic Co-operation and Development (OECD) countries in the late 1990s indicated that the use of SEA was already widespread (Fuller et al, 1998). Thirteen of the seventeen countries that responded to the survey claimed to have some provision for SEA. Of the four remaining countries one had definite plans to introduce SEA and two others would be obliged to do so when the European Directive on SEA was adopted. The means by which each country made provision for SEA varied from one country to another. In some, SEA was included in the EIA laws; in other cases other regulations triggered SEA; and in others the requirement for SEA was not legislated for, but was required as a result of a decree or as a matter of policy. In the UK, early SEA experience resulted from government policy to require an environmental appraisal of local development plans.

The results of the survey demonstrated that most of the experience with SEA was in the application to specific sectors or to land use planning. Experience with the systematic application to policy development was modest and remains so.

The Netherlands, New Zealand, Denmark, the UK and the US have been prominent in the development of SEA, together with the World Bank and the European Commission (EC).

Sectoral SEA

There is considerable experience with sectoral SEA. The National Environmental Policy Act (NEPA) that established the practice of EIA in the US did not specify that it should only apply to projects, although this is what happened for a period immediately following its enactment. When wider programmes were subjected to environmental analysis, it was sectoral programmes to which the requirements of NEPA were primarily applied. The World Bank has also adopted sectoral SEA as a means of assessing the environmental implications of lending for the purpose of the development of a particular sector within a receiving country. An example of a sectoral SEA is provided in Box 4.2.1.

In the UK the experience of sectoral SEA is limited, but is emerging. Notable examples of practice are SEA of multi-modal transport plans, SEA of offshore oil and gas development, and SEA of offshore renewable energy development.

Spatial SEA

SEA is applied to spatial plans more frequently than any other type of plan or policy. It is most prominently applied to land use plans. Provision for this has existed in the UK since 1992. Economic development strategies for a region have also been subjected to SEA, usually in the context of loans from the World Bank or aid from similar agencies, or structural adjustment funding from the EC. The purpose of applying SEA in this context is to ensure that decisions taken for the benefit of economic development are not taken at the expense of the environment. It is also an opportunity to take into account the environmental effects of locational decisions for major development. This should help to avoid the problem of project EIA being limited in its ability to minimize environmental effects by poor decisions that have been taken higher up the decision making hierarchy.

Box 4.2.1 *Dutch ten year programme on waste management*

The Dutch Waste Management Council developed a ten year programme on waste management and undertook a voluntary SEA. The purpose of the plan was to ensure that there was sufficient capacity for the final treatment of waste generated within the country.

To provide a basis for the development of alternatives, two scenarios formed the basis of the plan and the SEA. The 'policy scenario' assumed that national objectives for waste reduction, recycling and so on were met and the 'headwind' scenario assumed that these objectives would not be fully achieved and there would be a greater level of waste to deal with.

The SEA investigated three alternatives:

- maintenance of existing capacity for waste separation and incineration and landfilling of remaining waste;
- maximum increase in separation and incineration facilities and only landfilling of non-combustible waste; and
- maximum increase in separation facilities, but existing levels of incineration facilities.

Indicators were selected as the basis for assessing the environmental effects of the options. The indicators were drawn from the Dutch National Environmental Policy Plan.

The SEA demonstrated that the second alternative would have the least environmental impact. However, the necessary increase in separation and incineration facilities meant that it would not be feasible to fully implement this in the short term. The downsides of this option were also evident in terms of the acidification and dispersal of toxic materials and the large quantity of chemical residues.

Source: Verheem, 1996

In order to provide a closer integration of the economic, social and environmental considerations in spatial planning, the UK Government has been encouraging the extension of SEA to sustainability appraisal. This is similar in nature to SEA, but extends the analysis to the social and economic effects of decisions taken at this level. Critics of this approach argue that, given that social and economic factors dictate the content of such plans, there is little need for these issues to be systematically built into the assessment. In addition, there are suspicions that a sustainability analysis is a covert means of trading off adverse environmental effects for economic or social gains. An example of a sustainability appraisal of a spatial plan is shown in Box 4.2.2.

Policy SEA

Policy decisions are the most critical point at which SEA can influence the effect on the environment, as it is at the top of the decision making hierarchy and will dictate the nature of the decisions that are taken at lower levels. It has also proved to be the most difficult level at which to establish SEA. This is partly to do with a cultural resistance to its implementation and partly because policy making often does not follow the sort of systematic process to which you can apply an analysis tool. In addition, this level of decision making has a large degree of uncertainty with regard to outcomes and therefore predicting environmental effects with any precision or accuracy is a problem.

Nevertheless, there are examples of its application, usually undertaken as a matter of policy or ministerial decree rather than as a legal requirement. The approaches tend to be brief and concentrate on the provision of qualitative information. An example of a policy SEA is given in Box 4.2.3.

Box 4.2.2 *Sustainability appraisal of Cambridgeshire County Council and Peterborough City Council structure plan*

The sustainability appraisal was undertaken in the context of a review of the structure plan in order to make revisions to cover the period up to 2016. The appraisal was integrated into the development of the plan to facilitate an iterative process and was undertaken by consultants on behalf of the councils.

A sustainability appraisal framework was developed that set out 19 sustainability objectives that the plan should be aiming to pursue. They were grouped under the following four themes:

- safeguarding the environment through effective protection;
- providing for future generations through prudent use of natural resources;
- supporting communities through social progress that recognizes the needs of everyone; and
- promoting prosperity for all by maintaining high and stable levels of economic growth and employment.

These were supported by indicators that could be used to measure progress against the objectives and translated into criteria that formed the basis of the sustainability appraisal. Each of the draft structure plan policies was appraised using the appraisal framework.

Prior to undertaking a formal appraisal of the draft plan, the consultants commented on draft chapters to enable alterations to the plan to be made, in order to be more consistent with the sustainability objectives.

The appraisal focused on the broad direction of change, i.e. did the policy contribute to or move away from the achievement of the sustainability objective? An assessment of how well the policies fit together to provide a coherent plan for the area was also undertaken. A health impact review of the structure plan was also undertaken in parallel to the sustainability appraisal.

Following the appraisal, a conclusion was provided indicating how improvements in the plan had been made to place it on a more sustainable footing. A series of recommendations highlighted the issues that still needed to be addressed as they were currently detracting from the sustainability of the plan.

Source: Land Use Consultants et al, 2002

Box 4.2.3 *SEA of bills and other government proposals in Denmark*

The Danish system of SEA is based on an administrative order by the Office of the Prime Minister (1993, amended 1995). It applies to bills and other government proposals to be submitted to Parliament. The ministry preparing the legislation decides whether or not the proposal is likely to have significant environmental effects and whether an SEA is needed. About 15–20 per cent of draft laws are assessed.

Guidance on SEA procedures has been prepared by the Ministry of the Environment, which also provides advice on their application. This material includes a checklist for screening the potential environmental effects of a proposal and information on undertaking an assessment. The process is to be carried out to the extent that administrative and data limitations allow and so as to maintain applicability to the legislation process. A collection of case examples is included in the guidance material.

The commentary to the bill, which is part of the decision making basis for Parliament, includes a separate section on the environmental effects of the proposal. It is an easily understood non-technical statement. Background assessment statements and other relevant reports are to be publicly accessible.

Source: Sadler and Brooke, 1998

Applications within industry

Thus far SEA has been described as an environmental management tool that is applied by governments at a local or national level. Most of the experience is with such institutions, but there are examples of SEA approaches being used within industry to aid strategic decision making. Most examples are from privatized utilities that have to take strategic decisions with regard to the provision of public services. For example, a water company may have many strategic options open to them for the supply of water or the provision of wastewater treatment services. In the energy sector those responsible for the transmission lines are likely to have strategic decisions to make with regard to the routing and capacity of these lines. There are also examples of the oil and gas industry adopting an SEA approach to the development of oil and gas reserves in a new location. Each of these industries has found that an inappropriate strategic decision can make it very difficult to achieve consent for specific projects, regardless of how good the project EIA is. An example, of the application of an SEA type approach within a privatized utility is given in Box 4.2.4.

Box 4.2.4 *Strategic assessment and planning in the water sector*

Thames Water supplies water in the south east region of the UK. Demand for water is anticipated to exceed supply in the next 15–20 years, even if predicted savings are made from conservation. Several factors are considered to contribute to this, including:

- increased water use as a result of the predicted increases in population and housing;
- changes in rainfall frequency and distribution as a result of climate warming; and
- the need to reduce existing groundwater abstraction in areas where the environment is currently under stress through low levels and river flows.

In response to this Thames Water has developed a strategic approach to address these issues, comprising five steps:

1 needs statement, a prediction of the future demands for water and comparison with existing and future resources;
2 demand management studies, to evaluate the savings possible through leakage control, metering and other conservation measures;
3 best practicable environmental programme, a strategic review of the alternatives and options for meeting any predicted shortfall in water supply;
4 site selection study, to review sites for a potential reservoir as one of the options under investigation;
5 EIA of a reservoir, if adopted as one of the preferred options.

Source: Sadler and Fuller, 2002

The SEA Directive

Until recently there have been relatively few examples of SEA being given legal force. It is widely recognized as a good thing to do, but the culture shift of having decision making affected by an environmental analysis as a matter of law was too great. So, in many countries, a partial measure of requiring SEA as a matter of policy was adopted.

This approach is set to change. In June 2001, a directive was adopted by the EU 'on the assessment of the effects of certain plans and programmes on the environment'. While this does not contain the term 'SEA' within the title, this is commonly known as the 'SEA Directive'. The directive will become a legal requirement in all of the member states of the EU, including the accession countries that joined the EU in 2004. Member states were given three years to implement the requirements of the directive.

Main requirements

Scope: The directive applies to all 'plans and programmes' for specified sectors that set a framework for development consent for projects listed in the EIA Directive. These are to be prepared or adopted by an authority (including government) at a national, regional or local level. The directive only applies to plans and programmes that are required by legislative, regulatory or administrative provisions. Plans produced voluntarily are therefore likely to be exempt. The specified sectors are: agriculture, forestry, fisheries, energy, industry, transport, waste management, water management, telecommunications, tourism and town and country planning or land use planning.

Plans which require assessment as a result of the terms of the Habitats Directive are also covered by the directive. Member states are free to add to the list of plans that require SEA when incorporating the terms of the directive into their own domestic legislation. Plans for national defence, civil emergency and financial or budget plans are specifically exempted. Given that the directive covers plans that are adopted by, as well as produced by, 'an authority' it is thought that this is likely to require an assessment of the plans produced by privatized utilities that have to be approved by a government regulator.

Information requirements: The directive bears many similarities to the EIA Directive. The preparation of a report is required that provides information on the significant environmental effects of the implementation of the plan and reasonable alternatives. The specified information is:

- an outline of the contents, main objectives of the plan or programme and relationship with other relevant plans and programmes;
- the relevant aspects of the current state of the environment and the likely evolution thereof without implementation of the plan or programme;
- the environmental characteristics of areas likely to be significantly affected;
- any existing environmental problems which are relevant to the plan or programme including, in particular, those relating to any areas of a particular environmental importance, such as areas designated pursuant to Directives 79/409/EEC and 92/43/EEC;
- the environmental protection objectives, established at international, Community or member state level, which are relevant to the plan or programme and the way those objectives and any environmental considerations have been taken into account during its preparation;
- the likely significant effects on the environment, including on issues such as biodiversity, population, human health, fauna, flora, soil, water, air, climatic factors, material assets, cultural heritage including architectural and archaeological heritage, landscape, and the interrelationship between the above factors;

- the measures envisaged to prevent, reduce and as fully as possible offset any significant adverse effects on the environment of implementing the plan or programme;
- an outline of the reasons for selecting the alternatives dealt with, and a description of how the assessment was undertaken including any difficulties (such as technical deficiencies or lack of know-how) encountered in compiling the required information;
- a description of the measures envisaged concerning monitoring in accordance with Article 10; and
- a non-technical summary of the information provided under the above headings.

Public consultation: The directive requires a draft plan and the environmental report to be published and consulted on with authorities designated by the member states and the public. These consultations have to be taken into account as part of any amendments to the plan prior to its adoption. When the plan is adopted it is to be made available to the public together with a statement on how environmental considerations have been integrated into the plan and how the responses from the consultation were taken into account. The statement also needs to state the reasons for adopting the plan in its current form in the light of other reasonable alternatives.

Monitoring of the significant environmental effects of the plan is required with a view to identifying unanticipated significant effects and being able to implement remedial measures.

Application of the directive in the UK

At the time of writing no regulations have been passed to implement the terms of the directive. However, it is clear that local planning authorities are likely to experience the greatest impact of the directive. Development plans, minerals plans and transport plans will all require an SEA. Added to this, proposed changes to the planning system are likely to increase the number and diversity of plans that are produced by local authorities. While they should have been undertaking environmental appraisals of their plans since 1992, coverage has not been complete and the directive does add requirements to the process and the reporting.

At a regional level the government has been promoting the use of sustainability assessment and is keen to see this approach adopted at the local authority level. The Planning and Compulsory Purchase Bill currently includes a requirement for local development documents and regional spatial strategies to be subjected to a sustainability appraisal. Guidance on undertaking SEAs for planning authorities, issued by the Office of the Deputy Prime Minister (ODPM, 2003), includes some indications of how sustainability appraisal might be carried out while fulfilling the requirements of the SEA Directive. There is an intention to issue more detailed guidance on this matter as part of the implementation of the new planning system set out in the bill referred to above.

Local authorities are not alone in being affected by the directive. There is no definitive list of the different types of plan that are likely to be caught by the directive, but some estimates have indicated that there are over 100 different types of plan. While other government departments have tended to let the ODPM take the lead on EIA matters and then translate the requirements to apply to issues within their jurisdiction, this approach may be of limited value for implementing the SEA Directive. While different authorities will have the common requirements of the directive to meet, effective implementation will require the directive to be adapted to the different decision making contexts within each of the authorities.

Barriers to effective application

The implementation of the directive will mainstream the use of SEA within the plan making arena. Examples of implementation at the policy level do exist, but the extent to which the coverage is sufficient to provide significant advances in environmental protection is not clear. In the UK, tools for appraising policies have been available since 1991 (revised 1998), but evidence of their implementation is limited. In 2003 the Environmental Audit Committee reported on the degree to which environmental appraisals were conducted in government departments (EAC, 2003). Their results indicated that there were few appraisals being undertaken. It could be argued that this is because the various departments were not dealing with policy proposals that are likely to have significant environmental effects. However, the report of the committee also highlighted that few departments were screening policy proposals to determine whether they were likely to have significant effects and should be subjected to a detailed appraisal. It is clear that integrating SEA with policy making has proven hard to achieve and there are a number of reasons for this, as shown in Table 4.2.2.

Table 4.2.2   Problems in integrating SEA with policy making

Nature of problem	Description
Political unwillingness to subject high level decisions to external influences	In institutions where there is a tradition of secrecy and of not allowing external influence or scrutiny of policy proposals, and where the environment is not considered to be a primary responsibility of those tasked with policy development.
Ad hoc nature of policy making	Many policies are not developed within a systematic process to which SEA can be applied. For example, a ministerial speech could alter government policy overnight.
Lack of expertise and capacity in institutions	Those responsible for policy development may not have the environmental expertise to undertake an assessment, but the sensitive nature of some proposals means that they are unable to expose the policy proposals to external scrutiny.
Dealing with uncertainty	SEA at the policy level has a great deal of uncertainty associated with it, particularly with regard to the prediction of environmental effects. The absence of clear guidelines or frameworks for addressing this may mean that administrators prefer to avoid the issue.

Despite these barriers to policy SEA, there are examples of approaches that are designed to overcome them. For example, in the Netherlands an E-test is applied to policy proposals that are likely to have significant environmental effects. The analysis is undertaken by those responsible for the policy development with assistance from a support centre. The SEA is documented and is reviewed by the support centre and the Ministry of Justice to provide some assurance on the quality of the analysis. There is no provision for public involvement in the process. This approach to policy appraisal in the Netherlands demonstrates the need for SEA to be adapted to the decision making context in which it is being applied.

Does SEA eliminate the need for EIA?

One of the objectives of SEA was to address the limitations of EIA by considering the environmental effects of higher level decisions that dictate the nature of the project to which EIA is being applied. One might argue that a robust SEA system should therefore eliminate the need for project EIA as all of the major issues will have been dealt with at the strategic level. However, it is unlikely that this could be achieved. A consequence of addressing the issues at the strategic level is that there is still a great deal of uncertainty as to the size and design of a project and the processes that may form part of the development. As a result it will not be possible to predict with any precision the likely effects of a project or to design the appropriate mitigation.

Nevertheless, SEA should contribute to streamlining project EIA. Some of the significant environmental effects may be avoided by the examination of strategic alternatives (e.g. avoiding sensitive locations for the siting of projects). The SEA may also be able to advise on the scope for a project EIA.

Principles for undertaking SEA

The range of policy, plan and programme making contexts to which SEA is applied means that it isn't possible to set out a generic procedure that is applied in all circumstances. Experience with SEA has demonstrated that it is most effective, in terms of positively affecting the policy or plan, when it is undertaken by those responsible for developing the proposal. As a result there has to be a very tight fit between the policy or plan making context and the SEA process. Nevertheless, it is possible to identify some common features that are part of a good practice SEA process (Sadler and Fuller, 2002 adapted from Sadler and Verheem, 1996; Sadler and Brooke, 1998). An SEA should be:

- fit for purpose – the SEA process should be customized to the context and characteristics of policy and plan making;
- objectives led – the SEA process should be undertaken with reference to environmental goals and priorities;
- sustainability driven – the SEA process should identify how development options and proposals contribute toward environmentally sustainable development;
- comprehensive in scope – the SEA process should cover all levels and types of decision making likely to have significant environmental and health effects;
- decision relevant – the SEA process should focus on the issues and information that matter in decision making;
- integrated – the SEA process should include consideration of social, health and other effects as appropriate and necessary (e.g. if equivalent processes are absent);

- transparent – the SEA process should have clear, easily understood requirements and procedures;
- participative – the SEA process should provide for an appropriate level of public information and involvement;
- accountable – the SEA process should be carried out fairly, impartially and professionally having regard to the requirements in force and internationally accepted standards, and subject to independent oversight and review; and
- cost effective – the SEA process should achieve its objectives within limits of available policy, information, time and resources.

References and further reading

EAC (2003) 'House of Commons Environmental Audit Committee – Greening Government', 13th Report, The Stationery Office, London

EC (2001) 'Directive 2001/42/EC of the European Parliament and of the Council on the Assessment of the Effects of Certain Plans and Programmes on the Environment', *Official Journal of the European Community*, Brussels

EC (2003) 'Directive 2003/35/EC of the European Parliament and of the Council Providing for Public Participation in Respect of the Drawing Up of Certain Plans and Programmes Relating to the Environment and Amending with Regard to Public Participation and Access to Justice Council Directives 85/337/EEC and 96/61/EC', *Official Journal of the European Community*, L156, Brussels

Fuller, K. et al (1998) *The Status and Practice of Strategic Environmental Assessment, Report to the Japan Environment Agency*, Institute of Environmental Assessment, Lincoln

Land Use Consultants et al (2002) 'Cambridgeshire and Peterborough Structure Plan Review Sustainability Appraisal Stage 3 – Deposit Draft Plan', Land Use Consultants, London

ODPM (2003) 'The Strategic Environmental Assessment Directive: Guidance for Planning Authorities: Practical Guidance on Applying European Directive 2001/42/EC "on the Assessment of the Effects of Certain Plans and Programmes on the Environment" to Land Use and Spatial Plans in England', Office of the Deputy Prime Minister, London.

Sadler, B. and Brooke, C. (1998) *Strategic Environmental Appraisal, Report of the International Seminar – Ministry of the Environment and Energy, Denmark*, Institute of Environmental Assessment, Lincoln

Sadler, B. and Fuller, K. (2002) *UNEP Environmental Impact Assessment Training Resource Manual*, 2nd edn, United Nations Environment Programme, Geneva.

Sadler, B. and Verheem, R. (1996) *Strategic Environmental Assessment: Status, Challenges and Future Directions*, Ministry of Housing, Spatial Planning and the Environment of the Netherlands, International Study of Effectiveness of Environmental Assessment, The EIA Commission of the Netherlands, Zoetermeer

Verheem, R. (1996) 'SEA of the Dutch Ten-Year Programme on Waste Management 1992–2002', in R. Thérivel and M. R. Partidario (eds) (1996), *The Practice of Strategic Environmental Assessment*, Earthscan, London

Chapter 4.3

Environmental Risk Management

Risk, its assessment and management

Risk has become a familiar concept in the 21st century. The term is widely used and means different things to different people. We all live with risks – some we have control over; some we don't; some we understand in detail; others cause us alarm. This chapter is about environmental risk assessment and management. The management of risk, from or to the environment, has developed into a systematic process for making better and more accountable environmental decisions. We assess risks so we can manage them better – by focusing on the problems that are of greatest concern; and, because we all have different concerns, it is important that risk-informed decisions are influenced by a range of stakeholders, including those that bear the risk, and that decisions and the basis for them are communicated throughout the process.

Very often the questions faced by environmental professionals are not those where data is plentiful, the mechanisms fully understood or society's demands clearly stated. In uncertain circumstances, risk assessment can help balance technological development and society's need to protect the environment from harm. We generally assume that risks to or from the environment arise as an undesirable byproduct of some function or process, and need to be viewed against the accompanying benefits that such processes offer. There are also situations where risks exist naturally – such as flooding, or because of historic human activities such as land contamination – and in recognition of the risks inherent to these situations, regulatory and supervisory systems for their management have been devised.

Environmental risk assessment is a management tool for organizing and analysing the available information on an environmental problem. It has some aspects in common with other decision making tools, such as environmental impact assessment (EIA) and strategic environmental assessment (SEA), though its explicit treatment of probability and uncertainty makes it ideally suited to distinguishing between adverse environmental impacts (or consequences) that could occur, and the likelihood (probability) of the impacts actually occurring (see Figure 4.3.1). This is a function not performed by EIA and is an important distinction for those charged with managing risk because separate strategies exist for managing the probability and consequences of environmental impacts.

What does environmental risk assessment involve? Put simply, assessing the likelihood and consequences of events that impact on the environment; that is, understanding what might happen as a result of an activity and how likely it is to happen – and then making judgements on whether to be concerned about this combination of consequences and likelihood (risk) and how, and in what order, to manage unacceptable

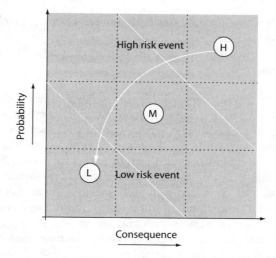

Figure 4.3.1   The concept of risk management, showing regions of high (H), medium (M) and low (L) risk, and objective of risk management

risks so they are no longer of concern. Risk assessment originated in the nuclear, chemical and oil industries where the language of risk was defined. The most important distinctions are those between:

- a 'hazard' – a substance or an activity with a potential for harm; the 'harm' – the undesirable consequence or damage that results from exposure to the hazard; and the 'risk' – the likelihood of the harm being realized;
- the 'probability' of an event (that is the likelihood of it occurring); and the 'consequences' if it were to occur; and
- the 'source' of a hazard, a 'receptor' (that which one wishes to protect) and the 'pathway' (the mechanism by which the receptor may suffer harm from the hazard).

The source–pathway–receptor approach can be illustrated by imagining being on holiday in a caravan park on the banks of a river. Under normal river flow conditions, this would be an attractive setting, but under extreme flood conditions, there is a risk that the caravan might be flooded or even washed away. The **source** of the hazard is unusually heavy rainfall. The **hazard** associated with this source is potential loss of life or property damage. The **pathway** is the passage of water through the catchment resulting in a rise in river level and the overwhelming of the flood defences. The **receptors** are the caravan and its occupants. If any one of these is absent, then **harm**, that is actual damage, cannot occur. So, for a risk to be present there must be a source of a hazard, a receptor and a pathway between the source and the receptor and these must be connected during the event. Understanding risk in these terms is essential to any assessment of risk and helps inform risk management because we manage risks by cutting the source–pathway–receptor linkage. We may:

- remove receptors (steer development away from areas that flood; use flood warning and evacuation);

- block or alter pathways (install flood defences, alleviation channels; or set up sustainable drainage systems); or
- address the source (difficult in this case for rainfall, but action on climate change may address the future severity).

Businesses need to take and manage risks to survive in a competitive market place. Like all organizations, they have to manage risks from hazards such as competition, from fluctuations in demand for their goods and services, from skill shortages and from damaged reputations. On the environmental side, they may be exposed to risks from historical land acquisitions, inherited safety cultures or through non-compliant, albeit accidental, environmental releases. Risk profiling across organizations has become essential to good corporate governance and a prerequisite for sound ethical, social and operational (including environmental) management. As a result, many large corporations have risk management committees that report periodically to the board and they have risk management systems that allow unacceptable risks to be managed.

Environmental risk is a concern to organizations because of the liabilities that may accrue and the damaged reputation that can result from the potential or actual harm caused to the environment. Businesses operate in a highly regulated environment. Regulatory decisions are made by close reference to the statutory duties and powers of the regulator and the responsibilities of operators. One aspect of the environment agencies' work includes the issuing, drafting and enforcement of environmental permits allowing business to discharge to, or abstract from, the environment. This is where most environmental professionals first encounter the requirement for an environmental risk assessment because the agencies often require an assessment of risk to inform the environmental permitting of industrial activities.

The regulatory context

In the UK, the application of environmental risk assessment within pollution control has grown substantially over recent years. It features as an explicit requirement of environmental planning and permitting and within the requirements of European and domestic legislation. The environment agencies take a risk based approach to regulating industry; that is, by targeting activities and operators posing the greatest likelihood of severe harm to the environment and public health.

Regulatory expectations of environmental risk assessment were first published in 1995, in the then Department of the Environment's Guide to Risk Assessment and Risk Management for Environmental Protection. These were revised and issued in 2000 as Guidelines for Environmental Risk Assessment and Management (DETR, 2000) for England and Wales. The Department for Environment, Food and Rural Affairs (Defra) re-endorsed their use in 2002. Good problem definition, use of a staged and tiered approach, the principles of proportionality and consistency of use, the explicit treatment of uncertainty and the need for presentational transparency are common themes in the revised guidelines, referred to as 'Green Leaves II'. The guidance provides a risk management framework (see Figure 4.3.2) to which specific risk guidance, such as that for waste management regulation, genetically modified

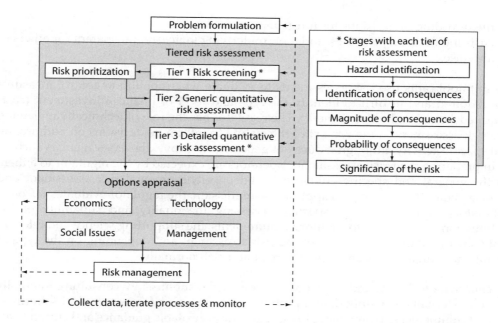

Figure 4.3.2 Framework for environmental risk assessment and management

organisms, historically contaminated land, groundwater protection and major accident hazards, for example, can in turn refer.

Operators and developers of a wide range of programmes, plans and projects are required to submit environmental risk assessments to local authorities and the environment agencies in support of their activities. Risk assessments help regulators assess the significance of the risks associated with these and then identify, and prioritize by reference to the risk, the risk management measures that are required to reduce risks to and from the environment and to human health. Regulators stipulate these measures as 'conditions' in their permits to develop land or operate plant. Preparation of the environmental risk assessment is usually the applicant's responsibility, in line with the polluter pays principle. Risk assessments are living documents requiring updating as and when modifications to an operation are proposed, or when new or additional information, relevant to the operation, becomes available.

Not all activities necessarily require complex risk assessment though – for example, where the risk is undisputedly negligible or the impacts well understood, or where there exist accepted mechanisms for control, a simple risk screening may be all that is necessary. As uncertainty increases and the likelihood of severe consequences becomes less clear, however, a formalized process of risk assessment assists in understanding the severity of the risk and how best to manage it. Advantages of risk assessment include:

- the distinction made between consequences (impacts) and the likelihood of occurrence;
- a structured approach to assessing risk and thus establishing a logical basis for managing risk;
- providing a basis for the prioritization of risk management actions and the targeting of regulatory effort;

- the recording of decisions for future use; and
- ensuring decision processes, and their underlying logic, are transparent for others to appraise.

Permit applicants use risk assessments to evaluate where pollution control measures are required and in turn to identify the type and level of financial investment (cost) required for risk reduction (benefit). The regulator has the role of technically reviewing the risk assessment in the context of the statute to inform its decisions on authorizing the specific activity although it does not generally 'approve' the assessment as such.

In preparing their risk assessments, operators are expected by the regulator to adhere to the general and specific guidance issued on environmental risk assessment and management. In reviewing an applicant's submission, the regulator evaluates it from a regulatory and technical perspective, assessing the quality and suitability of the submission, by reference to statutory requirements, the supporting science and relevant published guidance. On receipt of the risk assessment and depending on the type of facility and quality of submission, the regulator will normally:

- conduct a technical and regulatory review of the submission, consulting internally and externally as required, and probing the submission for its technical soundness and completeness by reference to the legislation, available guidance and current state of the science base;
- request further work of the operator, if deemed necessary;
- consider the need for an independent review of the operator's risk assessment where there are reasonable differences of opinion or where a second opinion might prove valuable;
- consider the need for an independent risk assessment for any operation or proposal; and
- review the operator's proposed risk management measures, or those additional measures that should be considered, to mitigate the risks to an acceptable level of residual risk.

Risk assessments are therefore used by both parties to: assess the magnitude and significance of the risk posed by the activity; identify the key drivers of the risk; prioritize risk reduction measures; and assess the level of residual risk following application of these measures.

Risk reduction is secured by applying conditions to the environmental permit, operating the process in accordance with the conditions as a minimum standard, and by the regulator enforcing the conditions. Measures may range from technological interventions (e.g. the application of best available technology) to a requirement for environmental management systems, training or even substitution of a product. Adherence to these measures is enforced through regulatory inspection and related regulatory mechanisms.

While individual legislation specifies the use of environmental risk assessment for specific regulatory processes, the environment agencies have general duties and powers (for the Environment Agency (EA), Sections 4 and 5 of the Environment Act 1995) they can use to request risk assessments of operators, permit holders and applicants. Furthermore, the adoption of various principles, tools and techniques for environmental decision making feature in the ministerial guidance provided to the EA on its contribution to sustainable development. In short, the agencies may generally request a risk assessment for any activity that they regulate where pollution of the environment is suspected. The general expectations of environmental risk assessment work submitted for regulatory review are set out in the revised Guidelines for Environmental Risk Assessment and Management (DETR, 2000).

Box 4.3.1 *Deciding on a risk assessment*

When do I need a risk assessment?
Usually when you are concerned about a known hazard and there is a sensitive receptor. A major chemical plant storing large quantities of hazardous bulk chemicals is an example of the former; residential housing close to a landfill site is an example of the latter. Risk assessments are not always required, however. Sometimes an accepted approach to managing a well recognized risk exists, such as bunding oil tanks or the use of wheel washes at waste transfer stations to avoid the release of mud or debris on approaching roads. In this type of circumstance, risk assessment may not be required unless you intend to depart from the accepted solution.

What will a risk assessment tell me?
A risk assessment will help determine how significant the probability of harm is and, usually, help establish what options there are to manage the harm. It won't make the decision over the various options for you, however. To do this, you will need to take account of economic, social and political factors and issues of practicality in making your final decision on whether, and how, to manage the risk. There are structured ways of doing this.

The application of risk assessment in regulation

Individual statutory instruments set out the context and objectives of the legislation and usually state whether risk assessment is to be applied and for what purpose. Supplementary guidance, whether statutory or non-statutory will usually describe the detail on how risk assessment should be used and what the regulatory expectations are. Further technical guidance is sometimes developed in support of this. Some of the more common regulatory applications of risk assessment, the specific context and the guidance that supports their application are discussed below.

Environmental planning

For certain development projects such as waste management facilities (incinerators, landfill, hazardous waste facilities), it has become commonplace for applicants to submit a project level environmental risk assessment as part of the EIA required under town and country planning legislation. Risk assessment offers greater resolution over EIA with respect to the relative likelihood of effects that the development may pose. It allows planners and their consultees the opportunity to scrutinize in detail the relative significance of potential impacts. With respect to the potential impacts of development projects on human health, the increasing application of health impact assessment (HIA) is seeing the outputs of project level EIA, risk assessment and HIA converge.

Risk assessments submitted during planning may be refined, adapted or expanded upon at the environmental permitting stage contingent on the requirements of the permitting regime. At the permitting stage, the environment agencies have powers to require permit applicants to furnish additional information, within a specified period, for the purposes of determining the application.

IPPC and COMAH

Risks from the process sector have historically been addressed through the integrated pollution control (IPC) regime. The IPC approach has been largely effects based and driven by the need to render releases from regulated processes to the environment harmless. In risk terms, the approach used environmental criteria, and their exceedence, as a surrogate for assessing the consequences and probability, respectively, of environmental harm.

Under integrated pollution prevention and control (IPPC) and control of major accident hazards (COMAH) legislation, risk assessment assumes a more formalized role. For COMAH, there is a fundamental requirement for operators to undertake an environmental risk assessment in a systematic way and to clearly demonstrate that risks have been identified, and all necessary measures put in place to prevent major accidents and to limit their consequences if they do occur. Each site is different and a systematic approach allows for the identification of the most important high risk accident scenarios and the prioritization of resources, resulting in a transparent, proportionate approach to the management of major hazards from dangerous substances. As a general principle, IPPC requires that all industrial operators applying for authorization assess the risk of accidents and their consequences and that necessary measures are taken to prevent accidents and limit their environmental consequences.

There is some element of overlap between IPPC and COMAH for certain sites and there is recognition that certain information required for both regimes may be interchangeable. However, the accident provisions for IPPC may fall beneath the threshold for COMAH classification. While IPPC risk assessments may require consideration to be given to smaller incidents, these may still have significant impacts on the environment, individually or cumulatively.

Contaminated land

Risks from land contamination have historically been addressed on a suitable-for-use basis with most sites being assessed for their future use under the planning regime. With the introduction of Part IIA of the Environmental Protection Act 1990 – the contaminated land regime – in 2000, an increased awareness by regulators and industry of the risks posed by land based on its current use has developed.

Part IIA has made much more explicit the role of risk assessment in contaminated land decision making. It firmly establishes the role of the conceptual model and the source–pathway–receptor relationship. A tiered approach to risk assessment is used with defined stages and roles for risk screening, generic and detailed quantitative risk assessment (Figure 4.3.2) as well as formalized options appraisal for risk management. Technical guidance is available to assist regulators and industry to assess risks to human health, controlled waters, and buildings. In addition, more general guidance covers the development of soil and groundwater sampling strategies and the communication of risk.

Planning and redevelopment of sites affected by land contamination still represent the most cost effective and beneficial way of dealing with such risks in the longer term. One of the likely benefits of Part IIA is that its explicit approach to the assessment of risks will raise the standards of such assessments under the planning regime, as its principles become more familiar among practitioners.

Waste management

Environmental risk assessment is fundamental to all phases of development for waste management facilities, from the strategic planning level through to the regulation of an individual facility. At the strategic level, risk assessment informs decisions about land use, and underpins assessment of the environmental impact associated with the site location considered, through the development planning process. In the context of environmental regulation, risk assessment is used to enable the operator and the environment agencies to identify whether, and what, risk management options or mitigation measures are required to adequately prevent, control, minimize and/or mitigate the identified risks to the environment from the facility. These measures are stipulated for waste management licences as licence conditions or in the working plan and for pollution prevention and control (PPC) permits in the conditions or in the PPC authorization.

Under the 1994 Waste Management Licensing Regulations applicants for waste management licences submit site specific risk assessments and previously, for landfill facilities, Regulation 15 (EU Groundwater Directive) risk assessments to the environment agencies in accordance with published guidance. Quantitative risk assessments, using the 'LandSim' probabilistic risk assessment tool for example, have represented good practice now for many years for the assessment of hydrogeological risks from landfill facilities. The risk management measures are subsequently addressed by specific licence conditions and working plan specifications. The complexity of the measures required depend upon the type and magnitude of risks that the operations present to the environment. Risk management measures may be relatively simple, such as operational procedures requiring simple action and documentation, or more complex, such as engineered systems with fully documented and quality assured stages of design, construction, testing and validation, operation and maintenance.

Some waste management facilities, including landfill facilities, now fall within the PPC Regulations 2000 as prescribed by Schedule 1, Section 5. Under the EU Landfill Directive, all landfills are now required to adhere to new requirements regarding their design and operation, with waste management licences being replaced with new PPC permits that comply with the directive's requirements. Under the Landfill (England and Wales) Regulations 2002, operators are required to demonstrate that necessary measures are taken to protect the environment and human health and to prevent accidents. The risk assessment requirements for the Landfill Regulations indicate the operator should have regard to:

- the generic government guidance on environmental risk assessment and management;
- the specific technical requirements for landfills falling under the Landfill Directive;

- the European Commission's decision establishing criteria and procedures for the acceptance of waste at landfills pursuant to Article 16 and Annex II of the Landfill Directive (1999/31/EC);
- the requirements of the Groundwater Directive; and hence
- EA guidance on 'Hydrogeological Risk Assessments for Landfills and the Derivation of Groundwater Control and Trigger Levels' (2002).

The latter document describes the framework for compliance with respect to groundwater for the above directives and sets out the requirements for environmental risk assessment under the new legislative regime. The framework is supported by the quantitative risk models – 'LandSim v2' which is familiar to many practitioners and now also the 'GasSim' model. In the future, the separate aspects of hydrogeological, human health and ecological risk, among others for waste management facilities, are expected to be drawn together within a single technical requirement.

Radioactive waste performance assessment

The Radioactive Substances Act 1993 provides the framework for controlling the creation and disposal of radioactive wastes so as to protect the public from hazards that may arise from their disposal to the environment. Regulatory guidance for disposal facilities sets down two criteria for assessment of the radiological safety of radioactive waste disposal facilities:

- a dose limit for a facility's operational phase; and
- a post closure radiological risk target.

Post closure, a radiological risk target is considered an appropriate protection standard because of the uncertainties inherent in assessment of future performance of a disposal system. The assessed radiological risk from a facility to a representative member of the potentially exposed group at greatest risk should be consistent with a risk target of less than one in a million risk per annum of a radiological health effect. Here, radiological risk is the product of the probability that a given dose will be received and the probability that the dose will result in a serious health effect, summed over all situations that could give rise to exposure to the group.

If, for a chosen facility design, the assessed risk exceeds the risk target, the developer should show that the design is 'optimized' and that the radiological risk has been reduced (benefit) to a level that represents a balance between radiological and other factors, including social and economic factors (cost). This is consistent with the 'as low as reasonably achievable' (ALARA) approach to risk management. Where the risk is below the risk target and the regulator is satisfied that the safety case has a sound scientific and technical basis and that good engineering principles and practice are being applied, then no further reductions in risk need be sought.

Groundwater Regulations

Activities likely to lead to the direct or indirect discharge of List I or List II substances, as defined by the Groundwater Directive, require prior authorization. Many activities authorized under the Groundwater Regulations are intermittent agricultural discharges or disposals, and due to the large numbers of authorizations, a tiered system of risk assessment has been developed. This approach allows the regulator to match the scale of the operation with the complexity of the assessment. A simple risk screening system is applied to the bulk of the applications. This risk screening system (Tier 1) uses several indicators that are readily ascertained from the application forms and readily accessible national data sets to score the application and determine whether the application for discharge can be approved subject to standard conditions, refused, or needs to be supported by further data or a more detailed analysis of the risk.

A second level risk assessment tool for the land spreading of wastes (the majority of activities) has now been developed that relies on soil property data and a soil leaching equation. Other tools such as the EA's 'ConSim' software package that takes account of processes within the unsaturated zone are available for more detailed assessment of point source disposals.

The close relationship between codes of good practice and risk assessment is stressed. Many of the risk assessments are predicated on adherence to good practice, as noted in recognized codes, a number of which are now statutory. The assumption of good practice is reflected in standard conditions on authorizations and a system of site inspection to check for compliance to the terms of authorizations.

Tools and techniques for practitioners

A wide range of tools and techniques are in use for undertaking risk assessments. They range from straightforward examinations of the connectivity between the source of a hazard and the receptor, to sophisticated numerical packages for dealing with probabilistic analysis. In practice, many risk problems can be addressed, at least initially, using a qualitative analysis, providing the logic is sound and transparent.

Box 4.3.2 *Qualitative risk assessment – tips for getting started*

Having established a risk assessment is required, think carefully about how you will use the assessment. Appreciate that people beyond those doing the assessment will also be interested in the results. Before undertaking any technical work, identify your audience and those who will be affected by the decision, and then plan how you will involve them and how you will communicate the results.

Be sure to use sound logic from the start and ensure the problem under study is properly described and understood by all the relevant parties. For example, have in mind what geographical area you are considering, and the time period that the study will address. You will need to have a very clear idea of what it is you are trying to protect (e.g. an ecosystem, human health, an aquifer) and be able to break down the problem into its main parts:

- What is at risk; what is it at risk from; and what might happen?
- How might it happen?
- How large will the consequences be and how probable are they?
- How significant are the probability and the consequences; what criteria will be used to judge their significance; and how certain are you about the assessment of probability and consequence?

Complex environmental issues with significant consequences will invariably require a combination of qualitative and quantitative analysis, usually because certain aspects of the system are better described than others. Fitness for purpose is the rule. For example, in radioactive waste disposal, while the engineering features of a disposal facility can be described in quantitative detail, future exposure scenarios in thousands of years' time can only ever be represented by illustrative futures. These types of complex assessment require formalized procedures for combining experimentally derived data with elicited expert judgement, predictive and illustrative exposure scenarios, and qualitative and quantitative expressions of risk with their associated uncertainties, all set within a risk assessment framework. Problems of this type rapidly become specialist activities.

A tiered approach to risk assessment allows for risk screening, prioritization and, in general, a qualitative treatment in advance of quantification. Because there is often considerable uncertainty involved in assessing environmental risk, particularly in the assessment of environmental exposures and impacts, resources should be targeted accordingly; that is where risks or uncertainties are high, or where the costs of the assessment are justified by the benefits to decision making. A simple risk screening approach is used first to determine the key risks and priorities. If the decision cannot be made based on this approach then more detailed approaches are used, focusing on the key risks identified at screening. A further consideration is the type of risk being assessed. One may be concerned with:

- the risk of an initiating event, or combination of events, occurring that subsequently results in a release to the environment (e.g. the over-topping of a coastal flood defence by large volumes of sea water; the release of firewater from an on site collection tank; a process plant failure; a landfill liner failure);
- the risk of exposure to an environmental receptor following a release (e.g. derogation of a drinking water supply by a leachate plume; grounding of a plume downwind of an incinerator stack; or the incidental exposure to contaminated soil);
- the risk of harm resulting from exposure (e.g. risks to human or ecological health as a result of exposure to toxic/asphyxiant gases; damage to property following the entry of floodwaters; harm to a wetland following over-abstraction or periods of drought; leaf damage to acid-sensitive trees following acid deposition).

Given these factors, experience has shown that it is invariably better to start simple and build in complexity as you need it. Start simply by drawing out your problem as a diagram. Include aspects you wish to assess; decide what aspects the assessment will and will not cover. Using your diagram (or conceptual model; Figure 4.3.3), write out possible source–pathway–receptor linkages; each linkage should have only one source, one pathway and one receptor. Ask whether, in each case, the source, pathway and receptor are linked or potentially linked; screen out those for which the answer is 'no'. Make simple but justifiable assessments (high, medium, low) separately for probability and consequence, for each linkage, recording your reasoning. In comparing probabilities, consider the nature of the pathway; in considering consequences think about the potency of the source and the receptor vulnerability/sensitivity. Establish your assessment criteria and then group linkages accordingly; for example those with high probability and high consequence, and prioritize the risks accordingly.

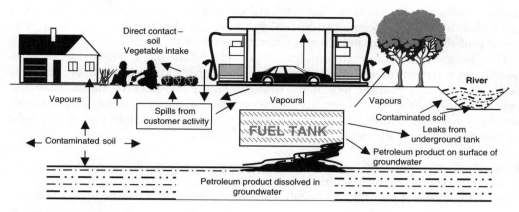

Figure 4.3.3   *The source–pathway–receptor conceptual model*

The type of risk influences the technique used to assess it. For example, event/fault tree analysis may be used to assess the performance characteristics of engineered systems and unit processes as there may be engineered safeguards to prevent the initiation or escalation of accident sequences (see Figure 4.3.4). The event tree structure provides

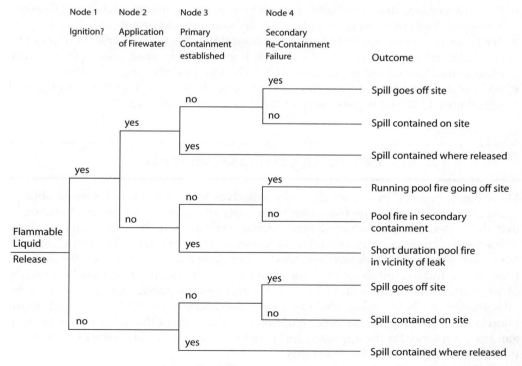

Figure 4.3.4   *Event tree for the release of flammable liquid from a process facility*

useful information by showing the combination of conditions required to achieve a particular undesired outcome. Additional value can be obtained by assigning conditional probabilities to each branch and quantifying the outcomes.

The quantification of environmental exposures following a release often relies heavily on distribution, including dispersion modelling, although event tree analysis can also be an important tool here. Understanding the risks of harm following exposure, beyond the reference to environmental criteria, requires a more detailed evaluation of physical, chemical or biological damage. Selecting the right tool, in the right circumstance and for the right purpose, requires both:

- selection of the appropriate level (tier) of sophistication as needs, complexities, priorities and data allow; and, within this,
- selection of the appropriate tool with reference to the type of risk being studied.

Complex risks may require a range of tools at various tiers of sophistication in order to manage the uncertainties inherent to the problem. Often there is insufficient data to be certain about what we are dealing with. Models may not be totally accurate or complete and we may not know what changes will take place in the future. It is important to be aware of these uncertainties when carrying out a risk assessment. A series of software packages are available for dealing with uncertainties in conceptual models, specific data and decision uncertainty. The following are practical pointers that can help with treating uncertainty:

- It is best to concentrate on the big picture before getting into the detail and to avoid a complex analysis of an issue unless you are sure it is important.
- Try to communicate where the greatest uncertainties lie. For example, you might be confident in the permeability of a landfill liner that is in good condition, but very uncertain as to whether the liner is likely to be torn or damaged.
- Be honest about uncertainties – use 'what if' questions, to explore the importance of uncertainty to the final assessment of risk (sensitivity analysis).

Evaluating risk assessments

Many environmental professionals find themselves in the position of commissioning, evaluating or reviewing the risk assessment work of experts. This can be daunting in that they often feel in uncharted professional territory and the complexity of many assessments can obscure the essential components. Below are some key principles.

Involve others: The risk assessor needs to understand the context of the decision being made and the full range of factors that might influence it. There may be a variety of audiences for the output and both stakeholders and the public may wish to have the opportunity to help frame the questions the assessment addresses, and input knowledge. Involving the audience early on and throughout the process may assist in gaining acceptance for the approach and in getting a wider buy-in to the final decision, though it would be naïve to expect this.

Good problem definition is essential: What is the environmental setting? What are the spatial and temporal aspects of the problem? Which aspects will the risk assessment address and which will it not address? This can often be set out schematically, or using a diagram often referred to as a conceptual model. Involving those with an interest in the risk assessment output at this stage is essential.

Taking a stepwise approach to the risk assessment is vital: The identification of hazards, the assessment of exposures and the estimation of risk and the subsequent evaluation of the significance of the risk follow a logical sequence: What is at risk and what is it at risk from? What and how might it happen? How large will the consequences be and how probable are they? What criteria will be used to judge their significance? How significant are the probabilities and consequences and how certain is the assessment of probability and consequence?

Be prepared to iterate: As the risk assessment proceeds, one often discovers new information that necessitates a revision of one's previous assumptions. Assessments that allow for iteration are useful because they facilitate review, may help avoid the incorporation of systematic bias and they ensure that the risk assessment process is developmental rather than being treated as a black box.

Risk assessments should be fit for purpose: Detailed quantitative work will not be required in every case and many potential risks can be screened out early on using a sound logic based on the source–pathway–receptor concept. Allowing for different tiers of sophistication of analysis ensures that a sound logic is established before progressing to quantitative assessment and, consequently, that resources are focused on the higher priority, more complex risks. An important aspect of tiering is ensuring that a defensible justification is provided for risks screened out and that the remaining risks are carried over into the next tier of analysis. At any point, the assessor may need to revisit the justification for screening a risk issue out.

The assessment–management interface: In practice, there is an iterative exchange of information throughout between risk assessment and management simply because certain practical management measures may often be anticipated or known quite early on in the assessment. Some frameworks explicitly emphasize a distinction between the risk analysis and assessing the significance of the risk. Communicating with, and involving, others is essential throughout.

Practicality: Risk assessments should not be overly complex, but guide the practitioner through the various steps and considerations. It should not force a level of analysis that is disproportionate to the risk. Throughout, the assessor should practice an approach to risk assessment that is commensurate with the supporting science.

Future trends

Future trends in the assessment of environmental risk are likely to see its continued expansion to more strategic levels of assessment (programmes of activity) and to the comparative assessment of many risks within an individual assessment. We can expect greater use of probabilistic techniques as these become more accessible and the current demand for greater openness in the process to continue.

References and further reading

Calow, P. (1997) *Handbook of Environmental Risk Assessment and Management*, Blackwell Science Limited, Oxford

DETR (2000) 'Environment Agency and IEH Guidelines for Environmental Risk Assessment and Management', The Stationery Office, London

EA (2000) *Introducing Environmental Risk Assessment*, HO-06/00 (reprint 2/02), Environment Agency, Bristol

EEA (1998) *Environmental Risk Assessment: Approaches, Experiences and Information Sources*, European Environment Agency, Copenhagen

HSE (2001) *Reducing Risks, Protecting People*, Health and Safety Executive Books, Sudbury

Presidential/Congressional Commission on Risk Assessment and Risk Management (1997) 'Volume I, Framework for Environmental Health Risk Management' and 'Volume II, Risk Assessment and Risk Management in Regulatory Decision-Making', Presidential/Congressional Commission on Risk Assessment and Risk Management, Washington DC, available at www.riskworld.com

SNIFFER (1999) *Communicating Understanding of Contaminated Land Risks*, Sniffer Publication SR97(11)F, Foundation for Water Research, London

Chapter 4.4

Life Cycle Assessment

Introduction

In the past, environmental management initiatives have tended to focus on specific sites. Examples include: an environmental impact assessment of a proposed new development, modifications to an industrial process in response to new emissions standards, and a company adopting an environmental management system. More recently a different approach to environmental management has become popular – this is life cycle thinking. In life cycle thinking, the focus is not on a specific site, process or organization but instead on an overall view of the impacts of products and services used in the economy.

For example, a washing machine provides the service of cleaned clothes to its owner and it uses electricity, water and detergents on a regular basis over a number of years to provide this service. However, in order to produce the washing machine, raw materials must be extracted, processed and manufactured. The machine is then delivered to the shop, and transported on to the consumer. The electricity, water and detergents used by the consumer all have their own upstream and downstream environmental impacts. And when the machine has reached the end of its service life, it becomes waste – to be disposed of, recycled or reused.

This way of thinking about products and services is illustrated in Figure 4.4.1. It involves looking along the whole life cycle from extraction of raw materials from the Earth all the way through to the return of these materials to the Earth. On the diagram, the arrows show the flows of materials and energy to and from the Earth for the different life cycle stages.

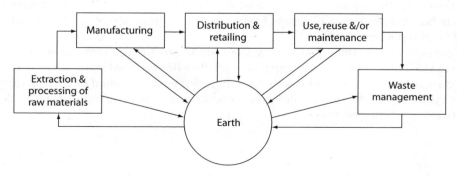

Figure 4.4.1   The life cycle approach

This systems approach is the basis of an environmental management tool called life cycle assessment (LCA) – the approach is summarized in Figure 4.4.2. This is an economic system that consists of a number of life cycle stages such as extraction of raw materials and manufacturing. The system produces one or more functional outputs; these may be products, but LCA defines them in terms of benefits, functions or services rather than materials. In order to produce these functional outputs, the economic system requires inputs of materials and energy and generates outputs of emissions to air, water and land. The inputs and outputs together are termed the environmental interventions associated with the economic system. They contribute to various environmental problems, and the magnitude of these contributions is assessed in LCA.

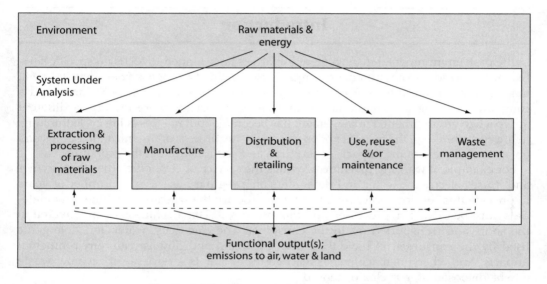

Figure 4.4.2   The systems approach in LCA

The benefits of LCA, compared with other environmental management tools, can be summarized as follows:

- In the evaluation of an existing system, significant impacts in the environmental life cycle become obvious. This helps in the prioritization of activities to improve environmental performance.
- In considering improvements to a system, trade-offs between improvements at one life cycle stage and increased impacts at another life cycle stage are revealed.
- In comparing two alternative systems with major environmental impacts at different life cycle stages, the assessment gives a comprehensive overview of the trade-offs between the two systems.

LCA methodology

The Society of Environmental Toxicology and Chemistry (SETAC) has acted as an umbrella body for the development of LCA methodology, and provides a forum for LCA practitioners. Recently, a series of standards (ISO, 1997) – the ISO 14040 series – has been developed to provide guidance on undertaking LCA studies. The description of LCA methodology in this section follows the approach taken in the ISO standards.

Four different phases of LCA have been identified. They are:

- **Goal and scope definition:** The goal and scope of the LCA study are defined in relation to the intended application.
- **Inventory analysis:** The inventory analysis involves the collection of data and the calculation procedures. The result of this phase is a table that quantifies the relevant inputs and outputs of the system under analysis.
- **Impact assessment:** The impact assessment translates the results of the inventory analysis into environmental impacts (e.g. ozone depletion). The aim of this phase is to evaluate the significance of environmental impacts.
- **Interpretation:** At this phase conclusions and recommendations for decision makers are drawn from the inventory analysis and impact assessment.

These phases are shown diagrammatically in Figure 4.4.3. The diagram shows that, in practice, LCA involves a series of iterations as its scope is redefined on the basis of insights gained throughout the study.

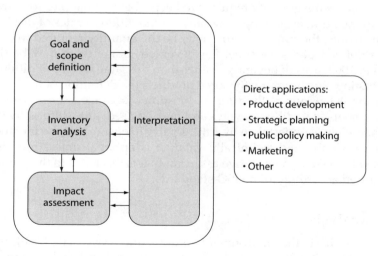

Source: ISO, 1997

Figure 4.4.3   The phases of life cycle assessment

Goal and scope definition

This first phase involves defining the goal of the study, its system boundaries, data requirements, functional unit and any need for critical review. The goal of the study is shaped by its sponsor, and it is important that it is clearly defined to avoid any subsequent misunderstandings about the wider applicability of the results. For example, a study carried out by a company to compare two alternative production processes may be adequate for internal decision making, but its results may not be appropriate for public policy making if the data are not representative of the national situation.

Having defined the goal, scoping involves defining system boundaries and other requirements for the study. These may include the geographical applicability of the results, time horizons over which the analysis is relevant, and the focus of the study, which could lead to omissions from the analysis of particular processes or stages of the life cycle.

Data requirements include the types of data to be collected, the quality of the data and the data collection process. Data are usually collected in three categories: physical inputs (energy and raw material inputs), products and emissions. Data quality tends to be a problem in LCAs, and has been the subject of a number of reports (Fava et al, 1994; Hemming, 1995; Beaufort-Langeveld et al, 2003). Various tagging systems have been suggested for indicating data quality, and database formats have been suggested to standardize data collection and facilitate compilation of common data sets. A complete absence of data is commonplace, and for these situations sensitivity analysis can be used to determine the impact of data deficiencies and omissions on the final LCA results. It is important that the data collection process is undertaken systematically and transparently.

Definition of an appropriate functional unit is fundamental to the credibility of an LCA. The functional unit is the unit of analysis for the study, and it provides a basis for comparison if more than one alternative is being studied. It should be defined in terms of the service(s) provided by any product, process or activity under analysis. For example, an appropriate functional unit for an LCA study of disposable and cloth nappies for babies is the quantity required to keep a baby in nappies for 6 months. This is preferred to the number of nappies because of the different rates of use for these two products. For paints, the functional unit may be the quantity required to cover $10m^2$ of surface for a defined period of time. For beverage containers it may be the quantity used to deliver 1000 litres of beverage, rather than the same weight of different types of paint or packaging. Furthermore, for some products the definition of the functional unit depends on the behaviour of the user or consumer, because alternative products are packaged or dispersed in different ways and may be used quite differently (Clift, 1993).

The critical review is undertaken by a third party to ensure that the methodology and report are scientifically and technically valid. It is optional unless the results of the study are used to make a comparative assertion that is disclosed to the public, in which case it is required according to the ISO standards.

Inventory analysis

At the inventory phase, the environmental interventions associated with the life cycle for the functional unit are quantified. These are the material and energy inputs, and product and emission outputs to air, water and land. The methodology involves drawing a boundary around the system under analysis and quantifying the inputs and outputs across this boundary. Within the system, a number of discrete unit processes are identified, and input–output analysis is undertaken for each unit process, including transportation. As an example, Figure 4.4.4 shows the unit processes that might be investigated in a life cycle assessment of apples.

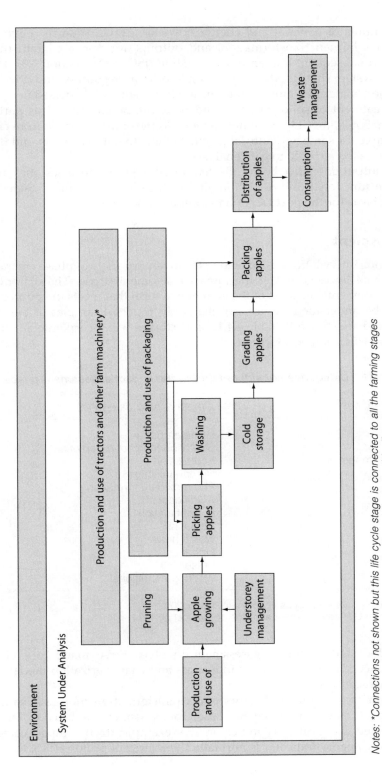

Notes: *Connections not shown but this life cycle stage is connected to all the farming stages
Energy is used in all the life cycle stages but is not shown on this diagram

Source: Cowell and Wright, 2002

Figure 4.4.4   Flow diagram for an LCA of apples

In an LCA, inputs of material and energy flows are drawn from the environment without previous human transformation, and outputs are discarded into the environment without subsequent human transformation (ISO, 1997, Section 3.3). Thus the overall product system should extend upstream to primary resources, and downstream to the point where material is emitted into the environment and dispersed in an uncontrolled way. Treatment of solid waste should therefore be considered as part of the product system. Sometimes LCAs do not encompass the entire life cycle from cradle to grave, for example for some agricultural products they do not extend beyond the farm gate, and this is called a cradle to gate analysis.

Once input–output data have been collected for all the unit processes, they are standardized to the functional unit, and compiled as a series of inventory tables. These tables form the basis for the next LCA phase: impact assessment.

Impact assessment

The environmental interventions calculated in the inventory analysis phase are translated into environmental impacts during the impact assessment phase. The objective is to present the environmental impacts of the system in a form that meets the purpose of the study and can be understood by users of the study results. Examples of the types of impact considered are shown in Table 4.4.1. Most studies will incorporate a majority of these impacts into their impact assessment.

Table 4.4.1   Categories considered during the impact assessment phase

Input related categories	Output related categories
Abiotic resources*	Climate change*
Biotic resources	Stratospheric ozone depletion*
Land use (land competition*)	Ecotoxicity*
Water use	Human toxicity*
	Photo-oxidant formation*
	Acidification*
	Eutrophication*
	Radiation
	Waste heat
	Odour
	Noise
	Working conditions

Note: *Described as baseline impact categories by Guinée, 2002
Source: Adapted from Guinée et al, 1993 and Udo de Haes et al, 1999

According to ISO 14042, impact assessment involves three mandatory elements: selection of impact categories, category indicators and characterization models; classification; and characterization.

Impact categories, category indicators and characterization models: Examples of the types of impact category that may be chosen for assessment are listed in Table 4.4.1. They are quantified using category indicators. For example, for the impact category of acidification, the category indicator is normally the release of protons (H^+). For climate change, the indicator is normally infrared radiative forcing in Watts per square metre (W/m^2). Characterization models are then used to model the process occurring in the cause–effect chain. For a number of categories, internationally agreed characterization models exist. An example is the Intergovernmental Panel on Climate Change (IPCC) computer model for climate change. For other categories, the development of characterization models is still the subject of research. Examples here include land use and depletion of biotic resources.

Classification: The inventory analysis data are assigned to certain impact assessment categories. Thus, in the life cycle of apples, sulphur dioxide emissions to air from energy consumption may contribute to the acidification and human toxicity categories, and nitrous oxide emissions to air from use of fertilizers and manure contribute to the climate change category.

Characterization: The data are aggregated within each impact assessment category to give one value for acidification, human toxicity, climate change and so on. This is accomplished by using conversion factors such as acidification potentials (APs) and global warming potentials (GWPs). For example, the IPCC publishes GWPs for carbon dioxide, methane, nitrous oxide and halocarbons (Houghton et al, 1996); global warming gas emissions calculated as part of the inventory analysis are multiplied by these factors and then aggregated to give an overall value for GWP relative to the functional unit.

At this stage there is still no way of ascertaining the relative importance of the different environmental impacts, or aggregating them to give an overall assessment of environmental impact. This can be done by normalizing the aggregated data in each impact category against the magnitude of that environmental impact within a certain area – for example, the UK or Europe. Thus, it is possible to estimate an overall value of GWP for the UK based on annual releases of global warming gases, and the impact assessment result can then be normalized against this value.

Each impact category can then be weighted and the weighted impact categories summed to give the overall environmental impact. This is the weighting element of impact assessment. It is obviously very subjective, and the results will depend upon the values and preferences of individuals involved in the assessment. It may be appropriate to use decision-theory techniques such as outranking methods (Seppälä et al, 2002) to decide on the weighting factors, or to undertake a qualitative final assessment without use of explicit weighting factors. In practice, most LCA studies omit the normalization and weighting elements of impact assessment, and proceed straight to the interpretation phase.

Interpretation

During the final phase of interpretation, the results of the analysis are discussed and opportunities for reducing the environmental impacts associated with the functional unit are identified and evaluated. ISO 14043 states that this phase should include communication of the study results in a form that is both comprehensible and useful to the decision maker.

ISO 14040 recommends that a critical review of the LCA study is undertaken if the results involve comparative assertions – for example, comparing plastic and glass bottles, or disposable versus reusable nappies – and particularly if they are to be disclosed to the public. The critical review may be undertaken by an internal expert who has not been involved in the LCA study, by an independent external expert or by an independent external expert with the support of a review panel of other independent experts.

Applications of LCA

LCA can be used to support strategic and operational decision making and awareness raising. In the latter case, the main focus is on the learning experience and educational benefits of undertaking an LCA study rather than on making a decision; however, it can be expected that the information provided by the study will affect subsequent decisions by those considering the LCA results. Application areas for LCA include:

- **Product design and product improvement:** Studies are conducted to provide information to support product design decisions, and to benchmark the environmental performance of products against others performing a similar function or against environmental standards. Design for the environment (DfE) is an approach incorporating simplified life cycle assessment techniques to enable a product developer to obtain a quick overview of the implications of design decisions.
- **Public policy making:** There is increasing interest in using LCA to underpin public sector decisions on policy and practice. For example, the Waste Strategy 2000 of the Department for Environment, Food and Rural Affairs (Defra, 2000) argues for a life cycle approach, and the WISARD LCA based software tool has been developed for use by local authorities to support implementation of that strategy.
- **Marketing:** Organizations may use LCA studies to market the environmental credentials of their products or services. One such mechanism is eco-labelling, where an environmental label is awarded to products meeting certain specified criteria in a product category (such as washing machines, toilet paper or paints). The product category criteria are generally established on the basis of LCA study results.
- **Strategic planning:** Studies are used to support decisions taken at an organizational level with a long term focus.
- **Supply chain management:** An LCA study may show that an organization, at one point in the life cycle of a product, may have the greatest scope to improve the product life cycle by selecting suppliers with better environmental performance rather than, or in addition to, focusing on its own operations.
- **Industrial ecology:** The idea behind industrial ecology is that wastes from one product or process can be used as inputs to another – industrial ecology goes beyond assessing the life cycle to closing it. One example is the systematic use and reuse of a material in a cascade of applications, usually with progressively lower performance specifications. Another embodiment is the linking of processes, rather than products, for systematic use and reuse of process streams, and the establishment of eco-industrial parks to facilitate these interactions (Ehrenfeld and Gertler, 1997).

Several common themes have emerged in the discussion on applications of LCA. They include: use of simplified life cycle approaches; integration of LCA with other environmental management approaches; combining the assessment of environmental impacts with economic and social impacts; and the most appropriate ways to communicate LCA results. The term 'life cycle management' (LCM) has been coined to embrace these themes, and take forward the research agenda on implementation of LCA (Sonnemann et al, 2001). LCM has been defined by the SETAC Europe Working Group on LCM as:

> an integrated framework of concepts, techniques and procedures to address environmental, economic, technological and social aspects of products and organizations to achieve continuous environmental improvement from a life cycle perspective (Hunkeler et al, 2001).

The three examples of LCA in use described below show how it can support decision making.

Unilever

Unilever has undertaken LCA studies over the last decade to inform and guide its environmental management activities. LCA experts in the company conduct comprehensive LCAs of selected products in order to identify critical environmental impacts and guide improvement initiatives; the information is conveyed to product developers and also used to support the launch of new products.

For example, reports are available on the Unilever web site summarizing the environmental trade-offs between using clothes washing tablets and unit dose capsules as opposed to self measured powders and liquids. LCAs have been used to make the comparisons and assess the whole life cycle of washing clothes, including the washing cycle and wastewater management as well as upstream production of the tablets/capsules, packaging, transport and so on (Unilever, 2000; 2001). More recently, Unilever has developed a set of simplified life cycle tools that are available on the Unilever intranet for product developers to use as an integral part of the design process. Unilever has also undertaken LCA studies of product categories such as tea, tomato sauces and frozen vegetables in order to identify opportunities for improvement.

Finally, strategic LCA studies have been undertaken using an approach called overall business impact assessment. This approach involves assessing the relative potential environmental life cycle impacts of business activities, compared with global potential environmental impacts, and scaling them against the company's contribution to the world economy measured as sales divided by global gross domestic product (Taylor, 1996; McKeown, 2000). The results have assisted the company in identifying where its operations are contributing more environmental impacts than economic value on a global scale.

Waste Strategy 2000

The UK Government's Waste Strategy 2000 for England and Wales, launched in summer 2000, states that decisions on waste management should be based on a local assessment of the best practicable environmental option. In order to facilitate such decisions by local authorities and businesses, the Environment Agency has developed a software tool called WISARD (Waste: Integrated Systems Assessment for Recovery and Disposal) which uses LCA to compare different waste management options at a local level. Use of LCA is encouraged because it assesses a number of environmental impacts, models impacts occurring outside the waste management system as well as within it, and takes account of the proximity principle through the inclusion of transport in the analysis (Defra, 2000, Chapter 3). In the most recent version of WISARD emphasis is placed on making the software user-friendly for non-experts, and it also offers flexibility in the formatting of results to suit the needs of a range of stakeholders.

EC Eco-labelling Scheme

The EC's Eco-labelling Scheme was established in 1992. It followed on from the success of various national schemes such as Germany's Blue Angel Scheme, which issued its first environmental label in 1978, Canada's Environmental Choice Programme founded in 1988, and Japan's Eco Mark Programme, which was launched in 1989 (OECD, 1991). These schemes award eco-labels to products in certain categories that meet specified environmental criteria. To date, eco-labelling criteria have been established for product categories as diverse as dishwashers, paints, portable computers, soil improvers and tourist accommodation.

According to the original EC Regulation on Eco-Labelling, criteria for eco-labelling product categories had to be established based on life cycle analyses. Therefore LCA studies have been undertaken to support development of criteria for the product categories. The challenges that have arisen in conducting the LCAs include: defining a common basis for comparing equivalent products, for example hairstyling aids that may be delivered using aerosols, hand-pumped dispensers or gels; defining criteria applicable on a Europe-wide basis when aspects such as power generation and waste management policies are so variable between countries (Clift, 1993); and whether relative weightings of different environmental impacts can be applied generically across all countries. In 2000, a revision of the EC regulation was adopted which replaced the original requirement to use comprehensive LCA by a requirement to use life cycle considerations. A main driver in this change has been a desire to speed up the whole process (ENDS, 2000).

References and further reading

Asian Institute of Technology (2003) 'Qualitative Life Cycle Study of a Whiteboard Marker and Quantitative LCA of Paperboard Packaging in Thailand', available from www.howproductsimpact.net/

Beaufort-Langeveld, A. de et al (2003) *Code of Life-cycle Inventory Practice*, SETAC-Europe, Brussels

Clift, R. (1993) 'Life Cycle Assessment and Ecolabelling', *Journal of Cleaner Production*, vol 1, nos 3–4, pp155–159

Cowell, S., Fairman, R. and Lofstedt, R. (2002) 'Risk Assessment and Life Cycle Assessment: A Common Research Agenda?', *Risk Analysis*, vol 22, no 5, pp879–894

Cowell, S., Nebel, B. and Clift, R. (2003) *Introduction To Life Cycle Assessment*, Centre for Environmental Strategy, University of Surrey, Guildford

Cowell, S. and Wright, E. (2002) 'Food Choices and Environmental Impacts', CD-ROM, Centre for Environmental Strategy, University of Surrey, Guildford

Defra (2000) 'Waste Strategy 2000 for England and Wales', Department of the Environment, Transport and Regions, www.defra.gov.uk/environment/waste/strategy/cm4693/index.htm

Ehrenfeld, J. and Gertler, N. (1997) 'Industrial Ecology in Practice. The Evolution of Interdependence at Kalundborg', *Journal of Industrial Ecology*, vol 1, no 1, pp67–79

ENDS (2000) *EC Eco-labelling Regulation Adopted*, The ENDS Report, 306, 39, London

Fava, J. et al (1994) *Life-cycle Assessment, Data Quality: A Conceptual Framework*, Society of Environmental Toxicology and Chemistry (SETAC) and SETAC Foundation, Pensacola

Guinée, J. (ed) (2002) *Handbook on Life Cycle Assessment. Operational Guide to the ISO Standards*, Kluwer Academic Publishers, Dordrecht

Guinée, J. et al (1993) 'Quantitative Life Cycle Assessment of Products 2. Classification, Valuation and Improvement Analysis', *Journal of Cleaner Production*, vol 1, no 2, pp81–91

Hemming, C. (1995) *Directory of Life Cycle Inventory Data Sources*, SPOLD, Brussels

Houghton, J. et al (eds) (1996) *Climate Change 1995. The Science of Climate Change*, contribution of Working Group I to the Second Assessment Report of the Intergovernmental Panel on Climate Change, Cambridge University Press, Cambridge

Hunkeler, D. et al (2001) *Life Cycle Management – Definitions, Case Studies and Corporate Applications*, preliminary edn, Society of Environmental Toxicology and Chemistry Working Group on LCM, Lausanne, cited in Sonnemann et al (2001)

ISO (1997) 'ISO 14040 Environmental Management – Life Cycle Assessment – Principles and Framework', International Organization for Standardization, Geneva

McKeown, P. (2000) 'Integrating LCA into an Organisation's EMS', presentation at Environmental Life Cycle Approaches course, University of Surrey, Guildford

OECD (1991) *Environmental Labelling in OECD Countries*, Organisation for Economic Co-operation and Development, Paris

Pré Consultants (2003) An introduction to LCA and a listing of related LCA links is available from www.pre.nl/life_cycle_assessment/

Seppälä, J., Basson, L. and Norris, G. (2002) 'Decision Analysis Frameworks for Life-cycle Impact Assessment', *Journal of Industrial Ecology*, vol 5, no 4, pp45–68

Sonnemann, G. et al (2001) 'Life Cycle Management: UNEP-Workshop. Sharing Experiences on LCM', *The International Journal of Life Cycle Assessment*, vol 6, no 6, pp325–333

Taylor, A. (1996) 'Overall Business Impact Assessment (OBIA)', Proceedings of 4th Symposium for Case Studies, Society of Environmental Toxicology and Chemistry, Brussels

Udo de Haes, H. et al (1999) 'Best Available Practice Regarding Impact Categories and Category Indicators in Life Cycle Impact Assessment', *The International Journal of Life Cycle Assessment*, vol 4, no 2, pp1–15

Unilever (2000) 'Tablet Detergents. Towards a More Sustainable Future', Unilever HPC, Europe, available from www.unilever.com/environmentsociety/environmentalmanagement/lifecycleassessment/

Unilever (2001) 'Unit Dose. A Sustainability Step for Fabrics Liquids', Unilever HPC, Europe, available from www.unilever.com/environmentsociety/environmentalmanagement/lifecycleassessment/

US EPA (2004) The Environmental Protection Agency's web pages are available at www.epa.gov/ord/

Wenzel, H., Hauschild, M. and Alting, L. (1997) *Environmental Assessment of Products, Volume 1, Methodology, Tools and Case Studies in Product Development*, Kluwer Academic Publishers, Dordrecht

Wenzel, H., Hauschild, M. and Alting, L. (1998) *Environmental Assessment of Products, Volume 2, Scientific Background*, Chapman & Hall, London

Other sources of information

Graedel, T. (1998) *Streamlined Life-cycle Assessment*, Prentice Hall Inc, New Jersey

Jensen, A. et al (1998) *Life Cycle Assessment. A Guide to Approaches, Experiences and Information Sources*, European Environment Agency, Copenhagen

Organizations and publications

The International Journal of Life Cycle Assessment provides the latest research findings on LCA methodology and reports of LCA case studies. For further information go to www.scientificjournals.com/sj/lca/welcome.htm.

The Society of Environmental Toxicology and Chemistry (SETAC) has acted as the umbrella body for the development of LCA methodology over the last decade. Its web site, www.setac.org/, gives details of upcoming events and LCA publications.

The UNEP SETAC Life Cycle Initiative is a collaborative project between UNEP and SETAC. This aims to put life cycle thinking into practice and improve the supporting tools through better data and indicators. The initiative can be viewed at www.uneptie.org/pc/sustain/lcinitiative/home.htm.

LCA software packages include

www.gabi-software.com gives details of GaBi software produced by P. E. Europe GmbH and the University of Stuttgart.

www.pre.nl/simapro/default.htm gives details of SimaPro software produced by Pré Consultants.

www.lcait.com/ gives details of LCAiT software produced by CIT Ekologik.

www.ecobalance.com/uk_team.php gives details of TEAM software produced by Ecobilan.

Section 5

Evaluating Environmental Performance

Chapter 5.1

Emissions and Contamination Standards

Emissions to atmosphere

Emissions to atmosphere can occur from a range of sources including heating and cooling equipment, industrial, commercial and domestic premises, waste disposal facilities and transportation – aircraft, trains, ships and road vehicles. These emissions can be discharged to atmosphere by design (through a stack, vent or other defined route), accidentally through leaking seals/joints or damaged equipment, or by diffusion through the ground. Many common emissions (e.g. nitrogen oxides, sulphur oxides, sulphides, methane and other organic compounds) also arise from natural sources such as forest fires, volcanic activity and natural biological decay.

This mixture of natural and man made emissions from both national and international sources combine through a number of dispersion (transport) processes to define air quality at any receptor location in the world. The relative fraction of each emission source to arrive at any receptor is determined by factors such as source strength, emission conditions, dispersive conditions, physical and chemical depletion mechanisms within the atmosphere and distance between the source and the receptor.

The sources from which emissions arise determine their chemical composition. This, together with subsequent chemical reactions in the atmosphere, determines the potential to cause harm to human health and the environment. The greater the potential to cause harm, the more stringent are the controls that are applied to the emission source.

The control of emissions from man made sources takes place by one of two processes. The first is the certification of an approved emission level, which is usually applied to transportation sources. The second is the specification of an emission concentration or emission rate to be achieved by process design, which is usually applied to industrial and commercial sources.

Emissions are subject to control through international protocols and agreements, and European and national legislation. There have been differences in English and Scottish law for some and since the establishment of the Welsh Assembly further differences have been introduced. For simplicity, in this section references are limited to legislation that applies in England. International protocols or treaties, for example the Montreal Protocol 1987 as amended (UNEP, 2000), are adopted to phase out emissions of substances that are damaging to the environment on a worldwide scale (e.g. ozone depletion in the upper atmosphere), which cannot be addressed at the national level.

International agreements are also used to regulate emissions from, for example, aircraft through an engine certification process (ICAO, 1995).

European Union (EU) directives are used to set uniform emission limits, and air quality standards, across member countries that are designed to protect human health and the environment while maintaining 'single market' economic conditions. National legislation is then used to implement these directives. National legislation is also used to control emissions of other polluting substances that are not subject to control through European legislation but are seen as damaging on a local scale. In this context national legislation has been applied, for example to the control of dark smoke (UK Parliament, 1993) and odours (UK Parliament, 1990a).

Emissions of exhaust gases from motor vehicles are controlled through national legislation that often differs from country to country. Emissions from vehicles therefore have to comply with the laws in the country where they are used and not necessarily those that apply in the manufacturing country. In Europe there are a series of directives that specify the maximum permissible emission rates of key pollutants for different engine types and sizes operating under specified conditions. These directives have been enacted in the UK. Emission legislation is gradually being extended to include off-road vehicles (e.g. construction plant) and shipping.

Improvements in certified emissions from transportation sources can and do occur as technology advances but the rate of change can be slow due to the low rate of introduction of new and scrapping of old vehicles and aircraft. Moreover, as the demand for travel is increasing, the value of technological improvements is reduced by the increases in distances travelled by more people. Some technological improvements (e.g. in aircraft engines) have successfully reduced the emission of some pollutants (noise, carbon monoxide and hydrocarbons) through better fuel combustion. These improvements have also reduced fuel consumption. These benefits, however, were obtained at a cost of increased emissions of nitrogen oxides.

The control of emissions from industrial premises and nuisance has a long history in the UK dating back to the Alkali and Public Health Acts of the late 1800s and early 1900s. In the last 30 years or so there has been a succession of new statutes and regulations to control emissions from not only the traditionally regulated chemical industry but also food processing, waste disposal, paint spraying, cremation and many other activities. Historically, regulation of emissions control was directed towards achieving a specified pollutant concentration (UK Parliament, 1906) using 'best practicable means' which was subsequently modified to have due regard to economics.

While this concept has been maintained through best available techniques not entailing excessive cost (BATNEEC) in the integrated pollution control (IPC) section of the Environmental Protection Act (EPA) (UK Parliament, 1990b), there is significant movement now towards the use of best available technology (BAT) in the current Pollution Prevention and Control (PPC) Act (UK Parliament, 1999). The IPC section of the EPA (UK Parliament, 1990b) was replaced by the PPC Act in order to implement the Integrated Pollution Prevention and Control (IPPC) Directive (EC, 1996). Implicit in the change is a movement away from specified emission limits towards minimizing emissions through the use of best available technology. It is evident, through this succession of legislative changes, that emission concentrations and total emissions have been progressively reduced. These tighter limits have also affected the operating economics of some processes and this has resulted in the closure of some plants.

The complexity of IPC and PPC legislation, and the number of process sectors that are subject to them, has necessitated the production of both general guidance (DoE, 1997a; Defra, 2002), and industry sector specific guidance (HMIP, 1990; EA, 2001a). As a consequence, a range of emission limits apply to IPC or PPC regulated processes. As an illustration, Table 5.1.1 shows the emissions to air that are associated with the use of BAT in ferrous foundries. The guidance in some sectors (e.g. incineration) is inherently more complex as it is necessary to take account of other directives (EEC, 1989a, 1989b; EC, 1994). Table 5.1.2 sets out the limit values from the Waste Incineration Directive (EC, 2000), which are used as the benchmark for incineration processes that fall within the definition of hazardous within the directive. It is recognized in the guidance that emissions from different types of incinerator will vary but will gradually converge on, if not improve on, those specified in the Waste Incineration Directive through the application of BAT.

Table 5.1.1   Interim emissions – ferrous foundry sector

Process	Emission	New Processes – Abated Release		
		Average concentration mg/m³	Peak concentration mg/m³	Mass emission g/tonne of product
Electric arc furnace (EAF) Secondary	Particulate	10	20	50
EAF combined extraction	Particulate	15	30	
Roof extraction	Particulate	10	20	20
Ladle treatment	Particulate	10	20	–
General local extraction	Particulate	10	–	–
Leaded steel processes	Lead	3	–	–
Stainless steel & special alloy processes	Chromium	4	–	–
	Nickel	2	–	–
All iron & steel processes	Dioxins (ITEQ)	1ng/m³	–	–
	Cadmium	0.2	–	–
	Lead	1	–	–
	Chromium	2	–	–
	Nickel	1	–	–
	VOCs* as total carbon	50	–	–
	Fluorides	5	–	–

Notes:
1 Figures are based on measurements taken at the point of discharge.
2 The average concentration figures refer to measurements taken over a complete process cycle for batch operations. For continuous processes, releases are based on an hourly average figure over a rolling 24 hour period taking into account only the hours when the plant is in actual operation, including startup and shutdown. The maximum hourly average value should not exceed the release level indicated in the table.
3 *The term 'volatile organic compounds' (VOCs) includes all organic compounds released to air in the gas phase. For details of the classification scheme see Appendix 1 of EA, 2001a.
4 Operators should be aware of the potential for the release of polychlorinated dibenzo-p-dioxins and polychlorinated dibenzofurans (dioxins) from metals processes particularly in secondary recovery/refining processes. An achievable release of 1ng/m³ international toxic equivalent (ITEQ) is appropriate.
5 All releases must be controlled and minimized to ensure that ambient air quality beyond the process boundary complies, as a minimum, with air quality standards (see Ref 11 of EA, 2001a).

Source: EA, 2001a

Table 5.1.2 Waste Incineration Directive Annex V: Air Emission Limit Values

Pollutant	Directive Requirement		
	ELV (mg/m³ unless stated)[1]	Averaging/Monitoring Period	Monitoring Frequency
Total Dust	10	Daily average	Continuous
Total Dust	30	100% ½ hourly averages	
Total Dust	10	97% ½ hourly averages	
VOCs (as total organic carbon – TOC)	10	Daily average	Continuous
VOCs (as TOC)	20	100% ½ hourly averages	
VOCs (as TOC)	10	97% ½ hourly averages	
Hydrogen chloride gas (HCl)	10	Daily average	Continuous (periodic may be used where emission *cannot* exceed ELV)
HCl	60	100% ½ hourly averages	
HCl	10	97% ½ hourly averages	
HF	1	Daily average	Continuous (periodic may be used where emission cannot exceed ELV or where HCl ELVs complied with)
HF	4	100% ½ hourly averages	
HF	2	97% ½ hourly averages	
SO_2	50	Daily average	Continuous (periodic may be used where emission cannot exceed ELV)
SO_2	200	100% ½ hourly averages	
SO_2	50	97% ½ hourly averages	
NO_x (nitrogen monoxide and nitrogen dioxide expressed as nitrogen dioxide)	200	Daily average	Continuous
NO_x (as above)	400	100% ½ hourly averages	
NO_x (as above)	200	97% ½ hourly averages	

Table 5.1.2 *continued*

CO	50	Daily average	
CO	150	95% of 10 minute averages	Continuous
CO	100	100% of ½ hourly averages	
Cd and Tl	Total 0.05		
Hg	0.05	All average values over the sample period (30 minutes to 8 hours) to be less than these limites	Periodic – 2 per year but 1 every 3 months during the first year of operation
Sb, As, Pb, Cr, Co, Cu, Mn, Ni and V	Total 0.5		
Dioxins and furans	0.1ng/m³ TEQ	CEN method (EN 1948, Parts 1, 2 and 3) sample period 6 to 8 hours	Periodic – 2 per year but 1 every 3 months during the first year of operation

Notes:
1   Reference conditions: 273K, 101.3kPa, 11% O_2, dry gas.
2   Emission limit values (ELVs) apply at all times when waste is being burned (except for CO during startup and shutdown).
3   The ELVs for metals include solid, gaseous and vapour forms as well as their compounds.
4   Toxic equivalent (TEQ) should be calculated as described in Annex 1 of the directive.
5   The directive provides for certain derogations in respect of NO_x and particulate emissions from existing plants. These are not generally expected to be applicable in the UK as BAT will achieve the required ELV.
6   The agency will generally apply the 100 percentile limits for both daily and ½ hourly ELVs.
7   Derogation from the above CO ELVs is available for fluidized beds up to 100mg/m³ as an hourly average.
8   The Waste Incineration Directive goes beyond ELVs. Permits will also be required to include an extensive range of conditions to ensure high operational standards.
9   Monitoring techniques should be European Committee for Standardization (CEN) or where not available, national or international standards. Further guidance is given in Section 2.10 of EA, 2001b.
Source: EA, 2001b

Emissions to atmosphere, administrative issues

In the early days of industrial emission regulation there was essentially a single agency, the Alkali Inspectorate, which was responsible for enforcement. The enforcement of environmental or public health regulation was undertaken by the local authority. This position remains broadly similar although the names of the enforcement agencies have changed (several times) and the extent of regulation is considerably wider.

The control of emissions from landfill waste disposal sites was achieved through licensing under the Control of Pollution Act 1974 (UK Parliament, 1974) by the Waste Disposal Authority. These powers were transferred to the Environment Agency (EA), which incorporated the National Rivers Authority (NRA), HM Inspectorate of Pollution (HMIP) and the Waste Disposal Authority, following the enactment of the Environment Act 1995 (UK Parliament, 1995a). The original licensing system was replaced by Waste Management Licensing Regulations under the EPA (UK Parliament, 1994). For some waste sites these regulations are incorporated into the PPC regime. Both sets of regulations continue to be enforced in England and Wales by the EA. The EA is also responsible for the enforcement of most industrial emissions legislation except for those from smaller processes that still fall to the local authority.

Activities that give rise to emissions to atmosphere are subject to a number of other regulations. For example, the Town and Country Planning Act 1990 (UK Parliament, 1990c) provides the framework for consenting the use and development of land. None of the activities mentioned above would be permitted if planning permission or some other historical established land use (pre-1948) existed. In the granting of consent for a change in land use (e.g. an application that increases the capacity of an existing industrial activity or introduces a new one) pollution issues are material considerations in the determination of the application by the planning authority (usually the local authority). If the emissions from the process are likely to compromise the achievement of one or more of the air quality objectives, this could be used as a reason for the refusal of planning consent.

Ambient air quality

Ambient air quality is itself subject to regulation, which sets a number of standards and objectives for specific pollutants as set out in Table 5.1.3. The establishment of air quality standards is the subject of much debate. The concentrations given in the regulations have been determined by expert panel reviews of the available scientific data on the observed effects on human health of individual pollutants at different concentrations, coupled with an evaluation of the costs, practicability and benefits of achieving lower standards.

The framework for improving air quality in the UK was set out in the Air Quality Strategy (DoE, 1997b), which was subsequently reviewed (DETR, 2000; Defra, 2003c). The strategy was enacted through the Environment Act 1995 (UK Parliament, 1995b) and associated Air Quality Regulations (UK Parliament, 2000, 2002a). In addition there are other regulations (UK Parliament, 2001, 2002b) that implement the European directives on air quality in the UK.

The Environment Act (UK Parliament, 1995b) imposes a duty on the local authority to undertake periodic reviews of air quality in its district to determine whether the objectives are likely to be achieved by the prescribed date for each pollutant, excluding ozone. Guidance (Defra, 2003a, 2003b) on how this review and assessment needs to be undertaken has been published.

If this review and assessment process indicates that one or more objectives will not be achieved by the due date, the local authority needs to declare an air quality management area (AQMA) covering the exceedence area. In this situation, the local authority needs to consult with key stakeholders in the AQMA to develop an action plan, which is designed to improve air quality, enabling the objectives to be attained. It is inevitable that if this occurs the local authority will look carefully at planning applications that might cause deterioration of air quality and recommend to their elected members that they refuse consent for the development. There is some evidence that planning authorities are using breaches, or potential breaches, of air quality objectives as one of the reasons for recommending refusal of planning consent for a range of developments including housing near to a motorway, a supermarket and a fast food outlet in the centre of a town.

If, following the implementation of the management plan, the objectives are not achieved, this would identify a need for further central government controls on emissions to atmosphere through tighter regulation. If this non-compliance arises from vehicle emissions alone then improved air quality may need to be achieved through traffic management and better use of public transport.

Table 5.1.3   Air quality objectives (statutory and non-statutory)

Substance	Statutory or non-statutory	Averaging period	Value ($\mu g/m^3$)	Date to be achieved
Benzene	S	Running annual mean (All UK)	16.25	31 Dec 2003
	S	Annual mean (England and Wales)	**5***	31 Dec 2010
	S	Annual mean (Scotland)	3.25	31 Dec 2010
1,3-Butadiene	S	Running annual mean	2.25	31 Dec 2003
Carbon monoxide	S	Maximum daily running 8 hour mean (equivalent of 100 percentile)	**10 mg/m^{-3}**	31 Dec 2003
Lead	S	Annual mean	**0.5**	31 Dec 2005
	S	Annual mean	0.25	31 Dec 2008
Nitrogen dioxide	S	Annual mean	**40**	31 Dec 2005
	N	Annual mean (for the protection of vegetation and ecosystems)	30	31 Dec 2000
	S	1 hour mean, not more than 18 exceedences a year (equivalent of 99.79 percentile)	**200**	31 Dec 2005
Ozone	N	8 hour mean, not more than 10 exceedences a year (equivalent of 99.1 percentile)	100	31 Dec 2005
PAH	N	Annual mean (to be set in future regulations)	0.25 ng/m^{-3}	31 Dec 2010
PM$_{10}$	S	Annual mean	**40**	31 Dec 2004
	N	Annual mean (England and Wales, not London)	20	31 Dec 2010

continued overleaf

Table 5.1.3   continued

Substance	Statutory or non-statutory	Averaging period	Value ($\mu g/m^3$)	Date to be achieved
PM$_{10}$ continued	S	1 hour mean, not more then 35 exceedences a year (equivalent of 90.41 percentile)	**50**	31 Dec 2004
	N	1 hour mean, not more than 7 exceedences a year (England and Wales, not London) (equivalent of 98.08 percentile)	50	31 Dec 2010
Sulphur dioxide	S	1 hour mean, not to be exceeded more than 24 times a year (equivalent of 99.73 percentile)	**350**	31 Dec 2004
	S	24 hour mean, not to be exceeded more than 3 times a year (equivalent of 99.18 percentile)	**125**	31 Dec 2004
	S	15 min mean, not to be exceeded more than 35 times a year (equivalent of 99.9 percentile)	266	31 Dec 2005
	N	Annual mean for the protection of vegetation and ecosystems	20	31 Dec 2000
	N	Winter mean (October –March) for the protection of vegetation and ecosystems	20	31 Dec 2000

Note: *Figures shown in **bold** are also limit values (UK Parliament, 2001) but the achievement dates may differ

Emissions to land

Land contamination standards are non-statutory in the UK, and are used primarily in the context of assessing whether land is suitable for either its current use or some future proposed use. The Department for Environment, Food and Rural Affairs (Defra) and the EA have developed the risk based Contaminated Land Exposure Assessment (CLEA) Model (Defra/EA, 2002c) for producing soil guideline values (SGVs).

SGVs are relevant when assessing chronic risks to human health from exposure to contaminants in the soil, but are not normally protective of acute exposure, except in specific circumstances where acute risk has been built into the modelling (for example the cyanide SGV is expected to be protective of human health for both short and long term exposure). Furthermore, they are not for use in the context of protection of non-human receptors such as ecological systems, and surface/groundwater. The general approach to protection of these other receptors is briefly described below.

SGVs may be used when making decisions about the need for action to protect human health in relation to land contamination under both the Town and Country Planning Act (UK Parliament, 1990c) and the Part IIA, Environmental Protection Act Contaminated Land Regime (UK Parliament, 1990a). In both regulatory frameworks, SGVs are used as intervention values (Defra/EA, 2002a), where, if a representative concentration of the contaminant in the land exceeds the SGV, then action should be taken to either:

- undertake further investigation to better characterize the site;
- undertake detailed quantitative risk assessment (DQRA) to allow more focused modelling of the circumstances of the particular site; or
- take remediation action to address the risks posed by exposure to the contaminants.

In the context of the planning regime, SGVs may be used to make judgements about action in relation to a proposed new use of land. Under the Part IIA Regime, they are used to deal with risks in relation to the current use of land.

SGVs are derived for different land uses, and hence reflect the risks posed to the most sensitive receptor likely to be present on the land. For example, the critical receptor for residential land use is the female child aged up to 6 years, whereas, the critical receptor for commercial/industrial use is a female adult over a working lifetime of 42 years (ages 17 to 59).

In deriving SGVs, a comparison is made between the average daily exposure of the critical receptor to the contaminant in the ground with the relevant health criteria value (HCV) – a measure of the toxicological properties of the contaminant (Defra/EA, 2002b). Two types of contaminant are considered:

- threshold substances, where there is a threshold of exposure below which no significant health effects are thought to occur; and
- non-threshold substances, where even the smallest exposure is thought to have some health effect.

For threshold substances, the HCV is termed the tolerable daily intake (TDI) – an estimate of the amount of a contaminant, expressed on a bodyweight basis, that can be ingested daily over a lifetime without appreciable health risk. In deriving an SGV, it is appropriate to take account of intakes of the substance from other sources, such as diet, drinking water and air pollution, and this background intake is defined as the mean daily intake (MDI). The amount of substance that can be accepted from exposure to a particular contaminated site is normally the TDI less the MDI (the difference between what can be tolerated and what we are already exposed to). Certain additional rules are applied where background exposure is already high or even exceeds the TDI.

For non-threshold substances, the HCV is based on the premise that exposure should be kept as low as reasonably practicable (the ALARP principle), and the HCV is known as the index dose – a dose which can be considered to present a minimal human health risk from exposure to soil contaminants. For such substances, background intake (the MDI) is not taken into account in defining an SGV as it is expected that exposure will be minimized by other initiatives.

There are three land uses for which SGVs have been published – see Table 5.1.4 – and these are linked to an assumed critical receptor.

Table 5.1.4   Critical receptors for three land uses

Land use	Critical receptor
Residential	Female child aged 0–6 years
Allotments	Female child aged 0–6 years
Commercial/industrial	Female adult aged 17–59 years

Residential land use is further divided to provide SGVs with or without plant uptake – to model the difference in exposure between houses that have gardens for vegetable growing, and town houses or flats where no such garden is available.

A rolling programme of publication of SGVs and supporting HCVs is in hand, as part of the EA/Defra research programme. Substances for which either HCVs or SGVs have been published are set out in Table 5.1.5 They are available on the Defra web site at www.defra.gov.uk.

Table 5.1.5   Substances with HCVs and SGVs*

Substance	Health Criteria Value	Soil Guideline Value
Arsenic	✓	✓
Benzene	✓	
Benzo(a)pyrene	✓	
Cadmium	✓	✓
Chromium	✓	✓
Dioxins, furans and dioxin-like PCBs	✓	
Inorganic cyanide	✓	
Lead	✓	✓
Mercury	✓	✓
Naphthalene	✓	
Nickel	✓	✓
Phenol	✓	
Selenium	✓	✓

Note: *up to December 2003

The publication of HCVs and SGVs is linked to very specific guidance for each substance, and particular caveats on the assumptions that accompany each set of values. For example, the SGV for cadmium is dependent on the pH of the soil. Further, cadmium exhibits threshold behaviour when intakes are by ingestion, but non-threshold behaviour when intakes are by inhalation. The substance has a TDI for ingestion pathways and an index dose for inhalation exposure pathways, and if only one set of pathways affects a particular receptor, then different assessment criteria will apply.

The approach to protection of surface and groundwater from land contamination is based on a tiered approach to risk assessment, and the preferred EA approach is set out in their guidance (EA, 1999). There are no prescribed contaminant concentrations in soil which are protective of controlled waters, but the leachability of substances is a key parameter in assessing the likely impact on underlying water bodies.

A framework to assess risks to ecological receptors from land contamination has been published by the Environment Agency and the Scotland and Northern Ireland Forum for Environmental Research (EA/SNIFFER, 2002a), and a series of ecotoxicological test methods is proposed for use within the framework (EA/SNIFFER, 2002b).

Discharges to water

Many human activities have the potential to pollute the aquatic environment. These include large and small scale industrial enterprises, agriculture, transport, mining, disposal of domestic sewage, urban drainage and deliberate or accidental pollution incidents. These activities can cause:

- persistent and extensive effects on water quality;
- major damage to the aquatic ecosystem (freshwater, estuarine or marine);
- closure of a potable abstraction;
- major impact on amenity value;
- major damage to agriculture and commerce; and
- serious impact on humans.

Classification and impact of pollutants

Aquatic pollutants can be broadly classified as being from either point or diffuse sources. A point source pollutant is one that reaches a watercourse from a defined location such as an outfall pipe. Diffuse source pollutants arise from widespread activities having no clearly defined point or origin, for example surface runoff from agricultural land. Generally, point source pollutants are easier to control than those from diffuse sources because they flow to a single location where the use of appropriate treatment can effectively remove them from the discharge. In contrast, such control is not usually possible over pollutants from diffuse sources, which contribute significantly to water pollution. These are best reduced by effective land use planning and catchment protection initiatives.

The impact of a particular discharge is the result of a number of factors relating to the strength (pollutant load), frequency, volume and rate of the discharge and the flow, quality and use of the receiving watercourse.

The frequency of a given discharge can be defined as being either continuous or intermittent. Continuous discharges are those that occur all the time, for example fully treated effluent discharges from sewage works. Intermittent discharges occur infrequently, for example storm discharges from overflows on urban drainage systems. Although the impacts from intermittent discharges are more transitory, they can result in acute pollution through sudden decreases in dissolved oxygen concentrations or disturbance of sediments resulting in the release of toxic substances.

Pollutants can be synthetic, but most are natural materials that are simply released in unacceptably high concentrations. Organic pollutants cause oxygen depletion in rivers, which can alter the aquatic ecosystem for a considerable distance downstream, while synthetic pollutants are problematic as no natural biogeochemical cycles exist for them and they cannot be readily broken down by natural processes and as such many are persistent. Some pollutants are highly toxic and are damaging at any concentration, whereas others are only a problem when they are present at critical concentrations. General types of water pollutants include pathogenic organisms, oxygen-demanding wastes, plant nutrients, synthetic organic chemicals, inorganic chemicals, sediments, radioactive substances, oil, heat and colour – the general impacts of which are outlined in Table 5.1.6.

Table 5.1.6   *Environmental implications of the discharge of pollutants*

Factor	Environmental effect	Potential ecological consequence
Microbiological organisms	Sewage contains many millions of micro-organisms per litre. The majority are relatively harmless coliforms but others are pathogenic microbes. This can impact on the recreational and amenity use of the watercourse.	Imbalance in aquatic community (trophic) structure leading to the dominance of competitive species.
Oxygen-demanding wastes	Oxygen depleters, e.g. biodegradable organic compounds and ammonia, lead to reduced dissolved oxygen levels in water. Oxygen concentration is directly influenced by temperature, which affects the solubility of oxygen in water, and the current velocity, which affects surface aeration.	Reductions in oxygen can result in changes in aquatic community structure through the elimination of sensitive oxygen-dependent species and the increase in some tolerant species.

The partial degradation of proteins and other nitrogenous material results in elevated ammonia, nitrate and nitrite concentrations. This leads to the elimination of intolerant species (as un-ionized ammonia is toxic) and the potential for increased plant growth especially in nutrient poor waters. |
| Plant nutrients | Nitrogen and phosphorous are the key nutrients responsible for eutrophication. | Excessive amounts can lead to eutrophic conditions notably the increased production of algae and/or other plants, affecting the quality of the water and community structure. |
| Toxic substances (e.g. metals, pesticides and oil) | All watercourses naturally have a low concentration of metals due to the nature of the underlying geology of the catchment. Pollution can result in concentrations in excess of those normally tolerated by aquatic fauna. | This can result in changes in community structure through the loss of sensitive species resulting in decreased biodiversity. Ammonia is a water soluble chemical compound, produced by the decomposition of organic material. It is widely used to characterize water quality since it is toxic to fish. |

Table 5.1.6   continued

Suspended solids	Particulate pollution from sediments, for example, can result in increased turbidity and reduction of light penetration. Deposition in slower flowing waters leading to modification of the substratum by a blanket of sludge. This can result in localized release of methane (CH_4) and hydrogen as sulphide (H_2S) as material decomposes anoxically.	Lower light levels can lead to reduced photosynthetic activity of submerged plants and loss of primary productivity and reduction in dissolved oxygen. Particulate matter can also cause abrasion to body surfaces (especially gills) or interference with the normal feeding behaviour of aquatic organisms. The sedimentation of particulates can result in the destruction of gravel riffles and natural pools and consequently a loss of fish breeding grounds.
Thermal energy (heat)	Thermal inputs affect the temperature of the water and can arise from waste heat from cooling towers or power generation and the manufacturing process.	Increased temperature affects chemical reactions and reduces dissolved oxygen concentrations, therefore reducing the potential for natural biochemical processes to occur optimally. Heat stress can lead to elimination of sensitive species, increased feeding and accelerated growth rates, shift in the timing of life cycles, changes in micro-organism respiratory rates, increased toxicity of substances and the enhanced survival of exotic species.
pH and salinity	pH strongly influences the rate of primary production since it affects micro-organisms and the availability of nutrients. Salinity alters the osmotic potential and proportional ionic composition of the water.	Outside of the range 5.0–9.0, a small change in pH can result in significant changes in community structure. It is generally accepted that as pH decreases, both the species diversity and the overall productivity of an aquatic ecosystem decline.
Colour	Primarily aesthetic resulting from the discharge of coloured effluents (e.g. dye manufacture or textiles), or it may appear as a result of different effluents combining in the watercourse.	Dependent on the light absorptive properties and the spectral requirements of algae and higher plants. These effects are usually minimal when compared with other factors.

Source: Adapted from Abel, 1989 and Hellawell, 1986

Water quality can be assessed on either a chemical or biological basis. Chemical assessment is often easier and more practical for routine use as it can be related more easily to readily measured parameters in a given discharge. In England and Wales, the general quality assessment (GQA) system is used to assess current inland water quality and consists of six classes ranging from A (the highest quality) to F (the lowest). Similarly, water quality objectives (WQOs) are used to determine the future desired quality of a given watercourse. They are based on the river ecosystem (RE) classification in which quality is defined in descending order from RE1 (cleanest) to RE5 (polluted) as shown in Table 5.1.7.

Table 5.1.7   Extract from the Surface Waters (River Ecosystem) (Classification) Regulations 1994

CLASS	Dissolved oyxgen (% saturation) 10 percentile	Biological oxygen demand (ATU) (mg/l) 90 percentile	Total ammonia (mgN/l) 90 percentile	Un-ionized ammonia (mgN/l) 95 percentile
RE1	80	2.5	0.25	0.021
RE2	70	4.0	0.6	0.021
RE3	60	6.0	1.3	0.021
RE4	50	8.0	2.5	–
RE5	20	15.0	9.0	–

Although water chemistry is useful as a technical tool for assessing the impact of discharges for planning or modelling purposes, a major drawback is that it only provides information about the watercourse at the time the sample was taken. In contrast, aquatic organisms are 'resident' 24 hours a day and therefore provide time integrated information on the impact of water chemistry on the various species which vary in their ability to tolerate pollution. Theoretically an unpolluted watercourse supports a diverse and balanced community, while watercourses exposed to severe pollution are associated with a decrease in the number of species present but an increase in their abundance due to the absence of competition. Biological information is of considerable importance where polluting discharges are intermittent and not detectable by other means, particularly as the effects of a combination of pollutants cannot be readily assessed by direct chemical determinations.

Pollution prevention and legislation

In developed countries, extensive measures are taken to prevent the pollution of natural waters. This is usually achieved through the treatment of the used waters from domestic and industrial sources prior to their release, necessitating the use of sophisticated technology. Since raw water must meet specific quality criteria to be suitable for potable treatment and the disposal of wastewaters is potentially a major source of pollution, an inherent conflict exists between these two uses of a river catchment. This is managed in the UK through a regulatory framework in which the control of discharges is governed by domestic (UK) and European (EC directives) legislation. These controls are based on the maintenance and improvement of water quality and the aquatic environment through meeting water quality objectives. Standards applied to discharges are set to safeguard the acceptable or required quality of water for a particular purpose. They make provision for the protection of the receiving watercourse or limit the quantity of the pollutant discharged in the form of a load limit based on either health criteria or environmental quality standards. These requirements are imposed through discharge consents. These are legal permits that allow a discharge to be made which contains potentially polluting substances, in which controls are used to ensure that no deterioration occurs. Consents can comprise either numeric and/or descriptive conditions:

Numeric conditions: Discharges that have the greatest potential to affect the quality of the receiving water have numeric concentration limits attached to their consents. These limits may apply to an individual substance or groups of substances, and include limits that are necessary to ensure compliance with a number of EC directives and with commitments made for various international conventions. There are approximately 30,000 numeric consents in England and Wales.

Descriptive conditions: Many small discharges to the aquatic environment have a low potential to adversely affect the receiving water (because of the nature and low volume of the discharge) and would be difficult to control by means of specific numeric values. In these cases, descriptive conditions are applied which can typically define the nature of the effluent treatment plant to be used and require that the plant is correctly operated and adequately maintained. There are currently approximately 50,000 discharges in England and Wales which are successfully controlled by descriptive consents.

Discharge consents were originally introduced by the 1951 Rivers (Prevention of Pollution) Act, which made it a statutory requirement for all new discharges to rivers to have a consent. This was extended under the 1961 Rivers Prevention of Pollution Act requiring all discharges to rivers to have a consent.

The overall responsibility for the maintenance and management of water resources in England and Wales rests with the Secretary of State for Environment, Food and Rural Affairs. This includes the responsibility for national policy on all matters of conservation and supply, sewerage and sewage disposal; the control of pollution in both inland and coastal waters; the use of inland waters for recreation and navigation; the control of marine pollution by oil and drainage; the protection of freshwater and marine fisheries; the disposal of wastes at sea; and the safe use of agricultural pesticides (NSCA, 2003). These functions are regulated by the EA whose responsibilities with regards to watercourses include:

- maintaining or improving water quality (including groundwater);
- maintaining watercourse flows and groundwater levels;
- monitoring and controlling emissions of dangerous substances;
- flood defence and land drainage; and
- fisheries and recreation.

The EA monitors water quality in order to assess compliance with UK legislation and various European directives (see Table 5.1.8), and to assess progress towards national water quality standards. Where standards are not met, the EA is responsible for identifying sources of pollution and ensuring that improvements are made. The majority of discharges to controlled waters are issued and regulated under the Water Resources Act

1991 (UK Parliament, 1991), which provides the statutory basis for the EA to control discharges to water. Under this act, the EA also checks compliance and prosecutes offences where necessary and may seek to recover the full costs from the responsible party for any remedial work carried out as the result of an incident.

In Scotland and Northern Ireland a similar role is undertaken by the Scottish Environment Protection Agency (SEPA) and the Environment and Heritage Service (Water Quality Unit), an agency of the Department of Environment in Northern Ireland.

Table 5.1.8   Examples of UK and EU legislation relating to inland water quality

UK Legislation	European Legislation (by year of introduction)
1951 – Rivers (Prevention of Pollution) Act	75/440/EEC – Surface Water Abstraction Directive
1960 – Clean Rivers (Estuaries and Tidal Waters) Act	76/160/EEC – Bathing Waters Directive
1961 – Rivers Prevention of Pollution Act	76/464/EEC – Dangerous Substances Directive
1963 – Water Resources Act	78/659/EEC – Freshwater Fish Directive
1974 – Control of Pollution Act (COPA)	79/923/EEC – Shellfish Waters Directive
1989 – Water Act	80/68/EEC – Groundwater Directive
1991 – Water Resources Act	91/676/EEC – Nitrate Directive
1991 – Water Industry Act	91/271/EEC – Urban Wastewater Directive
1994 – Urban Waste Water Treatment Regulations	2000/60/EC – Water Framework Directive
1995 – Environment Act	

References

Abel, P. D. (1989) *Water Pollution Biology*, Ellis Horwood, New York

Defra (2002) 'Integrated Pollution Prevention and Control: A Practical Guide', 2nd edn, Department for Environment, Food and Rural Affairs, London

Defra (2003a) 'Part IV of the Environment Act 1995 Local Air Quality Management Policy Guidance LAQM PG(03)', Department for Environment, Food and Rural Affairs, London

Defra (2003b) 'Part IV of the Environment Act 1995 Local Air Quality Management Technical Guidance LAQM TG(03) and Policy Guidance', Department for Environment, Food and Rural Affairs, London

Defra (2003c) 'The Air Quality Strategy for England, Scotland, Wales and Northern Ireland: Addendum', Department for Environment, Food and Rural Affairs, London

Defra/EA (2002a) 'Assessment of Risks to Human Health from Land Contamination: An Overview of the Development of Soil Guideline Values and Related Research, Report CLR 7', Department for Environment, Food and Rural Affairs and Environment Agency, R&D Dissemination Centre, WRC plc, Swindon

Defra/EA (2002b) 'Contaminants in Soil: Collation of Toxicological Data and Intake Values for Humans, Report CLR 9', Department for Environment, Food and Rural Affairs and Environment Agency, R&D Dissemination Centre, WRC plc, Swindon

Defra/EA (2002c) 'The Contaminated Land Exposure Assessment (CLEA) Model: Technical Basis and Algorithms, Report CLR 10', Department for Environment, Food and Rural Affairs and Environment Agency, R&D Dissemination Centre, WRC plc, Swindon

DETR (2000) 'The Air Quality Strategy for England, Scotland, Wales and Northern Ireland: Working Together for Clean Air', Cm 4548, SE 20003/3 and NIA 7, Department of the Environment, Transport and the Regions, London

DoE (1997a) 'Integrated Pollution Control – A Practical Guide', Department of the Environment, London

DoE (1997b) 'The United Kingdom National Air Quality Strategy', Department of the Environment, London

EA (1999) *Derivation of Remedial Targets for Soil and Groundwater to Protect Water Resources*, R&D Technical Report P20, Environment Agency, Bristol

EA (2001a) *Interim Guidance for the Ferrous Foundry Sector Integrated Pollution Prevention and Control*, S2.03 (Table 3.1), Environment Agency, Bristol

EA (2001b) *Interim Sector Guidance for the Incineration of Waste and Fuel Manufactured from or Including Waste, Integrated Pollution Prevention and Control & Integrated Pollution Control*, S5.01 (Table 3.1), Environment Agency, Bristol

EA/SNIFFER (2002a) *Assessing Risks to Ecosystems from Land Contamination*, R&D Technical Report P299, Environment Agency and the Scotland and Northern Ireland Forum for Environmental Research, R&D Dissemination Centre, WRC plc, Swindon

EA/SNIFFER (2002b) *Review of Ecotoxicological and Biological Test Methods for the Assessment of Contaminated Land*, R&D Technical Report P300, Environment Agency and the Scotland and Northern Ireland Forum for Environmental Research, R&D Dissemination Centre, WRC plc, Swindon

EC (1994) 'Council Directive 94/67/EC on the Incineration of Hazardous Waste', European Commission, Brussels

EC (1996) 'Council Directive 96/61/EC Concerning Integrated Pollution Prevention and Control', European Commission, Brussels

EC (2000) 'Directive 2000/76/EC of the European Parliament and of the Council on the Incineration of Waste', European Commission, Brussels

EEC (1989a) 'Council Directive 89/369/EEC on the Prevention of Air Pollution from New Municipal Waste Incineration Plants Directive 89/369/EEC', European Economic Community, Brussels

EEC (1989b) 'Council Directive 89/429/EEC on the Reduction of Air Pollutants from Existing Municipal Waste Incineration Plants', European Economic Community, Brussels

Hellawell, J. M. (1986) *Biological Indicators of Freshwater Pollution and Environmental Management*, Elsevier Applied Science Publishers, London

HMIP (1990) 'Chief Inspector's Guidance to Inspectors Waste Disposal & Recycling Merchant & In House Chemical Waste Incineration', Her Majesty's Inspectorate of Pollution, Process Guidance Note IPR 5/1, The Stationery Office, London

ICAO (1995) *ICAO Engine Exhaust Emission Data Bank*, Doc 9646 AN/943, 1st edn, International Civil Aviation Organization, Montreal

NSCA (2003) *Pollution Handbook 2003*, National Society for Clean Air and Environmental Protection, Brighton

UK Parliament (1906) 'Alkali & Works Regulation Act', The Stationery Office, London

UK Parliament (1974) 'Control of Pollution Act (Part 1)', The Stationery Office, London

UK Parliament (1990a) 'Environmental Protection Act', The Stationery Office, London

UK Parliament (1990b) 'Environmental Protection Act (Part I)', The Stationery Office, London

UK Parliament (1990c) 'Town and Country Planning Act', The Stationery Office, London

UK Parliament (1991) 'Water Resources Act (Sections 82–91 and Schedule 10)', The Stationery Office, London

UK Parliament (1993) 'Clean Air Act (Part III)', The Stationery Office, London

UK Parliament (1994) 'The Waste Management Licensing Regulations Statutory Instrument 1994, No 1056', The Stationery Office, London

UK Parliament (1995a) 'Environment Act (Part I)', The Stationery Office, London

UK Parliament (1995b) 'Environment Act (Part IV)', The Stationery Office, London

UK Parliament (1999) 'Pollution Prevention and Control Act', The Stationery Office, London

UK Parliament (2000) 'The Air Quality (England) Regulations, Statutory Instrument 2000, No 0928', The Stationery Office, London

UK Parliament (2001) 'The Air Quality Limit Values Regulations, Statutory Instrument 2001, No 2315', The Stationery Office, London

UK Parliament (2002a) 'The Air Quality (England) (Amendment) Regulations Statutory Instrument 2002, No 3043', The Stationery Office, London

UK Parliament (2002b) 'The Air Quality Limit Values (Amendment) Regulations, Statutory Instrument 2002, No 3117', The Stationery Office, London

UNEP (2000) *Handbook for the International Treaties for the Protection of the Ozone Layer*, 5th edn, United Nations Environment Programme, Paris

Further reading

Gray, N. F. (1999) *Water Technology – An Introduction for Environmental Scientists and Engineers*, Butterworth-Heinemann, London

Mason, C. F. (1991) *Biology of Freshwater Pollution*, 2nd edn, Longman, London

NRA (1994) 'Water Quality Objectives: Procedure used by the National Rivers Authority for the Purpose of the Surface Waters (River Ecosystem) (Classification) Regulations 1994', National Rivers Authority, London

Tebbutt, T. H. Y. (1998) *Principles of Water Quality Control*, 5th edn, Butterworth-Heinemann, London

Chapter 5.2

Measurement and Monitoring

Introduction

The terms 'measurement' and 'monitoring' and are often used interchangeably, but they have specific and different meanings. Measurement of an environmental parameter involves assigning a numerical quantity to its magnitude by carrying out some kind of gauging. Estimation, on the other hand, is the approximate judgement or opinion of this magnitude. Monitoring involves collecting and interpreting a number of measurements or estimates over a period of time. It usually involves an element of comparison, either with itself or with some external benchmark, such as an environmental quality standard or a guideline value.

An environmental measurement includes a sampling stage and an analysis stage though it can sometimes be difficult to say where one ends and the other begins. Sampling must be representative both spatially and temporally. Sampling is itself a very specialized subject and a number of publications including Pritchard (2001) and Burgess (2000) give a good introduction.

The fundamental principle of sampling is that a small amount of collected material should provide a reasonable estimate of the overall character of the material. For this to apply, it must be a representative sample. The number and locations of samples needed depend on how homogeneous the bulk material is, in both spatial and temporal terms. For a very homogeneous material, only a few samples are required; if it is non-homogeneous, many more samples will be needed. Other terms and concepts are defined in Table 5.2.1.

Table 5.2.1   Other terms and concepts

Monitoring approach	The term includes whether monitoring is continuous, periodic or surrogate; whether it is qualitative (measures what it is composed of), quantitative (measures how much of it is present), or semi-quantitative (whether it is present in trace, minor or major amounts).
Monitoring technique	The scientific principle behind the measurement, covering both the sampling and analysis.
Monitoring method	The documented procedure describing in detail how the monitoring technique should be used for a particular application. Official standard methods are published by the European Committee for Standardization (CEN), the International Organization for Standardization (ISO), the British Standards Institution (BSI), and others.

continued overleaf

Table 5.2.1   continued

Monitoring equipment	Some standard monitoring methods specify in detail the instruments and apparatus that must be used for the measurement, but many do not.
Analyte	The chemical species being investigated (qualitatively or quantitatively).
Measurand	Often, the analyte is not measured directly, but is inferred by measuring another parameter that is proportional to it. In such cases the term measurand (or sometimes determinand) is used. For example, in quantifying the temperature (the measurand) of gases emitted by a chimney stack using a thermocouple, the actual quantity measured is millivolts generated at the thermocouple junction.

Some of the techniques most commonly used to analyse environmental pollutants in the field and in the laboratory are listed in Table 5.2.2. However, analytical chemistry is a vast field that is continually developing and it is not possible to describe techniques in detail here. Further information is available from other published sources such as Radojevic and Bashkin (1999) and Harrison and Perry (1986).

Table 5.2.2   Common analytical principles used in environmental monitoring

Type of analysis	Brief description of principle	Examples of analytical techniques
Chromatography	Separates out the different analytes contained in a mixture, allowing them to be quantified individually by one of the other techniques.	Ion chromatography (IC); Gas chromatography (GC), usually coupled with a detector such as a flame ionization detector (FID), photo-ionization detector (PID) or electron capture detector (ECD); High pressure liquid chromatograph (HPLC); Liquid chromatography (LC).
Electrochemical	Measures electrical properties related to the chemical composition.	pH; Ion selective electrode (ISE); Conductivity; Redox potential.
Gravimetry	The amount of analyte present is found by measuring its mass.	Filtration techniques, e.g. total solids (TS) and suspended solids (SS) in water; PM_{10} and total suspended particulates (TSP) in air; Tapering element oscillating microbalance (TEOM).
Optical	The optical properties of the sample are assessed either qualitatively (e.g. colour) or quantitatively.	Colour; Turbidity; Obscuration; Opacity.
Spectrometry	Many different areas of the spectrum can be examined. From radiation absorbed or emitted, information is	Atomic absorption spectrometry (AAS); Chemiluminescence analysis; Infrared (IR) and Fourier transform infrared (FTIR) spectrometry;

Table 5.2.2   continued

Type of analysis	Brief description of principle	Examples of analytical techniques
Spectrometry continued	obtained on the composition of a sample and the amounts of different analytes.	Mass spectrometry (MS), often coupled with gas chromatography (GC-MS); Optical emission spectrometry (OES) using inductively coupled plasma (ICP); Photometry, including flame photometry (FP); Ultraviolet-visible spectrometry, including differential optical absorption spectrometry (DOAS) and colorimetry; X-ray diffraction (XRD); X-ray fluorescence (XRF).
Volumetric	By measuring the volume of one (known) substance reacting at a fixed stoichiometric ratio, the amount of the other (unknown) chemical can be inferred.	Titrations, for hardness, alkalinity etc.

Monitoring strategy and programmes

Quantification of pollution (usually for assessment of impacts) can be undertaken in two ways: firstly, by measuring and monitoring the pollution (either releases at source or in the ambient environment); and secondly, the pollution levels can be predicted by estimating source emissions using emissions factors or surrogate monitoring, and modelling dispersion of pollutants in the receiving medium, whether it be air, water or soil. While both approaches have their applications and are often complementary, the remainder of this chapter focuses solely on monitoring.

Monitoring is carried out for a variety of reasons. There may be legislative and regulatory requirements, often involving comparisons with environmental quality standards. Monitoring may be required for management and process control. It may be a response to complaints or for research purposes. The purpose will largely determine whether it is most appropriate to monitor pollutants as they emerge from the source (source monitoring) or once they have been dispersed into their receiving medium. The latter type is known as ambient monitoring (particularly when applied to air pollution).

Monitoring can be undertaken on very different geographic scales: from compliance monitoring of emissions from individual industrial processes; through ambient monitoring of regional geographical areas (e.g. the UK Automatic Urban and Rural Network) and national data initiatives (e.g. the Environment Agency's (EA's) Pollution Inventory and the Department for Environment, Food and Rural Affairs' (Defra's) local authority air emissions returns); up to a supranational level (e.g. the European Pollution Emissions Register). As the scale increases the focus tends to change from measurement of emissions to interpretations, comparisons and trend analyses.

Ambient monitoring usually aims to be fairly representative of the pollution experienced by the end receptor. For example an air quality monitoring station in a busy city street, or water samples collected from a particular depth in a receiving water. This allows it to be used in assessing environmental impacts for a particular area.

Emissions from specific pollution sources tend to be regulated by limits placed on the concentration or mass of pollutant emitted, for example limits on nitrogen oxides emitted from motor vehicle exhausts, limits on dioxins emitted from the stacks of incinerators and discharge limits on effluents released from outfalls into receiving waters. Regulatory policing of this involves source emissions monitoring.

There are some instances where source emissions monitoring and ambient monitoring work in concert. For example, when a new industrial process is being planned an environmental statement or an application for a Pollution Prevention and Control (PPC) permit to operate may be required. It would be necessary to show that the levels of pollution emitted were not going to cause significant environmental harm in the surrounding environment. Computer dispersion modelling can be used to predict the impact of source emissions that are controlled and monitored at source, but it is not uncommon to verify this subsequently by a period of direct ambient monitoring around the site.

A useful classification of monitoring types places them in one of the following three categories:

- **continuous monitoring** – measurements carried out continuously, with few if any gaps in the data produced;
- **periodic monitoring** – measurements carried out at periodic intervals, for example once every three months throughout the year; and
- **surrogate monitoring** – the pollutant itself is not measured. Instead, the level of pollutant is estimated from some other parameter. Typical examples are calculation of emissions using published emissions factors and estimation of volatile organic compounds (VOCs) emissions from solvent usage rates.

Both continuous and periodic monitoring can be carried out automatically or manually. Automatic monitoring uses an instrument that usually gives a direct read out of pollution levels in real time. Alternatively, a manual technique may be used where the pollutant is sampled on site and the sample is analysed later in the laboratory. Samples may be obtained over fairly lengthy periods of several hours, or may be so-called spot samples or grab samples collected over a period of seconds to a few minutes.

To be technically valid and cost effective, the objectives of the proposed monitoring programme should be clearly defined at the outset. This allows the design of a monitoring strategy to meet these needs. The key issues are described in detail in guidance published by the EA (2000, 2002a) but the four fundamental questions are reproduced in Table 5.2.3.

Table 5.2.3   Issues for a monitoring strategy

What?	What parameter(s) to measure? In many cases this may be obvious, but in others it merits careful consideration.
When?	When to sample and for how long? Should sampling be continuous or periodic? Factors to consider are: • Is the health impact or environmental impact acute or chronic? • What temporal resolution is required? • Is there an environmental quality standard (EQS) with a defined averaging period (e.g. one hour averages, daily averages, annual averages) which the data will be compared to?

Table 5.2.2   continued

Where?	Where to sample? Factors to consider are: • the relative locations of monitoring positions relative to the study area or emission source and the spatial resolution required; • suitability criteria for individual sampling sites, e.g. position relative to local emission sources and any interfering effects.
How?	How to measure? Both sampling and analysis techniques need to be considered. Selection involves an appraisal of cost versus performance, the latter including limits of detection, sensitivity, speed of instrument response, susceptibility to interfering species and the overall uncertainty of the measurement.

Monitoring of air

There are two main categories of industrial emissions to atmosphere, controlled releases and fugitive releases. Controlled releases are managed in some way, either as part of a process or as part of a control and abatement mechanism, and the emissions are therefore quantifiable. Fugitive releases are, literally, releases that cannot be captured. They are uncontrolled and often dependent on external conditions, such as the wind, which makes them difficult to quantify with any reasonable degree of certainty. Another definition of a fugitive emission is a release that is unintentional. An oil refinery may have a quarter of a million pumps, valves and flanges that can potentially leak, making it impractical to measure the emissions from every source.

Emissions can also be described in terms of their spatial characteristics, usually as a point source, line source or area source. It is important to recognize that each of these can be either controlled releases or fugitive releases, as shown in Table 5.2.4. It is controlled point sources, such as chimney stacks and vents, that are most commonly monitored.

Table 5.2.4   Categories of emissions to atmosphere

	Point source	Line source	Area source
Controlled release	Emissions from fixed location plant and often (but not always) released to atmosphere via a vent, duct or chimney stack.	Tailpipe emissions from vehicles driving along a road.	Open process tanks, storage tanks with floating roofs.
Fugitive release	Intermittently leaking valve.	Dust resuspended in a vehicle's wake; wind-whipping of dusty material on an open conveyor belt.	Wind-whipping of a stockpile of dusty material.

The main reasons for carrying out stack emissions monitoring are:

• compliance with environmental legislation, especially the Environmental Protection Act (EPA) 1990 and the PPC Regulations 2000;
• process data and control requirements;

- assessing the effectiveness of any abatement or control measures; and
- non-legislative environmental drivers such as environmental management systems, pressure groups and public opinion.

Deciding on the monitoring approach is the first step. Monitoring must be representative of emissions over a longer time period (e.g. a year). The EA's general preferred approach is for day to day monitoring using continuous emissions monitoring systems (CEMs) when possible, augmented by occasional checks using periodic monitoring. However, if intermittent monitoring will provide a reasonable estimate of longer term emissions then periodic monitoring alone may be acceptable. A further choice will then exist between carrying out periodic monitoring using automatic instruments giving a real-time read out or manual monitoring giving a result averaged over the sampling period.

Table 5.2.5 lists some of the popular monitoring techniques for common releases to air from controlled point sources. EA (2002a) gives more detailed descriptions and specifies the standard methods to be used.

Table 5.2.5 Popular techniques for source monitoring of controlled point releases to air

Category	Pollutant	Technique			
		CEMs		Periodic monitoring	
		Sampling	Analysis	Sampling	Analysis
Particulate matter	Total particulate matter	Cross duct/ in situ	Opacity; Light scattering; Tribo-electric probe	Extractive (isokinetic)	Gravimetric
		Extractive (isokinetic)	Gravimetric (TEOM); β radiation absorption		
	PM_{10}	Cross duct/ in situ	Light scattering	Extractive (isokinetic)	Gravimetric
		Extractive (isokinetic)	Photometric analyser		
Speciated particulates and phase-partitioned species	Heavy metals	Cross duct/ in situ	DOAS (Hg vapour only)	Extractive (isokinetic)	Digestion and AAS or ICP-OES
	Hydrogen chloride	Cross duct/ in situ	DOAS; IR; FTIR; Continuous flow IC and ISE	Extractive (isokinetic)	Aqueous extract and IC; IR; FTIR
	Dioxins and furans	Extractive (isokinetic) batch sampler	Solvent extract and GC-MS	Extractive (isokinetic)	Solvent extract and GC-MS

Table 5.2.5   continued

Category	Pollutant	Technique			
		CEMs		Periodic monitoring	
		Sampling	Analysis	Sampling	Analysis
Gaseous determinands (inorganic)	Sulphur dioxide	Cross duct/ in situ	DOAS; FTIR; UV	Extractive (non-isokinetic)	IC; titration; UV; IR; NDIR; FP, electochemical
		Extractive (non-isokinetic)	IR; FTIR; UV; FP		
	Nitrogen oxides	Cross duct/ in situ	UV; DOAS; IR; FTIR; chemilum-inescence; electrochemical	Extractive (non-isokinetic)	Chemilumin-escence; IR; UV; FTIR; IC; electrochemical; colorimetric
		Extractive (non-isokinetic)	UV; IR; FTIR; chemilumin-escence electrochemical		
	Carbon monoxide	Cross duct/ in situ	IR; DOAS	Extractive (non-isokinetic)	IR; FTIR; electrochemical
		Extractive (non-isokinetic)	IR; FTIR; electrochemical		
Gaseous determinands (organic)	Total VOCs	Extractive (non-isokinetic)	FID analyser	Extractive (non-isokinetic)	FID; IR; PID; electrochemical
	Speciated VOCs	Cross duct/ in situ	DOAS	Extractive (non-isokinetic)	FTIR; GC-FID/ECD/PID
		Extractive (non-isokinetic)	IR; FTIR; GC-FID/ECD/PID		

For ambient air quality monitoring, legislation is very much the primary driver. The Air Quality Strategy (AQS) for England, Scotland, Wales and Northern Ireland (2000 and 2003 Addendum) sets out air quality objectives for nine pollutants. These are: carbon monoxide (CO), benzene, 1,3-butadiene, lead (Pb), nitrogen dioxide (NO_2), sulphur dioxide (SO_2), PM_{10}, ozone (O_3) and polycyclic aromatic hydrocarbons (PAHs). The European Union has, or is, developing limit values for 12 pollutants, which include all of those in the AQS – with the exception of 1,3-butadiene – but with the addition of heavy metals (cadmium (Cd), mercury (Hg), arsenic (As) and nickel (Ni)). Other non-regulated pollutants may be of concern at a local level, for example various organic compounds such as formaldehyde, dioxins and furans.

Techniques for monitoring pollutants in ambient air may be divided broadly into those which provide continuous, automatic measurements, and those which are based on manual techniques or which require some form of post sampling laboratory analysis to be performed. The main techniques are summarized in Tables 5.2.6, 5.2.7 and 5.2.8.

Table 5.2.6   Common ambient particulate monitoring techniques

Suspended particulate matter[1]	Deposited particulate matter
Filter-paper samplers	Frisbee gauge
β-gauge instruments	Deposit gauges[2]
Impingers	Dust slides/soiling meter
TEOM	Sticky plates
Light-scattering systems	

Notes:
1 Includes total suspended particulates (TSP) and specific fractions, e.g. PM_{10}.
2 Includes ISO deposit gauge, BS bowl gauge and CERL-type directional gauge

Table 5.2.7   Common automatic techniques for monitoring ambient gaseous air pollutants

	CO	SO_2	NO_x	O_3	Organics
NDIR	●				
NDUV		●			
UV fluorescence		●			
Chemiluminescence			●		
Flame photometric		●			
FID, PID					●
DOAS		●	●	●	●
FTIR					●
UV absorption				●	

Table 5.2.8   Common manual sampling techniques for ambient gaseous air pollutants

Absorption sampling	Adsorption sampling	Cryogenic sampling	Grab sampling	Passive sampling
Bubblers	Sorbent tubes	Cryogenic traps	Tedlar bags	Diffusion tubes
	Coated filters Denuder tubes		Evacuated flasks Evacuated canisters	

Continuous analysers for CO, NO_2, SO_2, PM_{10} and ozone are widely used in the UK, including the UK Automatic Urban and Rural Network (AURN). Further details of the network can be found at www.airquality.co.uk. Continuous analysers are also available for organic pollutants, such as benzene and 1,3-butadiene. These analysers can provide high quality data with a short time resolution (less than one hour) but are relatively expensive to purchase and operate.

Manual monitoring techniques are frequently used for monitoring of particulates, including PM_{10}, and heavy metal species. This involves drawing air through a filter (usually via a size-selective inlet to provide a PM_{10} fraction) which collects the particulate material. The filter may then be weighed, to provide PM_{10} mass, or subjected to various laboratory analytical procedures to determine the heavy metal, PAH or dioxin content. Where there is a significant proportion of the pollutant species in the vapour phase (as with some PAH and dioxins/furans) then a foam plug may be placed downstream of the filter.

Passive (diffusion) sampling devices are also widely used in the UK. These devices sample passively from the atmosphere by collecting the target pollutant species onto an adsorbing medium, which is subsequently analysed in the laboratory. Diffusion tubes for NO_2 are widely used in the UK, and form the basis of the UK Nitrogen Dioxide Diffusion Tube Network. Further details of this network may also be found at www.airquality.co.uk. Passive devices for NO_2 and benzene are also commonly used, and samplers are also available for other species such as ozone and SO_2. The principal advantage of these devices is that they are relatively cheap, they allow wide scale surveys to be carried out, and require no electrical power. Their main disadvantage is that they only provide a concentration averaged over the period of exposure (typically two to four weeks) and results may differ significantly from one laboratory to another. Some form of validation or bias correction of the results is therefore usually required.

Many established methods are becoming obsolete as better techniques are developed that are more sensitive, less prone to interference and more automated. However, care must be taken to avoid over-specification. It should be emphasized that monitoring surveys may be based on more than one technique. For example, ambient NO_2 concentrations can be assessed by a small number of chemiluminescence analyser sites supplemented by a larger number of cheaper diffusion tube sites.

Monitoring of water

Measurements of water quality tend to be carried out either to check a water's fitness for purpose (e.g. as potable water, or as bathing water) or as a means of monitoring or controlling pollution in bodies of water. Primary sources of water pollution include industry, wastewater (sewage), agriculture and land drainage, and oil spills. The water bodies affected may be coastal waters, inland surface waters (rivers and lakes) and groundwaters. Water quality is monitored routinely:

- around the UK coastline, under the Bathing Waters (Classification) Regulations 1991;
- in the water supply system, under the Water Supply (Water Quality) Regulations 2000;
- in the wastewater industries, usually as part of the discharge consent under the Water Resources Act 1991; and
- increasingly from other industries, under environmental protection legislation.

Water pollutants can be chemical (e.g. nitrates, heavy metals such as lead and arsenic, and pesticides), radiochemical, biological (bacteria such as faecal coliforms, viruses and parasites) and thermal (e.g. from the cooling water outfalls of power stations). The subject is reviewed thoroughly by Harrison (1992). There are European (CEN) standards, British standards (especially the BS 6068 series) and ISO standards covering methods for water sampling and a wide range of chemical, radiochemical and biological water quality analyses.

Sampling must be spatially representative, both in terms of the geographical location where the sample is taken, and – for source releases – the sampling points within the discharge flow profile. Sampling must also be representative over the required time frame. For source emissions this may mean either repeated periodic spot samples, or continuous monitoring. For the latter, the EA has set a minimum performance specification for automatic wastewater samplers used to provide compliance data. For environmental monitoring of water, the spatial consideration must include whether samples are to be obtained at the surface of the body of water, or at depth – for which special samplers must be used.

Table 5.2.9 shows some commonly used techniques for analysis of a selection of water quality parameters, including those priority parameters covered by the agency's operator monitoring assessment (OMA) audit scheme.

Table 5.2.9 Selected water quality analyses

Parameter	Techniques
pH	Electrochemical (pH meter)
Ammonia	Spectrometric
Ammonium	Spectrometric
	Distillation and titration
	Potentiometric
BOD	DO determined before and after incubation
COD	Oxidation with dichromate followed by redox back-titration
Conductivity	Electrochemical (conductivity meter)
Total cyanide	Potentiometric or titrimetric
Dissolved oxygen (DO)	Iodometric titration
Hardness	EDTA titration
Heavy metals	ICP-AES
	AAS
Nitrate and other anions (fluoride, chloride, bromide, sulphate, nitrite, orthophosphate)	Ion chromatography
Phosphorous	Spectrometric (ammonium molybdate method)
Suspended solids	Filtration and gravimetry
TOC	FID
Turbidity	Optical

Monitoring of land

In the context of this handbook the discussions in this section are restricted to the measurement and monitoring of pollution in the ground. This is often carried out in response to:

- Part IIA of the Environmental Protection Act 1990 which places a duty on local authorities to identify contaminated sites within their area;
- other environmental protection legislation, such as integrated pollution prevention and control (IPPC), PPC, the Groundwater Regulations, and the Landfill Directive;
- planning policies and guidance, requiring investigation if the site history indicates potential for contamination;
- social factors, such as housing and development pressure and the need to develop brownfield sites, some of which may have historical contamination; and
- legal requirements, such as checking for land contamination as part of due diligence for a corporate acquisition.

Source emissions potentially leading to pollution of land include industrial wastes (e.g. gasworks residues), domestic and municipal wastes (e.g. to landfills), accidental spills and leakages, and application of agricultural chemicals (e.g. fertilizers, sewage sludge and pesticides). However, unlike emissions to air and releases to water, emissions to land are rarely monitored at source other than as part of their control under waste regulations. For land, the focus is on environmental monitoring of the pollutants once they have been deposited, and perhaps dispersed, in the ground. For example, a key requirement of the PPC Regulations is the preparation of a site condition report showing baseline ground contamination. When the PPC permit is eventually surrendered, a second survey will be carried out and the operator will be required to restore the land to the baseline condition.

Contamination may not be limited to the soil. There may also be pollution of aquifers and groundwaters, and the possible generation of leachates and runoff, and the build up of gases. Measurements of groundwaters, and leachates and methane gas from landfill sites, are often carried out repeatedly over extended periods of time to provide information on trends and so can be considered as monitoring in the true sense of the word. In contrast, many surveys of the contaminated soil are carried out only once or twice at the same location, and so should be classified as measurements rather than true monitoring. Soil samples must undergo some sample pre-treatment involving the extraction of the analyte species and their conversion to a form suitable for chemical analysis.

Sampling of contaminated land must be planned to address both horizontal and vertical variations of pollutants. On modern landfill sites, sampling of leachates is often carried out from purpose built wells and monitoring of landfill gas is carried out at well defined extraction points or boreholes in and around the site. However, for sampling soils and groundwaters one must first decide if the objective is:

- to obtain an average value for the whole area of land; or
- to assess the spatial variability of contamination in the area of land.

For investigations of contaminated land, it is usually the latter and trial pits or boreholes are dug to allow samples of soil and groundwater to be collected. Contaminants in soil are usually dispersed less homogeneously than those in air and water and this makes the sampling strategy of crucial importance. Firstly, the required spatial resolution for the contamination survey should be agreed. Secondly, the number of samples and sample density required to deliver this resolution should be established. There are several different random or systematic sampling patterns that can be adopted, including grids and traverses (Radojevic and Bashkin, 1999). Further guidance on site investigation techniques is available in a British standard (BSI, 1999). The EA's contaminated land exposure assessment (CLEA) model gives suitable approaches for assessment of exposure from contaminated land.

For soils the sample preparation stage is very important. Contaminants can exist in different forms in soils and the procedure to be used depends on whether one wishes to measure the total amount of the contaminant present or just that available for incorporation into the food chain. For determination of total inorganic species, the sample preparation involves direct dissolution using a hydrofluoric acid digestion, or dissolution after fusing at high temperature with sodium carbonate (Radojevic and Bashkin, 1999). Available species are separated by extraction with ammonium acetate and acetic acid. Sample preparation for the analysis of organic species can be by extraction into organic solvent, headspace analysis or purge-and-trap.

The species to be analysed will of course depend upon the sources of contamination. Some substances are tightly regulated: for example, the Groundwater Regulations specify List I substances (oil, fuel and toxic substances) which are prohibited from entry to groundwater; and List II substances (e.g. heavy metals), the entry of which are tightly controlled. Table 5.2.10 shows a selection of contaminated soil parameters and some commonly used techniques for their analysis. The parameters in bold are those covered by the Laboratory of the Government Chemist (LGC) Contaminated Land Proficiency Testing (CONTEST) scheme for checking the quality of analyses of soils and soil extracts.

Table 5.2.10   Selected contaminated soil analyses

Parameter		Analytical techniques
pH		Electrochemical (pH meter)
Heavy metals		AAS; ICP-AES
Inorganic species:	**anions, e.g. sulphate**	IC
	sulphide	Spectrophotometric
	cyanide	IC; ISE
Organic species:	**phenols**	HPLC
	PAHs	HPLC; GC-MS
	PCBs	GC-MS; GC-ECD

Monitoring of nuisance – noise

For the most part, noise measurements are ultimately an attempt to quantify, objectively, a subjective response. There are exceptions, of course: measurement of noise for health and safety purposes is an attempt to quantify the amount of sound energy that a person is exposed to. Other objective measurements may be made to define the sound attenuating performance of items such as partitions and enclosures. In general, noise tends to be measured for the following reasons:

- to check on compliance with conditions that may have been set with regard to planning, licensing or IPPC;
- to check compliance with regulations (e.g. the Noise at Work Regulations);
- to make comparisons with predicted noise levels;
- to describe and characterize the baseline situation as the first stage towards an impact assessment; and
- to assist in solving a problem.

The decision on what to measure depends on the purpose of the measurements. For compliance or comparison monitoring, the parameter, units, measurement period, measurement location and time of measurement should already be stated in the licence condition. Baseline monitoring and problem solving require consideration to be given to the features of the noise that are of interest.

Although the noise level is important, there are other features of noise that can be important and that need to be reflected in what is measured. Table 5.2.11 shows different features of noise and how they might be captured during monitoring.

Table 5.2.11   *Different characteristics of noise and their measurement*

Feature	What to measure
Continuous noise at a constant level	Short sample only needed to characterize it.
Continuous noise that fluctuates in level	Statistical sampling needed (L_{10}, L_{90}); or Total energy in representative measurement period, T, ($L_{eq,T}$).
Intermittent noise	Total energy of an individual event (SEL); or Average energy of a number of events over period, T, ($L_{eq,T}$); or Average maximum level of the events (L_{max}); or How the maximum compares with the noise between the events (L_{max} (of the events) compared with L_{eq} or L_{90} (no events)); or The number of events in a period.
Frequency content of noise	Linear or A-weighting. (C-weighting may be useful if the noise has a strong low frequency component); Octave or 1/3rd octave frequency bands.
Time of day noise occurs	Time of day of interest (although it is sometimes possible to extrapolate results from one time of day to another).

Other issues that need to be considered with regard to noise measurements include the following:

- A microphone is indiscriminate. It will measure the noise from all sources and not just the source of interest. The degree of potential interference will depend on the noise source being investigated and the noise parameter being used to define it.

- The weather conditions, including wind speed and direction and temperature gradients, will affect propagation – especially over longer distances. Adverse weather conditions can also directly affect the measurements: measurements in wind speeds of more than 5m per second are not likely to be valid, even if the microphone is fitted with a windshield.
- The type of meter used in terms of accuracy, frequency response and dynamic range.
- Being aware of the uncertainty of the results. Guidance on this has been published recently (see University of Salford, 2001).

Monitoring of nuisance – odour

Odours are measured for a number of reasons, including: in response to odour complaints; as part of a local authority's duty (under the Environmental Protection Act Part III) to inspect their areas and detect if nuisance exists; to check the efficiency of odour control measures; and to meet conditions included in authorizations, licences and permits issued under environmental legislation. The latter may require predictive assessments of odour impacts, which usually involve measured odour emissions or odour emission factors in combination with the latest computer based atmospheric dispersion models or indicative spreadsheet models. The three main approaches to measuring and monitoring odours are:

- sampling combined with conventional analytical end techniques;
- sampling combined with dynamic olfactometry; and
- field odour assessment.

These are described briefly in Table 5.2.12. The EA (2002c) and Woodfield and Hall (1994) give more detailed descriptions.

Table 5.2.12   Odour monitoring techniques

Analysis technique	Sampling technique	Advantages	Limitations
1. Dynamic olfactometry (uses a panel of people to assess odour strength under controlled conditions in a laboratory)	Collected in inert bags using: 'lung sampler' for point sources; sampling hoods for area sources; gas purging for bulk materials (sewage)	Produces numerical value for overall odour strength exactly as people perceive it. Popular for assessing annoyance impact	No information on the chemical constituents of the odour. Can only be used for source monitoring, not ambient monitoring

Table 5.2.12 continued

Analysis technique	Sampling technique	Advantages	Limitations
2. Conventional chemical analysis	Full analysis, e.g. by GC-MS	Collected onto sorbent tubes using: 'lung sampler' for point sources; sampling hoods for area sources; gas purging for bulk materials (sewage)	Gives a quantitative chemical breakdown of chemical species present. Useful for assessing health impacts and abatement options	Though can compare each chemical with its odour threshold, cannot simulate the synergistic and additive effects of chemicals in a mixture to assess true impact of odour as people perceive it
	Analysis of single species as a surrogate for odour, e.g. H_2S at sewage works	As above, or using a continuous instrument, e.g. gold-film detector for H_2S	Measurement can be carried out quickly (often in real time) and cheaply. Can be used as a CEM for stack emissions	Only suitable if single, known species is the predominant source of the odour
3. Field odour assessments ('sniff testing' using a single person in the field)			Uses the human nose, which is the best 'instrument' for assessing ambient odour. Daily monitoring along site boundary is a common permit condition under IPC/IPPC	People react differently to odour, so assessors must be certified as having 'normal' sensitivity and must be trained to work to strict, documented protocols

Monitoring of nuisance – deposited dust

Dust can be an issue around minerals workings, mines and quarries, foundries, construction and demolition sites, and waste establishments such as landfills. There are three main quantitative approaches to monitoring deposited dust, as summarized in Table 5.2.13. Dust gauges are better suited for monitoring bulk dust deposition around the site perimeter, whereas dust slides (see Schwar, 1994) and sticky pads (see Bearman and Kingsbury, 1994) are excellent means of measuring dust nuisance at sensitive receptors. Often these approaches are used together in a complementary fashion. More details are given in official guidance (see DETR, 2000; EA, 2002b).

Table 5.2.13 Deposited dust monitoring techniques

	Sampling technique	Analysis technique	Advantages	Limitations
1. Deposit gauge monitoring	Gravitational settling into a collection container	Usually gravimetric, but sometimes by optical obscuration of dust washings	Gives an overall measure of dustfall. Popular, long track record, well documented standard methods	Different types of dust gauge exist, having different collection efficiencies. Some require long sampling durations
2. Dust slide monitoring	Gravitational settling onto a glass microscope slide	Measure reduction in reflectance compared to a clean slide	Gives a measure of the annoyance effect of dust on cars, window sills, etc. Large surveys can be carried out in duplicate at modest cost.	Cannot be compared with deposit gauge monitoring results
3. Sticky pad monitoring	Gravitational settling onto white, self adhesive Fablon pad	Measure reduction in reflectance compared to a clean pad	Gives application to dust slide method. Large surveys can be carried out in duplicate at modest cost	Cannot be compared with deposit gauge monitoring results.

Quality assurance and control

Monitoring involves measurements and the drawing of inferences on trends, exceedences, and so on. These measurements are of little value unless we have some confidence in their reliability. The uncertainty of a measurement is an estimate of the range of values that the true value can be expected to fall within. Quality control (QC) procedures are designed to reduce uncertainties to a minimum. Quality assurance (QA) is the effective management of the quality control tasks so that all measurements are carried out to the same standard and are comparable. General principles of QA/QC to environmental monitoring are described in several publications (notably EA, 2000, 2002a, 2002b, 2002c). The quality systems of organizations carrying out monitoring should conform to the requirements of EN ISO/IEC 17025: 2000.

A series of measurements can be precise (i.e. the results are grouped closely together) without actually being accurate (i.e. close to the true value). Both precision and accuracy are important and the concept of uncertainty is an attempt to combine them into a single, convenient value. The uncertainty is conventionally reported in the form:

$$\text{Result} = X \pm U \text{ (units)}$$

for example:

$$NO_x = 247 \text{ mg/m}^3 \pm 5 \text{ mg/m}^3$$

It is unique to the particular combination of measurement technique, method and apparatus used in the analysis.

Without knowledge of the uncertainty, it is not possible to make valid judgements on, for example, compliance with an environmental limit value. The value of pollutant release inventories is diminished if the source data has an unknown uncertainty. For trading in carbon emissions, knowledge of the measurement uncertainty makes it possible to estimate the accounting uncertainty on the traded pollutant. Corporate environmental reports should take care not to claim reductions in emission that are smaller than the uncertainty of the technique used to measure them.

There are a number of different variants on the basic principle for assessing uncertainty and further details can be obtained from published guidance on uncertainty. General guidance on uncertainty has been published by the ISO (1995), while Eurochem and the Royal Society of Chemistry address uncertainty as applied to analytical measurements (Eurochem, 1995; Farrant, 1997). The Source Testing Association has produced guidance for stack emissions monitoring specifically (STA, 1998).

The EA has established a monitoring certification scheme, known as MCERTS, and a number of subschemes covering different applications. The CEMs scheme covering continuous monitoring of releases to air from chimney stacks gives type-approval to instruments shown to meet certain technical specifications. The scheme covering manual stack emissions monitoring is very different, being broken down into two parts: one covering the personal registration and certification of technicians carrying out manual stack emissions monitoring; the other part covering certification of organizations meeting the requirements of EN ISO/IEC 17025: 2000, with some additional, specific requirements. Further information can be found at the EA's web site, www.environment-agency.gov.uk – search for 'MCERTS'.

Operator monitoring assessment (OMA) is the EA's audit based assessment of the quality and reliability of monitoring data submitted to them by process operators themselves. OMA focused initially on emissions to air from chimney stacks of integrated pollution control (IPC) processes, but it is now being extended to releases to water and to PPC regulated premises. The scheme covers monitoring carried out using CEMs, periodic monitoring and surrogate monitoring.

OMA will contribute towards targeting the EA's own check-monitoring visits according to risk, hence sites awarded a high OMA score may be less likely to be targeted. The EA expects to place a greater reliance on self monitoring as its transparency and quality improve. OMA, in combination with MCERTS, will act as a driver towards improved data quality. The OMA guidance on scoring of particular areas can be found on the EA's web site, www.environment-agency.gov.uk – search for 'OMA'.

References

Bearman, A. and Kingsbury, B. (1994) 'Assessment of Nuisance from Deposited Particulates Using a Simple and Inexpensive Measuring System', *Journal of Clean Air*, vol 24, no 4, pp164–169

BSI (1999) 'BS 5390 Site Investigations and BS 10175 Investigation of Potentially Contaminated Sites', British Standards Institution, London

Burgess, C. (2000) *Valid Analytical Methods and Procedures*, Royal Society of Chemistry, London

DETR (2000) 'Minerals Planning Guidance Note 11, Controlling and Mitigating the Environmental Effects of Minerals Extraction in England', Department of the Environment, Transport and the Regions, London

EA (2000) 'Technical Guidance Note M8 Environmental Monitoring Strategy – Ambient Air', The Stationery Office, London

EA (2002a) 'Technical Guidance Document (Monitoring) M2, Monitoring of Stack Emissions to Air', Environment Agency, Bristol

EA (2002b) 'Technical Guidance Document (Monitoring) M17, Monitoring of Particulate Matter in Ambient Air Around Waste Facilities, (Consultation Draft)', Environment Agency, Bristol

EA (2002c) 'Technical Guidance Note IPPC H4, Horizontal Guidance for Odour, (Consultation Draft)', Environment Agency, Bristol

Eurochem (1995) *Quantifying Uncertainty in Analytical Measurements*, Eurochem Secretariat, Teddington

Farrant, T. (1997) *Practical Statistics for the Analytical Scientist – A Bench Guide*, Royal Society of Chemistry, London

Harrison, E. (ed) (1992) *Pollution: Causes, Effects and Controls*, Royal Society of Chemistry, London

Harrison, R. and Perry, R. (1986) *Handbook of Air Pollution Analysis*, 2nd edn, Chapman & Hall, London

ISO (1995) 'Guide to the Expression of Uncertainty in Analytical Measurement', International Organization for Standardization, Geneva

Pritchard, E. (2001) *Analytical Measurement Terminology*, Royal Society of Chemistry, London

Radojevic, M. and Bashkin, V. (1999) *Practical Environmental Analysis*, Royal Society of Chemistry, London

Schwar, M. (1994) 'A Dust Meter for Measuring Dust Deposition and Soiling of Glossy Surfaces', *Journal of Clean Air*, vol 24, no 4, pp164–169

STA (1998) *Quality Guidance Note QGN1, Guidance on Assessing Measurement Uncertainty in Stack Emissions Monitoring*, Source Testing Association, London

University of Salford (2001) *A Good Practice Guide on the Sources and Magnitudes of Uncertainty Arising in the Practical Measurement of Environmental Noise*, University of Salford, Salford

Woodfield, M. and Hall, D. (1994) *'Odour Measurement and Control – An Update*, AEA Technology, Oxford

Chapter 5.3

Auditing in Environmental Management

Introduction

What management tool was used by large and high profile companies (mostly in the US and Europe) in the mid-1980s and early 1990s, but by the late 1990s was being used by thousands of organizations in the public and private sectors across the world? The answer is environmental auditing. Except that by the late 1990s the nature of environmental auditing had altered quite significantly. From its original use as a strategic tool in the development of environmental policies and strategies it has evolved to become a multipurpose tool with both strategic and operational applications. In many ways it is the Swiss Army knife of environmental management.

The two driving forces behind the development of environmental auditing as a management tool and its wider application have undoubtedly been:

- the emergence of standards for environmental management systems – BS 7750 in 1994, EU Eco-management and Audit Scheme Regulation (EMAS) in 1993, and ISO 14001 in 1996; and
- the need for managers to demonstrate improvements in environmental performance, and to provide assurance on environmental risks, to a greater number of stakeholders.

Environmental auditing is now an integral part of environmental management and is, in particular, a major requirement of the standards for environmental management systems (EMS). As the focus shifts from purely environmental goals towards sustainability (encompassing social, ethical and economic dimensions), environmental auditing is beginning to assume an even larger role. In the context of environmental auditing this has to do with interest in environmental performance being, necessarily, extended beyond the boundaries of a company or organization to suppliers, customers and users.

Definitions

Environmental auditing is a generic term for a range of investigative and checking activities, based on a common methodology and related protocols, aimed at supporting different management processes and decision making in relation to environmental performance. While an essential component of an EMS, it is by no means limited to the role of verifying compliance with management systems standards. Although the EMS has provided the platform for recent developments, environmental auditing still has a much wider role.

The environmental review was considered to be an early form of environmental auditing although there was no common understanding of how it should be done. The definition given in the latest version of the EMAS Regulation and the requirements set out in Annex VII indicate that environmental reviews can be carried out as either information gathering exercises or as a form of audit. The review is defined as 'an initial comprehensive analysis of the environmental issues, impacts and performance related to activities of an organization' (EU, 2001).

Most other modern definitions either refer directly to or are based on the classic International Chamber of Commerce (ICC) definition, which states that the environmental audit is:

> a management tool comprising a systematic, documented, periodic, and objective evaluation of how well organizations, management and equipment are performing with the aim of contributing to safeguard the environment by facilitating management control of practices, and assessing compliance with company policies, which would include meeting regulatory requirements and standards applicable.

The evaluation of performance in the EMAS definition covers processes rather than just equipment, and the aim is to facilitate 'management control of practices which may have an impact on the environment' (EU, 2001), thereby making it more prescriptive in terms of scope. Similarly, the assessment of compliance also covers 'objectives and targets of the organization'. The audit should be an evaluation of performance rather than a check for compliance with practices. The ICC definition could be interpreted in a similar way.

The definition in ISO 14001 is similar to that in EMAS, but focuses more strongly on management systems, both in the title – environmental management systems audit – and in the definition itself – whether the 'environmental management system conforms to the environmental management systems audit criteria set by the organization'. There is no direct reference to performance. While the achievement of performance is implicit in the aims of EMS, not everybody sees the audit as being an evaluation of performance.

The definition in ISO 19011 – guidelines for quality and/or environmental management systems auditing – is interesting as it is evidently linked to the way in which the financial professional defines auditing. In this standard an audit is a 'systematic, independent and documented process for obtaining audit evidence ... and evaluating it objectively to determine the extent to which audit criteria ... are fulfilled'.

In most audits there must be some reference point or norm against which the subject of the audit is being investigated; for example to audit an effluent treatment plant against its operating instructions and against the terms and conditions of its discharge consent under the Water Industry Act. The role of the audit, therefore, is to certify the validity of a statement that may be implicit (e.g. we comply with all company policies and procedures) or explicit (e.g. text in an environmental report that states that 'this is a true and fair representation of performance').

For those involved in environmental management, as in other areas of management, auditing is clearly an important tool. The expectation is that environmental auditing will be used in different ways at different times, including:

- at the time of major investment decision making – such as a company merger or acquisition – to investigate environmental risks and potential liabilities;
- in product development to check for conformity with company targets and legal requirements;
- in supplier evaluation either as part of selection or an ongoing performance evaluation;
- in reviewing current environmental performance as the basis for developing objectives and targets for future performance; and
- in checking whether EMS requirements are being met.

This chapter aims to guide the reader in determining the type of environmental auditing that may be appropriate and to provide some useful references to key standards and guidance.

Scope and objectives of auditing

The different definitions of auditing can be confusing but we cannot be prescriptive about what an environmental audit should be for every organization and for all circumstances. If we accept that environmental auditing in all its forms involves a common methodology of investigating and checking existing conditions (practices, procedures, processes and systems) against predetermined criteria (technical specifications, operating instructions, standards, regulations, policies and performance objectives) then we have a ready means of determining scope and objectives for an audit. A number of key variables need to be considered in determining scope, in particular:

- geographic location (country, region, site);
- organizational unit (company, division, department);
- processes (manufacturing and managerial/administrative, including design, procurement and distribution);
- products/services (design, performance in use and disposal); and
- system elements (e.g. procedures for assuring regulatory compliance).

The selection of the appropriate mix of the above variables together with the relevant specifications or standards will enable audit scope to be determined.

For environmental auditing to be successful it is essential that the objectives are clearly defined, and it is likely that these will have a significant bearing on the scope that is selected. Environmental auditing objectives can vary. References are made to compliance, effectiveness and performance. In the case of an environmental review there is reference to analysis. In broad terms auditing objectives can be classified into three types as follows, although these are not meant to be mutually exclusive:

Management (internal) assurance

- Internal audit of EMS – is the EMS operating as intended, in accordance with defined responsibilities and procedures?
- Environmental performance – how well are objectives and targets being met?
- Risk management – how well are risks being identified and managed?
- Regulatory compliance – are operations within regulatory limits? Are consent, permit and authorization conditions being met?
- Supplier audit – how well do suppliers meet requirements related to products and services supplied?

Information for decision making

Due diligence audits are concerned with the acquisition of sites and companies. Questions might include: 'how well is the company managing environmental performance?' and 'is the site or company being operated in accordance with relevant environmental regulations?' They can include some assessment of compliance as the basis for determining potential liabilities. When applied to land transactions the audit aims to determine the presence of any pollutants that may have caused environmental damage, or may do so in the future.

Environmental risk assessment is often undertaken for investment or insurance purposes. For example, have hazards been identified and have appropriate management practices been put in place for prevention and mitigation?

An environmental review is normally undertaken for the purposes of development of environmental policy and strategy. Questions could include: 'how do the activities, products and services of the organization impact on the environment?', 'what are the relevant regulations and standards to which the organization should operate?', 'what are the current practices for managing environmental performance?' and 'what changes should be made to existing systems and operations?'

A supplier audit is used for selection purposes. The question might be: 'do suppliers meet company specified criteria for products and services and for their own operations?'

Stakeholder (external) assurance

These environmental audits are intended primarily for external consumption, either through information publication or certification. Certain other audits, such as due diligence and risk assessment, will also be used by external stakeholders as part of their decision making processes. The results, however, are rarely made publicly available. Examples include:

- EMS – does the EMS meet the ISO 14001 specification?
- EMAS – do the EMS and the published environmental statement meet the requirements?
- Environmental and sustainability reports – does the report meet Global Reporting Initiative guidelines?
- Environmental performance data, including greenhouse gas emissions – can it be verified that data provide a complete and accurate representation of performance and have data been calculated and presented according to specified requirements such as the UK Emissions Trading Scheme or Climate Change Agreement?

- Product audit in relation to eco-labelling – do products meet specified environmental performance criteria such as energy efficiency, resource and materials use, and toxicity, emissions and waste byproducts?

First, second and third party audits

A further significant variable in determining the scope and objectives of an environmental audit concerns who should be the auditors. In broad terms auditors can be internal or external to the organization being audited.

Internal audits (sometimes called first party audits) are carried out by or on behalf of the organization for management control or other internal purposes. They can either be carried out by the organization's own employees or by appointed representatives.

External audits can be referred to as second or third party audits. The distinction lies mainly in the degree of independence and objectivity that can be provided by the auditors. Second party auditors are likely to come from, or to represent, organizations that have a direct interest in the organization being audited (such as a bank, insurance company, customer or potential investor, and shareholders including the parent organization).

Third party auditors, although still being paid by the organization or one of its stakeholder groups, are considered to be the most independent. Typically, these audits will belong to commercial auditing firms, particularly for ISO certification. Such firms are regulated by other authorities to ensure their impartiality and that appropriate auditing standards are being met.

In practice the distinctions between first, second and third party audits are not important or useful. The most important consideration will be the degree of independence required of the auditors, and therefore who should carry out the audit in accordance with the determined scope and objectives.

Sustainability – broadening the scope and objectives

Developments in corporate social responsibility and in guidelines for sustainability management raise the question of the role of environmental auditing in these areas. It is clear that sustainability criteria include environmental as well as social and economic factors. In one way, therefore, the role of environmental auditing may be quite obvious. In another way, it is clear that the common auditing methodology can be extended to cover social, ethical and economic requirements. However, environmental auditing should at least be extended to cover environmental requirements beyond the boundaries of the organization. Extending environmental auditing throughout the supply chain will be an important aspect of sustainability management, assuming of course that the organizations involved have determined or accepted specifications of environmental performance for the materials and services supplied, as well as products and services provided to customers. Sustainability management can, to some extent, be accommodated by suitably broadening the scope and objectives of environmental auditing.

Standards for environmental auditing

The emergence of national and international standards for EMS together with the 1993 EU Regulation for EMAS, has led to a significant growth in the numbers of environmental auditors. Environmental auditing has become an essential component of EMS. However, the EMS standards (including EMAS) are in themselves not entirely adequate for providing guidance on how environmental auditing should be carried out and on how environmental auditors should be qualified. In 1996, the International Organization for Standardization (ISO) introduced guidelines for environmental auditing covering general principles (ISO 14010), audit procedures for EMS (ISO 14011) and qualification criteria for environmental auditors (ISO 14012). All of these guidelines have since been replaced by one single standard that covers both quality and EMS auditing – ISO 19011.

ISO 14001: 1996

Clause 4.5.4 requires that programmes and procedures be established for periodic EMS auditing. The aim of auditing should be to determine whether the EMS conforms to planned arrangements (including the ISO 14001 specification), and whether it has been properly established and maintained. Results should be reported to management.

These requirements are effectively for internal audits. In its annex, however, the ISO 14001 specification states that external persons can be appointed as auditors, provided that the audits can be carried out impartially and objectively.

ISO 14001 should be seen as providing the basic requirements for environmental auditing. There is little guidance on how environmental auditing should be implemented in terms of principles and process although the annex does list what the audit programme and procedures should cover, namely: scope, frequency, responsibilities, process, reporting and auditor competence.

EMAS: 2001

The 2001 version of EMAS (replacing the 1993 regulation), incorporates the same requirements for EMS as ISO 14001, as well as requiring an environmental review to be conducted and the preparation of an environmental statement. EMAS is more prescriptive in its requirements for EMS, including environmental auditing.

Although the ISO 14001 text is used in Annex I, it must be noted that Article 3, in relation to environmental auditing, states that 'audits shall be designed to assess environmental performance of the organization'. This is a much stronger statement of requirement than 'conformance to planned arrangements', as required for ISO 14001.

Annex II of EMAS is useful, furthermore, because it provides more detailed requirements for how auditing should be carried out, covering: objectives, scope, organization and resources, planning and preparation, activities, reporting, follow up and frequency.

ISO 19011

This single standard covers auditing principles and procedures and auditor qualifications for both quality and EMS. As the most recent management systems standard it is based on generic principles that have evolved over time and reflects commonly accepted auditing practices.

ISO 19011 is probably the most useful reference document for anybody interested in learning about and implementing environmental auditing. It is both comprehensive and consistent with ISO 14001 and EMAS requirements. Although its focus is on management systems, it addresses principles and protocols that are applicable to all forms of environmental auditing.

The essentials of standards for environmental auditing

The standards discussed in this section provide what could be considered as a core set of norms for environmental auditing. The standards provide some concentrated guidance. More detailed guidance is available in the references at the end of this chapter (see Grayson, 1992; Hoggart, 2001; Pearson et al, 1992; Welford, 1996). In summary, the essential elements of environmental auditing are:

- a predetermined scope and objectives, including criteria against which performance can be assessed;
- defined procedures that can be applied consistently to different organizational areas, including methods for selecting or sampling the areas and the records to be covered;
- clear records of evidence that provide the basis of audit findings and conclusions;
- competent auditors who have the skills and knowledge (through suitable experience and training) to be able to meet audit objectives (typically an assessment of performance); and
- auditors appointed who can conduct the audit with impartiality and objectivity, and who will conduct themselves ethically and with due professional care, so that audit results will be truthful, accurate and based on professional judgement (refer to ISO 19011 for more detail).

Management systems auditing

Most environmental audits are connected with EMS in some way, whether or not the organization concerned is aiming for ISO 14001 certification or EMAS registration. Implementing and operating an EMS will require environmental auditors to work to different scopes and objectives at different stages of development. These will encompass not only environmental review and management systems audits, but also performance audits in key areas such as waste, water, energy and materials/resources.

Overall EMS auditing system and external audits

Figure 5.3.1 shows the key players involved in management systems auditing and notes the respective standards to which they must work. They all have a bearing on how environmental auditing should be implemented.

For both ISO 14001 and EMAS the organization must undertake an external audit of its EMS, with the aim of demonstrating that the requirements of the ISO 14001 standard or EMAS Regulation are satisfied. Certification/registration provides the organization

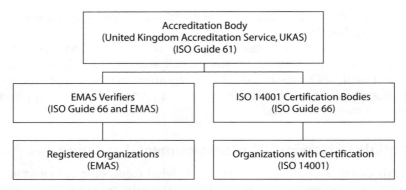

Figure 5.3.1   Management systems auditing

with external recognition of conformity with the standards. Some organizations do, however, use the standards as a framework for implementing an EMS without necessarily having the external audits.

In the case of EMAS registration, the regulation requires that external audits are carried out by accredited verifiers. The requirements for accreditation and verification are set out in the regulation articles and annexes. In the UK, the accreditation body is the United Kingdom Accreditation Service (UKAS). UKAS assesses, or audits, EMAS verifiers against the requirements of EMAS and those of ISO Guide 66 (UKAS, 2001). Guidance produced by the International Accreditation Forum is also used. For EMAS there is also a supplement to ISO Guide 66, which has been produced by UKAS for use in the UK.

The ISO 14001 standard does not stipulate who should carry out the external EMS audit. There are two types of certification body; bodies that are accredited by UKAS in the UK and, somewhat controversially, those that are not. Accredited certification bodies must be audited by UKAS to check that they meet the requirements of ISO Guide 66 for procedures and systems as well as against competence requirements. The accreditation system therefore acts as a quality control mechanism, which is independent and impartial. In the case of non-accredited bodies, any quality control is internal and self determined. To many people this means that accredited EMS auditing is more robust and more reliable, and less likely to be influenced as a result of conflicts of interest.

UKAS itself is also subject to audit by specially selected international teams brought together from other accreditation bodies, outside the UK. This is largely a peer review process, but UKAS must demonstrate that it meets relevant standards; in this case ISO Guide 61.

The main point of all this is to help the reader understand the system that affects the external auditors. There is no question that, within ISO 14001 and EMAS certification/registration, the way in which the EMS is implemented and operated will be influenced to some extent by how the auditors do their work – what areas they pay particular attention to, and how they interpret the respective standards. Hopefully this is mostly for the better. However, ISO 14001 and EMAS only provide a framework of generic requirements for EMS. Each organization must then decide how to interpret and put these requirements into practice.

Accordingly, one role of ISO Guide 66 is to guide certification bodies and EMAS verifiers in how they audit certain elements of EMS. In effect this provides some interpretation of EMS requirements. Organizations seeking to implement EMS and achieve ISO 14001 certification or EMAS registration would, therefore, be well advised to take ISO Guide 66 guidance into account as far as possible.

EMS internal audits

The different types of EMS audit that an organization may itself undertake at some stage, assuming that the fundamental goal is to improve environmental performance, are: the environmental review; an EMS implementation audit; an EMS effectiveness audit; an environmental performance audit; and a supplier audit.

Environmental review

An environmental review is not mandatory for EMS development, although it is an advisable step to take. The review is a useful tool, and can be carried out as a form of audit, as it can provide a strategic basis for the development of an EMS. It can also be useful in developing an environmental policy, as well as identifying specific areas for improvement. However, as with all audits, much depends on how the scope and objectives are set. The best guidance for environmental review can be found in Annex VII of the EMAS Regulation, which suggests that the review should cover:

- legislative, regulatory and other requirements;
- organization and systems, including responsibilities, practices and procedures;
- environmental aspects and impacts of activities, products and services; and
- results of investigations of previous incidents and performance problems.

Organizations working to the EMAS standard should make sure that the environmental review requirements are met (Article 3). However, this might not necessarily need to be a separate exercise, and it is possible to incorporate the requirements into the environmental aspects identification and evaluation as required by ISO 14001. Conversely, an environmental review can be used to identify environmental aspects and impacts in sufficient detail to form the basis for EMS development, in line with ISO 14001 requirements.

EMS implementation audit

For any organization implementing an EMS to ISO 14001 or EMAS it is worthwhile for auditing to be carried out at different stages. Clearly the audit scope and objectives would need to vary. We have already seen how the environmental review is a form of environmental auditing that may be valuable pre-EMS implementation, during the design stage. The term 'EMS implementation audit' is being used here to differentiate between audits that can take place during, and therefore facilitate, implementation, and those that are used predominately after implementation to assess the effectiveness of EMS.

Audits can be useful at more than one point during implementation and should certainly not be left to the later stages (as indeed the sequence of ISO 14001 clause numbers may imply). The scope and objectives are of course variable but typically would be to:

- cover one or more EMS elements, according to ISO 14001 or EMAS specification, within specified organization units (sites/departments);
- determine whether EMS elements are being put in place and adequately designed to meet EMS specifications;
- evaluate the extent of implementation to date – to ensure that EMS elements are suitably designed and documented and have all necessary procedures; and
- determine whether adequate plans are in place to complete the implementation.

Tables 5.3.1.and 5.3.2 give some guidance on implementation audits. The tables illustrate the key points that should be covered by the audit in two areas of the EMS. As such they are not intended as a checklist or to be comprehensive.

Table 5.3.1   Guidance on environmental aspects

- all activities, products and services covered (including past activities and processes);
- all types of aspects covered (air, land, water, waste, natural habitat, resources/materials, energy);
- procedure for identification;
- procedure covers significance evaluation; are criteria specified and sound/workable?
- data gathered in relation to recent/current performance;
- aspects include risk of impacts/pollution (aspects that may have an impact on the environment);
- covering aspects associated with product/service use and disposal, and with supply of materials and goods (indirect).

Table 5.3.2   Guidance on objectives and targets

- set for all significant environmental aspects;
- targets incorporate dates for achievement and quantifiable measures;
- consideration evidently given to interests of key stakeholders (interested parties);
- set on basis of evaluation of alternative technological and operational options (rather than just subjective estimates);
- set at all organization levels commensurate with managerial responsibilities or ability to control or make a difference.

EMS effectiveness audit

The prime purpose of an EMS is to achieve a desired standard of performance, whether this be to control performance within prescribed limits (as in regulatory compliance) or to improve performance to meet targeted levels (either voluntary or to meet new regulations). Audits aimed at determining whether the EMS is effective should therefore be performance oriented, regardless of scope, focusing on results and outputs rather than merely on the existence of procedures, responsibilities, training, objectives and targets and so on (these are inputs).

Effectiveness audits can take place at different times. External auditors, such as for certification purposes, would be expected to fully assess the EMS effectiveness. Therefore, it would be quite normal for part of the internal audit programme to be set to emulate the external audit, in preparation for certification audits. However, organizations would also benefit significantly from ensuring that internal audits were routinely programmed to cover EMS effectiveness and environmental performance. It is often the case that those operating an EMS will be influenced in how they do so by the approach taken by auditors. Therefore, internal auditors who consistently focus on outputs and performance are likely to encourage a stronger emphasis on similar areas throughout the organization. Auditing, done well, can therefore have a positive impact on environmental performance and should not be seen as merely a controlling function.

Two simple examples of how auditing can focus on performance are as follows:

- Has the EMS, as operated at the wastewater treatment plant, led to an achievement of regulatory standards (e.g. chemical oxygen demand (COD), suspended solids, acidity, temperature, oil)?
- Have risk assessments resulted in a reduction in the number of spills in line with targets, and a reduction in the hazard rating at the plant?

As with all other audits, the scope can be adjusted to meet specific objectives, although for certification purposes the organization and its EMS should be audited as a whole. For internal purposes it is also worth bearing in mind that it can be difficult to assess effectiveness if the scope is too narrow. Very often the auditor will need to determine whether different parts of the system operate well together. Typical objectives, as might be amended by varying scope, are to determine whether:

- the EMS, or specified parts, are achieving the desired results – for example people have been trained in accordance with plans and are operating in line with EMS requirements; and
- the EMS is resulting in intended performance in key areas – for example packaging waste has been reduced to the targeted level of 20kg per vehicle.

In evaluating EMS effectiveness in terms of environmental performance, the auditor should be dealing with quantitative results (as opposed to qualitative ones) and measurements. The ISO 14001 definition of environmental performance is useful here: 'Environmental performance: measurable results of the environmental management system, related to an organization's control of its environmental aspects, based on its environmental policy, objectives and targets' (BSI, 1996).

It is important to note that to audit in accordance with the above objectives the auditors need to go into much greater depth and detail. Information and evidence need to be gathered often directly from auditees, and direct reference will need to be made to records and sources of information. Where data are concerned, auditors should aim to trace back to source data, and should also aim to test and validate any calculations performed in data processing.

A major challenge here is how the auditor should best plan time to cover enough of the system and environmental performance areas, while also going into sufficient depth. Some form of sampling will be necessary. But this must not be completely at random or ad hoc. Sampling should be done systematically in accordance with prede-termined criteria, and recorded. At least, the auditor should make conscious decisions about how big the sample should be, how far back in record keeping to go, and if, for example, 12 measurement points are in place using three different types of technology, how many should be checked. It is the case rather too often in EMS auditing that ad hoc samples are taken without any understanding of nature and scale of the whole (from which the sample is taken). Accordingly auditors are mostly not in a position to state with confidence whether their sample is representative or adequate.

In evaluating performance it is also important to determine whether improvement has been achieved as a result of the operation of the EMS or for other reasons. It can be important to understand how performance has been achieved, as much as why it has not. This will then enable further improvements to be made to the EMS, and give the organization greater assurance that performance is sustainable.

Two examples of how auditing can contribute to achieving improvements in environ-mental performance are given in Table 5.3.3.

Table 5.3.3   Auditing for environmental improvement

Regulatory compliance example
- Are limits as set by consents/permits/authorizations being achieved?
- Is there compliance with other, non-measurable conditions (e.g. how waste is stored, record keeping)?
- Check a sample of records as evidence of performance. Check some data to find the source of measurements or data inputs. Determine the validity of key data upon which analysis and reporting of performance is dependent (e.g. calibration of measuring equipment).
- In view of the importance of regulatory compliance, it is advisable to audit all applicable regulatory requirements more frequently and within a reasonable time period, if not during the same audit.

Performance measurement example
- Check data and quantitative information used to report performance for significant environmental aspects.
- As with regulatory compliance, check the validity of data and information (is it sufficiently accurate?)
- How have performance information and data been reported; have they been communicated and used as intended?
- Have actions been taken as a result of performance analysis and review, and have these been implemented?
- Have the actions had the planned effect in terms of performance?

Environmental performance audit

There are other ways to test the effectiveness of an EMS than focusing on organization units or parts of the EMS, especially if the audit is being used to identify opportunities for improvement. Some organizations, and indeed some certification auditors, will scope the audit to investigate a cross-section of the EMS for a particular performance area (such as energy, waste, emissions, resource/material usage or product disposal), as illustrated in Table 5.3.4.

Table 5.3.4   Auditing for waste

Objective: to audit the effectiveness of the EMS with respect to the handling, storage and disposal of waste.

Scope: all processes and areas of the site which are involved in generating, handling, storing, treating and disposing of liquid and solid waste (excluding effluents and wastewaters).

Target Performance: quantity of waste, by type, by key area.
Current Performance: quantity of waste, by type, by key area.
Baseline Performance: quantity of waste, by type, by key area.

Identify all relevant requirements of EMS and related responsibilities.

Develop an audit plan, and review documents and records in preparation for the audit. Decide on key waste streams and areas to audit. Visit relevant site areas and departments.

Key elements of the EMS should at least include (but may need to be more comprehensive):

- identification and evaluation of environmental aspects;
- risk assessment and emergency response planning;
- objectives and targets;
- responsibilities;
- training;
- performance measurement;
- management reporting/review.

Supplier audit

Some organizations, particularly those working towards sustainability, wish to extend the EMS beyond the boundaries of their own organization. One way of doing this, especially if product stewardship policies and programmes are being put in place, is to work with suppliers. The ISO 14001 requirement is quite basic with respect to suppliers in that organizations only need to communicate relevant EMS requirements to their suppliers. This may or may not involve specifying particular requirements, and the typical response is often to encourage suppliers to obtain ISO 14001 certification. However, this in itself will provide no assurance regarding any aspect of performance. Those organizations seeking more assurance or wishing to influence environmental performance in other parts of the supply chain or product life cycle will take more proactive steps. Often this will concern materials and resources used, and the specification of good practices such as with waste and recycling. Supplier audits can cover:

- regulatory compliance – for example waste contractors complying with waste licensing and disposal regulations;
- product and service specifications – for example elimination of cadmium and lead in automotive products; and
- environmental practices or management systems – for example methods for material and wastes storage and handling, including those in developing industrial countries.

In summary, EMS auditing, in all its different forms, has the potential to make a significant contribution to improving environmental performance and directing an organization towards sustainability. However, to do so it must be properly designed and planned so that the effectiveness of the system is tested and the reasons for good and poor performance are understood. The goal must be to make improvements to the systems and practices of the organization with the specific aim of improving environmental performance.

Auditor qualifications

Environmental auditing is clearly a key part of an EMS. It has a major role to play in ensuring that the EMS is effective and environmental performance requirements are met, whether the scope and objectives of the audit are purely to check conformity with EMS requirements (as with ISO 14001 certification) or to identify opportunities for improvement. It goes without saying that effective environmental auditing is essential if the EMS is to be effective.

While a sound auditing procedure together with good protocols (planning, checklists, reporting and follow up) is important, the key to effective environmental auditing rests with the competence of the auditors. A suitable combination of education, training and experience, at least within the team as a whole, is needed. There are those people who argue that an auditor who is experienced at auditing management systems will be able to audit other management systems – whether between quality and environment, or between EMS in industrial sectors that are significantly different. It seems that, for some, general environmental training is considered to be adequate for most if not all EMS auditing. This cannot be a good recipe for achieving better environmental performance.

But if we are to gain real value from environmental auditing, then the auditors must be capable of auditing EMS effectiveness in terms of environmental performance achieved. This means being able to recognize good performance and poor performance, and being able to investigate and identify the causes. One of the real tests of auditor competence is whether or not errors of omission are identified; for example:

- A manufacturer operating straightforward machining processes, discharging wastewater without a consent has not recognized that one is required. Does the auditor pick this up?
- In risk assessment, are all significant risk events and hazards covered or does the auditor just consider those that have been identified and assessed by the client?

Personal attributes are also important: the ability to operate professionally; asking the right kinds of question and following a line of investigation; and being able to work impartially and objectively.

However, competence (training, knowledge and experience) is the single most important requirement. Of course, not all auditors can be as highly qualified, or need to be. Whether auditing internally or externally, in (environmentally) simple or complex organizations, the important thing is to put together a team that, basically, knows about what they are auditing and what they should expect in terms of performance and how it should be managed.

Auditor registration schemes

There are different schemes around the world, and two in the UK in particular, operated by the Institute of Quality Assurance (IQA) – the International Register for Certificated Auditors (IRCA) – and the Institute of Environmental Management and Assessment (IEMA). Individuals can gain registration by meeting specified criteria for education/training and auditing experience. These registration schemes must, however, be seen for what they are. They provide a general indication of auditor qualification and experience, but do not provide any indication of competence to carry out a specific audit in a particular type of operation. They are therefore not reliable indicators of competence and should not be used alone as criteria for selecting auditors.

ISO 19011

ISO 19011 provides a useful framework for establishing qualification criteria for auditors, and their evaluation. The guidelines are predominantly written for external (certification) auditors. Those organizations seeking to set criteria for internal auditors are likely to take a simpler approach, albeit based on the same principles.

The standard sets out guidelines for personal attributes and generic skills required for management systems auditing. There are then guidelines for specific knowledge and skills of environmental management systems auditors, namely:

- environmental management methods and technologies – how an EMS works;
- environmental science and technology – how human activities interact with the environment;
- technical and environmental aspects of operations – how the auditee organization's activities, products and services interact with the environment; and
- knowledge of applicable laws, regulations and other requirements.

These broad criteria are clearly open to considerable interpretation. Indeed, one should expect that external auditors are far more knowledgeable and have wider, possibly more specialized, experience, given that auditing is their day to day work. For internal auditors, less knowledge and experience will be adequate provided it is relevant to the operations being audited.

Table 1 in ISO 19011 gives an illustration of how these criteria might be quantified, although no direct reference is made to the different areas of specific knowledge and skills. The danger here is that people will take the figures provided as the norm, whereas for some external auditors they could be wholly inadequate and for many internal auditors they will be too stringent.

External (certification) auditors must interpret the ISO 19011 guidelines and develop their own more specific criteria for knowledge and experience. This is a requirement for their accreditation under ISO guidelines and they are assessed accordingly, by UKAS assessors in the UK.

For internal auditors, there is no explicit requirement to develop specific criteria or to evaluate audit qualifications and performance. However, the ISO 19011 principles and guidelines are sound, and to gain value from environmental auditing, all organizations should be encouraged to develop suitable, relevant criteria for qualification. Table 5.3.5 gives an example of how qualification criteria can be set.

Table 5.3.5   Setting auditor qualification criteria

- **Training**
Attendance on environmental training and EMS internal auditor training courses (between 5 and 15 days' training in total, which can lead to a professional qualification and EMS auditor status).
- **Process knowledge**
How much does an auditor need to know about operations to be able to audit EMS for effectiveness (x years in the company or working with specific or similar processes)?
- **Familiarity with EMS**
Attendance at internal environmental awareness sessions; study of EMS manuals and procedures; internal auditor training based on the EMS.
- **Auditing experience**
Auditing of different parts of EMS under supervision/coaching.

Links with other business systems

There has been much talk about integrated management systems since the introduction of ISO 14001 in 1996. At one time there was even a proposal under consideration by ISO and other standards organizations to develop a separate specification for integrated systems. However, at the time of writing the desire for integration has been typically translated into developments that provide greater consistency and some common elements between business systems.

If we consider the areas of quality systems and health and safety systems, and possibly sustainability, as being those most closely linked with the environment, then there have been several significant developments since 1996, as follows:

- The standards for quality management systems were revised in 2000 and adopted certain key principles from the EMS standards. The most notable was that organizations should set objectives and targets for quality performance that are, as far as possible, quantifiable and measurable; performance against these targets should be measured and monitored. Accordingly, the audit processes should by now also be more performance oriented as described earlier. This is not to say, of course, that some organizations did not run their quality management systems with the aim of achieving specified performance objectives.
- Guidelines have been introduced by the British Standards Institution for the implementation of occupational health and safety management systems – OHSAS 18001 (BSI, 1999). The guidelines have been modelled very closely on ISO 14001, although there is additionally an explicit requirement for risk assessment (something that many claim the EMS standard lacks); there is a very similar requirement for internal auditing of health and safety management systems.
- There has been some development of guidelines for sustainability management, under the title of Project Sigma, which has been co-sponsored by the DTI, BSI and

Forum for the Future. Some people may question the validity of applying the management systems model to sustainable development; but there is undoubtedly a need for companies that are seeking to develop strategies towards sustainability to be able to see the links between sustainability programmes and other management systems. In their present form the guidelines are similar to ISO 14001 (based on the same model) and also have a requirement for auditing.

Given the commonality between these systems and between different types of auditing, many organizations are likely to integrate their auditing procedures and protocols. However, it is important to acknowledge that, while some savings may accrue, they will not get three audits for the price of one, as sometimes is the expectation. Some systems elements will be common (for example the way responsibilities are defined, communication methods, the way in which objectives and targets are set, the management reporting and review processes) and can be audited simultaneously. However, it is essential to remember that there are fundamental differences between quality performance, health and safety performance and environmental performance. In fact there may even be conflicts between them (for example extending process time for product quality purposes, which increases energy and resource use). These differences should translate into differences in key areas such as audit plans, checklists (the nature of evidence needed) and reporting. There will also be implications for who should carry out the audits, to ensure that suitably qualified auditors are involved as required in each area.

The integration of management systems auditing can be beneficial but requires careful planning to ensure that the effectiveness of each system is adequately assessed by competent auditors. In particular where combined audits are carried out it is important to ensure that a proper balance is achieved between the environment, quality and health and safety performance, as appropriate.

Conclusions

Environmental auditing plays a key role in environmental management whether in the day to day management of environmental performance, in decision making or in providing assurance to stakeholders. If performed well, auditing can have a positive impact on the effectiveness of environmental management systems and in the achievement of better performance. To do this, however, requires a clear scope, objectives to be set for assessing effectiveness and performance, and auditors to be suitably qualified.

It is in these areas that the value of environmental management systems auditing is being questioned. There have been claims that the operation of a certified EMS (to ISO 14001 or EMAS) does not ensure compliance with environmental regulations or improvement in performance. Indeed, there have been cases where some organizations have been prosecuted in spite of having a recently audited EMS. Of course this is bound to call into question the integrity of the overall system – whether the standards are strong enough, whether auditors are sufficiently qualified, whether the right auditors are selected and whether the accreditation of auditors is sufficiently based on an evaluation of environmental competence. Of course, it is possible that other factors can come into play; but it is fair to say that environmental auditing, especially for management systems, is under the spotlight and needs to be strengthened at all levels.

The various standards for environmental auditing (ISO 14001 and EMAS), and others that are relevant, provide good frameworks. In the case of ISO 19011 there is sound and detailed guidance for auditing; but this is mostly generic and largely process oriented (how to plan and carry out auditing). Of course this is inevitable with any standard that needs to be widely applicable across many types of organization and in different countries. It is essential for all those involved with environmental auditing (internal as well as external) to study the standards carefully and to apply them robustly in a way that genuinely assesses effectiveness. This has implications for the training and selection of environmental auditors who need to be sufficiently knowledgeable to interpret and apply the standards in the areas in which they are working. The acid test should be whether they are adequately qualified and experienced so as to be able to identify what is missing, rather than merely auditing what is already in place. Only then will you find that environmental auditing is of real benefit to the organization and to the environment.

References and further reading

BSI (1996) 'BS EN ISO 14001:1996, Environmental Management Systems – Specification with Guidance for Use', British Standards Institution, London or www.iema.net/shop

BSI (1999) 'OHSAS 18001:1999, Occupational Health and Safety Management Systems – Specification', British Standards Institution, London or www.iema.net/shop

BSI (2002) 'BS EN ISO 19011, Guidelines for Quality and/or Environmental Management Systems Auditing', British Standards Institution, London or www.iema.net/shop

EU (2001) 'European Parliament and the Council of the European Union Regulation 761/2001 Allowing Voluntary Participation by Organisations in a Community Eco-management and Audit Scheme (EMAS)', *Official Journal of the European Community*, L114/1 24/4/2001, Brussels

Grayson, L. (1992) *Environmental Auditing: A Guide to Best Practice in the UK and Europe*, Earthscan, London

Hoggart, C. (2001) *Environmental Auditing for the Non-specialist*, Chadwick House Group, London

ICC (1991) *ICC Guide, Effective Environmental Auditing*, International Chamber of Commerce, London

Pearson, B., Little, B. and Brierley, M. (1992) *Using Environmental Management Systems to Improve Profits*, Kluwer Publishers, Dordrecht

UKAS (1996) 'ISO Guide 61, General Requirements for Bodies Operating Assessment and Registration of Accreditation Bodies', United Kingdom Accreditation Service, London

UKAS (2001) 'ISO Guide 66, General Requirements for Bodies Operating Assessment and Certification/Registration of Environmental Management Systems (EMS) Issue 2 and Related Guidance Issued by IAF – International Accreditation Forum', United Kingdom Accreditation Service, London

Welford, R. (1996) *Corporate Environmental Management: Systems and Strategies*, Earthscan, London

Section 6

Communicating with Stakeholders

Chapter 6.1

Indicators

Introduction

From the point of view of all the interrelations between the different media and living species, our environment is a complex system; but it is also complex in the way that organizations interact and have an impact on it. To be able to manage the way organizations impact on the environment we need management tools that provide useful information and help us deal with this complexity and interaction.

Active management of these interrelations requires the identification and understanding of the particular aspects of our activities, products and services that impact on the environment. Aspects are defined in the ISO 14000 series as 'element(s) of an organization's activities, products or services that can interact with the environment' (ISO, 1996). Furthermore, the prioritization and allocation of resources need to be based on some notion of the scale of these impacts.

Indicators seek to capture the magnitude and direction of change of aspects and impacts, and by using indicators properly we can develop a picture of an organization's environmental performance. From an organization's perspective it is important that indicators enable decision making to be based on an understanding of the environmental and business implications; it also helps if the format and units strike a cord with senior management.

The use of indicators presents a number of difficulties. For example, the lack of standard environmental measures and the general poor quality or lack of data might mean that proxy or qualitative measures are the best available option. Additionally, the often-times iterative process of defining, measuring and redefining indicators might halt the process before arriving at the best option.

In overcoming these challenges it will be important that the limitations and biases inherent in some indicators are carefully considered during their development. It is also important to recognize that no single approach to environmental performance measurement is appropriate for all organizations. While there are difficulties, progress in the field demonstrates that it is possible to reap the benefits of measurement by improving environmental performance.

Organizations need to be aware of the risks and opportunities arising from their interactions with the environment. For successful management, these risks and opportunities should be accounted for in the measurement of environmental performance and embedded in core business processes. In this way indicators will provide the right information at the right time to the right person to make the right decisions.

This chapter offers an insight into the subject of environmental indicators. The subject is explored from three different angles, namely:

- the use of indicators for internal management;
- the use of indicators to measure performance from the perspective of an external stakeholder; and
- future trends and market expectations in terms of the overall subject.

Indicators as an internal management tool

The International Organization for Standardization published the standard ISO 14031, guidelines for environmental performance evaluation (EPE), in 1999 (ISO, 1999a). ISO 14031 is a systematic way (but not the only one available) of approaching the subject. It is not a certifiable standard but is a guidance document that is intended to support the development of EPE systems.

The guidelines propose a simple but systematic approach to EPE using the plan–do–check–act process. The basic steps are identified in the guidelines along with some key considerations in undertaking these steps. Examples are given and lists of potential indicators are contained in Annex A. Case studies on the application of EPE can be found in the technical report ISO/TR 14032 (ISO, 1999b).

The key to EPE is to identify an organization's activities, products and services that are relevant from an environmental point of view. This process needs to be informed by considerations of the magnitude of the impacts on the environment, the interests and pressures from internal and external stakeholders, and relevant criteria for performance.

Following broadly the same process described above, the UK has developed a strategy for sustainable development and within it a number of national headline environmental indicators have been identified such as: greenhouse gas (GHG) emissions, road traffic by type of road, populations of farmland or woodland birds, and percentages of river length of good biological or chemical quality. Indicators have also been developed to measure the quality of life in the UK – examples include domestic water use and noise. Industry bodies have developed industry specific schemes; examples include the Responsible Care Programme for the Chemical Industries Association (CIA, 2004) and the sustainability indicators project for the water industry (Luckhurst, 2003).

The point is that there are many different indicators. Some of them might not be directly applicable to particular organizations, but they point to areas that the UK Government and other stakeholders think are significant. These are important considerations that should inform an organization's decision making process of selecting relevant environmental issues to measure and manage.

Measurement should be of value in the management of an organization, but it is not an end in itself. A very common problem with environmental indicators is where organizations identify the need to measure their environmental performance but do not follow a systematic process to select indicators. Resources are wasted and ultimately the organization might decide that it is not worthwhile maintaining the indicators as they do not add any value; the consequence is a failure to manage the risks or to seize the opportunities that the environment presents.

To ensure that an indicator will be of value we need to consider its users – indicators should be developed in consultation with them, so that the information and the form in which the indicator is presented are appropriate. In particular, users need to be fully aware of related assumptions and limitations so that interpretations are valid.

It is important to consider existing data availability. In many cases the data required for the indicators does not exist, does not have the form or quality required or has to be collated from many different departments and systems within the organization. Depending on the use of the indicators, a validation or auditing process might be required to ensure the robustness of the information. Therefore, from the outset the scope and key attributes of the indicator should be clearly defined. Additionally, there is the need to identify, communicate and provide training and documentation where required in relation to the responsibilities for data collection, management and decision making.

Indicator design and implementation require careful consideration of organizational structures, resources, data availability and supporting systems. The process tends to be iterative, coming back and forth between user and other stakeholders. Within these iterations it is important to check that the indicator is indeed driving the desired behaviour. Actively engaging stakeholders to obtain feedback might be particularly relevant if the indicator is to be used as an external communication tool.

The first classification: ECIs, OPIs and MPIs

Two classifications are presented in ISO 14031, the first relating to what is measured and the second to how information is presented. The first classification works on the principle that an aspect of an organization's environmental performance can be measured in three main ways; namely:

- by directly measuring a particular environmental condition affected by the organization (environmental condition indicator or ECI). An ECI records changes in an environmental condition, and this can help an organization to identify whether the impact is relevant;
- by using an operational performance indicator or OPI. This is a more direct measure of environmental performance. It tracks an organization's operational inputs and outputs that can have an impact on the environment; and
- by using a management performance indicator or MPI. This measures the effort invested by an organization to reduce or control an impact on the environment.

Each type of indicator has its strengths and weaknesses. An MPI can be used to predict OPIs and ECIs, but they are usually difficult to quantify and evaluate. On the other hand an OPI is usually easy to quantify and tends to identify the root causes of an impact, but it can only provide information on previous performance. An ECI can be the most difficult to use because some environmental conditions are particularly difficult to measure. Moreover, the environment may suffer changes due to many variables outside the control of the organization. Thus, establishing a clear link with a selected OPI is not always possible.

This classification is of greatest value when the three types of indicator complement each other. So, for example, an organization can identify the number of species (ECI) in a local lake that are affected by their effluent discharge into the lake (OPI), and that the quality of the effluent discharge is influenced by the number of trained operators (MPI). This method of action – reaction using ECIs, OPIs and MPIs – can be very useful; however, as we have seen it has its limitations.

The second classification: presentation of indicators

The second classification of indicators in ISO 14031 is based on how the information is presented. Indicators are made up of different data sets, which are related by a mathematical formula. The formula could be very simple, such as the sum of individual components or a division or ratio, or it could be a complex algorithm with many variables. This second classification identifies six basic approaches, namely:

- **Direct indicators:** These are the simplest type in which a data set is assembled from the point of measurement.
- **Aggregated indicators:** A number of data sets of the same nature can be aggregated – for example aggregating waste arising from all sites within an organization.
- **Index indicators:** An alternative is to create an index, by taking a baseline (for example a particular year's performance or a standard performance) and then producing a ratio to compare it to the present performance.
- **Relative indicators:** When it is important to account for the variability of a particular factor it can be correlated in a relative indicator by, for example, relating emissions to production. The World Business Council for Sustainable Development introduced the concept of eco-efficiency using this type of indicator. Eco-efficiency is the ratio of the value of products or services to the magnitude of the environmental impact.
- **Weighted indicators:** An indicator can also have data sets weighted differently depending on certain criteria.
- **Qualitative indicators:** Although not included in ISO 14031, this is in some cases the most suitable.

There are particular strengths and weaknesses to each of these types of indicator. For example, a relative indicator might not work well if there are changes in variables not considered in the design of the indicator. An index indicator might provide a useful tool to benchmark facilities in the same organization, but it is unlikely to allow external benchmarking. In selecting a weighted indicator as a function of the significance of multiple environmental aspects, there is no exact science to determine which aspects should have more weight and by how much. Qualitative indicators are particularly difficult to interpret and evaluate; however, it is important to recognize that not every single aspect related to environmental management can be measured quantitatively. For example, the assessment of the level of implementation of a policy might be better measured with a qualitative description.

In the literature and in practice there are many more types and classifications of indicator. Nevertheless, the message here is that environmental performance can be measured in many different ways and a combination is usually the most effective way to use indicators as internal management tools.

Many organizations have experimented with and developed environmental balanced scorecards (for example Kaplan and Norton, 1992). The balanced scorecard is like an aeroplane's cockpit – it contains a number of indicators that provide condensed information at a glance to allow the pilot to make decisions on how to fly the plane. The environmental balanced scorecard provides key indicators that inform an organization's decision making processes. However, users of this technique have frequently pointed out that a scorecard does not provide a bottom line score and in some cases it might not be helpful in predicting the impacts a particular indicator has on other parts of the scorecard.

Indicators can be used to measure progress towards an improvement target. A common problem is that targets are not based on robust and tested indicators. This makes it impossible to determine whether they have been achieved. Another common problem with targets is that the baseline is not known. An indicator can help to determine where the baseline is. This allows an organization to make a much more informed decision on where the target should be set, which increases the chances of success and strengthens the push towards environmental improvement.

Targets are a crucial element of an environmental management system (EMS). It is perhaps the monitoring and measuring clause (4.5.1) in ISO 14001 (ISO, 1996) that is most directly relevant to indicators. The clause states that:

> The organization shall establish and maintain documented procedure(s) to monitor and measure, on a regular basis, the key characteristics of its operations and activities that can have a significant impact on the environment.

This clause has implications for other clauses and thus extends the importance of indicators in the context of the EMS – for example by using indicators to help maintain operational control (Clause 4.4.6) and legal compliance (actually included in the monitoring and measuring Clause 4.5.1). Records (Clause 4.5.3) are likely to hold the data required for the indicators.

It is actually possible to develop performance indicators for most of the clauses in ISO 14001; for example, MPIs could be based on the results of the audits or on progress with the training programme. Many organizations have actually followed this idea by using indicators, which measure the progress of sites towards the implementation of an EMS. BSI has recently published BS 8555 (BSI, 2003) as a guiding standard for the phased implementation of EMS incorporating EPE. The method embeds performance indicators into all phases of EMS development and the phases allow the tracking of progress with implementation.

Indicators from the perspective of an external stakeholder

As environmental awareness has increased so has the number of stakeholders interested in an organization's environmental performance. This trend has led to the development of approaches, external to organizations, to measure the environmental performance of organizations. Indicators are at the centre of this relatively recent development, and they provide the key building blocks in many stakeholder valuations.

Stakeholders are interested in an organization's environmental performance for a variety of reasons. Many of them seek to measure environmental performance but their different drivers and aims have an impact on how this is done. As a consequence there are now a multitude of performance measurement initiatives, using different measures, measuring different issues and using different measuring processes – these initiatives exert pressure on organizations in different ways.

There are four well known initiatives relevant to the UK market. They are discussed here in terms of: what they measure, how they measure, the value they bring, their impacts on the organizations they measure, and some of the key considerations in the interpretation of their outcomes.

Business in the Environment (BiE) Index of Corporate Environmental Engagement: BiE's main objective is to drive continuous improvement in corporate environmental performance through yearly reporting of benchmarking results for individual companies and industrial sectors in the UK. FTSE 350 companies are the main target, although non-FTSE companies are included based on their environmental leadership – regional benchmarks have also been produced. So far BiE has produced seven annual reports (BiE, 2004).

Global Reporting Initiative (GRI): The GRI aims to develop and disseminate guidelines for a globally applicable voluntary reporting framework on sustainability (incorporating economic, social and environmental criteria). The guidelines are aimed in principle at all industry sectors although some sector specific supplements have already been developed (GRI, 2004).

FTSE4Good and Dow Jones Sustainability Index (DJSI): These are socially responsible investment (SRI) indices managed respectively by FTSE and Dow Jones. Through specific selection criteria, these indices (as with other SRIs) place significantly more weight on the importance of good environmental, social and ethical performance of companies than conventional investment practices do (FTSE4Good and DJSI, 2004).

Moving on to the question of 'what they measure', the scopes of the FTSE4Good and DJSI indices as well as of the GRI are wider than environment. They include issues such as social, ethical and economic performance. In this context most initiatives use MPIs and OPIs to develop a picture of an organization's environmental performance.

Currently most MPIs in these initiatives attempt to measure the development of management structures or systems elements. The implicit assumption is that the path towards environmental improvement requires the right management structures. For example BiE uses a number of questions to produce indicators of the degree to which an organization has developed or integrated environment into management systems elements; these include board member responsibility and policy, objectives and targets, communication, management systems and audit, supplier programme and product stewardship.

The GRI, FTSE4Good and DJSI address similar issues, although they cover some areas in more detail and use different nomenclature. A notable difference is the inclusion in FTSE4Good and the DJSI of reporting as a specific element of performance measurement.

All these issues need to be translated into some form of indicator that can be measured. Indicators from the different initiatives might have very different structures or approach an issue from different angles even if obtaining information from the same subject. For example, BiE's indicator for policy is part of the management section – it aims to measure the level of approval, scope, dissemination and review process. In contrast, in the GRI, policy is part of the governance structure and management systems and requires qualitative descriptions of policy related elements and their level of implementation. Finally, for FTSE4Good, the indicators related to policy depend on the level of impact of the company.

Matters get a bit more complicated when the measurement of operational performance is being considered. In general most management elements are common to all organizations, but not all elements of operational performance are relevant or have the same significance. Nevertheless, there are some global issues such as energy, waste and water.

With regard to 'how to measure', the indicators for operational performance are varied. BiE, for example, focuses on the level to which a company measures and reports its performance as well as on a measure of performance data assurance. Note that the selected indicators are not based on actual performance. On the other hand the indicator used by the GRI is actual environmental performance (energy use for example).

FTSE4Good takes a different approach by classifying industries into high, medium and low impact based on the magnitude of their impacts in relation to their economic size. The classification is used to indicate the level of management controls required for the required performance to be included in the index. Similarly, the DJSI uses materiality considerations by having industry specific criteria as part of the evaluation methodology. To address this problem of materiality, the GRI has been developing sector specific guidance and indicators.

'How to measure' requires consideration of the processes by which indicators are developed and data is collected. Both processes have significant impact on the selected indicators and the value of the information obtained. All four initiatives have undertaken in-depth stakeholder consultation exercises to help them determine what to measure and how to measure it. However, the processes of collation of information are significantly different, and these can have an impact on the value of the information collated.

At present BiE sends companies a self assessment questionnaire. They provide some guidance and actively engage with organizations to support the process of answering the questionnaire. Nevertheless there is a potential problem of inconsistent interpretation of the questions, and this can have an adverse impact on the reliability, completeness and consistency of the information. In other words, if the indicators are not well defined they might lead companies to adopt their own interpretation.

Indicators used by these initiatives are presented as qualitative (text) information, as quantitative data and as multiple options (including yes and no). To reduce subjectivity many initiatives use multiple option questions and avoid, as far as is possible, the use of qualitative indicators. Moreover, both FTSE4Good and the DJSI use external agencies to collect information directly from organizations and from publicly available sources. The DJSI undertakes a formal process of data verification by an external third party. External and independent expert agencies help to reduce subjectivity and bias; however, to some extent the process still relies on the quality of the data provided by the organization and obtained from the public domain.

The choice of indicators should be driven by their intended use, but the issues to be measured and the process of measuring have a clear impact on the indicators. For the

GRI the main focus is reporting, whereas the aim of BiE, FTSE4Good and the DJSI is to develop indicators within a robust benchmarking framework. To be able to benchmark, mathematical algorithms are used to aggregate data, produce individual indicators and overall results. The algorithms are often complex and not always transparent, and organizations cannot always explain or predict the outcome.

We now have a better idea of 'what to measure' and 'how to measure', but what is their value? A company will not (and should not) participate or join any of these initiatives if they can't derive value from the process. Also, it is important to keep in mind that the benefits are not only for the participating company but for external stakeholders as well.

The work of these four initiatives has contributed greatly to the development of environmental performance indicators. They have helped to identify the issues and key process considerations, and to identify which areas in environmental management need more work. Benchmarking has helped to identify the leading organizations and industry sectors in terms of environmental and sustainability performance. The initiatives have informed organizations of the nature of the interest shown by their stakeholders as well as providing them with a mechanism to report on their performance.

Stakeholder systems of measurement have also provided organizations with ideas on how to develop their own performance measuring systems; although organizations should recognize that no single approach fits all situations. Most of these initiatives have been developed with larger companies in mind. Smaller companies are still finding it difficult to adapt them to their circumstances. Whether small or large, an organization needs to understand clearly the limitations of these indicator sets.

It is important to keep in mind that external indicators can have consequences for the development and use of internal indicators. For example, an organization might need to translate external indicators to be able to measure and collect data. Because methods and best practice are constantly evolving with stakeholder consultation, they might also require internal changes. All of these changes require resources and the increasing number of ever-changing initiatives is currently creating significant pressures on organizations – the process of external performance measurement needs to be streamlined so that they can focus on improving and not only measuring.

Indicators – market analysis and future trends

It is becoming increasingly clear that the environment is only one aspect of an organization's overall responsibility to society, and that it fits within the concept of corporate governance. An example of this trend is the initiative from BiE to combine their environmental initiative with their Corporate Responsibility Index (CRI). Organizations are in general better at measuring environmental impacts than social impacts; therefore, there might be scope for transferring some of the lessons learned from environmental indicators. The trend towards sustainability measures also coincides with a shift away from compliance driven measures.

In its environmental performance review of the UK, the Organisation for Economic Co-operation and Development sheds some light on possible future trends (OECD, 2004). The review recommends further integration of environmental concerns with economic and social factors. It identifies as priorities for action environmental issues such as waste management, soil and water management, and climate protection for which there is already a wealth of indicators and measurement frameworks. It also identifies issues such as landscape, biodiversity, conservation and diffuse pollution. These are areas where work needs to be done to develop useful indicators.

Knowledge about how our actions impact on the environment is continually increasing, and we are likely to see more and more information becoming available to enable us to translate our actions into environmental impacts. However, an interesting development to follow will be the effect that integration of sustainability measures has on the development of impact measures.

Stakeholders will continue to have an important influence on the development of indicators. The understanding that different stakeholders need different information could possibly lead to the development of tailor-made reporting indicators for specific stakeholders; however, this will require further discussion and careful assessment of the costs and benefits.

Although environmental data is often found in many different systems and parts of an organization, there is an increasing use of environmental management information systems (EMIS). An EMIS places environmental data into a single framework so that it is easier to manage and obtain the desired indicators. There is the potential for these systems to produce web based reporting indicators with the aim of having online environmental performance data. There is some way to go with this idea; data collection processes and data verification in particular still need significant improvements.

Organizations and stakeholders are showing an increasing interest in understanding and addressing indirect impacts along the value chain, from the supplier to the client. In the same vein, BiE identifies sustainable supply chain management and understanding an organization's indirect impacts as two of the next key challenges. Information from the OECD review on the increasing growth of the UK's service sector further supports the idea that more will need to be done to develop supply chain and indirect impacts indicators.

Further external performance measurement initiatives are likely following the debate on materiality, driven in part by the UK Government's White Paper, Modernising Company Law (OFRWG, 2002). These proposals would require companies over a certain size to undertake and publish an operating and financial review (OFR). Besides traditional financial measures, the OFR requires companies to include an account of how intangible assets contribute to its overall value generation and how conflicting stakeholder interests are balanced. Directors will need to decide precisely what information is material to their particular business and publish it in their OFR. Clearly, this will have an impact on the development of reporting indicators.

A survey by Deloitte & Touche (2002) indicated that interest in SRI would continue to grow during 2003. The survey also identified that the SRI market has yet to make a decision on how success will be measured. This is a critical issue that will have a major bearing on the future development of indicators.

Interestingly, the same survey also identified that the potential for SRI based investments to outperform the market might not necessarily be important in driving the growth of SRI – client demands and government pressures were identified as the most significant factors. This suggests that future SRI indicators might not have strong links to financial business performance. Further than pure financial indicators, quality of management is sought as a key characteristic for investment. It is possible that the investment market has now started using measures of corporate social responsibility as an indicator of quality management to inform investment decisions.

References

BiE (2004) For information on performance measures developed by BiE, go to www.bitc.org.uk/programmes/programme_directory/business_in_the_environment/index.html

BSI (2003) 'BS 8555: Environmental Management Systems – Guide to the Phased Implementation of an Environmental Management System Including the Use of Environmental Performance Evaluation', British Standards Institution, London

CIA (2004) For details of the Chemical Industries Association's Responsible Care Programme go to www.cia.org.uk/newsite/responsible_care/care.htm

Deloitte & Touche (2002) *Socially Responsible Investment Survey 2002*, Deloitte & Touche, Environment and Sustainability Services, London

FTSE4Good and DJSI (2004) For information on these two initiatives go to www.ftse.com/ftse4good and www.sustainability-index.com

GRI (2004) For information on performance measures developed by the GRI go to www.globalreporting.org

ISO (1996) 'ISO 14001: Environmental Management Systems – Specification with Guidance for Use', International Organization for Standardization, Geneva

ISO (1999a) 'ISO 14031: Environmental Management – Environmental Performance Evaluation – Guidelines', International Organization for Standardization, Geneva

ISO (1999b) 'ISO 14032: Environmental Management – Examples of Environmental Performance Evaluation', International Organization for Standardization, Geneva

Kaplan, R. and Norton, D. (1992) 'The Balanced Scorecard: Measures that Drive Performance', *Harvard Business Review*, vol 70, no 1, January/February 1992, pp71–79

Luckhurst, J. (2003) 'Sustainability Indicators for the Water Industry', *the environmentalist*, no 20, December, pp19–21

OECD (2004) For information on the Organisation for Economic Co-operation and Development go to www.oecd.org/env

OFRWG (2002) 'Modernising Company Law, Consultation Document on Materiality' UK Government White Paper, Operating and Financial Review Working Group, London

Chapter 6.2

Reporting and Accounting

Introduction

Environmental accounting and reporting is not a single, tidy and coherent area of activity. It comprises a number of quite different strands and, for the purposes of this chapter, we will think of these strands as being:

- the environmental impact on financial statements and auditing (financial accounting);
- accounting in support of environmental management (management accounting);
- environmental reporting;
- social reporting, the Global Reporting Initiative (GRI) and towards the 'triple bottom line'; and
- accounting and reporting for sustainable development and sustainability.

The first two of these strands principally involve interaction between the environmental manager and the accountants in the organization. This interaction may be of the form of the accountants (or auditors) coming to you asking for your advice and help as would usually be the case with financial accounting. Or it may be that you are trying to get the accountants to work in a way that helps you more – as will be the case with management accounting. The next two strands refer to the increasingly high profile activity of reporting to external stakeholders. Environmental reporting has had a very successful, if relatively short, history but is now usually seen as part of 'environmental and social' or, increasingly, triple bottom line reporting. Finally, there are the more experimental – though no less urgent – moves towards accounting and reporting for sustainability.

Financial statements, financial auditing and environmental issues

Virtually all organizations are required to produce some form of financial statements on a regular basis. In many cases, these statements are subject to extensive regulation and checking. This is at its most obvious in the case of companies – especially large companies – whose financial statements are governed by both companies acts and financial reporting standards. They are also subject to statutory audit. This form of audit should be distinguished from an environmental audit for two reasons. First, it is statutory in nature, and second, this sort of audit is exclusively designed to express an opinion about whether or not the financial statements show a 'true and fair view'. Financial statements (which include a profit and loss account – sometimes called an income statement – and a balance sheet) are typically produced as part of the organization's annual report – a document primarily intended for shareholders.

Historically, there has been no requirement to separately recognize environmental issues of any sort in financial statements and, while this is still the case in most countries (including the UK), there is slow progress towards some limited acknowledgement of such matters as impairment of assets and environmental liabilities. For example, in the EU, the Commission Recommendation on the Recognition, Measurement and Disclosure of Environmental Issues in the Annual Accounts and Annual Reports of Companies (2001) has emphasized the need to integrate financial and environmental reporting. Mandatory environmental reporting already applies in some countries – both inside and outside Europe.

The pace in the area has been set by the US, which since 1980 has had what is colloquially known as the Superfund. This is a major set of regulations that require that contaminated land be remediated by the owners and/or the responsible parties. The potential liabilities this imposes on, in particular, companies can still, even now, only be estimated but they are probably enough to force a great many companies into receivership.

The crucial thing to recognize in this area is that the financial statements have no intrinsic interest in the environment as such. The financial statements only recognize matters that will have a material financial impact on the organization. The impact must be of sufficiently large financial size to alter the economic story told by the financial statements. The environmental materiality is of no consequence here. In practice the impact of environmental issues will typically play out through changes in the market for one's products, changes from suppliers and/or – most significantly – changes in legislation (as with the Superfund).

And so the financial accountants and, more importantly, the financial auditors will be looking out for environmental (typically legal or regulatory) changes that will, for example, prevent the sale of goods in stock, will make products obsolete, will require major capital expenditure to meet consent levels and so forth. On finding such potential financial hazards, the accountants or the auditors will come to the environmental manager looking for guidance and assistance in dealing with the issue and limiting its financial impact. This is something a good environmental management system (EMS) would typically have spotted anyway and so, in practice, apart from an annual visit from the auditors, this area is unlikely to have a big impact on environmental management practice in the near future. Monitoring developments in this area should be relatively simple. Within Europe the Fédération des Experts Comptables Européens is a useful source of information.

Of much greater significance is the interplay between the EMS and the management accountants.

What accounting can do for environmental management

A crucial factor in determining the success or otherwise of an EMS will be the extent to which it articulates with and is informed by the management accounting system of the organization. At a very crude level one can think of management accounting as the system that identifies, tracks and offers alternatives for the financial manifestations and consequences of the activities and aspirations of the organization. More prosaically, everything from strategic possibilities through to budgeting, performance appraisal and capital expenditure appraisal need to be explored and justified in, ultimately, financial terms. The more pressing the financial control in the organization, the more this will be the case. The EMS will have to justify its existence; the environmental management department (if there is one), will have a budget; and the case for the new equipment which is needed to bring the organization back into line with consent levels will have to be financially justified.

Increasingly, every action must be explored through the business case – which, at its crudest level, means 'will it make us – or stop us losing – money?' No environmental manager who ignores the financial exigencies of the business will make much progress. However, the successful environmental manager will work with the grain of the organization and will make the economics work for her or him. That is, the environmental manager should be constantly searching for what are known as the win–win scenarios and working with the accountants and the accounting system to make the best environmental management also in the best economic interests of the organization.

Win–win scenarios: The simplest examples of win–win scenarios are in aspects of the business where a reduction in usage of a resource, for example, reduces costs and reduces environmental impact. Reductions in energy usage or waste produced are the most obvious examples of this. But any reduction in resource use either on a per unit (efficiency) or a total (ecological footprint) basis has this potential. The difficulty, however, is that not all accounting systems will separately identify these costs and so the financial savings may not be obvious. Ensuring that the accountants amend the system to track and identify such numbers can often be the key to exploiting win–win potential.

Hidden costs: This becomes even more important when it comes to many of the existing environmentally related costs that are currently buried in overheads. Safety costs, emergency procedures, costs of dealing with the regulators, and so on are important costs that are essential to any organization. They are not, however, typically identified separately and are not, therefore, typically identified as needing control. Moreover, these sorts of cost, although critical to the projects and processes to which they relate, are often not allocated to those projects or processes. Such omissions can have a considerable effect on both the actual and the perceived viability of such activities.

Exploiting uncertainty: More subtle win–win situations can arise as a result of the uncertainties inherent in performance and accounting measurement. So much of short term (e.g. monthly or even yearly) performance assessment depends upon assumptions built into the longer term decisions about the future. Thus, for example, scenario planning and, most especially, capital expenditure and new project decisions involve considerable uncertainty about the future and also have a direct impact on current organizational activity. The trick for the environmental manager is to exploit this uncertainty in order to encourage the organization to adopt the more environmentally benign options. Key to this can often be changes to the performance appraisal system, which can be used to redirect managers' behaviour away from environmentally malign – but (apparently) economically attractive – activities. The nub is that in a great many organizations, short term financial exigencies will normally dominate decision making. Such exigencies can often be in conflict with longer term environmental, social and, indeed, often economic desiderata. Careful management and exploitation of the doubts and uncertainties embedded in the measurement and accounting system can work to lessen the extent of such conflict.

Environmental reporting

Environmental reporting, as we currently know it, emerged in the early 1990s. Companies such as Norsk Hydro, BA, Noranda and BSO/Origin produced innovative, standalone, voluntary environmental reports that have pretty much set the standard ever since. Since that time, environmental reporting has grown as a voluntary activity mainly among companies, but it has remained a predominantly partial phenomenon and is dominated by the larger companies. The KPMG International Survey of Corporate Sustainability Reporting (KPMG, 2002) reported that nearly half of the top 250 in the Global Fortune 500 had produced such reports in the previous two to three years. It is increasingly a mandatory issue; countries with some mandatory requirement for environmental reporting include Denmark, the Netherlands, Sweden, France, Australia and Korea. The prospect of British and/or pan-European legislation to require environmental reports by large organizations remains a distinct possibility.

Environmental reporting can be thought of as communicating an accurate, although much simplified, overview of the organization's environmental interactions to its stakeholders. It is most likely to undertake this communication: in the annual report (in which case it is likely to be very simplified); in a standalone environmental (or other – see later in this chapter) report; on the company's web site; or by a combination of these methods.

The current state of the art in environmental reporting sits between two poles. On the one hand the audiences for the report (shareholders, the City, employees, non-governmental organizations (NGOs), the press, and so on) will not tolerate anything that looks too much like a 'greenwash'. A bland, glossy publication, which is heavy on beautiful pictures and low on data and which paints a rosy glow around the company, is likely to do more harm than good. No organization is squeaky clean and a report that claims otherwise will invite unwelcome (but well deserved) attention. On the other hand, the activity of environmental reporting is largely voluntary and no organization will willingly subject itself to the painful rigour of a full, complete and honest accountability statement. Consequently, most reports are substantial and honest, but partial and selective.

There have been many guidelines issued on how to construct an environmental report and what such a report should contain. Of these it is probably the GRI that currently sets the pace. The flow of guidelines shows no sign of easing off – even though they mostly say the same basic things. A credible environmental report must contain (or, at a minimum, reference):

- the organization's policy statement;
- identification of principal environmental impacts;
- plans, structure and organization – who is responsible for what?
- status and position of the EMS, levels of accreditation and so on (typically ISO 14000 and EMAS);
- detailed data on targets and performance against those targets in key areas such as water, land, air, energy and other resource use;
- analysis of performance and plans for continual improvement;
- links to sustainable development (see later in this chapter); and
- probably an attestation (audit) statement.

What such a report does, in effect, is emphasize the environmental management procedures in the organization and pay particular attention to eco-efficiency issues. What it does not do is give a complete outline of the organization's environmental interactions. For an environmental report to approach that ideal it would also have to include data on:

- the organization's eco-balance (a concept pioneered by German and Austrian researchers and organizations) – at least in outline;
- the organization's ecological footprint and its change over time;
- country by country, site by site breakdowns with particular reference to local ecosystems and habitats;
- detailed compliance with standards; and
- key environmental/social issues such as biodiversity, carbon footprinting/climate change, transport and so on.

Such complete environmental reports are very scarce indeed but, perhaps surprisingly, reporters are rarely chastised for failing to address these more complex and testing issues. However, continual monitoring of the environmental agenda is essential – for example, the last few years saw the issue of climate change, greenhouse gas emissions and carbon equivalents rising in importance and becoming an essential component of substantial environmental reports.

At the heart of an environmental report – especially a voluntary environmental report – is the question 'why report?' There are many reasons why an organization might report and it certainly makes life simpler if an organization can work out in advance what its motives and goals actually are. Sadly, it remains rare – and will remain rare until substantive regulation requires it – that an organization reports because it believes itself to be accountable and wishes to discharge that accountability.

Accountability is principally about the 'rights' that society has to information about the activities of an organization. Such rights range from the extent to which the organization has complied with law, the extent to which it has complied with its own standards and the extent to which it has improved (or more likely worsened) the potential sustainability of the planet. It is far more likely that the organization is reporting for a complex set of reasons that include the desire to:

- educate stakeholders;
- explain the organization's achievements;
- indicate to potential regulators that legislation is unnecessary;

- persuade stakeholders that the organization is 'walking the talk' – whether or not this is the case;
- counter environmentalists' claims;
- legitimate the industry;
- express a personal commitment by the board;
- signal to financial stakeholders that environmental risk is managed sensibly; and
- provide an external focus for the EMS.

A well balanced, substantive report which is reaching towards completeness can have value – to both society and the organization itself – in all of these areas. However, a key factor in determining how to manifest the organization's objectives vis-à-vis the environmental report is to ensure that the principal stakeholders to whom the report is addressed are properly understood. This is doubly important because experience shows that an organization is unlikely to receive much in the way of substantive feedback on their published environmental (and social) report. This is not because stakeholders are uninterested in the environmental activities of the organization but rather because of time, effort, commitment and so on. It therefore behoves the reporting organization to be satisfied that the report is meeting their own intended aims.

While all the organization's stakeholders are likely to have an environmental interest in the organization (although not all may want an environmental report), the probability is that their interests will differ. For example:

- Financial stakeholders (shareholders, bankers etc.) may be concerned with environmental risks as well as with the management of environmental issues as an indicator of management competence – this audience will typically be best addressed through the annual report not through a standalone report.
- Customers may be concerned by ethical purchasing considerations or with the contents of their supply chain.
- Employees may be looking to defend or take pride in their employer – as well as wanting reassurance that health and safety issues are seen as paramount.
- Local communities may be concerned by local hazards and whether or not the organization is acting as a good neighbour.
- Suppliers may be concerned with responsible care; NGOs with compliance with ethical codes; ... and so on.

One of the principal ways through which the organization will gain an understanding of what stakeholders want from it, what information they require and how they react to reporting and other initiatives is through stakeholder dialogue. Formal and informal consultation, market research, focus groups and community advisory panels are just some of the ways in which this can be achieved and, consequently, the reporting (and, indeed, other environmental initiatives) more carefully and efficiently focused. Such mechanisms (as long as they are not treated either cynically or as a glamorous version of market research) try to bring the concerns of the stakeholder and the organization closer together – where that is possible – and to help each other understand differences of view – where it is not. Then environmental (and social etc.) reporting becomes just one important part in the whole reporting and communication strategy of the organization.

For the organization keen to develop a credible environmental reporting strategy but not intent upon pushing the envelope too far, there is no shortage of guidance. But rather than wading through endless and largely repetitive guidelines, the GRI guidelines (see the next section) are as likely as any to illustrate the leading edge of reporting while current best practice can be very confidently gauged through three major sources: the KPMG annual survey(s) of reporting, the SustainAbility/United Nations Environment Programme (UNEP) project monitoring worldwide reporting and the Association of Chartered Certified Accountants (ACCA) reporting awards schemes.

The KPMG report has been produced in one form or another for several years. Its focus (e.g. environmental reporting, sustainability reporting) and its coverage (e.g. the largest worldwide companies) have developed over the years but the report provides as good a snapshot as any of who is reporting what globally (KPMG, 2002).

The alliance of UNEP and the consultancy SustainAbility has resulted in the Engaging Stakeholders project. This project produces periodic reports on such matters as: stakeholder views on reporting; experiences of companies with reporting; analysis of leading edge reporters; industry trends plus predictions as to future directions. From these reports one is not only taking the pulse in environmental (and related) reporting but is receiving detailed guidance on what makes a good report together with a distillation of widespread experience in reporting (SustainAbility/UNEP, 2002).

The ACCA reporting awards schemes have been in place since the early 1990s. They began as a UK-only, environment-only scheme and have mushroomed. The UK scheme covers environmental, social and sustainability reporting and there are now commensurate schemes all over the world – including a pan-European awards scheme. The ACCA awards' criteria have evolved over time and, in effect, reflect the changing patterns of, and attitudes to, reporting. These criteria are published from time to time.

More usefully for the reporting environmental manager, ACCA also publish a detailed judges' report which itemizes the strengths and weaknesses of the shortlisted reports. These judges' reports are also, very usefully, illustrated by examples of good (and not so good) practice from the shortlisted reports. These reports can then be obtained (and studied) by interested parties. In addition ACCA also publish relevant research reports, republish guidelines and produce a periodic e-magazine on accounting and sustainability which covers all developments in the field. Much of this experience and output has been condensed on to the ACCA and Sustainability CD-ROM (ACCA, 2002).

In addition to providing excellent guidance on approaches to reporting and the current state of the art these sources will keep you abreast of changes in attitude and focus. The most important of recent years has been the move beyond purely environmental reporting, via social reporting towards triple bottom line reporting and, as it is sometimes inaccurately called, 'sustainability' reporting.

Social reporting, the GRI and towards the triple bottom line

The term 'triple bottom line' was coined by John Elkington of SustainAbility. It is an effective notion and suggests that any organization must be operated to produce positive economic, social and environmental benefits. The importance of the concept lies in the realization that it is probably impossible for any organization to produce a net economic and social and environmental benefit from its activities and virtually certainly true that no commercial organization can give all three elements equal weight (the economic will always dominate). But it focuses the mind (or it least it should do so) on the trade-offs that every organization makes in pursuing economic returns. The move towards triple bottom line reporting was intended to make explicit the 'beyond the financial' aspects of organizational behaviour and in so doing to communicate to stakeholders the extent to which the organization was coping with that trade-off. Thus, it was envisaged, organizations would produce full financial, social and environmental accounts of their activities and, thereby, indicate the trade-offs, difficulties and choices made (the social and/or environmental eggs broken in making the profitable omelette).

Most organizations already produce full – perhaps too full – financial reports. We now know, as described in the last section, what a full environmental report (based around an eco-balance and estimates of ecological footprint) might look like. The upsurge of social reporting in the early 1990s produced a range of experimentation with social reporting. However, like environmental reporting before it, much of the really path-breaking reports were the early ones. Most notably, the early reports produced by: the small fair trade company Traidcraft plc; its charitable foundation Traidcraft Exchange; the Body Shop; and, later, the Co-operative Bank remain among the most complete reports of this type.

A complete social report involves more complex notions than does a complete environmental report. Such a report might comprise (and the best of the Traidcraft reports did comprise) inter alia:

- values and mission statements;
- an identification of stakeholders – the stakeholder map;
- an explanation of how selected stakeholders have been prioritized;
- for each stakeholder group:
  - descriptive information about the organization–stakeholder relationship;
  - legal and quasi-legal standards and the organization's performance against those standards;
  - the organization's performance against its own values and standards; and
  - the voices of the stakeholders. The voices of the stakeholders was a very significant initiative begun by New Economics Foundation in the Traidcraft report and developed in the Institute for Social and Ethical Accountability (ISEA) standards on social reporting and auditing – the AA1000 series.
- plans and intentions based on these data; and
- an attestation (audit) statement.

The idea of a triple bottom line is certainly, therefore, feasible. But for this to become a reality it requires that organizations produce detailed and comprehensive reports in sound and inclusive ways. In the absence of regulation it seems very unlikely that many organizations will do so. This point is crucial because while there is a considerable discussion about triple bottom line reporting, virtually nobody is actually doing it. This is dishonest and misleading and certainly does not advance the case for the reliability of voluntary responsibility and accountability.

In summary, reporting has developed since about 1990:

- from reporting about the environment (correctly called environmental reporting);
- through reporting on aspects of social interaction (often correctly called social reporting or rather less accurately social responsibility reporting);
- to reporting about the environment and some aspects of social interaction (incorrectly called triple bottom line reporting);
- which has been repackaged as sustainability reporting. This is wholly inaccurate (see later in this section), as triple bottom line reporting is only a dim relation of sustainability reporting.

The issue of terminology is crucial because there is no point in talking about a triple bottom line reporting strategy when, in fact, one is talking about something else. This confusion has, to an extent and understandably, been increased by the GRI.

The GRI is a voluntary, cross-sectoral initiative involving both companies and NGOs. Established in 1997 by the Coalition for Environmentally Responsible Economies as a successful attempt to combine all the disparate efforts that were going into voluntary reporting, the GRI's primary task is to produce a single set of guidelines that will slowly take organizations' reporting towards sustainability reporting. These guidelines (which are updated as needed) have effectively reified the (incomplete) environmental and social reporting practices that we discussed earlier. They have done this in order to, firstly, bring more organizations into the reporting experience and, secondly, to then have a base from which to steadily ratchet up the standards of reporting.

Although the GRI remains the front runner in terms of widespread acceptance of reporting guidelines and although they have set reasonable standards in environmental reporting, they have yet to develop any serious standards in social reporting and are, therefore, still someway off decent triple bottom line reporting. They are, despite the title of their guidelines, a very long way off indeed from sustainability reporting.

Accounting and reporting for sustainability and sustainable development

Sustainability is a complex and demanding notion. For an organization to be contributing to sustainability it needs to be, somewhat simplistically perhaps, reducing its ecological footprint and increasing equality of access to environmental resources. Neither of these conditions is very likely for an organization with commercial imperatives and the first will be unlikely for an organization that is growing.

An account or report of sustainability – a 'sustainability report' – should, presumably, allow one to assess the extent to which an organization was contributing to or (more likely) reducing planetary sustainability. Certainly, the full social and environmental reports we have discussed in this chapter (but which are rare in practice) could not tell a reader whether or not an organization was moving towards or away from sustainability. Whatever the label might say, sustainability reports are not about sustainability – or not yet anyway.

Experiments have been undertaken to try and work out how an account of an organization's sustainability might be constructed. Progress is promising but slow and seems to confirm that few, if any, Western organizations are currently sustainable. For more detail see Gray and Bebbington, (2001, Chapter 14) and the ACCA (2002) CD-ROM. In essence, the problem is that companies are designed to grow (which will typically increase their ecological footprint) and to ensure that the wealthy (shareholders) as opposed to the poor (the excluded and those in emerging nations for example) earn a high return.

It seems likely that much more work will need to be done before organizations will voluntarily start reporting on their (un)sustainability, so a key factor for any organization will be monitoring the developments in this debate. The ACCA web site and publications, as well as the SustainAbility/UNEP publications, are the best source of information for this.

But it is as well to bear in mind that, while we are developing ways of thinking about sustainability at the organizational level because that is where the power and decision making over resources currently lie, sustainability, may not be accurately located at the organizational level. Sustainability is, first, a planetary concept and working out the relationship between planetary sustainability and an organization's use of resources and its impacts on justice require a calculus far beyond our capacities. Second, sustainability is an ecosystems concept. Very few organizations are coterminous with ecosystems. As the ecosystems cannot adapt to the shape of organizations it might be that organizations will have to adapt to the shape of ecosystems. All this suggests that the very best accounts of sustainability can only ever be broad approximations of organizational sustainability.

Conclusions

Environmental managers will have many occasions when they interface with, or come up against, conflicts with the accounting systems of their organizations. Accountants and the accounting system will not always be the ally of the environmental manager and the EMS. However, a carefully developed understanding between the accountants and the environmental manager can bring major benefits to both – as well as to the organization. It is not a natural relationship and so it will require effort to understand other, often quite different, points of view.

The organization's environmental and social (and/or triple bottom line or sustainability) reporting regime is less likely to involve the accountants to any great extent. A key part of the environmental manager's role will be monitoring developments in this rapidly changing arena. The organization's own reporting strategy must make sense – to the organization and to the stakeholders – and it must avoid the all too easy trap of taking too glib an approach to what are greatly complex and challenging matters. Monitoring the web sites given below should keep the organization informed about the opportunities and challenges that face it in this difficult but exciting area.

References and further reading

ACCA (2002) 'ACCA and Sustainability', CD-ROM, Association of Chartered Certified Accountants, London

Gray, R. H. and Bebbington, K. J. (2001) *Accounting for the Environment*, 2nd edn, Sage, London

KPMG (2002) 'KPMG 4th International Survey of Corporate Sustainability Reporting', KPMG/WIMM, the Netherlands, www.kpmg.com

Milne, M. and Gray, R. (2002) 'Sustainability Reporting: Who's Kidding Whom?', *Chartered Accountants Journal of New Zealand*, vol 81, no 6, July, pp66–70. Reprinted in the *ICFAI Journal of Accounting Research*, Institute of Chartered Financial Analysts of India and in the *Accounting & Sustainability* e-newsletter, no 6, August, ACCA, London, www.accaglobal.com/publications/as_index

Schaltegger, S. and Burritt, R. (2000) *Contemporary Environmental Accounting: Issues, Concepts and Practices*, Greenleaf Publishing, Sheffield

SustainAbility/UNEP (2002) 'Trust Us: The 2002 Global Reporters Survey of Corporate Sustainability Reporting', SustainAbility/United Nations Environment Programme, London, www.sustainability.com

Web sites

The Association of Chartered Certified Accountants (ACCA), www.accaglobal.com/sustainability

The Centre for Social and Environmental Accounting Research (CSEAR), www.gla.ac.uk/departments/accounting/csear

The Environmental Management Accounting Research and Information Center, www.emawebsite.org

Fédération des Experts Comptables Européens (FEE), www.fee.be

The Global Reporting Initiative (GRI), www.globalreporting.org

The Institute for Social and Ethical Accountability (AccountAbility), www.accountability.org.uk

Chapter 6.3

Engaging with Stakeholders

Introduction

Until recently there has been a tendency for developers, local government and environmental agencies to only consider public and stakeholder concerns when they disagree with a proposal or a decision. There are exceptions to this generalization, such as British Petroleum actively engaging with a wide range of stakeholders in developing oil and gas facilities in Scotland in the 1970s. While there was no legal requirement to do so, the company considered this approach to be beneficial. As a result of this openness they faced no public inquiries during this early phase of development.

However, changes in society are now occurring. These changes can be seen at both global and local scales. At the global scale are issues such as climate change, the role of multinational companies in developing countries, environmental aid programmes of bi- and multilateral agencies, and the reality of stakeholder engagement as inevitable and powerful forces as witnessed at the Rio and Johannesburg summits. At the local scale in the UK are issues such as the development of river catchment management plans (CMPs), 'planning for real', local waste initiatives and an increasing emphasis on developing partnerships to achieve environmental enhancement – direct and proactive participation and stakeholder engagement are now central features.

A recent multinational government initiative, The Aarhus Convention (UNECE, 1998), represents a major step forward in ensuring that the public has a say in decisions taken that affect the quality of their environment. The convention gives the public certain rights and represents 'a commitment to access to information, participation in decision-making and access to justice on environmental matters'.

At the national level, 'modernizing government' initiatives in England, Scotland and Wales now require that local authorities and government agencies modernize their systems and enhance public participation. As clearly stated in the 1998 Royal Commission on Environmental Pollution's report, 'Setting Environmental Standards', it is necessary for governments to use more direct methods to ensure that people's values, along with lay knowledge and understanding, are articulated and taken into account alongside technical and scientific considerations.

Who are the stakeholders?

Both within the scientific literature and in the real world of decision making there is no clear and unambiguous agreement as to who are stakeholders. In one sense every citizen must be considered as a stakeholder. At a global scale, the population of Britain was represented in the negotiations on the Rio Declaration, the Climate Change Convention and the Kyoto Protocol by UK Government ministers and civil servants. Essentially this was negotiation by global stakeholders. For practical purposes, and particularly as the emphasis in this chapter is on national, regional and local scales of stakeholder engagement, two definitional approaches can be adopted. First, that proposed in the Institute of Environmental Management and Assessment's (IEMA's) *Guidelines on Participation in Environmental Decision-making* (IEMA, 2002) and secondly the categorization in 'Managing Radioactive Waste Safely' (Defra, 2003). The two approaches should be considered as complementary to each other.

Stakeholder definition according to the IEMA

According to the IEMA's guidelines the term 'stakeholder' encompasses all individuals, groups or organizations with a stake or interest in an issue. Stakeholders can be grouped into three categories as follows:

- The proponent is the organization or individual proposing a particular policy, plan, programme, project or activity.
- The decision maker is the individual or organization responsible for making decisions during the development of a proposal and also, ultimately, as to whether a proposal is acceptable or not. The decision maker may be the same individual or organization for both of these types of decision or they may be different depending on the type of proposal. For example, a local policy may be developed and given authorization by the local authority whereas a project could be developed by a proponent and authorized by a local authority. Ongoing project management decisions could also require consents from the environmental agencies.
- Third parties include statutory consultees who are required by law to be involved in particular processes of environmental decision making. Third parties also include national and local interest groups, businesses, trade bodies and trade unions, residents, customers, suppliers, the media, academics and any other group or individual with a stake or an interest in an issue.

Stakeholder definition according to 'Managing Radioactive Waste Safely'

The differentiation of stakeholders into the following three categories, suggested by the UK Government (Defra, 2003), is of potential use on a wide range of environmental issues:

- **Professional stakeholders** encompass public and private sector organizations, and professional voluntary groups. Professional stakeholders include government departments and agencies, local authorities, business, industry, academia/research, and non-governmental organizations (NGOs). Professional stakeholders tend to possess specialist (expert) and procedural knowledge. They work at (or are well linked into) the national level, as well as local and regional levels. When engaged in participatory processes, professional stakeholders will normally represent their organizational perspectives and strategic/tactical interests.

- **Local stakeholder groups** are non-professional, organized groups that operate within specific localities. It is possible to distinguish between three types of local stakeholder group, they are: people who come together around a common interest such as autonomous local environmental groups; people who have an attachment to a particular place such as residents' associations, amenity groups and parish councils; and people who are united by feelings of a common identity such as the Women's Institute, church groups and youth clubs. Local stakeholders may lack specialist (expert) and procedural knowledge, but possess rich understandings of local knowledge through their active engagement with others. Individual members of local stakeholder groups are usually enrolled in participatory processes to represent the views of their group and, often, to act as surrogates for the general public.

- **The public, or citizens,** is by far the largest category of potential participants that covers individuals who represent no one else other than themselves in an institutional sense but who are representative of the diverse elements which constitute civil society as a whole. No prior assumptions can be made about their specialist, procedural or local knowledge. Qualitative approaches to public engagement often recruit individuals into focus groups characterized by one or more shared demographic features (e.g. mothers with children under five, Muslim men in financial services).

The objectives of stakeholder dialogue

A wide range of aims and objectives has been identified for the role and function of stakeholder dialogue. Four broad perspectives can be listed. These are: the political–philosophical role – good government and the role of citizens; improved planning – public input to decision making; political – demands of the electorate; and conflict resolution – reducing or avoiding conflict and developing support for environmental decisions. However, many other roles can be identified including validation, education, accountability, competence, equity, legitimization and transparency. The objectives of stakeholder engagement listed in Box 6.3.1 apply to a wide range of environmental issues.

If we apply these broad objectives to environmental impact assessment (EIA) and strategic environmental assessment (SEA), a number of practical issues arise. People who may be directly or indirectly affected by a proposal will clearly be a focus for public involvement. Those directly affected can often be easily identified. They may be project beneficiaries or those likely to be adversely affected. The identification of those indirectly affected is more difficult, and to some extent will be a subjective judgement. For this reason it is good practice to have a very wide definition of those who should be involved, and to include any person or group who thinks that they have an interest. Sometimes it may be easier to consult with a representative from a particular interest group. In this case the choice of group representative should be left to the group itself. Care is required to ensure that a fair and balanced representation of views is sought and that the views of poor people or minority groups are not overwhelmed by those of the more influential or wealthy.

Box 6.3.1 *Objectives of stakeholder engagement*

- informing stakeholders about what is proposed and providing the opportunity for creating a sense of ownership of the proposal;
- providing an opportunity for those otherwise unrepresented to present their views and values, therefore allowing more sensitive consideration of mitigatory measures and trade-offs;
- providing those involved in planning the proposal with an opportunity to ensure that the benefits are maximized and that no major impacts have been overlooked;
- providing an opportunity for the public to influence project design in a positive manner;
- obtaining local and traditional knowledge before decision making;
- increasing public confidence in decision makers;
- providing better transparency and accountability in decision making;
- reducing conflict through the early identification of contentious issues.

Source: UNEP, 1996

An alternative approach was recently proposed by Michael Meacher, the former UK Government Minister of Environment. It encapsulates the idea that objectives of stakeholder dialogue have to be translated into transparent rules of engagement (see Box 6.3.2).

Box 6.3.2 *Rules of engagement*

A – Accessibility

R – Responsiveness in taking views into account

T – Transparency and clarity – who is responsible, how are decisions made, are consultation points taken into account, what will be done to make a decision, when will the decision be made?

I – Intelligibility – speak the language of the stakeholders, keep it simple and interpret all technical jargon

C – Consultation through genuine dialogue – links to the above principles. Those doing the consultation must really intend to use the results. More is lost by doing a bad piece of consultation than by not doing one at all.

Source: EA, 2000

The form and structure of stakeholder dialogue can vary greatly. Much depends on the nature of the activity. In certain cases, such as in EIA and SEA, the role of participation can be defined by legal requirements. In other cases (e.g. in the formulation of area waste plans) participation and public involvement, while not formal legal requirements, are central to the whole objective of the environmental initiative. Objectives of stakeholder dialogue therefore depend to a large extent on the nature of the environmental issue, scale and time elements, legal or best practice concerns, and whether the process is genuinely transparent and open or mere tokenism. What is clear, however, is that stakeholder dialogue should be seen as a process whose objectives are most likely to be achieved if started early, rather than when problems arise.

Levels of stakeholder engagement

In a broad sense stakeholder engagement varies along a continuum from the provision of information by a developer, agency or other initiator to delegation of decision making powers by an authority to the public and stakeholders. Figure 6.3.1 illustrates this continuum.

Education and information provision is the most basic form of stakeholder engagement. Material on a proposal or environmental topic is widely disseminated to create awareness of an issue. Normally there are no explicit mechanisms to encourage formal responses, but in many cases this may occur if the issue is contentious.

At the **information provision and feedback** level, the public and stakeholders are encouraged by various means, such as surveys, staffed exhibits and displays or by telephone, to comment on a specific proposal or issue to solicit the range of views.

Involvement and consultation involves either formal or informal discussion to identify issues of concern. Processes may involve face to face interaction between professional stakeholders, local interest groups and the public.

Extended involvement is the most open form of participation. It allows participants to contribute to the formulation of a plan or proposal and to influence the ultimate decision in an explicit manner.

A key element of any stakeholder dialogue, from the perspectives of an environmental initiator, stakeholders and the public, is to attempt to achieve agreement by consensus, with all parties being committed to any agreement reached. This should not assume that any divergence between the knowledge claims and values of participants should be ignored. If the dialogue has been conducted transparently to arrive at a consensus decision, it can often lead to continuing cooperation, even from objectors to the proposal.

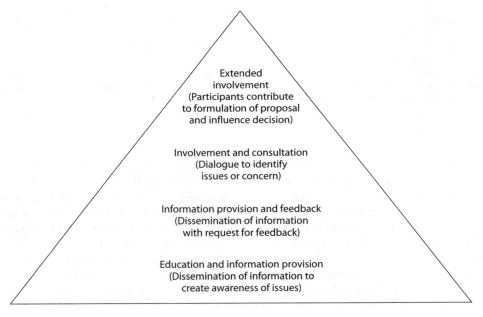

Source: Adapted from IEMA, 2002

Figure 6.3.1   Levels of stakeholder participation

Techniques for stakeholder engagement and participation in environmental decision making

The choice of techniques to stimulate participation and engage with stakeholders on a wide range of environmental issues is complicated by the myriad of approaches that exist. One of the most useful summaries of techniques for participating in environmental decision making is contained in the IEMA guidelines (IEMA, 2002, pp34–39). As well as outlining a wide range of methods it also describes their usage and perceived advantages and disadvantages.

As well as the techniques described in the IEMA guidelines, other approaches to stakeholder involvement have been developed to meet legal requirements in a country or to cope with a specific environmental issue. An example of the former is the role of the review panel in Canada. For major projects, an independent review panel is set up to facilitate the EIA process. It has powers to help formulate the scope of the assessment, engage with all interested stakeholders, and where necessary propose appropriate compensation to those negatively impacted (usually in the form of community facilities enhancement). In its decision report to the appropriate government minister, the nature and results of the public consultation must be stated clearly. The panel also has powers to stipulate that financial assistance should be provided to selected stakeholders, usually potential objectors, who might be disadvantaged given the financial resources of a major developer. When considered appropriate, a mediator may be appointed instead of a review panel. The mediator would consult with all interested stakeholders, with the aim of achieving consensus out of potential conflict.

Examples of techniques, or more appropriately frameworks, to deal with specific environmental issues also exist. In Britain these include Local Agenda 21 groups, regional sustainable development frameworks and river basin management (RBM) planning. Given the importance of the Water Framework Directive, considerable debate is now taking place as to the most appropriate techniques to engage the multiplicity of stakeholders in RBM planning.

Table 6.3.1 is a summary of the wide range of techniques for communicating with the public. Broadly the techniques are similar to those proposed by the IEMA in their guidelines. What is of value is the attempt, based on empirical evidence of what works and what doesn't, to relate techniques to communication characteristics, participation objectives and levels of participation.

In summary, the selection of the most appropriate technique will depend on many factors. These include: the specific purpose of the participation exercise; the degree of interaction required between participants; whether participants can influence decisions; the time available for participation; the resources available; and the complexity, controversy and level of interest in the environmental issue under consideration. Therefore, a number of principles need to be considered when selecting the most appropriate involvement technique. For example:

- Sufficient relevant information must be provided in a form that is easily understood by non-experts, without being simplistic or insulting.
- Sufficient time must be allowed for stakeholders to read, discuss and consider the information and its implications.

Table 6.3.1   Techniques for communicating with the public

Communication characteristics				Public information and participation objectives					
Level of public contact achieved	Ability to handle specific interest	Degree of two way communication	Public participation/ communication techniques	Inform/ educate	Identify problems/ values	Get ideas/ solve problems	Feedback	Evaluate	Resolve conflict/ consensus
2	1	1	Public hearings		X		X		
2	1	2	Public meetings	X	X		X		
1	2	3	Informal small group meetings	X	X	X	X	X	X
2	1	2	General public information meetings	X					
1	2	2	Presentations to community organizations	X	X		X		
1	3	3	Information coordination seminars	X			X		
1	2	1	Operating field offices		X	X	X	X	
1	3	3	Local planning visits		X		X	X	
2	2	1	Information brochures and pamphlets	X					
1	3	3	Field trips and site visits	X	X				
3	1	2	Public displays	X		X	X		
2	1	2	Model demonstration projects	X			X	X	X
3	1	1	Material for mass media	X					
1	3	2	Response to public inquiries	X					
3	1	1	Press releases inviting comments	X			X		
1	3	1	Letter requests for comments			X	X		
1	3	3	Workshops		X	X	X	X	X
1	3	3	Advisory committees		X	X	X	X	
1	3	3	Task forces		X	X		X	
1	3	3	Employment of community residents		X	X			X
1	3	3	Community interest advocates			X		X	X
1	3	3	Ombudsman or representative		X	X	X	X	X
2	3	1	Public review of decision documents	X	X	X	X	X	X

Note: Level of participation: 1 = low, 2 = medium, 3 = high
Source: UNEP, 1996

- Sufficient time must be allowed to enable stakeholders to present their views.
- Responses should be provided to issues and problems raised or comments made by stakeholders – this enables public confidence in the involvement process to be maintained.
- The selection of venues and the timing of events should encourage maximum attendance and a free exchange of views by all stakeholders, including those that may feel less confident about expressing their views.

Stakeholder engagement and participation: case studies

Managing Radioactive Waste Safely

On 12 September 2001, the UK Government and the devolved administrations for Northern Ireland, Scotland and Wales published a joint consultation paper on Managing Radioactive Waste Safety. It proposed a review of a range of options, including public debate and research, leading to a decision on how to manage the waste for thousands of years. This consultation closed in March 2002 and later that year government ministers decided to go ahead with a review of all the options, which would include seeking the views of the public and stakeholder groups. An independent body (The Committee on Radioactive Waste Management – CoRWM) will oversee the review process with the government wanting to promote a dynamic and extensive process of engagement with the public and stakeholder groups. It was felt that this approach would reach far more people and encourage active involvement in decision making, compared to occasional opportunities to respond to consultation papers (Defra, 2003).

Table 6.3.2 presents different engagement techniques, from the earlier consultation process, which could be utilized to inform the debate on options. Its interest lies in the fact that for different levels of engagement, a multiplicity of methods are proposed – selecting the most relevant and appropriate ones is what makes stakeholder engagement such a challenging activity.

Table 6.3.2   Stratagies for stakeholder engagement in radioactive waste management

Engagement Strategy	Description	Methods
1. Education and information provision	Communication of information and educational material to individual members of the public and stakeholders with no feedback mechanism. The main purpose is to raise awareness and increase understanding. It is equally applicable from local through to national scale levels.	• Leaflets, brochures, information packs, videos, newsletters; • Exhibitions/displays (non-staffed); • Advertising; • Media (TV, radio, newspapers); • Internet (information provision).

continued overleaf

Table 6.3.2   continued

Engagement Strategy	Description	Methods
2. Consultation (predominantly open to all)	Various approaches to providing information and receiving feedback that are potentially open to all types of participant (i.e. professional and local stakeholders, and the public). Engagement can either be at a distance or face to face (with individuals or groups) and tends to be in the form of one-off events or initiatives.	• Site visits; • Exhibitions/displays (staffed); • Open house; • Public meetings; • Consultation workshops; • Consultation documents; • Internet (information/ feedback); • Free telephone lines (automated or staffed); • Teleconferencing; • Public inquiries.
3. Consultation (targeting the public/citizens)	Citizens are targeted through statistically representative samples to take part in quantitative surveys to test public opinion, or are recruited to participate in qualitative approaches based on shared demographic features. Quantitative surveys can be at a distance allowing wide national coverage, but lack in-depth reasoned responses. In-depth qualitative approaches allow face to face individual or group deliberation and thus tend to be locally situated (but can reach national coverage through multiple processes throughout the country).	• Questionnaire surveys (postal, web); • Telephone surveys; • Interview surveys; • Focus groups; • Discussion groups; • Deliberative opinion polls.
4. Deliberation/ dialogue (groups of citizens and specialists)	Innovative deliberative approaches that engage citizens, often recruited to be representative of the wider public, in panels over extended periods of responsive information provision, considering issues, and providing recommendations to decision makers. Citizens interact with specialists (or experts) at various points throughout the process – available methods differ in the degree and nature of this interaction and thus the extent of mutual learning and capacity building between panellists and specialists.	• Research panels; • Interactive panels; • Citizens' juries (citizens' panels; planning cells, etc.); • Consensus conferences; • Deliberative mapping.
5. Deliberation/ dialogue (groups of predominantly local stakeholders)	Methods that seek to engage (predominantly) local stakeholders, selected to represent the interests of others or as surrogates of the general public, over extended periods in group deliberation and dialogue. Participants identify local issues and concerns, set priorities and agree on recommendations for action. Some approaches involve stakeholders in framing and actively engaging in technical-analytic aspects of decision processes (e.g. joint fact finding; participatory research), while others involve local stakeholders in the evaluation and prioritization of policy options.	• Community advisory committees (CAS); • Planning for Real; • Visioning; • Workshops; • Stakeholder dialogue; • Joint fact finding (and other forms of collaborative analysis); • Stakeholder decision analysis; • Participatory research/ participatory appraisal; • Internet dialogue.

Table 6.3.2 continued

Engagement Strategy	Description	Methods
6. Deliberation/ dialogue (groups of predominantly professional stakeholders)	Approaches that seek to engage (predominantly) professional stakeholders, selected to represent the interests of others, over extended periods in group deliberation and dialogue. The most common approaches for this strategy are stakeholder workshops and stakeholder dialogue.	• Workshops; • Stakeholder dialogue; • Joint fact finding (and other forms of collaborative analysis); • Stakeholder decision analysis; • Multi-criteria mapping; • Internet dialogue, Delphi process.
7. Existing engagement processes initiated and carried out by others	Engagement structures already in place at the local authority, regional and national levels could be used to engage the public and stakeholders in radioactive waste issues. The nature of processes would depend on existing structures, meaning limited control over who participates and how. It might be necessary to provide funds and resources to assist those undertaking engagement processes.	• Local Agenda 21 processes; • Regional sustainable development frameworks; • Community planning networks; • Scottish Civil Forum.

Source: Defra, 2003

Area Waste Plan for North East Scotland (SEPA, 2003)

The draft area waste plan was published for consultation in July 2002. Copies were sent to community councils, local businesses and special interest groups. Copies were also distributed by the area's local authorities for wider coverage such as to elected council members as well as being placed in libraries and council offices. Notifications were also made through the Scottish Environment Protection Agency's (SEPA's) press releases and by local radio broadcasts. All documents were made available on SEPA's web site – this included a dedicated email address for responses. About 2500 non-technical summaries with a returnable freepost comment sheet were distributed throughout the waste strategy area. In addition, about 400 individual invitations were sent out for participation in workshops, which were held throughout July and August 2002.

The workshops were chaired by officers representing the local authority, and SEPA officials were in attendance at all workshops. A standard presentation format was adopted which included a presentation from SEPA officials outlining the draft area plan and the rationale for the decisions made, and the best practicable environmental option (BPEO) was described. This was followed by a question and answer session. The numbers of delegates attending workshops ranged from 6 in Elgin to 30 in Aberdeen City.

Given the importance of the issues at stake this appears to be a very poor response to an extensive engagement exercise. However, there was general agreement at all the workshops as to what the key issues were. They were: concern over excessive packaging; how to raise awareness and education; use and location of recycling facilities; and opposition to incineration.

As well as comments received at the workshops, over 75 letters, written comment sheets and email responses were received. Views on the plan ranged from positive to negative in almost equal measure. The majority of comments came from local authorities, community councils, and a wide range of NGOs. Inevitably, the greatest concerns were expressed by those community councils that believed that they would be adversely affected by a proposed incinerator.

The Area Waste Strategy Group (AWSG) considered these responses and, as a result, a number of modifications were made to the way the BPEO is to be implemented. In particular there is to be:

- earlier and a more extensive introduction of kerbside collection of materials for recycling;
- a commitment to achieve the Scottish Executive targets on recycling;
- targets for waste reduction at source and expanded partnership working with the key stakeholders; and
- the AWSG has entered into dialogue with representatives of trade bodies with regard to commercial waste.

This case study illustrates that, despite adopting extensive and wide ranging engagement techniques, results can be disappointing. A genuine attempt was made to actively involve the wider public but their input was minimal. Instead it was those with a vested interest who actively engaged in the process. If the exercise is repeated it is difficult to know what other stakeholder engagement techniques could be used. This suggests that even though there was a willingness to engage in a proactive manner, and apply a wide range of engagement techniques, satisfactory outcomes do not always materialize.

The River Spey Catchment Management Plan (Spey Catchment Steering Group, 2003)

The River Spey Catchment Management Plan (CMP) sets out a strategic framework for the wise and sustainable use of the water resource, and for the protection and enhancement of water quality and natural heritage within the River Spey catchment. In so doing, it recognizes the need to accommodate the social and economic wellbeing of communities along the river and its tributaries. A fundamental principle behind the development of the plan was to secure the support, and encourage participation, of all those with an interest in the River Spey and its tributaries. Through the development of the plan, a strong commitment was shown by organizations, agencies and individuals towards working together to tackle some of the more difficult and contentious issues and to ensure the future sustainable management of this valuable resource. The success of this plan will be measured by the continuing level of cooperation and commitment to achieving the management objectives and delivery of the recommended actions.

How the CMP was developed: The development of the CMP evolved in five stages. The first stage was an initial public consultation seeking people's views on key water resource management issues within the catchment. In the second and third stages some of the key issues were considered in more depth by five working groups, each of which made recommendations for action. The fourth stage was the collation of these recommendations into a consultative draft CMP. This was followed by the fifth and final stage of reviewing the draft document and producing a fully integrated CMP.

The Steering Group undertook an extensive public consultation in the summer of 2000 to elicit people's views and concerns, and to provide comment on the key issues facing the River Spey and its tributaries. Public participation in this exercise was sought through a consultative document (Spey Catchment Steering Group, 2000). This was made widely available to people throughout the river catchment and promoted by the partner organizations themselves through the media and on web sites. The consultation generated considerable interest and views and comments were received from a wide range of organizations and individuals with an interest in the future management of the water resources of the River Spey catchment.

There followed a period of further discussion of the key issues by five working groups, made up of a number of representatives from organizations and agencies, plus individuals, who had volunteered to contribute time, knowledge and expertise to the process. The issues identified during the initial public consultation were divided into five broad topic areas as follows: water quality; management and control of river water; fisheries management; nature conservation, agriculture and forestry; and community economic development and recreation.

The remit of these working groups was to discuss the key issues in more depth and to draw up a series of recommendations for future action that would help to address these issues and contribute to a more integrated approach to the management of the water resources. Culminating in a workshop in May 2002, the output from these working groups marked the completion of a third stage in the development of the CMP. The fourth stage comprised a public consultation on a draft plan containing recommendations from the five working groups. The fifth and final stage was a review of the draft plan in the light of feedback from the consultation, followed by publication of the final report.

Management objectives provide the foundation of the River Spey CMP. These, together with the recommendations for action, were derived through a collaborative and consultative process. The initial public consultation on key issues provided a focus for deliberation on the activities that take place within the catchment and impact in some way on the water resources. Organizations, agencies, associations, communities and individuals who contributed their time and expertise to the working groups all helped to shape the plan. The second public consultation, on the consultative draft CMP, provided further opportunity for interested parties to help focus the plan and to define a series of actions that would help to ensure future sustainable management of this valuable resource.

Given the actual and potential conflicts that exist in the Spey catchment between various stakeholders, this plan indicates that interactive and open processes of participation can lead to consensus being achieved. It should act as a model as to how sound river basin management plans might evolve.

Mendip District Council's village visions planning days (IEMA, 2002)

Mendip District Council held a series of visioning days as part of the process of producing a new local plan for the area. The planning days, as they were called, were used to get a picture of local residents' aspirations for their village prior to a draft of the local plan being drawn up.

Mechanism for participation: A series of planning days was held, covering groups of two or three neighbouring villages. Events were publicized with the help of the parish councils. A series of stations was set up, at which residents were asked to respond to a variety of questions. The answers were posted onto boards or written on feedback sheets. Answers were visible for others to read but non-attributable. Questions included:

- What would you like your village to be like in 2011?
- What do you like about your village? What do you dislike about your village? What would you like to change? (The Good, The Bad and the Ugly).
- What makes your village special?
- What are the priorities for change?

Finally a large scale map was provided and residents were invited to highlight problems, areas where development could take place, and areas that were highly valued.

Outcomes: A permanent record of each event was made and circulated in the villages. It continues to be used as a tool in the district and parish council's work. The planning days were well attended and provided an interactive and open forum for residents to express their views on the future of their villages. Discussion was frequently generated between residents as well as with council staff. People stayed on average for about an hour and often revisited stations as new issues were raised. Comments indicated that people generally found the events thought provoking.

The events generated a great deal of information, which has been used in local plan preparation and by other sections of the council. The issues that raised the most universal concerns were traffic and access, and work is continuing to address these problems. The open and interactive format was widely welcomed, helping to show how the council is listening and being responsive to local views. It also allowed people who would not otherwise have become involved in the local plan process to participate. The events started the process of generating a consensus among local residents as to what the future of their villages should be.

Testwood Lakes (Clark, 1994)

This case study concerns a proposal to extract sand and gravel from a 58ha site in Hampshire, southern England, in preparation for the construction of water storage reservoirs. Southern Water had to apply to the local planning authority for planning consent and under the EU EIA Directive was required to carry out an environmental assessment of the proposal.

The company consulted with its stakeholders before undertaking the assessment. Consultations were carried out with official bodies, interest groups, local residents and the general public. Participation methods included presentations, exhibitions and public meetings. Alternatives, such as water conservation, desalination, use of existing lakes, as well as alternative sites for the project, were all considered and the public was consulted. The consultations provided views from all concerned parties on the principle of development; the site; alternatives; and impacts, both positive and negative, of the project. The wider implications of the project for the hydrology of the area, effects on water quality and fishing, and the opportunities for recreation and nature conservation were all reviewed. The consultation process was therefore used as a scoping exercise, to identify the key environmental implications to be assessed in more detail.

The environmental assessment itself was carried out by a team of specialists, and the concerns raised during the consultation process were addressed in the final environmental statement. This document was circulated free of charge and detailed technical reports on individual topics were given to those who asked for them. At no stage were there any complaints about lack of information on the development.

Outcome of the proposal: There were very few objections to the project, and planning permission was granted without the case going to appeal, which suggests that the consultation process was effective in allaying any concerns over the project. The proponents of the development maintained good consultation procedures after the project was granted planning permission, with letters to local residents, and exhibitions to keep people informed of progress.

Contacts with the Hampshire Wildlife Trust have also been maintained as they jointly manage the nature conservation and interpretative centres. The general acceptance of the project is indicative of good consultation procedures, with the concerns of affected parties being sought early in the EIA process, leading to modifications to the project design to make it more acceptable. This is a good example of how public consultation in the EIA process can be effective in enabling a project to proceed by introducing measures to prevent or mitigate impacts and satisfy the concerns raised by all affected parties.

Taking stock and future directions

Perhaps the key message that came out of the Rio Summit in 1992 was that models for sustainable development required a paradigm shift from a top-down to a bottom-up approach. As a major contributor to achieving more sustainable types of development, many forms of environmental management will play a key role, and stakeholder engagement and more active participation are prerequisites of such an approach.

In some quarters, however, there is still opposition to increasing stakeholder engagement. Arguments include a belief by some proponents of environmental policies and projects that more active participation and dialogue can lead to delays, incur excessive costs, raise expectations that cannot be met, and that issues cannot be understood by a non-technical public. Also, decision makers might be nervous about increased stakeholder involvement as it could delay them making rational decisions. At the same time many members of the public are cynical about their ability to have any real input. A lack of awareness of their rights, apathy and a 'sleeping with the enemy' attitude have all been noted as reasons for lack of engagement.

On the other hand there is now strong empirical evidence that open and transparent engagement can be of benefit to all parties. Proponents can legitimize their proposals and ensure public acceptance and support. They can improve public trust and, perhaps most important of all, good early consultation can often help to avoid possible costly delays by resolving conflicts early on in the process. Equally there are benefits to decision makers and the public that help to ensure there is an open and transparent process that sees empowerment of the public contributing to more democratic decision making.

A good example of this can be seen in Figure 6.3.2, which illustrates the engagement process used to develop Agenda 21 for Vale Royal, Cheshire. Cooperation between the decision maker, a wide range of stakeholders and interest groups has led to a highly effective, and bought-into process, of which ownership by the community is a core feature.

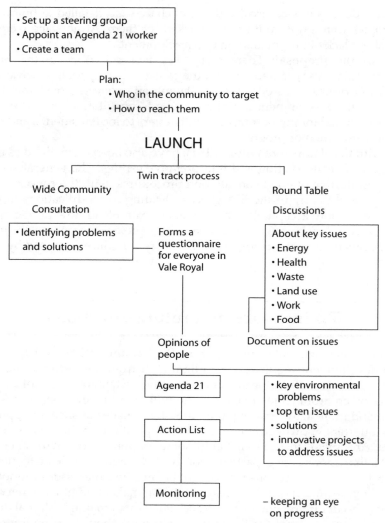

Source: Hughes, 1998

Figure 6.3.2   Agenda 21 in Vale Royal

Many lessons have been learned from the wide range of stakeholder dialogues that have now taken place. Key elements that can lead to positive outcomes, whether in EIA, formulation of environmental management plans, or a range of other initiatives include the following:

- Start the process early, rather than when problems arise.
- Involve senior management in the process.
- Use trained facilitators rather than see participation and engagement as a public relations function.
- Attempt to be inclusive; while this may take more time and resources, the pay off will usually be greater.

- Be flexible in the way that stakeholders are dealt with.
- Information provided should be simple, jargon free but not patronizing.
- Provide feedback as to how stakeholders influenced the decision.

Stakeholder engagement and greater participation is now entering a period of experimentation. This is partly the result of pressure from government to ensure that the public has a greater say in environmental decision making and a major input into issues of environmental justice. It is also because of a growing confidence in local government and environmental agencies, that while they are predominantly regulators, they can make a major contribution to achieving more sustainable forms of development, by working in partnership with a diverse range of stakeholders. As an example, SEPA is now developing a wide range of engagement activities. Stakeholder partnerships are now growing in significance. Regional boards of SEPA are meeting with stakeholders to evaluate the effectiveness of regulatory regimes, partnerships and how to improve awareness of environmental issues. Thus, while many of the tried and tested methods of stakeholder engagement will continue to be utilized, it is likely that increased emphasis in the future will be placed on mediation and consensus building approaches.

References and further reading

Audit Commission (1999) *Listen Up, Effective Community Consultation*, Audit Commission, London

Clark, B. D. (1994) 'Improving Public Participation in EIA', *Built Environment*, vol 20, no 4, pp249–309

Defra (2003) 'Managing Radioactive Waste Safely – Participatory Methods Workshop Report', vol 2, Background Papers (Defra/RAS/03.001), Department for Environment, Food and Rural Affairs, London

EA (2000) *Public Involvement in Agency Activities*, Report no 22, National Centre for Risk Analysis and Options Appraisal, Environment Agency, Bristol

Environmental Resolve (1995) *Beyond Compromise: Building Consensus in Environmental Planning and Decision Making*, Environmental Council, London

Hughes, K. (1998) 'Agenda 21 and Local Agenda 21: Principles and Practice', conference paper, Centre for Environmental Management and Planning, Aberdeen

IEMA (2002) *Guidelines on Participation in Environmental Decision-making*, Institute of Environmental Management and Assessment, Lincoln

Tóth Nagy, M. et al (1994) 'Manual on Public Participation in Environmental Decisionmaking: Current Practice and Future Possibilities in Central and Eastern Europe', Regional Environmental Center for Central and Eastern Europe, Budapest, www.rec.org/REC/Publications/PPManual/Default.html

LGIU (1994) 'Consulting and Involving the Public', Local Government Information Unit, London

Morgan, R. (1998) *Environmental Impact Assessment – A Methodological Perspective*, Kluwer Academic Publishers, Dordrecht

NEF (1998) *Participation Works, 21 Techniques of Community Participation for the 21st Century*, New Economics Foundation, London

NEPA (2001) 'Fact Sheet: Public Participation under NEPA', National Environmental Protection Act, http://gsa.gov (search for NEPA)

Petts, J. (1999) 'Public Participation and Environmental Impact Assessment', in Petts, J. (ed) *Handbook of Environmental Impact Assessment. Vol 1 – Environmental Impact Assessment: Process Methods and Potential*, Blackwell Science, London

RCEP (1998) 'Setting Environmental Standards', 21st report, Cm 4053, Royal Commission on Environmental Pollution, The Stationery Office, London

SEPA (2003) 'National Waste Strategy, Scotland – Aberdeenshire, City of Aberdeen and Moray', Scottish Environment Protection Agency, Stirling

Spey Catchment Steering Group (2000) *River Spey – Towards a Catchment Management Plan*, Spey Catchment Steering Group, Aviemore

Spey Catchment Steering Group (2003) *River Spey: Catchment Management Plan*, Spey Catchment Steering Group, Aviemore

UNECE (1998) 'Convention on Access to Information, Public Participation in Decision Making and Access to Justice in Environmental Matters', (The Aarhus Convention), UN Economic Commission for Europe, Geneva

UNEP (1996) 'Public Involvement', in *EIA Resource Training Manual*, United Nations Environment Programme, Nairobi

Wilcox, D. (1994) *The Guide to Effective Participation*, Partnership Books, Brighton

World Bank (2001) 'Public Participation', World Bank, Washington DC, www.worldbank.org/wbi/sourcebook/sb0003.htm

Section 7

Key Environmental Themes

Chapter 7.1

Pollution Prevention and Control

Introduction

Pollution prevention and control (PPC) is core to effective environmental protection. It is very much about making a difference, the achievement of a better quality of life and a key component of the delivery of sustainable development.

Historically, the objective of PPC has been to prevent further deterioration of the environment as a result of industrial activity or the achievement and maintenance of a particular standard. More recently we have recognized that there are a range of interests at play including social and economic considerations that have to be integrated into environmental decision making.

There are very few pollutants, if any, where we can say that a particular level of pollution is safe to human health or environmentally benign. As a result, instead, we are increasingly asking what can be achieved by the technology and techniques available to us, at what environmental, economic and social cost. This has shifted the focus from the source of the pollution to the individual, animal, plant, natural or man made feature that is affected. As releases of pollution from high profile sources are successfully reduced, the focus must shift to the many smaller, contained and diffuse sources. One molecule of sulphur dioxide, whatever its source, will have the same impact on a particular limestone pavement or habitat.

A wide range of tools are available for PPC to tackle the diversity of sources and achieve the desired environmental outcome. At the same time we must take account of the factors affecting the different sources, industries and individuals, which include:

- the individual company and its culture;
- the national and local economic profile – is it in growth or decline?
- the size of organizations – are there many SMEs or a few dominant players?
- environmental awareness – is the organization committed or determinedly non-compliant?

Increasingly, organizations are seeing environmental commitment as an asset. Regulation is seen less as a burden and more as a complement to the effective operation of their business and their markets. For the smaller operator regulation is often more of an issue, as it can appear disproportionate to the benefits obtained. Not only is a proportionate approach required, but often different techniques are required to achieve environmental goals. For many operators, ensuring that they have an effective management system, akin to a tachograph in the cab, could be more effective than placing them under surveillance. Support can often be achieved from a far larger number of organizations at lower cost by a successful information/education programme compared with the resources required to pursue a single prosecution. However, prosecution can also have a significant effect in reminding those in a similar position of their obligations.

In order to achieve transparent and consistent environmental protection clear objectives and milestones are required whatever the approach used. This means that if one tool or mix of tools is not achieving an environmental objective, it is obvious and other approaches can be deployed. Robust enforcement is required to maintain respect for and the integrity of regulation, the tools used, and the standards to be achieved. The tool, standard or commitment is sustained and enhanced by prosecution, withdrawal of certification or expulsion from a voluntary agreement.

Guiding principles

Increasing public expectation, more complex issues, many new environmental initiatives and regulations from UK legislators, Europe and internationally, all mean that demands on organizations and their regulators are increasing. The efforts of operators and regulators have to be strictly managed and prioritized. Both operators and regulators are answerable to their shareholders, boards of management or funding bodies to ensure that they operate efficiently and effectively.

The guiding principles of environmental protection for the process operator are:

- prevention – not using or not producing specific substances, designing out the problem;
- minimizing the problem – using the best techniques, continuous processes, minimal inventories;
- effective control – identifying the risks and hazards, and designing and operating to control them, bunding, containment;
- minimizing the effects – dispersion, dilution;
- monitoring – process, releases, the receiving environment, the effects; and
- reporting to the public, the regulator and other interested parties – not only must operators get it right, they need to be seen to be getting it right.

Where practicable, regulators must seek to simplify and rationalize existing regulatory regimes, reducing administration and bureaucracy. Environmental regulators are moving to a more risk based approach to target and allocate resources and provide incentives for better performers and to match their approach to operator performance and attitude. Wherever practicable, regulators are seeking to work in partnership with responsible industry, working with trade associations and individual companies to inform, influence and educate to achieve environmental goals. At the same time, to be effective, regulators must use their powers of enforcement where necessary.

The guiding principles of environmental protection for the modern regulator are:

- that environmental objectives are delivered in the most efficient and effective manner;
- that the regulated organizations take responsibility for their environmental performance, including environmental improvements where these are needed;

- to assess the effectiveness of the operators' processes and systems and to take a lighter touch for those who earn it and apply tougher regulation for those who need it;
- to match the regulatory resource with income;
- to allocate effort according to risk and the potential for outcomes; and
- to identify and secure minimum standards.

In the UK, industrial regulation is primarily activity focused with some outcome based controls. The type of industry and its scale of operations and releases determines the type and level of regulatory control. For the simplest activities the requirement is to prevent nuisance: for example the release of an odorous substance or noise. For industries with more than minimal pollution potential, technology derived standard limits are applied. Where their potential impact is primarily local, simplified permits could be used. Standardized permits are suitable for industry sectors where the technology and standards are relatively consistent across the industry. For technically complex industries with more significant environmental impact bespoke permits are required.

The performance of an operator can then be based on an assessment of:

- systems – procedures, training, maintenance, monitoring and so on;
- emissions – compliance with permit conditions;
- administrative aspects – reporting requirements and notifications;
- compliance with improvement programmes;
- compliance with other permit conditions; and
- incidents and complaints.

The integrated approach

The Environmental Protection Act 1990 paved the way for integrated pollution control (IPC) for a wide range of industrial sectors and provided significant experience to industry, regulators, public and government of the strengths and pitfalls of cross-media regulation. It introduced the concept of 'best available techniques not entailing excessive cost' (BATNEEC) and 'best practicable environmental option' (BPEO). The latter attempts to compare impacts of substances on different media. The analogy of seeking to compare apples and pears captures the difficulty experienced by both regulators and industry in making the assessment. The Environment Agency (EA), following its predecessor – Her Majesty's Inspectorate of Pollution – was given responsibility in England and Wales to deliver this integrated approach to specified industries and developed 'horizontal guidance' (which was designated EI and is now designated H1) to assist operators. The 1990 Act also introduced local air pollution control (LAPC) by local authorities and the application of BATNEEC for generally less technically complex industrial processes with the potential to have a significant environmental impact on the air alone.

The European Community Directive 96/61/EC on Integrated Pollution Prevention and Control (the IPPC Directive) was implemented through the Pollution Prevention and Control (England and Wales) Regulations 2000, SI 1973 made under the Pollution

Prevention and Control Act 1999. Similar provisions applied the IPPC Directive in Scotland and are expected to apply in Northern Ireland. The regulations apply a two-part approach to PPC:

- Part A applies an integrated approach to controlling a wide variety of industrial activities, from chemical plants and power stations through to food factories and intensive pig and chicken farms. Air and water pollution, protection of the land and management of waste are all considered in a single regulatory regime. In addition energy efficiency, the prevention of accidents, noise and compliance with other EU directives, regulations and environmental quality standards must also be addressed.
- Part B deals with emissions to air only – local air pollution prevention and control (LAPPC) – and is a continuation of the LAPC regime.

In England and Wales, local authorities (district or metropolitan councils) regulate Part B installations. Part A installations are split between the EA – Part A (1) and local authorities – Part A (2). In Scotland, the Scottish Environment Protection Agency (SEPA) regulates all the installations. The operator of an activity must submit a permit application describing the installation and its environmental impacts. The regulator then consults the public and other statutory consultees before deciding whether to issue a permit. Emissions to air, land and water including discharges to sewer plus other environmental effects must be considered together. The aim of IPPC is to achieve 'a high level of protection of the environment as a whole' and requires the regulator to ensure that 'installations are operated in such a way that all appropriate measures are taken against pollution, in particular through the application of best available techniques'. Permit conditions are based on the use of the best available techniques (BATs) for the sector, which balances the costs to the operator with the benefits to the environment.

The agencies have published a large amount of guidance to help industry, much of it based on the BAT reference (BREF) documents produced by the European Commission through the European IPPC Bureau in Seville. Permits for new installations normally require operators to meet, as a minimum, the standards in the BREF documents immediately. Permits for existing installations will often include improvement requirements to bring the installation up to the standards in the BREF document over the appropriate length of time.

The permitting of existing installations has to be complete by October 2007, which creates a considerable workload challenge. The legislation sets out a transitional timetable under which industries come within the ambit of IPPC on a sector by sector basis. This approach contrasts with many other EU countries, which are planning to implement IPPC by, but closer to, the 2007 deadline.

In applying IPPC, it is also necessary to meet the requirements of other EU directives. Examples include the revised Large Combustion Plants Directive, the Waste Incineration Directive and the Landfill Directive. This has led to some complex regulatory requirements, and has also revealed some areas where the standards or definitions of different pieces of legislation are inconsistent or in conflict. The UK Government continues to support the development of a more coherent approach to legislation, which would support greater efficiency and effectiveness in implementation.

The commission is reviewing the current state of play on implementing the IPPC Directive and the regulation of large industrial point sources and their impact on the environment. In 2003 the commission issued a communication to help promote this review. Specifically the commission has identified major suspected or confirmed short-comings in the legislation of most member states, identified difficulties in the implementation of the directive and raised a number of key questions. The national responses to this review will influence the future development of environmental regulation.

Certain IPPC installations are also subject to the requirements of the Control of Major Accident Hazards Regulations 1999 (COMAH). COMAH applies because of the presence or anticipated presence of threshold quantities of certain dangerous substances. COMAH requires operators to take all necessary measures to prevent major accidents and limit their consequences to persons and the environment. A joint competent authority comprising the agency, SEPA and the Health and Safety Executive (HSE) enforces COMAH. There are also additional planning consent requirements of sites subject to COMAH under the Planning (Control of Major Accident Hazards) Regulations 1999 (P(COMAH)). The environment agencies and the HSE work closely together in the assessment of safety cases, inspection and enforcement on COMAH sites.

In England and Wales the EA is required to assess the state of the environment. As a result it is in a strong position to see what needs to be done for the environment, and influence other agencies including government and industry to take the right steps towards appropriate environmental outcomes. This holistic approach to the environment is one of the strongest aspects of environmental regulation in the UK.

Regulation

Regulation is not an end in itself but rather a means to an end. It is important to focus on the environmental outcome to be achieved through regulation in addition to the permitting and compliance assessment process. Historically, industrial regulation has been activity focused with technology derived standard limits applied to all industries in each sector. The application of limits and standards on releases can then be directly linked to environmental effects or impacts. This approach is of particular value for processes where their impact is primarily local. Where there are many potential sources of the pollution or particular sources disperse their releases more widely through tall stacks, for example, connections are less easy to make. Where possible the key pollutants arising from each industry and the technologies available to the operator provide the focus for regulation.

The UK environment agencies have produced guidance on applying for permits and on the techniques and standards they expect. The guidance identifies the key pollutants for each industry and the technologies expected to be addressed by the operator in his or her application and the regulator in compliance assessment. The EA, on behalf of the Environment Department of the government, also produces guidance on the processes regulated by local authorities. The government-run Envirowise programme provides information on waste minimization and environmental best practice.

For each significant regulated industry the EA is producing sector plans. The plans set the context for the industry, identifying technical, economic and some social aspects of the industry, and inform the sector plans. They then set out the desired environmental outcomes, balance key sector drivers (including economic issues) and identify strategic tools relevant to the sector. The plans are prepared in cooperation with the industry and reflect the agency's assessment of the priority of substances released by that industry and their impact on the environment. They also set out the permitting strategy including, for example, permit type and sector permit conditions, and detail the key performance indicators for that sector. For each sector, the agency is preparing a sector compliance assessment plan which identifies national compliance issues and enables it to prioritize the regulatory workload on a sector by sector basis.

The regulatory process consists of several elements, which apply to both new and existing activities. The principles apply to most permitting regimes applied by local authorities and national regulators. The stages described below are particularly pertinent to PPC regulation:

- permitting;
- compliance assessment; and
- closure and surrender.

Even before an operator starts the formal application process he or she should engage with the stakeholders, as a minimum the regulator and local public who will be impacted by the activity. Time invested with the regulator pre-application will pay dividends in optimizing the work and time for the permit application and determination. The public have considerable sway in deciding whether an application has a quick, smooth ride or a difficult, slow one through their own action, as well as through the actions of those they can influence such as local politicians and the healthcare trusts. Operators are required to advertise and the regulator, on receipt of the application, will consult the statutory consultees.

In making an application the operator must address the following issues:

- management of the installation;
- identity and quantity of polluting releases;
- identification and justification of BAT;
- compliance monitoring;
- compliance with environmental quality standards and other regulations;
- energy efficiency;
- waste minimization;
- accident prevention; and
- site condition.

The regulator must be satisfied that the operator has addressed these points – the onus is on the applicant. In determining the PPC permit the regulator will consider the following issues:

- management systems – training, use of environmental management systems (EMS);
- raw materials – minimize use, type and quantity, historical production methods;
- energy efficiency – how it will be improved;
- operating techniques – review, new technology, comparison with other processes in the sector;
- groundwater protection;

- habitats – impact on Natura 2000 sites and sites of special scientific interest (SSSIs);
- waste handling, storage and disposal;
- accident prevention and control – the COMAH interface;
- release monitoring – quality of data and consistency of approach; and
- site reports – the need for an intrusive investigation.

Only if the regulator is satisfied with the application can it issue the permit. In most cases the permit will contain improvement conditions to demonstrate ongoing compliance and that the technology is consistent with BAT. The permit may be varied at any time at the instigation of either the regulator or the operator, which may also include further public consultation. Reviews may be required when the operator wishes to undertake a process development, or when there has been a significant pollution incident or development in a related industry sector.

When an installation closes, the operator should apply to surrender the permit. The operator must include a site report identifying any changes to the condition of the site. The operator must satisfy the regulator that he or she has removed any pollution risks and returned the site to a satisfactory state. Only if the regulator is satisfied will it accept the surrender of the permit.

Complementary approaches

Over the past few years, more use has been made of complementary approaches to the achievement of environmental goals. They are to be welcomed if they bring forward the achievement of environmental goals, achieve goals in a more cost effective way, or go beyond the goals achievable by statutory means in terms of improvement or scope. However, there is a need for a more strategic approach to the achievement of environmental objectives in the UK and in Europe. This will require more integrated thinking and working in UK legislation and, because of the EU driver behind much of our environmental legislation, in the European Commission as well.

The interactions between relevant Community legislation on the environment present difficult challenges to regulators, for example the interface between the IPPC Directive and the Landfill Directive is far from clear. The IPPC Directive and the Trading Directive refer to installations but they are not always consistent. The European Polluting Emissions Register refers to facilities rather than installations and the Solvents Emissions Directive contains a different definition of installation to that in the IPPC Directive despite controlling similar activities.

Operators must take responsibility for the environmental impacts of their activities. They have to take a structured approach in order to deliver consistent and continuing management of environmental impacts. EMS provide a way for businesses to do this.

Many organizations choose to operate in-house, or informal, EMS to manage their environmental impacts. Others use the recognized worldwide standard ISO 14001, or go on to achieve a higher standard through the EU Eco-management and Audit Scheme (EMAS). EMAS requires, for example, legal compliance, independent verification and public access to company environmental reports. However, having a site with an EMS is not a guarantee of good environmental performance. There needs to be a continuing management commitment.

Legal compliance and good environmental performance are fundamental. The EA recognizes EMS in its risk based approach to regulation via the operator and pollution risk appraisal (OPRA) schemes.

There are still a number of unanswered questions in relation to EMS. Studies suggest that sites with EMS don't necessarily deliver better compliance with permit conditions, have fewer incidents or better general environmental performance than those that do not have them. However, the scope of a site EMS will often address issues that go beyond regulatory requirements. It may be that by introducing an EMS, a site's environmental performance will improve at a faster rate than if it does not implement one. Further work is required to better understand these issues.

The EA has stated that it considers that possession of EMAS or ISO 14001 accreditation is likely to demonstrate a high standard of environmental management and should simplify the application and determination process. However, until the EU funded REMAS study, which the EA is helping to conduct, is completed, the EA does not consider that there is sufficient objective evidence to justify a significant relaxation in regulatory approach under the directive.

To improve the uptake and effectiveness of robust EMS:

- industry needs to recognize their benefits;
- third party certification schemes should focus on legal compliance and improvements in environmental performance;
- greater consistency is required between the different certification schemes, as are agreed minimum competency standards;
- a coordinated approach to the recognition of EMS at a European level is required;
- the UK Government should encourage higher standards of certification, through bodies such as the United Kingdom Accreditation Service (UKAS).

EMS can benefit a company or organization by:

- facilitating greater awareness of legislative requirements as all relevant legislation should be identified and plans put in place to achieve compliance;
- identifying the potential for cost savings through improved efficiency in the use of materials and energy;
- providing a better understanding and greater control of processes thereby reducing emissions and the risk of pollution incidents; and
- improving its public image as environmental performance is increasingly important to, among others, customers, insurers and local residents.

Emissions trading can be a more cost effective method for delivering certain environmental outcomes, but its use is currently constrained by the IPPC Directive requirement to apply emission limit values (ELVs) within individual permits. This is incompatible with the collective target approach of trading which requires individual installations to be given some flexibility in the level of emissions they release, provided that the overall collective target is met. An integrated approach for the environment allows the collective target of an appropriately designed trading scheme to substitute for installation-specific BAT-based ELVs for specific substances, provided that the scheme meets all of the equivalent objectives of BAT, including protection of the local environment. An example of such an integrated approach would be the use of installation based ELVs set at the minimum level to ensure the local environment is protected, combined with trading as an instrument to deliver further reductions in long range, transboundary pollution.

The EU Greenhouse Gas Emissions Allowances Trading Directive has put in place a mechanism for trading emissions from 1 January 2005. This required installations to be permitted by 31 March 2004. The UK already has some experience of trading greenhouse gases and sees trading as a valuable tool to achieve its Kyoto commitments.

Emissions trading has the potential to make a significant difference to the regulation of the principal pollutants from the power industry. In the UK, the industries capable of achieving major reductions in emissions of sulphur dioxide and nitrogen oxides are the electricity supply industry, refineries, the iron and steel industry and other large combustion processes. Together these contribute some 77 per cent and 25 per cent of total UK emissions of sulphur dioxide and nitrogen oxides, respectively. Therefore, efforts to reduce the national emissions are best targeted at these industrial processes.

To achieve the greatest impact, the EA has worked with the devolved administrations and other regulators to devise a UK strategy. The strategy will set reduction targets for 2010. These targets will be based on the costs to industry and the resulting environmental benefits. Any regulatory approach adopted by the EA for this sector needs to secure the optimum environmental protection consistent with the application of BAT through controls on emissions and operation. It also needs to be sufficiently flexible to allow industry and, in this case, the electricity supply market to operate, facilitate competition and support fuel diversity. The approach must encourage the switch to cleaner fuels/renewables. Any arrangement also needs to be consistent with commercial operation of sites and portfolios.

Environmental outcomes

Outcome focused environmental protection requires a good knowledge of the environmental impact of human activity. In general we fail to recognize that most of our landscape is man made and we tend to react against proposals to allow it to revert to thick forest cover. We also tend to ignore the implications of our own individual lifestyle and impact. The waste we produce each week for disposal by the local authority is only recently being recognized as our responsibility. We consume industrial products but resist the operation of industry in our neighbourhood no matter how environmentally clean it is.

In order to establish and maintain public confidence, regulators have to ensure that information on emissions, site hazards and risks, operator performance and compliance with permit conditions is readily available to the public, industry and other interested parties. To improve understanding it is important that industry and regulators work closely with many key stakeholders, some of whom are represented through local and central government, statutory committees and environment groups. These are vital links to the wider community. Under PPC there are many statutory consultees but the level of engagement is very variable and dependent on the installation.

The PPC statutory consultees are:

- Health Authority/Primary Healthcare Trust;
- Food Standards Agency;
- English Nature/Countryside Council for Wales;

- Harbour Authority;
- Local Fisheries Committee;
- Local Authority/EA;
- Planning Authority;
- Health and Safety Executive;
- Sewerage Undertaker.

The challenge is to achieve a high level of clarity and consistency of message with all stakeholders and the general public. Different methods are required for each audience but in all cases they must not be underestimated. Parties interested in any proposed change or development tend to be very well informed – both technically and in the way they present their case. It is essential to use the best possible methods for getting to the right people with the right information at the right time.

The challenge is to be sure that the information provided to the public through the internet, face to face, by telephone, via the media and in correspondence is up to date, appropriate and delivered on time.

Enforcement

The regulator will achieve many of its objectives through education, by providing advice and by regulating the activities of others. Securing compliance with legal regulatory requirements, using enforcement powers including prosecution, is an important part of achieving this aim. Prevention is better than cure. The regulators offer information and advice and seek to secure cooperation avoiding bureaucracy or excessive cost. They encourage individuals and businesses to put the environment first and to integrate good environmental practices into normal working methods.

The purpose of enforcement is to ensure that preventative or remedial action is taken to protect the environment or to secure compliance with a regulatory system. The need for enforcement may stem from an unlicensed incident or from a breach of the conditions of a licensed activity. Although regulators expect full voluntary compliance with relevant legislative requirements and licence provisions, they do not hesitate to use their enforcement powers where necessary.

The powers available to the regulator include:

- enforcement notices and works notices (where contravention can be prevented or needs to be remedied);
- prohibition notices (where there is an imminent risk of serious environmental damage);
- suspension or revocation of environmental licences;
- variation of licence conditions;
- injunctions; and
- the carrying out of remedial works (where the regulator has carried out remedial works, it would seek to recover the full costs incurred from those responsible).

Where a criminal offence has been committed, in addition to any other enforcement action, the regulator will consider instituting a prosecution, administering a caution or issuing a warning.

Effective environmental protection requires firm but fair regulation. Underlying this policy are the principles of proportionality in the application of the law and in securing compliance, consistency of approach, transparency about how the regulator operates and what those regulated may expect from the regulator, and targeting of enforcement action.

Achievement

For industries with the potential to make a significant environmental impact, more effective environmental protection can be achieved through regulation based on the risk to the environment. The EA has developed its OPRA tool, which is designed to reflect its regulatory effort for industries coming under PPC. It assesses the company against the following attributes:

- **Complexity:** The effort needed to understand the processes, their interactions, and pollution potential.
- **Emissions:** The use of an emission index for air, land and water that is generated from assessing the annual permitted load and the pollutants' potential to cause environmental harm. It utilizes environmental quality standards (EQSs), occupational exposure limits (OEC), waste inputs as surrogates for emissions, and provides reductions for third party disposals, recycling and reuse.
- **Location:** The proximity to humans, habitats, groundwater protection zones, the potential for direct releases, sensitivity of receiving waters, flooding potential and air quality zones.
- **Operator management:** This has two parts, management systems and compliance history. The management systems elements assessed are operations and maintenance, competence and training, emergency planning and organization. An operator having ISO 14001 or EMAS is rewarded under the organization section. Compliance history is based on criminal convictions, enforcement/prohibitions notices, and formal cautions; this also includes health and safety and food hygiene offences if relevant to management competence.

This assessment tool has built on the experience of the use of a similar OPRA assessment system used for industries regulated by the EA under Part I of the Environmental Protection Act 1990. The resulting score is used to inform work planning and charging. The EA also intends to use the scores in its reporting of industrial performance in *Spotlight on the Environment*, published each year.

The EA has introduced a scheme known as operator monitoring assessment (OMA) to strengthen its auditing of operators' self monitoring arrangements. OMA was launched in November 2001 and initially applied to the monitoring of emissions to air from industrial processes regulated under IPC.

The EA is to use the OMA scheme to:

- assess operators' self monitoring, including monitoring undertaken on behalf of operators by contractors, using a consistent and transparent approach;
- provide a driver for necessary improvements; and

- contribute to the targeting and prioritization of the agency's check monitoring programme.

Challenges to industry

The requirements of PPC pose a challenge to industry but one that can be minimized and even used to commercial advantage by those who are environmentally committed. The environmental regulation of industry will be a success if:

- industry operates in a way that minimizes adverse effects on people and the environment;
- freeloaders are prevented from undermining the commitment of the majority;
- clear requirements are established and maintained;
- public confidence is established and maintained; and
- real environmental improvements are delivered.

Further reading

Defra (2002) 'Integrated Pollution Prevention and Control: A Practical Guide', 2nd edn, Department for Environment, Food and Rural Affairs, London

Environment Agency publications: information is available on the EA's web site at www.environment-agency.gov.uk

Envirowise publications: information is available on the Envirowise web site at www.envirowise.gov.uk

European Union (1996) 'Council Directive 96/61/EC Concerning Integrated Pollution Prevention and Control', *Official Journal of the European Community*, L257 10/10/1996, pp 26–40, Brussels

NSCA (2001) *Report of the NSCA Commission on Industrial Regulation and Sustainable Development*, National Society for Clean Air and Environmental Protection, Brighton

UK Parliament (2000) 'Pollution Prevention and Control (England and Wales) Regulations 2000 (SI 1973)', The Stationery Office, London

Chapter 7.2

Biodiversity and Conservation

What is biodiversity?

Biological diversity or biodiversity is the variety of life on earth. It is nature's variety of plants, animals, micro-organisms, habitats and ecological systems, from the everyday to the highly endangered – from the blackbird and the urban park to the Sumatran tiger and tropical rainforest. The concept was placed firmly on the international agenda by the 1992 Convention on Biological Diversity (CBD). Article 2 of the convention formally defines biodiversity as:

> The variability among living organisms from all sources including, inter alia, terrestrial, marine and other aquatic ecosystems and the ecological complexes of which they are part; this includes diversity within species, between species and of ecosystems.

Biodiversity conservation is similar to the more traditional nature conservation, but takes a holistic approach, giving greater recognition to the social, cultural and economic values of the variety of life; it also includes genetic diversity.

Why does conserving biodiversity matter?

The conservation of biodiversity is a key test of sustainable development. Economic and social development is simply not sustainable if it is achieved while diminishing biodiversity. Biodiversity has economic, ecological, aesthetic and ethical value. Box 7.2.1 summarizes why biodiversity matters.

The economic value of biodiversity is difficult to calculate. This is because many of biodiversity's benefits do not impact on markets and so do not have prices. The market economic impacts of biodiversity can nevertheless be significant, particularly at a regional or local scale.

Globally – Economists have put the value of nature's services at about US$38 trillion a year, roughly equal to the global economy itself (Constanza et al, 1997). This figure demonstrates biodiversity's high overall value, but economic decisions are based on changes in value, which for biodiversity is even more difficult to measure. One study that has attempted this estimated that a single year's loss of natural habitats costs humanity more than US$200 billion, and the same amount every year thereafter. (Balmford et al, 2002).

Box 7.2.1 *Biodiversity matters because ...*

- **it supports life itself** – every species plays a role in the Earth's wellbeing;
- **it provides direct economic benefits** – for example in farming, fisheries, forestry, pharmaceuticals, manufacturing;
- **it provides indirect economic benefits** – for example flood control, wastewater systems, soil stabilization;
- **it has an economic and social value for recreation** – for example recreation, enjoyment of the countryside, wildlife tourism;
- **it has aesthetic and spiritual value** – it enriches our quality of life, it inspires, entertains and motivates us. It makes the world a better, healthier place to live;
- **people value the existence of biodiversity and care whether or not it is conserved** – people place a value on knowing a species or habitat exists and are worried about the loss of UK plants and animals.

Nationally – Biodiversity in the UK supports direct employment on the natural environment (the equivalent of 18,000 full time jobs) and indirect employment in tourism. For example, geese in Scotland benefit tourism by attracting winter bird watchers and goose shooters. Goose watching alone was estimated to attract £1.5 million per annum, which is significant when calculating the net local economic impact of the geese (Rayment and Dickie, 2001). By comparison, the Scottish population has a willingness to pay for policies to conserve geese at £5.2 million to £10.2 million (MacMillan et al, 2001).

Regionally – An increasing number of studies has shown that the environment (including biodiversity) makes a significant contribution to regional economies. For example, it is estimated that the East of England's environmental economy supports between 108,000 and 180,000 jobs, amounting to 6 to 9 per cent of total regional employment (Environmental Posterity Partnership, 2001).

Locally – Biodiversity often helps to bring employment and income generation to rural areas. For example, the management of the Royal Society for the Protection of Birds' (RSPB's) Abernethy nature reserve supports 25 jobs, and spending by the 70,000 visitors attracted to the reserve each year supports an additional 40 jobs in the local area (Shiel et al, 2002). Visitors to the natural environment of the North Norfolk Coast spend £21 million each year, supporting over 3000 jobs in the region. Birds and wildlife are a key attraction for visitors to this area (Rayment and Dickie, 2001).

Conserving biodiversity also has considerable benefits for our quality of life in terms of our mental and physical wellbeing. For example, walking in a 'natural' environment increases mental restoration more significantly than walking in a city or relaxing at home (Hartig et al, 1991). It is now widely accepted that physical activity brings numerous health benefits including reduced risk from heart disease, stroke and bowel cancer as illustrated by the Countryside Agency's Walking the Way to Health Initiative (www.countryside.gov.uk/). What is not so widely recognized is the important role that biodiversity plays in encouraging people to maintain exercise through walking, running, cycling or riding in the countryside.

We are losing biodiversity at an alarming rate (equivalent to prehistoric mass extinctions) both worldwide and in the UK. For example, in less than a human lifetime, 98 per cent of wildflower meadows, 448,000km of hedgerows, over 2 million skylarks and 95 per cent of high brown fritillary butterflies have been lost from the UK. What is unprecedented is that the current loss is predominantly because of human activity.

At a global level, habitat loss and fragmentation is the biggest threat for 85 per cent of all threatened species. Invasive non-native species are the second greatest threat to biodiversity after habitat loss. Pollution, climate change, desertification, human population growth and unsustainable use are also significant threats to the world's variety of life (http://iucn.org/).

Recent analysis of the factors causing loss or decline of priority species and habitats in the UK shows that habitat loss or degradation is the most significant threat followed by pollution. Agriculture, inappropriate management and infrastructure development are the most significant causes of habitat loss or degradation (www.ukbap.org.uk).

International legislation and policy

The key piece of international legislation is the Convention on Biological Diversity (CBD) from the 1992 United Nations Conference on Environment and Development in Rio de Janeiro, Brazil – the 'Earth Summit' (www.biodiv.org). This has now been adopted by 187 parties, including the UK and the European Union (EU). The three key goals of the CBD are shown in Box 7.2.2, and other relevant international obligations and initiatives are listed in Box 7.2.3.

Box 7.2.2 *The key goals of the CBD*

- **Conservation of biodiversity:** the CBD advocates the protection of species and ecosystems through in situ conservation, including nature reserves and policies to save endangered species. However, it acknowledges the need for ex situ conservation, such as zoos and seed banks in some cases.
- **The sustainable use of the components of biodiversity:** the CBD promotes measures to ensure that future generations will benefit (economically and otherwise) from today's biological resources.
- **The fair and equitable sharing of benefits arising from the use of genetic resources:** the CBD sets ground rules for access to genetic resources (chromosomes, genes and DNA) by acknowledging that when a microbe, plant or animal is used for a commercial application (e.g. biotechnology and the development of new pharmaceuticals) the country of origin should benefit.

In furtherance of these three goals, the CBD places various obligations on parties, including requirements to:

- produce a national biodiversity plan and to ensure that strategies for conserving biodiversity are integrated into sectoral policies;
- identify and monitor biodiversity;
- establish in situ and ex situ conservation goals and goals for the sustainable use of biological resources and on access to genetic resources;
- introduce procedures and arrangements to ensure that impacts of projects, programmes and policies on biodiversity are assessed; and
- make provisions relating to the transfer of technology.

Box 7.2.3 *Other relevant international obligations and initiatives*

The Ramsar Convention on Wetlands of International Importance 1971 (**Ramsar Convention**) for the conservation and wise use of all wetlands and their resources (www.ramsar.org).

The Convention on International Trade in Endangered Species of Fauna and Flora 1973 (**CITES**) aims to ensure that international trade in specimens of wild animals and plants does not threaten their survival (www.cites.org).

The Bonn Convention on Migratory Species of Wild Animals 1979 (**CMS or Bonn Convention**) aims to conserve terrestrial, marine and avian migratory species throughout their range (www.cms.int).

The Convention Concerning the Protection of the World Cultural and Natural Heritage 1972 (**World Heritage Convention**) aims to protect cultural and natural heritage (http://whc.unesco.org/).

The Cartagena Protocol on Biosafety (a supplementary agreement to the CBD which came into force in 2003) seeks to protect biodiversity from potential risks from modified living organisms resulting from modern biotechnology (www.biodiv.org/).

The Pan-European Biological and Landscape Diversity Strategy (**PEBLDS**), a European response to support implementation of the CBD, aims to stop and reverse the degradation of biological and landscape diversity in Europe (www.strategyguide.org).

The Convention on the Conservation of European Wildlife and Natural Habitats 1979 (**Berne Convention**) aims to conserve wild flora and fauna and their natural habitats, with an emphasis on the protection of endangered and vulnerable species and their habitats, particularly migratory species (http://europa.eu.int).

European Union policy and legislation

The EU Biodiversity Strategy aims to anticipate, prevent and address the causes of significant reduction or loss of biodiversity at the source and is supported by sectoral action plans for the Conservation of Natural Resources, Agriculture, Fisheries, and Development and Economic Co-operation; see http://biodiversity.eea.eu.int/.

The EC Council Directive on the Conservation of Wild Birds 1979 (**Birds Directive**) aims to protect wild birds, and to provide sufficient diversity of habitats for all bird species so as to maintain populations at a sound ecological level. It lists 175 bird species requiring special conservation measures and provides for the selection of areas to be designated as special protection areas (SPAs); see http://europa.eu.int/eur-lex/en/consleg.

The EC Council Directive on the Conservation of Habitats and of Wild Fauna and Flora 1992 (**Habitats Directive**) complements the Birds Directive and covers species other than birds. It identifies habitats and species of **community interest**, which must be maintained at **favourable conservation status**. The key mechanism for protection is through designation of special areas of conservation (SACs) both for habitats and certain species; see http://europa.eu.int/comm/environment/nature.

Natura 2000: together SACs and SPAs make up a network called Natura 2000. The aim of this network is to establish a coherent European ecological network of protected areas; see http://europa.eu.int/comm/environment/nature.htm.

Draft environmental liability legislation is currently under negotiation. It aims to establish a civil liability regime for environmental damage including damage to biodiversity; see http://europa.eu.int/comm/environment/liability/.

UK policy and legislation

UK policy on the conservation of biodiversity was first set out in the UK Action Plan (UK Government, 1994). This was the UK's initial response to Article 6 of the Biodiversity Convention, to develop a national strategy for the conservation of biological diversity and the sustainable use of biological resources. It incorporates three elements: assessment, strategy and an action plan. Box 7.2.4 provides more details on the action plan.

Box 7.2.4 *Biodiversity: the UK Action Plan*

Overall goal
To conserve and enhance biological diversity within the UK and to contribute to the conservation of global biodiversity through all appropriate mechanisms.

Underlying principles
- Where biological resources are used, such use should be sustainable.
- Wise use should be ensured for non-renewable resources.
- The conservation of biodiversity requires the care and involvement of individuals and communities as well as government processes.
- Conservation of biodiversity should be an integral part of government programmes, policy and action.
- Conservation practice and policy should be based upon a sound knowledge base.
- The precautionary principle should guide decisions.

Objectives for conserving biodiversity
- To conserve and where practicable to enhance:
  - the overall populations and natural ranges of native species and the quality and range of wildlife habitats and ecosystems;
  - internationally important and threatened species, habitats and ecosystems;
  - species, habitats and natural and managed ecosystems that are characteristic of local areas; and
  - the biodiversity of natural and semi-natural habitats where this has been diminished over recent decades.
- To increase public awareness of, and involvement in, conserving biodiversity.
- To contribute to the conservation of biodiversity on a European and global scale.

The action plan was not an end in itself, but the start of a dynamic process of biodiversity action planning in the UK. The plan included two features of particular note.

First, it identified 59 tasks for the UK Government and its nature conservation agencies (in conjunction with others) over a 20 year period. These became known as 'the 59 steps' and included a wide range of tasks, from preparing and implementing management plans for every Site of Special Scientific Interest (SSSI) by 2004, to updating species and habitat legislation in dependent territories.

Second, the plan recognized the need to develop specific UK species and habitat action plans for the highest priorities. To take this forward a UK Biodiversity Steering Group was formed which has now been superseded by the UK Biodiversity Partnership; see www.ukbap.org.uk.

The development of UK species and habitat action plans and, more broadly, the UK approach to biodiversity conservation are based on a simple but very effective concept, as illustrated in Figure 7.2.1.

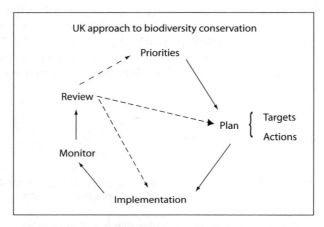

Figure 7.2.1   Managing biodiversity conservation

The **priorities** for action are identified based on a scientific **audit** against agreed criteria and using the best available data. This acknowledges that resources and time for action are limited. Therefore, choices have to be made. Top priorities are those species or habitats that are globally threatened, those confined to the UK or those that have declined significantly within recent decades.

Clear biological **objectives and targets** have been agreed for UK priority species and habitats. These can be **maintenance** targets, which represent a declaration of holding on to what we have; or **enhancement** targets, which set out what we want to bring back. Enhancement targets should represent either favourable conservation status or measurable milestones towards this end. Targets are important, they help to encourage real progress and enable us to measure outcomes much more effectively.

UK action plans have been produced for priority species and habitats. Between 1995 and 1999, the UK Biodiversity Steering Group published 391 species action plans and 45 habitat action plans. Each plan summarized: current status, factors causing loss or decline and action already underway. Targets were set and actions were proposed identifying the lead agencies for delivery. A broad costing was provided for each plan. All the UK biodiversity action plans (BAPs) can be viewed at www.ukbap.org.uk.

Monitoring and review are essential to assess progress against targets and to judge whether priorities, targets or actions need to be adjusted. Progress on UK species and habitat plans has been assessed in 1999 and 2002. The results of the 1999 review were incorporated into a five year review of progress on the UK BAP overall (UK Biodiversity Group, 2001). The detailed results of the latter review are available on the

UK BAP web site (www.ukbap.org.uk). This shows that although there has been some important progress and some, particularly species, targets have been met, there is still much to do. This includes some conspicuous gaps in knowledge on the distribution and status of species and habitats.

Plans are only effective if they are implemented and if they remain dynamic tools that help to deliver conservation on the ground. Therefore, probably the most important aspect of the development of the UK BAP was the identification of lead partners to lead, coordinate and encourage conservation action for each priority species and habitat. For species, the lead partner can be a government agency or a non-governmental organization (NGO). For example, the RSPB is the lead partner for 36 species (25 birds and 11 other species where the organization's nature reserves or management knowledge are important components of plan delivery) and Plantlife International for 75 species. Box 7.2.5 explains the role of lead partner.

Box 7.2.5 *The role of lead partner*

Lead partners are identified because of their acknowledged conservation competence. They are voluntary appointments and are responsible for coordinating an action plan. This includes:

- establishing and running steering groups of key players (where appropriate);
- developing a coherent work programme across key players;
- seeking resources for plan implementation;
- coordinating progress reporting; and
- maintaining support and ownership of the plan across key partners.

Lead partners (or their organization) are not expected to deliver the action plan single-handed or provide all the necessary resources – these are shared responsibilities with the rest of the steering group) – but to use their knowledge, expertise and enthusiasm to galvanize implementation (DETR, 1999a).

For many BAP species and habitats, it is appropriate and effective to coordinate conservation work from a national level. Lead partners can help to connect national policy work with specific conservation projects on the ground.

Work on habitat conservation can bring benefits for a wide number of species but it is important never to lose sight of the needs of individual species. Accepting or adopting generalized habitat management across the board can lead to the loss of species even though their habitat remains. It is also important to appreciate that work on some flagship species can bring wider benefits for other species, for habitat conservation and restoration and in helping to deliver conservation at a landscape scale. The UK BAP has provided impetus to this work for a number of species including the bittern – see Box 7.2.6.

Another key aspect of the UK BAP has been the development of local biodiversity action plans (LBAPs). These were encouraged by the UK Biodiversity Steering Group Report to complement the delivery of UK action plans. The aim of these plans was to 'focus resources to conserve and enhance the biodiversity resource by means of local partnerships, taking account of both national and local priorities' (UK Local Issues Advisory Group, 1997). The functions of LBAPS are explained in Box 7.2.7.

Box 7.2.6 *The booming bitterns*

The deep booming sound of courting male bitterns was formerly a much more common sound around the wetlands of southern Britain. Major decline caused this bird to be included in the UK BAP. Action plan targets for the bittern included:

- arrest the decline of the bittern, maintaining at least 20 booming birds;
- increase the population before the year 2000; and
- increase the population to 50 booming males by 2010.

By 1997, there were only 11 booming bitterns in the UK. However, detailed research by the RSPB and English Nature had revealed the importance of wet reedbeds as part of its ecological requirements and an extensive programme of habitat restoration and (re)creation was underway. This work is bringing success. By 2000, the population had increased to 22 males and there were at least 42 in 2003. While this represents great progress, it is still only half the population in the 1950s.

The programme of habitat work continues across a strategic network of sites from Kent and Suffolk in the east to Cornwall in the west and Lancashire in the north. The current project, which is coordinated by the RSPB and includes eight partners, has been successful in attracting significant funding from the EU LIFE fund (www.bitterns.org.uk).

In considering the habitat management requirements for bitterns, it has been important to look at the potential effects on other species. The work has brought considerable benefits for other BAP priorities such as the otter and water vole but there is a potential conflict with species of moth that favour drier conditions. However, by encouraging the development of new and larger reedbeds the extent of habitat for these species should also be increased (see also the case study on Needingworth in Box 7.2.14).

Box 7.2.7 *Functions of LBAPs*

- To ensure that national targets for species and habitats, as specified in the UK Action Plan, are translated into effective action at the local level.
- To identify targets for species and habitats appropriate to the local area, reflecting the values of people locally.
- To develop local partnerships to ensure that programmes for biodiversity conservation are maintained in the long term.
- To raise awareness of the need for biodiversity conservation in the local context.
- To ensure that opportunities for conservation and enhancement of the whole biodiversity resource are fully considered.
- To provide a basis for monitoring progress in biodiversity conservation, at both national and local level.

Source: UK Local Issues Advisory Group, 1997

LBAPs have been produced throughout much of England, Scotland and Wales, at various geographical scales from parish to region, but most frequently at county or equivalent level. As they have been produced by local partnerships with different composition depending on local circumstances and resources, they have developed at different rates and, in some cases, taken different approaches to national and local priorities. Good guidance and case studies have been produced centrally (CoSLA and Scottish Biodiversity Group, 1997; UK Local Issues Advisory Group, 1997).

LBAPs are a key way for local authorities to get involved in biodiversity conservation. They can provide vital strategic guidance, both for local authority activity and for a range of land use issues at a local level. LBAPs can also play an important role in raising public awareness about biodiversity conservation. Many LBAP partnerships have appointed an LBAP officer to coordinate work on the plan and act as a point of contact with lead partners. Details of LBAP coverage can be found on the UK BAP web site (www.ukbap.org.uk). An example of an LBAP project is shown in Box 7.2.8.

Box 7.2.8 *Farming for partridges and sparrows: a Scottish Borders LBAP project*

Set up in 2002 by the Scottish Borders Local Biodiversity Action Plan Partnership, this project targets habitat management for grey partridge and tree sparrows. Both birds are priority species under the UK BAP.

Farmers are encouraged to create a tailor-made habitat for grey partridge and tree sparrow using the Wild Bird Cover option of set-aside. Seed from a choice of three crop mixes is offered free of charge. The broad based partnership is providing free technical advice on crop establishment and placement.

Under the project, each farm grows around 1ha of the Wild Bird Cover. By 2003, 45 farms were within the scheme and 40 farms were on a waiting list for inclusion in 2004. Events have been held at three project demonstration farms to discuss habitat management, monitoring and sharing ideas with farmers. Farmers in the project are eligible for extra points for Rural Stewardship Scheme applications.

The project is being led and coordinated by the natural heritage officer of the Scottish Borders Council, with funding from SBC and Scottish Natural Heritage. The project partnership consists of a wide range of conservation, farming and landowner organizations and the farmers themselves.

Species and habitat action plans and LBAPs do not address all of the issues that are necessary for biodiversity conservation to be delivered on the ground. An essential further step is to identify the common issues (including social, economic and policy factors) that affect the state of the UK's biodiversity. Areas of government policy on agriculture, forestry, fisheries and water have huge impacts on biodiversity but so do transport, energy and treasury policies. These broad policy issues have to be addressed if biodiversity goals are to be met.

In theory, this was the role of the '59 steps' (see earlier in this section). However, many of these were rather vague and, crucially, there was no clear allocation of responsibility or means of reporting. With devolution, the responsibility for ensuring that this happens has passed to the country biodiversity groups and the relevant administrations. A key approach to this is the development of country biodiversity or sustainable development strategies (see Defra, 2002).

Initially, there was no legal basis for the UK BAP process. The plans were produced by consensus, by a steering group involving representatives from inside and outside government and its agencies. However, the opportunity was taken to give some legislative backing to biodiversity conservation for England and Wales in the Countryside and Rights of Way Act 2000. Box 7.2.9 lists the duties in the act. At the time of writing, the draft Nature Conservation (Scotland) Bill also contained some biodiversity duties and legal underpinning for biodiversity conservation in Scotland.

Box 7.2.9 *Section 74 of the Countryside and Rights of Way Act 2000*

The three main elements of the new duties are:

- a general duty on all ministers, government departments and the National Assembly of Wales to have regard to the Biodiversity Convention;
- a duty to list the most important species and habitat types for biodiversity conservation; and
- a specific duty, on the Secretary of State in England and the National Assembly of Wales, to further their conservation and to encourage others to do likewise.

The Wales Biodiversity Group has taken the opportunity provided by the second duty in Box 7.2.9 to refine the UK list of priorities as it applies to Wales. They have included in their list all those UK priority species that occur in Wales and, in addition, a number of species that are in need of conservation action in Wales, for example chough, brown hairstreak and wild chamomile (Welsh Assembly Government, 2003).

Unlike the UK BAP, LBAPs do not have any statutory backing or legal force behind them. They are documents produced by agreement within a partnership and the actions they contain are not binding. However, Section 4 of the Local Government Act 2000 requires local authorities in England and Wales to prepare community strategies for the economic, social and environmental wellbeing of their area. Government advice is that LBAPs are among the elements that local authorities should draw on when preparing these community strategies (DETR, 2001).

Conservation of our biodiversity is a key test of sustainable development, and to that end progress with BAPs has been adopted by the UK Government as one of the 'quality of life counts' indicators of sustainable development (DETR, 1999b). This has been refined to cover:

- the proportion of action plans making progress towards their targets; and
- the numbers of BAP priority species and habitats showing signs of recovery, those which are stable and those still in decline.

It is also recognized that an indicator on the proportion of action plan targets that are being met should also be developed (UK Biodiversity Group, 2001).

Other quality of life indicators that relate to biodiversity are: populations of wild birds, trends in plant diversity, extent and management of SSSIs, numbers of native species at risk and area of ancient semi-natural woodland in Great Britain.

Organizations' approaches to biodiversity conservation

If biodiversity conservation is to be successful, it is essential that biodiversity concerns are integrated into sectoral practices and decision making. This includes government at national and local levels and the business community. Box 7.2.10 describes the cornerstones of this integration with government thinking.

Box 7.2.10 *Biodiversity and government decision making*

Sustainable development in government
Biodiversity is a key test of sustainable development. Government has pledged to promote biodiversity in their policies and programmes and in the management of their own estates. In 2003, they agreed a set of biodiversity targets for the management of the Government Estate (www.sustainable-development.gov.uk/sdig/improving). This provides a framework for measuring progress.

Local government – best value for biodiversity
Under the Local Government Act 1999 local authorities in England and Wales have a duty to ensure they achieve and demonstrate the best possible service for their communities – the best value duty. In 2001, the Association of Local Government Ecologists (ALGE) produced Best Value for Biodiversity: Helping to Achieve Continuous Improvement for Biodiversity Conservation within Local Government (www.alge.org.uk). This provides guidance on how local authorities can incorporate biodiversity fully and effectively into the best value review of their overall service delivery. This includes: a review of current and potential local authority biodiversity actions; recommendations for voluntary best value biodiversity performance indicators; and examples of realistic biodiversity targets.

Biodiversity and land use planning

While there are benefits in integrating biodiversity into all strands of local government activity, one of the most crucial areas is in land use planning.

The use and development of land brings both threats and opportunities for bio-diversity. The cumulative effects of all planning decisions should contribute to biodiversity. Planning should promote the highest quality development and the most beneficial land use changes, and produce a net improvement. It should help put back some of our lost natural environments. Large scale habitat creation makes a 'big bang' but small scale opportunities for habitat creation or enhancement can be significant and build into major contributions over time. Conversely, individual adverse changes that may seem insignificant can combine to cause serious damage to the integrity or coherence of habitat networks. If biodiversity targets are to be met, it will be important to ensure that spatial plans maximize opportunities to enhance biodiversity and support large scale habitat creation and strategic links, corridors and stepping stones.

The Royal Town Planning Institute has produced a good practice guide (RTPI, 1999). This sets out principles that planners should take into account. Their five point approach is reproduced in Box 7.2.11.

Box 7.2.11 *The RTPI's five point approach*

Information: Is more information needed about the site's biodiversity or the development, its potential effects and their significance?

Avoidance: Have all adverse effects on wildlife species and habitats been avoided wherever possible?

Mitigation: Where adverse effects are unavoidable, have they been or can they be minimized by the use of mitigation measures that can be guaranteed, for example by conditions or planning obligations and agreements?

Compensation: Where, despite mitigation, there will be residual adverse effects, have they been or can they be compensated for by measures that offset the harm? Can these measures be guaranteed by conditions or planning obligations/agreements?

New benefits: Where there would be no significant harm to wildlife species or habitats, are there opportunities to provide new benefits, for example by habitat creation or enhancement? Can these be guaranteed by planning obligations/agreements?

Emphasis is also placed on the need for planners to have access to the specialist advice of qualified and experienced ecologists and the relevant data.

Two case studies that illustrate some of the valuable work that local authorities have undertaken are presented in Box 7.2.12.

Box 7.2.12 *Two local authority case studies*

Rhondda Cynon Taff County Borough Council
In 2000, Rhondda Cynon Taff County Borough Council in Wales became the first unitary authority in the UK to adopt its LBAP as supplementary planning guidance (SPG) to ensure that the LBAP was recognized as a material consideration in the council's planning matters (www.rhondda-cynon-taff.gov.uk/countryside). This positive approach has subsequently been adopted by some other authorities.

Cambridgeshire County Council
Cambridgeshire County Council has published guidance on biodiversity for planners, developers and householders (www.cambridgeshire.gov.uk):

The *Biodiversity Checklist for Land Use Planners* (2001):

- sets out **five main objectives** for planners (protect existing habitats and species particularly those with BAPs; enhance existing environments and create new where possible; mitigate against potentially adverse impacts; compensate for biodiversity losses where loss is unavoidable; monitor and enforce conditions/agreements);
- provides a **flowchart** to identify where the checklist and associated guidance can be used, lists steps that can be taken for minor developments;
- gives **recommendations** for different types of development (e.g. housing, mineral workings, water development, road and rail) to benefit biodiversity;
- gives an overview of **priority habitats** in different locations in the county.

Delivering biodiversity through community strategies

Community strategies are a new government initiative led by local authorities aimed at improving the quality of life and contributing to sustainable development. Planning for local action on biodiversity should be a key element of community strategies. Two examples of local action are shown in Boxes 7.2.13 and 7.2.14.

Box 7.2.13 *Natural Communities*

Natural Communities (2002) produced by English Nature, the RSPB and the Wildlife Trusts provides guidance on biodiversity and community strategies including objectives that should be included and how wildlife organizations can contribute to community strategies. Such objectives include protecting and enhancing wildlife and promoting targets contained within local Agenda 21 and LBAPs (www.rspb.org.uk).

Pilot studies
Although some biodiversity groups are successfully influencing community strategies for biodiversity, many LBAP partnerships are finding it difficult to engage in the community strategy process. To share information from positive experiences the Welsh and English biodiversity groups have produced a series of case studies. These look at Cardiff, Herefordshire, Nottinghamshire, Cheshire, Staffordshire and Kent and draw out lessons learned. These are available from www.ukbap.org.uk.

Box 7.2.14 *Case study: Needingworth wetland project*

Needingworth quarry, Cambridgeshire, will be turned into a huge new wetland over the next 30 years as sand and gravel is extracted and a new landscape created. The restoration of this 700ha site is happening due to a partnership between Hanson Aggregates and the RSPB, facilitated by Cambridgeshire County Council. The wetland will include nearly 40 per cent of the UK biodiversity target for reedbed creation, will provide vital habitat for a range of wildlife (including bitterns) and 32km of new rights of way. The project was awarded an RTPI National Planning Award in 2000 and described as setting 'a new standard for future restoration projects following mineral extraction on a major scale'.

Biodiversity and business

Businesses and industry, large and small, can also play an important part in the conservation of biodiversity through the management of land, their supply chain and the involvement of their workforce. Many large companies have developed or are developing environmental management systems (EMSs) to help reduce risks and to maximize opportunities in a planned way. Companies that do not have the resources to develop a formal EMS can undertake the five basics steps, which are:

- identify activities, products and services and the habitats and species these might affect;
- assess the potential importance of environmental impacts;
- decide which of the impacts are significant and set priorities for action;
- plan a management programme; and
- integrate the action plan into business processes.

Earthwatch have produced a series of useful publications providing guidance on how biodiversity can be integrated into business processes (see www.businessandbiodiversity.org).

In recognition of the importance of the construction industry in shaping the quality of life, in 2000 the Government published a strategy for more sustainable construction, Building a Better Quality of Life (see www.dti.gov.uk/construction/sustain/bql).

The Construction Industry Research and Information Association (CIRIA) is producing a training pack on Working with Wildlife (see www.ciria.org/), for the construction industry and its clients. This training pack aims to promote good practice in relation to wildlife on development and construction projects, including: how to comply with the law; how to go beyond compliance and make a contribution to the achievement of LBAP targets; how to involve all levels of staff in improving industry performance; what to do when wildlife crops up on site; and whom to ask for assistance and what to expect of them.

Conclusions

Biodiversity action planning in the UK is an important and ambitious approach to conserving and enhancing species and habitats. Identifying priorities and setting clear biological targets can help to galvanize real action on the ground. It goes well beyond simply protecting nature reserves by including policy, research and education actions. If carried out well it can help to address conservation at a landscape or ecosystem scale. For this to be fully realized it is vital that biodiversity becomes a mainstream consideration in the policies and practices of all sectors (including agriculture, forestry, development and transport). Only then will biodiversity achieve its rightful place as a fundamental pillar of sustainable development.

References and further reading

Balmford, A. et al (2002) 'Economic Reasons for Conserving Wild Nature', Science, no 55583, 9 August, pp950–953

Constanza, R. et al (1997) 'The Value of the World's Ecosystem Services and Natural Capital', Nature, vol 387, pp 253–260

CoSLA and Scottish Biodiversity Group (1997) *Local Biodiversity Action Plans: A Manual*, Convention of Scottish Local Authorities (CoSLA), Edinburgh

Defra (2002) 'Working with the Grain of Nature: A Biodiversity Strategy for England', Department for Environment, Food and Rural Affairs, London

DETR (1999a) 'Lead Partner Guidance Notes 1–4', Department of the Environment, Transport and the Regions, London

DETR (1999b) 'Quality of Life Counts', Department of the Environment, Transport and the Regions, London

DETR (2001) 'Countryside and Rights of Way Act 2000', Circular 04/2001, Department of the Environment Transport and the Regions, London

Environmental Posterity Partnership (2001) 'Business and the Environment in the East of England: Summary', Environmental Posterity, Sandy

Hartig, T. et al (1991) 'Restorative Effects of Natural Environment Experiences', *Environment and Behaviour*, vol 1, pp11–23

MacMillan, D. et al (2001) *The Costs and Benefits of Managing Wild Geese in Scotland*, Scottish Executive Central Research Unit, Edinburgh

Rayment, M. and Dickie, I. (2001) *Conservation Works*, Royal Society for the Protection of Birds, Sandy

RTPI (1999) *Planning for Biodiversity: Good Practice Guide*, Royal Town Planning Institute, London

Shiel, A. et al (2002) *Reserves and Local Economies*, Royal Society for the Protection of Birds, Sandy

UK Biodiversity Group (2001) 'Sustaining the Variety of Life: 5 years of the UK Biodiversity Action Plan', Department of the Environment Transport and the Regions, London

UK Government (1994) 'Biodiversity: The UK Action Plan', Cm2428, The Stationery Office, London

UK Government (1995) 'Biodiversity: The UK Steering Group Report. Volume 1, Meeting the Rio Challenge', The Stationery Office, London

UK Local Issues Advisory Group (1997) 'Guidance for Local Biodiversity Action Plans. Guidance Note 1: An Introduction', Local Government Management Board and UK Biodiversity Group, London

Welsh Assembly Government (2003) 'Going Wild in Wales: List of Species and Habitats of Principal Importance for the Conservation of Biological Diversity', Welsh Assembly Government, Cardiff

Chapter 7.3

Climate Change and Energy

The science of climate change

The greenhouse effect is a natural phenomenon linked to the absorption of solar energy by the Earth's atmosphere. Part of the long-wave infrared radiation emitted by the sun is not reflected back into space by the Earth's surface but is absorbed by greenhouse gases naturally occurring in the atmosphere. This radiation is transformed into heat, resulting in a stable average temperature of 15°C in the Earth's atmosphere. However, through the sustained release and accumulation in the atmosphere of greenhouse gases since the industrial revolution, human societies are affecting this natural balance, resulting in the disturbance of normal climatic cycles. Because of the long residence times of greenhouse gases in the atmosphere, measured in centuries in the case of carbon dioxide, and the inertia of the climate system, climate change would still constitute a risk, as a result of past emissions, even if human induced emissions suddenly ceased.

The potential impacts are complex and far-reaching, involving global climate dynamics, varying in timing and severity. The main documented observed changes attributable to human activity are the gradual increase of global mean temperatures of approximately 0.45°C and the associated sea level rise, caused by thermal expansion, of approximately 18cm. Other potential natural impacts are the increased incidence of floods and droughts, changes to biodiversity and ecosystems, including risks to unique and threatened ecosystems such as coral reefs and alpine systems. Consequences to human societies are expected to be most severe in the poorest countries, with damage to human health, a decrease of agricultural output and damage to infrastructure. Any action to reduce greenhouse gases or adapt to the impact of their build up has direct and immediate economic impacts on nations and industry.

Despite the record of observed changes, there remains a large amount of uncertainty regarding the future dynamics of climate change, particularly on the precise nature, scale and location of impacts, as well as future emission trends. Nevertheless, the risks, particularly that of catastrophic events, such as the collapse of the ice sheets and large scale discontinuities such as the disturbance of the Gulf Stream, lead to the recognition that scientific uncertainty should not constitute an obstacle to action. Therefore the precautionary principle is the starting point for negotiations to address the issue.

There are sceptics to the existence of human induced climate change but the broad scientific consensus on climate change is unequivocally represented by the Intergovernmental Panel on Climate Change (IPCC). The IPCC was formed in 1998 under the auspices of the World Meteorological Organization (WMO) and the United

Nations Environment Programme (UNEP). The IPCC reports on international research efforts carried out in the atmospheric, social and economic sciences, documented into assessment reports on the three themes of science, mitigation options and adaptation measures. A key feature of these reports is the record of simulated projections of future trends of emissions and impacts based on a range of scenarios of future global socio-economic patterns. Although it doesn't conduct research itself, the IPCC provides an authoritative assessment on the state of knowledge on climate change, and its conclusions, notably on the human causality of climate change, provide the political impetus for action, making the IPCC the recognized international institution that underpins the diplomatic process of the Climate Convention.

Some 30 gases contribute to the anthropogenic greenhouse effect, but only six are regulated by the Kyoto Protocol. Many of the other gases are already regulated by other international protocols, for example the Montreal Protocol on substances that deplete the ozone layer, or are not released in sufficient quantities to be regulated or, like water vapour, are not controllable by human intervention. The six greenhouse gases specified in the Kyoto Protocol are set out in Table 7.3.1.

Table 7.3.1 Greenhouse gases covered by the Kyoto Protocol

Chemical species	Formula	Abundance (ppb) 1750	Abundance (ppb) 1998	100-year GWP*	Main sources
Carbon dioxide	CO_2	278,000	365,000	1	Combustion of hydrocarbons for energy; deforestation
Methane	CH_4	700	1745	21	Waste management; agriculture (rice paddies, enteric fermentation), flaring
Nitrous oxide	N_2O	270	341	296	Agricultural soils; biomass burning
Hydrofluoro-carbons	HFCs	0	7	120–1200	Mostly refrigerant fluids
Perfluoro-carbons	PFCs	20	40	6000–12,000	Industrial processes – e.g. production of aluminium; electronics
Sulphur hexafluoride	SF_6	0	4.2	22,200	Industrial processes – e.g. magnesium foundries; semiconductor manufacture

Note: *The GWP Index indicates the relative impact compared to carbon dioxide (CO_2), also termed 'CO_2 equivalent', and is a function of species' strength and residence time in the atmosphere, per molecule
Source: IPCC, 2004

The basics of carbon management

Carbon dioxide from fossil fuel combustion for energy generation and consumption is the most abundant anthropogenic greenhouse gas. According to 1999 National

Inventory figures published in the UK's latest national communication to the UN Framework Convention on Climate Change (UNFCCC) of 2001, the energy sector is responsible for 84 per cent of national greenhouse gas emissions in the UK. Sources include the combustion of, and fugitive emissions from, fuel for the generation of public electricity and heat production, for consumption in manufacturing industries, and in transport (civil aviation and road transportation mainly). Therefore, any action that aims to mitigate human induced climate change needs to be directed primarily at energy related activities.

Fundamental ways to reduce emissions include:

- increasing the share, in a country's energy mix, of carbon based fuels with a lesser carbon content, which emit less carbon dioxide for the same amount of energy supplied;
- increasing the share of renewable energy sources (e.g. solar, wind, biomass);
- improving efficiency in the generation and transmission of energy;
- improving the efficiency of energy end use (e.g. fuel efficient engines, energy efficient light bulbs); and
- increasing the use of public transport.

Many emissions-cutting technologies already exist. These include wind turbines, efficient hybrid engine cars, fuel cells, and energy efficiency measures in buildings, transport and the manufacturing industries. However, these need to be supported by governments in order to maximize their market penetration and effective contribution to emission reductions.

As well as reducing emissions at source, it is possible to offset emissions. Offsetting activities, also termed 'carbon sinks' by virtue of their capacity to absorb atmospheric greenhouse gases, include forestry and geological storage. The degree to which sinks can be used remains a contentious issue due to the temporary nature of the measure and technical issues surrounding carbon accounting. The preferred environmental option is therefore energy reduction and energy efficiency before the end-of-pipe solution of offsetting. Carbon sinks are viewed as a way of buying time while the carbon intensity of the world's economy is reduced.

Significant greenhouse gas reductions have already occurred as a result of major changes, for example by the breakdown of the communist system in the USSR and the associated collapse of industrial production in Russia and the new independent states. Another example is the shift of a main energy source to one of a lesser carbon content. This is the case in the UK, where the shift from coal to gas in the 1990s resulted in achieving half the UK's international emissions reduction target. Aside from such economic and structural changes, national governments can influence carbon conservation and efficiency through a range of climate policy measures. Governments have three broad policy options to control pollutant emissions:

- Command and control mechanisms where the regulator defines minimum environmental standards and all emitters are required to meet these requirements irrespective of cost. There is no financial benefit for overcomplying.
- Taxation, whereby financial penalties are applied to greenhouse gas emissions. Organizations have a financial incentive to reduce emissions only up to the point where the cost of reduction is lower than the per unit level of the tax.

- The market based mechanism, or 'emissions trading', is a newer policy instrument where regulation sets emissions targets and lets the market decide how to allocate actual emission reductions among participants in the most economically efficient manner.

The choice or mix of policy is a complicated task that requires consideration of the major issues of social and political acceptability, trade-offs between environmental and economic goals, and existing institutional and legal frameworks. Specifically, issues concerning the safeguard of international competitiveness, job preservation and economic growth are pivotal to the balance to be achieved when introducing climate policy measures.

Traditionally, regulators are mostly accustomed to the command and control or taxation approach. However, greenhouse gas emissions trading provides advantages for both the selling and buying activities. It provides the incentive to companies of maximizing their own reductions with a view of selling the credits thus achieved, which contributes toward the mitigation effort, and provides least-cost solutions for companies that need to reach beyond their own set of solutions to capture reduction opportunities in other sectors with lower marginal abatement costs.

In parallel with emissions control, governments can choose between a range of instruments to encourage the development and market take up of renewable energy and carbon and energy efficient technologies.

The policy framework

In recognition of the findings of the IPCC and of the fact that a global problem requires an international solution, the Climate Convention was signed in Rio de Janeiro in 1992 with almost global adherence. Its ultimate objective is the stabilization of greenhouse gas concentrations in the atmosphere at a level that would prevent dangerous anthropogenic interference with the climate system. This overall aim is to be achieved with the leadership of industrialized countries, in keeping with the agreed principle of common but differentiated responsibility between industrialized and developing countries, relative to their historic contributions to human induced climate change. In the convention's language, these are referred to respectively as Annex I and non-Annex I Parties.

Parties meet annually to monitor the implementation of the convention and continue negotiations on unresolved or further issues, in open and closed meetings. The Convention of the Parties (COP) is the supreme body of the convention. As well as governmental delegates, plenary sessions are open to many observers from the press, and the environmental, business and academic communities, who also take part in corridor debates. Significant milestones are: the Berlin Mandate decision at COP1 in 1995 launching the round of talks on industrialized-country commitments; the adoption of the Kyoto Protocol at COP3; and the breakdown of the negotiations at COP6 in The Hague, followed by the much publicized rejection of the Kyoto process by the US. In recent talks, the Bonn Agreement (COP6.5), the Marrakech Accord (COP7) and the Delhi Declaration (COP8) established a detailed rulebook on the operational detail of the convention especially with regards to funding and the clean development mechanism (CDM).

The Kyoto Protocol, signed in 1997, is one of the instruments of the Climate Convention and provides quantified emissions reduction targets for each country included in Annex I, corresponding to an aggregate reduction of 5.2 per cent, to be met over the first commitment period of 2008–2012, relative to the 1990 base year. For the protocol to enter into force, it must be ratified by 55 countries, accounting for 55 per cent of Annex I emissions. By August 2003, 113 parties representing 44 per cent of required emissions have ratified the protocol, now making ratification by Russia a prerequisite for its entry into force without US participation.

One of the protocol's aims is to achieve these reductions at least economic cost, and to this end the protocol contains mechanisms which would enable industrialized countries to benefit from opportunities in other countries where marginal abatement costs are lower. There are three flexibility mechanisms in the protocol; these are:

- **International emissions trading:** This provides for the creation of a market in greenhouse gas allowances, tradable between Annex I countries. Ultimately it is expected that emissions trading markets at national and regional levels will be compatible with this mechanism.
- **Joint implementation (JI):** This allows credits from emissions reduction projects in an Annex I country to be used for compliance by another Annex I country. The experience gained from a pilot phase suggests that most JI projects are likely to take place in economies in transition and be based upon the application of energy efficiency technologies used in district heating, small scale fuel switching from coal to biomass, the installation of efficient boilers and fuel efficiency improvements in power plants.
- **The clean development mechanism (CDM):** This is also a project based mechanism where the project is undertaken in a developing country and must contribute to the host country's stated sustainable development goals. The CDM has the effect of assisting developing countries reduce the carbon intensity of their economies and participate in the Kyoto Protocol.

While emissions trading involves the direct transfer of instruments without associated project activity, JI and CDM generate credits from specific projects that reduce emissions below a business as usual scenario. These mechanisms are intended to facilitate cooperative development projects that seek to reduce, avoid or sequester greenhouse gas emissions, contributing to the commitments of an Annex I Party from 2008 onwards. Project activities will most likely lie in the energy sector, involving renewable energy (e.g. wind, biomass, solar, hydro and wave), energy efficiency, but also in landfill methane recovery and forestry activities.

The Kyoto process is unprecedented in terms of international environmental agreements. Aside from its institutional complexity and a technically detailed rulebook, the need to ally both political and technical matters in areas which are at the heart of all countries' economies leads to very complex negotiations, with political issues at stake that represent fundamentally different interests linked to economic development and financing.

Negotiations on the next Kyoto Protocol commitment period (post 2012) begin in 2005 with debates on broadening the list of parties with emission reduction targets to include larger developing countries. The issue of developing-country participation is a contentious one. This challenge of greater developing-country action, along with enhanced Annex I targets and the role of the US remains to be addressed at future COPs.

The global effort to achieve effective climate protection is a long term process and the Kyoto Protocol supports this process through clearly defined and binding targets defined over five-year commitment periods in line with a long term basis for action. In keeping with this goal and to support actual progress towards the targets, it requests parties to develop and report on domestic policies and measures and their predicted contribution to the country's mitigation effort. Most policies and measures reported are not motivated by climate change objectives alone but are associated with the restructuring of national energy sectors, improvements in energy efficiency motivated by competitive liberalized markets, and improvement of local air quality and congestion conditions.

The main policy objectives reported by parties are in the field of energy and comprise:

- efficiency improvements in energy production and transformation;
- fuel switching from coal and fuel oil to natural gas;
- restructuring and liberalization of energy markets;
- increase in the share of renewable energy sources;
- increase in end use energy efficiency; and
- improved vehicle fuel efficiency.

In the UK, the range of national measures is documented in the UK Climate Change Programme (see Box 7.3.1) launched in 2000 with the dual objective of meeting the UK's emission reduction commitments while safeguarding the international competitiveness of the UK's businesses.

Box 7.3.1 *Summary of the UK Climate Change Programme*

The UK target under the Kyoto Protocol is for a 12.5 per cent reduction by 2008–2012 over 1990 levels. The UK Government has set itself a stronger domestic goal of a 20 per cent reduction in carbon dioxide emissions.

The Climate Change Levy (CCL)

Electricity	0.43 p/kWh	
Gas	0.15 p/kWh	
Coal and lignite; coke and semi coke or lignite; petroleum coke	1.17 p/kg	**Levied on commercial energy users**
LPG	0.96 p/kg	
Electricity from renewable sources; combined heat and power	Exempt	

The Climate Change Levy Agreements (CCLAs) provide an 80 per cent discount on the levy to 44 energy intensive sectors in exchange for agreed energy efficiency improvements (output-weighted), until 2010.

The Carbon Trust was established in 2001 to assist businesses and local authorities with energy efficiency and develop a low carbon industrial base in the UK.

The Domestic Emissions Trading Scheme is a voluntary scheme for companies to take emission reduction commitments in exchange for a financial incentive. Thirty-four companies took part in its first phase. The scheme is also open to CCLA entities to assist them in achieving their target.

Source: Defra, 2004 and HM Customs and Excise, 2003

The programme is a package of policies and measures comprising regulations, economic instruments, information programmes and public expenditure initiatives. More importantly, the programme is designed to be as flexible as possible, with a focus on the use of economic instruments – for example a climate change levy and emissions trading. It reflects the specific circumstances of energy intensive sectors competing internationally, through the proposed lower rate of climate change levy for sectors that agree to meet energy efficiency improvement targets.

Other measures include the promotion of renewable energy and fuel efficient technologies, changes to electricity generation and distribution, improvements to the transport planning system, support of EU level efforts on integrated product policy and the use of the Kyoto mechanisms.

Despite an early start and effective progress toward the UK target, there are some incompatibilities between the UK Programme and EU level policy, particularly with respect to the Directive on Emissions Trading. Under the directive, National Allocation Plans, setting out the elements for implementing the directive at the national level, had to be submitted by member states no later than March 2004. Policy discontinuities and double counting between the EU Emissions Trading Scheme (EU-ETS) and the CCL, the CCLA and the UK Emissions Trading Scheme (UK-ETS) is a challenge for present and future UK climate policy. Indeed, climate policy is a moving target, due to the lack of synchrony between the international, regional and national levels, in keeping with differing national circumstances and policy traditions.

Emissions trading and renewable energy

Emissions trading is a market mechanism that seeks to achieve an environmental outcome (e.g. to reduce pollutant emissions) in the most economically efficient way. A regulator places a limit on the total emissions of the defined pollutant. The regulator shares out this overall limit by giving (or selling) allowances to each emitter, the total number of allowances being equal to the overall cap. One allowance might be equal to, for example, one tonne of carbon dioxide emitted. In order to comply with the regulations, each emitter must hold allowances equal to its total emissions for the period (usually measured on an annual basis). The allowances are tradable and a market price will emerge based on supply and demand factors. Emitters who expect to exceed their targets must decide whether to reduce their physical emissions or buy additional allowances. Those with surplus allowances may sell the excess.

The approach described above is known as a cap-and-trade scheme. In this case the regulator creates the currency used in the scheme (the 'allowance'). An enhancement to this approach is the use of emission credits. Emitters who fall outside the scheme may choose to reduce their own emissions below an agreed baseline (or remove the pollutant from the atmosphere through sequestration). This action reduces emissions below what they would have been in the absence of this activity. The promoter of the emission reduction project receives a credit which may be sold into the cap-and-trade scheme.

Emissions trading and the use of market mechanisms are not new. Schemes have been implemented around the world in a variety of markets. The earliest examples are the various sulphur dioxide and nitrogen oxides allowance trading schemes in the US. Tradable fishing quotas were used in New Zealand and later adopted by Australia, Canada and the EU. In the greenhouse gas sphere, there has been significant voluntary activity, including early (pre-compliance) trades between corporations and voluntary exchange based schemes such as the Chicago Climate Exchange in the US. The World Bank Prototype Carbon Fund and the Dutch CERUPT programme, as the most significant buyers of CDM credits, have helped prompt the development of an institutional framework for this mechanism. National greenhouse gas trading schemes have emerged in the UK and Denmark, ahead of the EU-wide scheme.

Of the existing instruments for greenhouse gas emissions management, the following are specifically relevant to the UK.

The UK-ETS

The pioneering UK-ETS is the first cross-industry, national greenhouse gas emissions trading scheme. It applies to emissions primarily from energy consumption and runs from 2002–2006. There are three ways of participating:

- Direct participants entered on a voluntary basis (in return for government subsidies) and committed to absolute targets, where emission reductions are expressed as tonnes of carbon dioxide equivalent (t CO_2eq) over an annual compliance period. Some 34 companies joined the scheme as direct participants through an incentive auction in April 2002. This represents a classic cap-and-trade system.
- CCLA participants also have access to the scheme and may trade to meet their energy efficiency targets. Targets are typically expressed per unit of output (%kWh/tonne of output). CCLA participants operate along a baseline and credit approach with two-yearly milestone periods.
- Projects that reduce greenhouse gas emissions below a business as usual baseline represent a third route into the scheme. However, the development of the EU-ETS may supersede this option.

The government expects that the scheme will result in greenhouse gas emission reductions of 12 million tonnes of carbon dioxide equivalent over its duration, representing 16 per cent of the UK's Kyoto emissions reduction target. The scheme has assisted UK firms gain early experience in emissions trading and allowed the development of institutional and business capacity, for example verifiers, consultants and emission brokers in the City of London. Over the next few years the UK-ETS will briefly co-exist and subsequently be subsumed under the EU-ETS.

The EU-ETS

The EU-ETS is the largest greenhouse gas emissions trading scheme to date. This cap-and-trade scheme commences in 2005 and covers carbon dioxide emissions from energy production in the energy and industrial sectors, representing almost 50 per cent of EU-wide emissions (in 2010). The reductions sought by the EU-ETS will constitute roughly half the EU's mitigation effort required by the Kyoto Protocol. It is an economy-wide scheme, set out by a directive, and scheduled to run over rolling five year periods starting in 2008 in parallel with the Kyoto Protocol's commitment periods, following a three year (2005–2007) pilot phase.

The scheme covers the energy, industrial and manufacturing sectors – see Table 7.3.2 – and applies to installations physically located in the EU. Accession countries will be incorporated as of 2005, although in practice there may be a number of opt-outs prior to 2008. Certain countries in the European Economic Area may also join the scheme (e.g. Norway).

Table 7.3.2   EU-ETS sectors

Sector	Description
Energy activities	Combustion installations greater than 20MW, mineral oil refineries, coke ovens
Ferrous metals	Metal ore roasting/sintering Iron/steel production
Mineral industry	Cement clinker production Glass manufacture Ceramic manufacture
Other activities	Pulp, paper and board

It is expected that other sectors, most likely aluminium, chemicals and transport, will be included from 2008. For the first period of the scheme (2005–2007) only carbon dioxide will be regulated. From 2008 other greenhouse gases such as methane and nitrous oxide are likely to be included.

Emission targets are set at the installation level and each installation is allocated allowances, denominated in tonnes of carbon dioxide equivalent. At the end of each compliance (calendar) year, an installation must reconcile allowances against verified emissions data. In order to comply with its target (and avoid financial penalties) an installation must surrender allowances equal to its carbon dioxide emissions in the year concerned.

Installations may trade allowances at any time, and there is a four month true-up period after each compliance year where an installation may continue to buy or sell allowances to ensure it achieves compliance for the prior year. Allowances may be banked for use in subsequent years within the same period, but may not necessarily be carried across periods (that is, from 2005–2007 to 2008–2012).

If an installation fails to meet its target it faces a fine of €40/t CO_2eq for 2005 rising to €100/t CO_2eq for 2008. The installation will also be required to make good this shortfall in the next compliance year, and may face additional penalties.

The scheme requires installations to report carbon dioxide emissions on an annual basis. In practice, installations are likely to monitor emissions on a quarterly, monthly or even a continuous basis for management purposes. An independent, third party is required to verify the emissions report by 31 March of the following year.

The EU-ETS provides for a linkage to the Kyoto Protocol project based mechanisms – JI and the CDM – subject to the ratification of Kyoto.

The opt-out clause in the EU directive provides for individual installations to be excluded from the pilot phase of the scheme, provided it can be demonstrated that each installation is subject to domestic legislation that has an equivalent impact on emission levels. Despite efforts to secure opt-out for certain UK sectors, the EU-ETS probably signals the end of the development of the UK-ETS, due to incompatibilities between the two schemes. These relate to their respective scopes, the upstream versus the downstream treatment of greenhouse gas emissions from energy, and the type of targets and coverage of gases. The EU scheme is economy-wide and compulsory whereas the UK scheme applies to a small group of companies that agreed to abatement action in exchange for financial incentives. The EU-ETS sets absolute caps on carbon dioxide emissions whereas these targets are mostly relative under the CCLA and apply to all greenhouse gases. And crucially, the EU-ETS will require UK electricity generators to comply with caps, whereas under UK policy, it is the electricity consumers that are responsible for emissions from electricity generation.

UK renewables obligation certificates

The Renewables Obligation Order 2001 entered into force on 1 April 2002. The order is part of the UK Government's objective of stimulating renewable energy generating capacity by increasing its contribution to the energy supply sector. Through the Utilities Act 2000, licensed electricity suppliers in the UK have to source specified amounts of electricity from eligible renewable sources based on a 2003 target of 3 per cent, increasing annually to 10.4 per cent in 2011. Eligible sources are solar energy (including photovoltaics), hydro, wave power, tidal energy, geothermal energy, biofuels (including energy crops) and on- and offshore wind. Starting from 2002, obligation periods last a year from 1 April to 31 March. The supplier needs to demonstrate compliance to the regulator, OFGEM, via a system of renewables obligation certificates (ROCs) issued by OFGEM to the generator.

A renewable generator that qualifies under the scheme will produce one ROC for every MWh of electricity produced. In order to comply with the obligation, an electricity supplier must purchase sufficient ROCs to meet its target. It may either purchase physical renewable energy and receive the certificates as part of the package, or it may simply purchase them alone, separate from the physical renewable electricity. In either case, the same amount of renewable energy will be produced system-wide.

Should a supplier fail to hold enough ROCs, it must pay the buy-out price, an economic safety mechanism, initially set at £30 per MWh. The revenue generated from buy-out is pooled and redistributed on a pro rata basis to any entity that used a certificate for compliance purposes. The value of the ROC is the sum of the £30 buy-out plus the share of the buy-out pool. The effect of the buy-out mechanism is to increase the support for renewable energy when compliance is low – that is, many electricity suppliers will pay the buy-out, leading to a large buy-out pool, a relatively high share paid to ROC holders and a high ROC price.

In the first year, the ROC price traded in the range of £45–£50 per/MWh. Consequently, renewable generators received a total price per MWh in the range of £60–£70, which is the sum of the standard price of black electricity (£15–£20) during that period, plus the market price of the ROC. Therefore the market price of renewable electricity is approximately 200 per cent greater than non-renewable electricity.

The Renewables Obligation provides a market based support mechanism where the level of financial support varies with the compliance level. This can be contrasted with the tariff based scheme that preceded it – the non-fossil fuel order where the regulator would negotiate long term fixed tariffs (per MWh) with renewable generators.

Greenhouse gas mitigation is not the only policy objective of the Renewables Obligation which also seeks to incentivize the development of an industry with export potential, increase the energy mix of the UK and improve its security of supply, develop rural enterprise, and improve air quality.

References and further reading

Climate Action Network (2004) The web site of this environmental NGO is www.climatenetwork.org

Defra (2004) For a presentation of UK policy and scientific background go to www.defra.gov.uk/environment/climatechange

EU (2004) For a presentation of EU policy go to the European Union web site at http://europa.eu.int/comm/environment/climat/home_en.htm

Grubb M. et al (2003) 'Keeping Kyoto' is a demonstration of the role of the Kyoto Protocol in the international effort to mitigate climate change. This can be found at www.climate-strategies.org/keepingkyoto.pdf

HM Customs and Excise (2003) For further information on the Climate Change Levy go to www.hmce.gov.uk/business/othertaxes/ccl.htm

IEMA (2001) *Managing Climate Change Emissions: A Business* Guide, vol 1, Institute of Environmental Management and Assessment, Lincoln

IETA (2004) The web site of the International Emissions Trading Association is www.ieta.org

IPCC (2004) For further information on the Intergovernmental Panel on Climate Change go to www.ipcc.ch

UNFCCC (2004a) For a comprehensive account of the negotiation process and the scientific issues go to the official site of the United Nations Framework Convention on Climate Change at www.unfccc.int

UNFCCC (2004b) For the full texts of the Climate Convention and the Kyoto Protocol go to the official sites of the United Nations Framework Convention on Climate Change as follows: http://unfccc.int/resource/docs/convkp/conveng.pdf http://unfccc.int/resource/docs/convkp/kpeng.pdf

Chapter 7.4

Transport

Environmental impacts of transport

Some of the best known environmental impacts of road transport are emissions, mainly from exhaust gases, which affect local and regional air quality. Nitrogen oxides (NO_x) are emitted from all internal combustion engines, and are hard to avoid as they result primarily from the nitrogen and oxygen in the air combining under the high temperatures and pressures of combustion. NO_x is known to exacerbate respiratory illnesses, and is also a major component of acid rain.

Carbon monoxide (CO) arises from incomplete combustion, primarily in petrol engines, and can adversely affect mental capacity and exacerbate circulatory problems. Unburnt or partially burnt hydrocarbons (HC) can also have a range of adverse health effects, and, together with NO_x, also contribute to the formation of ozone in the lower atmosphere. This too can have damaging effects on human, animal and plant tissues. Particulates, which are related to but not synonymous with visible smoke, have also been a concern for some time with diesel engines in particular, and fears over the health implications of small particles continue to grow.

One of the most important exhaust emissions from petrol and diesel engines is carbon dioxide (CO_2), the most important greenhouse gas. Transport gives rise to about one quarter of all the carbon dioxide emitted in the UK, and is unavoidably produced when carbon based fossil fuels are burnt. The only way to avoid this is to move away from fossil based fuels such as petrol and diesel, or at least to use them more efficiently.

Noise is a further environmental problem in both urban and rural areas, and road and air transport are the two most important generators of noise nuisance. This adversely affects both human settlements, and the peace and tranquillity of the countryside. Car engines in particular are getting quieter over time, but at high speeds most of the noise is caused by the impact of tyres on the road, and this is much harder to deal with.

Further threats to the environment result from the provision of transport infrastructure – particularly, but not exclusively, roads. Demands for large areas of land for roads, car parks, and service stations continue to destroy not only wildlife habitats and areas of natural beauty, but also parts of our towns, homes, historic sites and the more mundane landscapes and recreational areas which add to the quality of life for many people.

Congestion also results from increasing levels of traffic. This is not strictly an environmental impact, but it can exacerbate other impacts by making traffic flow less efficiently. It also has obvious detrimental effects on economies and society more generally.

Organizations as traffic generators

In congested traffic, all road users are inconvenienced, but they in turn obstruct all others. Thus it is important to be aware of the transport 'footprint' of an organization, as this not only has an impact upon the total level of traffic and congestion, but also is an indicator of how much an organization's own activities are being compromised by delays imposed by congestion.

Virtually all organizations generate travel and traffic in a number of ways:

- Most staff commute regularly to work, and the distance and mode of travel used will be influenced by the location of the organization and the incentives and facilities available to them. In addition, some staff will travel substantial distances in the course of work.
- Most installations require a quite wide range of supplies and services to be delivered to them. Manufacturers, shippers and distributors give rise to even greater movements of goods, and many products are composed of numerous components which themselves have to be transported for assembly.
- Many public and commercial buildings generate significant numbers of visitors, such as patients and their visitors to hospitals, and shoppers to shopping centres. Again, location and the availability of services and facilities can make a great difference to numbers of visitors, distances travelled and mode of travel.

New technologies and fuels for the future

Liquefied petroleum gas (LPG) has been promoted for some years now as a road fuel; the fuel duty payable is much lower than for petrol and diesel; grants are available from the Energy Saving Trust to convert cars to LPG; and they are exempt from the London congestion charge. LPG offers some environmental benefits over petrol and diesel cars, but these are not large and will be eroded as conventional petrol and diesel cars become cleaner and more efficient in the coming years. The Energy Saving Trust now argues that the development of high-compression dedicated LPG engines will be essential if LPG is to maintain its environmental credentials (Energy Saving Trust, 2003).

Compressed natural gas (CNG) offers advantages in terms of emissions and noise in particular for heavy diesels, where few alternatives exist (Cleaner Vehicles Task Force, 2001). This option is in principle attractive for urban fleet vehicles such as municipal vehicles and buses, but users must install their own refuelling infrastructure at depots, and the compressors needed to pump the gas into a pressurized tank on the vehicle are expensive.

Biofuels offer the possibility of producing liquid fuels for conventional motor vehicles from non-fossil sources. In principle they can offer diversification away from oil dependence and a substantial reduction in carbon dioxide emissions, although in practice, the scope is rather more limited.

For the UK, the most promising source of domestically produced biofuel is rape methyl ester made from rapeseed oil. This biodiesel can be used as a direct 100 per cent substitute for mineral diesel fuel, and a few firms are considering this option, but it presents some technical problems and requires minor engine modifications. Given the likely limitations on supply, blending up to five per cent of this fuel into conventional diesel is generally a preferable approach that presents no significant technical problems. These biodiesel blends are now becoming available at a few commercial outlets around the UK, and several firms can supply biodiesel blends to fleet operators.

Bioethanol can be manufactured from wheat or sugar beet, and blended into petrol as rape methyl ester can be in diesel. Some quantities of this biopetrol may appear on the market shortly, and, if so, these will again be able to be substituted directly for conventional petrol, giving some carbon dioxide savings.

Battery electric vehicles pre-date the internal combustion engine. In spite of their obvious benefits (zero emissions at the point of use, and very low noise levels), they continue to suffer major limitations in terms of performance, range, recharging times, and availability of recharging infrastructure. There is still no prospect of a dramatic improvement in battery performance, so it seems likely that they will remain restricted to specialist uses such as milk floats, handcarts and in-building vehicles.

Improved conventional vehicles: In the short to medium term we can expect to see sustained improvements in the fuel efficiency of conventional engines, in part through increased use of hybrids in many classes of vehicle. The latter are already on the market for a small number of car types. These allow much cleaner, quieter and more efficient running because they smooth out the stop–start profile of urban traffic. In a hybrid, a small internal combustion engine generates power much more efficiently than in a conventional vehicle, not only because it is smaller, but also because it can be operated at near maximum efficiency during most of its operating time, because it does not need to provide all the power required during periods of high engine load. In a parallel hybrid, auxiliary power is supplied by an electric motor during startup and acceleration, using electricity generated by the internal combustion engine and stored in a battery, thus providing greater efficiency overall.

There are already certain truck engines that offer substantially better economy than the average, and these should be encouraged. There are important improvements to vehicle design that could reduce total weight, and some lighter vehicles for light payloads are already marketed, thus allowing an increase in payload for the same power requirements.

In the longer term, hydrogen used in fuel cell engines offers the prospect of zero emissions – always assuming that the hydrogen comes from renewable sources, which is not an imminent prospect. Such vehicles would also be virtually silent and possibly very reliable, and would offer a range of other benefits to users. However, it is likely to be several decades before such vehicles become commercially available.

In summary, there is no easy or perfect technological solution yet available to the emissions problems of road transport. Operators of heavy fleets might consider switching to CNG; in most other cases the best practicable option is to get the most efficient vehicles available, and then fuel these with appropriate biofuel blends where possible.

Improving the environmental performance of transport

Freight transport

While most company vehicles are essential business tools they do contribute to both global and local air pollution and congestion as outlined earlier. By implementing effective and responsible fleet management measures, organizations can not only help improve their environmental performance, but also cut their operating costs.

A recent survey found that there is considerable variation in fuel consumption rates among UK car and van fleets. Those fleets that were aware of their fuel consumption achieved significantly lower costs than those that were not. Monitoring mileage and fuel consumption can help to establish a baseline against which any future reductions can be measured and can also help to identify ways in which reductions can be made. For further information see the TransportEnergy Best Practice web site at www.transportenergy.org.uk.

Driver behaviour is also fundamental to attaining high levels of fleet efficiency. Efficient driving techniques can help reduce fuel consumption considerably: they can also mean fewer accidents and reduce the cost of insurance premiums. Effective route planning also cuts fuel costs and pollution, saves time, reduces stress and increases efficiency. Increasing use is being made of in-vehicle navigational aids that advise on the best routes and how to avoid congestion.

Just in time (JIT) entails a complex system of computer based ordering, delivery planning and distribution centres whereby goods are delivered 'just in time' to be utilized. The purpose is to turn goods over as quickly as possible, and reduce stockholding to a low level. Costs are saved on warehousing and inventory because at any one time they are only holding what is required to replenish supplies within the delivery time frame; however, JIT requires more frequent deliveries of smaller quantities and the efficiency of vehicle utilization is reduced considerably. On the other hand, one expert argues that the negative effects of JIT on vehicle utilization may have been exaggerated as many firms using this system have taken measures to minimize the downward pressure on vehicle load factors. This can be achieved, for instance, by including additional consolidation points into the supply chain, where a number of small consignments can be consolidated into a single truckload. The 'milk-round' collection of orders and the single-sourcing of supplies are further possibilities (McKinnon, 2002).

Conversely, increasing vehicle load factors can help towards reducing the levels of traffic required to move a given quantity of freight. Improved loading can also lead to improved efficiency of delivery operations, therefore yielding both environmental and economic benefits. UK statistics show that load factors (excluding empty running) remained fairly stable at around 63 per cent between 1986 and 1996 (DETR, 1998). The proportion of empty runs declined from about 33 per cent to 29 per cent between 1980 and 1996, but can still vary enormously between apparently similar organizations (DfT, 2003).

Travel plans are increasingly being used by organizations to help reduce the amount of traffic they generate. While more frequently associated with dealing with staff and commuter travel, travel plans are also an effective tool to help reduce business related travel.

Travel plans involve a package of practical measures designed to establish ways in which journeys generated by businesses can be reduced or eliminated. Managing the business fleet more efficiently to reduce the environmental impact of journeys, primarily through reduction in fuel consumption, would form an integral part of a travel plan. However a travel plan also addresses ways to eliminate some journeys altogether. For instance, through utilizing internet opportunities and tele/videoconferencing some journeys can be completely avoided. Not only can this result in environmental impacts being reduced but also time and money savings for companies employing such measures. For instance the Royal Bank of Scotland estimates that it saves more than £70,000 per month on corporate travel through videoconferencing (TransportEnergy, 2003).

Personal travel

While workplace travel plans are intended to address all areas of business travel, they are more commonly associated with employee travel. In particular most travel plans aim to reduce single occupancy car use and encourage employees to travel to and from work by alternative modes such as walking, cycling, public transport and car sharing. A recent study carried out by the Department for Transport (DfT, 2002) based on the findings of 20 UK organizations with travel plans found on average the proportion of commuter journeys made by a car driver was reduced by at least 18 per cent.

Although not an exhaustive list, typically a travel plan would include measures such as:

- provision of secure cycle storage and showers (to encourage cycling);
- promotion of car sharing;
- provision of public transport information;
- provision of pool cars and pool bicycles (for business journeys);
- flexible homeworking arrangements for staff; and
- loans for rail and bus season tickets.

Organizations with parking problems are increasingly implementing travel plans, and this can make sound business sense. While the average cost of maintaining a car parking space is typically £300–£500, the average cost of running a travel plan was approximately £47 a year per employee (DfT, 2002). The introduction of pool cars is put forward as one possible solution to help reduce parking problems. Pool cars are a fleet of vehicles available for use by employees on the basis of operational needs. An efficient booking system guarantees a vehicle is available when required. Often people say that they drive to work because they need their car during the day. A pool car scheme can solve this problem. Pool cars could also result in considerable savings for companies by replacing the need for company cars. The true cost of a company car is not always apparent, especially when the car is left at work all day in the best parking space, a space that could be utilized by a customer or client instead, for example.

Organizations that implement travel plans can appear more responsible towards their employees, the local community and the environment. Indeed, staff that cycle and walk to work can benefit from improved health, cost/time savings and reduced stress levels. Travel plans can also be used to gain environmental accreditations such as ISO 14001 and EMAS.

The policy framework

Taxation and charging: The UK Government applies a range of taxes and charges on transport fuels and vehicles. Increasingly, the government is incorporating an environmental component into the various taxation systems, as will be highlighted later, in order to encourage more environmentally sound behaviour. In addition to taxes, it must be remembered that VAT is additionally charged on the purchase of fuel and vehicles.

Fuel tax: The most significant, and recently most controversial, tax on transport is fuel duties. In 1993, the former Conservative Government introduced an environmental element into fuel duty through the so-called 'fuel duty escalator'. The aim of the escalator was to increase the relative price of fuel in an attempt to reduce demand, thereby restricting the growth in carbon dioxide emissions from the transport sector. This was the primary domestic measure to limit carbon dioxide emissions. Under the escalator, the price of fuel rose by a fixed percentage above the rate of inflation each year from 1993 to 1999. When the policy was introduced by the former government, duties rose annually by 3 per cent above the rate of inflation, which was quickly increased to 5 per cent and then to 6 per cent by the incoming Labour Government. However, the policy was abandoned as a result of increasing public resistance to high fuel prices.

Even though these automatic increases in fuel duty have been abandoned, fuel duty in the UK is still differentiated according to the environmental impact of fuels. For example, there is a differential between petrol and diesel in favour of the former. While diesel vehicles are more efficient in terms of their fuel consumption than petrol vehicles, the UK Government has been reluctant to encourage the 'dieselization' of the UK vehicle fleet, owing to concerns over particulates.

Differential fuel duties have also been used to encourage the introduction of environmentally less damaging versions of the same fuel, first for unleaded petrol. Duty differentials were applied in the UK more recently to encourage the introduction of ultra low sulphur diesel and petrol, and we can expect to see a similar approach in the next couple of years to bring in sulphur free motor fuels.

Similarly, fuel duty differentials already exist in favour of LPG, CNG and biofuels compared to petrol and diesel. In the future, we can expect to see these policies extended further to encourage the introduction of other fuels, such as, possibly, hydrogen.

Vehicle excise duty (VED) and grants for cleaner vehicles: The UK Government also differentiates VED, i.e. the annual vehicle tax, for cars based on environmental criteria. In this case, the differentiation is based on a car's carbon dioxide emissions and owners of cars that emit less are charged less VED. This is a relatively recent innovation and one that critics argue could do with refining and extending. However, the principle is a good one and is likely to be developed, as a result of the various measures, both EU and domestic, to reduce carbon dioxide emissions from new cars. These include informing potential car buyers of the emissions and energy consumption of vehicles, through a labelling scheme and other publicity material, to an agreement between the European Commission and car manufacturers to reduce emissions from new passenger cars. Such policies are expected to be expanded to light commercial vehicles and other vehicles in the near future.

While the differentiation of VED attempts to steer purchasing behaviour towards cars that emit less carbon dioxide, the Energy Saving Trust, a government agency set up, inter alia, to encourage the use of cleaner vehicles, awards grants for converting vehicles to cleaner fuels such as LPG and CNG, and for the purchase of hybrid vehicles.

Company car taxation in the UK has also recently been reformed to reflect the carbon dioxide emissions of the different vehicles, and early indications are that this has had a significant effect on the average emissions of new company cars.

Road user charging and workplace parking levies: In recent years, there has been increasing interest in the application of road user charging as a measure to reduce congestion and also emissions from transport. While the feasibility of some sort of user charging was being investigated in the early 1990s by the former Conservative Government, it was the incoming Labour Government that introduced legislation to enable local authorities to introduce congestion charging and workplace parking levies if they so desired. While the former was clearly aimed at addressing congestion, the aim of the latter was to reduce the number of free private commercial parking spaces by taxing them.

In the event, workplace parking levies have not been introduced in any UK city to date, although Nottingham is the most advanced in considering such a move. A form of congestion charging has been introduced on one street in Durham and, famously, the entire central area in London. To date, this appears to have been more successful in reducing the amount of traffic in the city centre than even the London authorities could have hoped for, even though clean-fuelled vehicles are exempt and residents benefit from reduced rates.

The government is also planning to introduce a distance charging scheme for heavy goods vehicles around 2006. The aim of the scheme is to encourage more efficient use of vehicles, as vehicles would be taxed according to the distance they travelled – other taxes on heavy commercial vehicles, such as VED or diesel duty, would be reduced proportionately. Road hauliers' groups are generally in favour of the scheme in the anticipation that it will soon be introduced for all vehicles and thus reduce congestion, particularly on inter-urban routes. The Secretary of State for Transport has recently raised the possibility of extending distance charging to other road users and it is likely that, in time, such a policy will be adopted.

Tax breaks for green travel plans: When an employer contributes to the costs of benefits such as travel facilities for employers to get to and from work there would normally be tax and national insurance contributions to pay. However, in an attempt to encourage more sustainable means of transport, the government has introduced tax breaks for various measures. These include, inter alia, free or subsidized works' buses, cycle mileage for employees using cycles for business purposes, and cycle and safety equipment. The Inland Revenue has produced a leaflet, IR176, providing more details on the various tax breaks available, which can be viewed at their web site (Inland Revenue, 2003).

Other relevant policy: Increasingly, many local authorities recognize the importance of securing travel plans through the planning process. This means that any business wishing to relocate or extend its premises will need to draw up a travel plan in order to gain planning permission. Planning Policy Guidance Note 13 (PPG13) sets out a basis for requiring and securing travel plans, although it recognizes that there is no standard format or content of a travel plan (DETR, 1994). PPG13 clarifies that either a planning condition or a Section 106 agreement can be appropriate to legally secure a travel plan. However, approaches and mechanisms vary greatly from one local authority to the next. The size and nature of the development will also play a fundamental role in determining which legal mechanism is used.

Managing travel

Dealing effectively with transport issues is vital for organizations; those that address their transport needs in a comprehensive manner can derive many benefits. Looking at all aspects of travel within an organization necessarily requires an assessment of employee travel patterns, fleet management and issues dealing with information and communication technologies, as a means to reduce or eliminate transport and associated transport cost. However, assessment of such a broad range of issues can be problematic, as they are often complex and each one is not confined to a single area of the organization. For instance, while consideration of switching fleet vehicles to an alternative fuel may fall under the remit of someone in transport operations or a fleet manager, it is unlikely that the same person would have responsibilities for the introduction of homeworking or flexible hours for staff. The lack of a comprehensive approach may result in actions be taken, albeit unintentionally, without consideration of other actors which may in turn cause problems. For instance, a facilities manager may be striving to find extra space for car parking, unaware that elsewhere the organization is seeking to promote cycling or car sharing among employees.

Nonetheless the responsibility of transport issues falling to different people does not necessarily need to cause problems, rather an awareness of potential drawbacks is necessary. Organizations implementing travel plans have generally found that such problems can be overcome by nominating a travel plan coordinator. While the coordinator would not take over the roles and duties of existing staff with responsibilities for transport, they would oversee all aspects of transport policy within an organization and ensure a comprehensive approach is taken.

Motivations for tackling an organization's travel and transport issues can vary widely and include economic, environmental and legal considerations. However, regardless of the motivation for change, the impacts usually result in benefits that are more far-reaching than initially envisaged. For instance, encouraging employees to walk and cycle to work may derive from the need to reduce car parking demand, but it can also lead to improved health and reduced stress levels for staff. This in turn can result in staff taking fewer days off sick and thus improving levels of productivity. Such benefits should act as an incentive to organizations to reassess their current transportation needs and use patterns. Indeed countless studies have shown that major cost savings and environmental and health benefits can all be derived by implementing the various measures outlined in this chapter.

References

Cleaner Vehicles Task Force (2001) 'The Impacts of Road Vehicles in Use – Air Quality, Climate Change and Noise Pollution', Department for Transport, London

DETR (1994) 'Planning Policy Guidance Note 13 (PPG13) (Revised)', Department of the Environment, Transport and the Regions, London

DETR (1998) 'A New Deal for Transport: Better for Everyone' CM3950, Department of the Environment, Transport and the Regions, The Stationery Office, London

DfT (2002) 'Making Travel Plans Work', Department for Transport, The Stationery Office, London

DfT (2003) 'Benchmarking Guide 78 – Key Performance Indicators for the Food Supply Chain', Department for Transport, available at www.transportenergy.org.uk/best-practice/

Energy Saving Trust (2003) For further information on the use of liquefied petroleum gas go to www.est.org.uk

Inland Revenue (2003) Leaflet IR176 provides details on the various tax breaks for vehicles. This can be viewed at www.inlandrevenue.gov.uk/cars/green_travel.htm

McKinnon, A (2002) 'Influencing Company Logistics Management', European Conference of Ministers of Transport, International Seminar Managing the Fundamental Drivers of Transport Demand, Brussels

TransportEnergy (2003) For further information on the measurement and monitoring of fleet fuel consumption, and on the videoconferencing experiences of the Royal Bank of Scotland, see the TransportEnergy Best Practice web site at www.transportenergy.org.uk

Chapter 7.5

Food and Agriculture

Introduction

The major product of the agriculture sector is, of course, food, and an environmentally sound agricultural production system is a prerequisite for an environmentally sound food industry overall. It therefore makes sense to consider environmental management in the food industry in terms of the supply chain – that is, all those activities that contribute to the production of primary food products, and their processing, distribution and retailing. In generic terms these activities are common to wider economic sectors such as manufacturing and retailing, but in this case the products concerned simply happen to be food.

In many respects, therefore, environmental management in the food industry is little different from environmental management in other economic sectors, and as such it is addressed elsewhere in this handbook. As a consequence, these more generic aspects of environmental management will not be considered closely here. For example, while the concept of food miles is an important one, the principles that help us decide whether or not it is environmentally sustainable to import food from overseas in substitution for food produced locally are largely standard questions of environmental procurement and life cycle analysis. Issues of food packaging can be considered in the context of the chapter on packaging and packaging waste, and while food manufacturing is a sector with specific integrated pollution prevention and control (IPPC) obligations, these issues can be considered in the more general context of pollution prevention and control.

The emphasis of this chapter is therefore on environmental policy and management in the agriculture sector, and how these primary food production issues relate to the downstream links of the supply chain.

Policy background

Environmental management has become an increasingly important component of farm management practice, particularly since the European Commission's 1992 so-called MacSharry reforms. These signalled an acknowledgement that agricultural policy in Europe could no longer be based purely on the driver of economically efficient food production. The share of agriculture and forestry in the gross domestic product (GDP) of the European Community in 1973 was 4.8 per cent. By 2001 it had fallen to 2 per cent. As this primary agricultural production came to represent a continually declining share of European economic activity, so the non-economic impacts of agriculture began to carry more policy significance. These included concerns about food safety, access to the countryside and, increasingly high on the public agenda, the issues of conservation, landscape management, animal welfare and environmental protection.

The shift towards the integration of environmental goals into policy development accelerated during the 1990s. At the European level, the commissioner in charge of the agriculture portfolio became the commissioner for agriculture and rural affairs, indicating a broadening of the portfolio towards a recognition of the whole spectrum of rural stakeholders.

The commission's Agenda 2000 policy paper, published in 1997, established rural development as the second pillar of the Common Agricultural Policy (CAP), with sustainability objectives at its core. The Rural Development Regulation 1999 (Regulation 1257/99) required all EU member states to develop rural development plans, of which the only compulsory component was for each member state to establish an agri-environment scheme.

In the UK, a parallel development in national policy was the abolition of the Ministry of Agriculture, Fisheries and Foods (MAFF), long criticized as being too farmer focused, and its subsumption in June 2001 into the Department for Environment, Food and Rural Affairs (Defra). Agricultural policy was repositioned, almost at a stroke, to become a subset of a much wider policy portfolio. Agricultural policy, and indirectly environment policy as it relates to agriculture, is now driven by several forces at the national, European and global levels.

National and European policy

National policy in the EU's member states varies according to the place of agriculture within each country's economy and socio-cultural tradition. In both France and the UK, for example, agricultural output accounts for a mere 1 to 2 per cent of GDP. However, the agricultural sector carries much more political weight in France, arguably because of the country's more rural nature – and possibly because of a different social perspective on, and greater tolerance of, civil disobedience. In theory, French farmers can appeal more effectively to the French electorate, more of whom live in rural areas than in Britain, and who are sympathetic to farming problems as a result. In practice, therefore, France has pursued a very conservative approach to farm policy reform, which reflects the vested interests of its farm sector. This is in contrast to the UK, whose government has led the push within Europe towards a reduction in emphasis on production related subsidies, and an increase in the emphasis on environmentally responsible farm policies. Contrasts such as this, of which there are many between all EU member states, make policy development a highly dynamic but incremental process, subject to protracted negotiation.

European agriculture policy, therefore, is largely a compromise that arises from the meeting of conflicting national policies, but in the context of an essentially reformist European Commission. It has also developed more recently in the light of the expected impact of ten new member states. By and large these candidate countries (with the exception of countries such as Malta) have large agricultural sectors within relatively small economies, and farm policy threatens to be heavily influenced by their arrival in the EU. So the current membership tried to define policy in a way that would be sustainable after EU enlargement in 2004.

The latest stage in this policy definition was marked by the agreement of the member states in the Agriculture Council at the end of June 2003. The agreement included explicit moves towards a more environmentally friendly agriculture policy by decoupling the calculation of the subsidies farmers receive from their levels of agricultural production, and by applying the principle of cross-compliance, making such payments conditional upon good agricultural practice.

Global influence

The policy developments outlined here are taking shape in a world of international trading agreements, dominated by the World Trade Organization (WTO). As of April 2003, the WTO consists of 146 member states (with another 30 negotiating membership), and its members account for approximately 97 per cent of world trade. The WTO's aim is to remove barriers to trade between member countries by negotiated multilateral agreements. The traditional support given to agricultural industries around the world has long been seen as one of the most problematic of such trade barriers, because it gives advantages to local producers over competing food imports. In extreme cases, such as the agricultural subsidies provided by the EU or the US, the policy leads to overproduction which is then exported to other countries, often undercutting local produce and distorting local markets, to the disadvantage of the farmers there.

The WTO has been attempting to reach agreement on cutting trade-distorting agricultural subsidies since 1986. Progress is slow, because member states do not wish to tie themselves into agreements that will not be popular at home. However, because important economic benefits are perceived to arise from agreement on trade liberalization in other economic sectors, they are under pressure to avoid the situation where lack of agreement on farm trade talks disrupts the entire WTO process. At national and European level, therefore, farm ministers are under pressure from their governments to produce a farm policy that will allow progress to be made in the WTO. In a nutshell, this means a farm policy that distorts markets as little as possible.

Implementing good environmental practice in farming

There have been a number of contradictions in British farming since the middle of the last century. As the predominant economic (and social) activity in rural areas, the farming industry considered itself, at the end of the Second World War, as the guardian of the natural environment. The landscape of the British and European countryside has been largely shaped by farming activities over hundreds of years, to create artificial but valuable landscapes which conservationists now seek to protect.

At the same time, agriculture was called upon to feed the hungry post war populations of Europe, and it responded by embracing new technologies enthusiastically, as a result of which the output of domestic (i.e. European) food production increased.

These new technologies were primarily engineering and chemical in nature, in the form of increasingly sophisticated farm and processing equipment, and new uses for agrochemicals to eliminate the pests and diseases that suppress yields. As concern over food and environmental safety rose following observation of the adverse effects of the profligate use of farm chemicals (see, most famously, Carson, 1963), new approaches to agrochemicals saw the accelerated development of synthetic materials, and more stringent testing and safety regimes. These appeared to offer more and safer food from Europe's fields, although continued concerns about long term or hidden adverse effects resulted in a continuing and growing interest in alternative, chiefly organic, systems of production which do not rely so heavily on artificial chemical technologies.

This debate has taken on a new dimension with the advent of genetically modified (GM) food. Concerns expressed about GM food include:

- the unknown impact on human health over the long term of eating such food;
- the potential impact on the environment of introducing GM crops into it; and
- the implications for agriculture in developing countries where small and subsistence farmers may see their traditionally diverse sources of home produced crop varieties displaced by dominant GM varieties, under the control of multinational corporations.

The debates over these issues remain unresolved, despite extensive scientific trials into some of them. While the debates continue, farmers have found themselves perceived, not necessarily as guardians of the countryside, but sometimes as its ravagers. Indicators such as declining numbers of farmland birds, loss of hedgerows and increased levels of diffuse pollution from agriculture are cited as evidence of this.

For example, farmland birds are considered to be a useful indicator of environmental health because of their dependence on a wide range of habitats, and their position near the top of the food chain. Their populations declined by nearly 50 per cent between 1978 and 1993, although they have since stabilized. It is largely through the implementation of the environmental aspects of European agricultural policy that farmers are able to respond to these environmental concerns, by undertaking measurable actions to demonstrate good environmental practice.

A central problem of the GM debate is the opposition of the arguments. The case against GM on environmental grounds (where the precautionary principle can be invoked to prohibit the development of an unnecessary technology which may be damaging) is set against the argument that the world desperately needs the yield-enhancing benefits of the GM technology to feed its growing populations. Current estimates suggest that about 800 million people are undernourished or hungry. In other words, the debate is not just about a confrontation between environmental concern and big business profitability, but between the three corners of the sustainability triangle: environment versus community versus economics.

The arguments are complex, and interested readers may explore them further as follows:

- GM technologies offer potentially enormous benefits, but must be developed with extreme caution and due regard for avoidance of adverse environmental impact.
- The development of existing technologies, by supporting third world farmers more effectively, can provide enough food sustainably for growing populations without recourse to intensive GM based systems controlled by Western transnational corporations.

For accessible discussions of these arguments see, for example, the scientific assessment by the Royal Society et al (2000) and Pretty (2002).

Environment and rural development – the second pillar of the CAP

The reformed CAP distinguishes between the policy aimed at supporting agriculture as an economic sector, and that which aims to achieve sustainable rural areas, by supporting and promoting rural development that optimizes environmental, social and economic outcomes for all rural stakeholders, including those in the farm industry. This rural development policy is known as the second pillar of the CAP, and it uses both sticks and carrots to achieve its aims.

Sticks and carrots

Following the June 2003 CAP reforms the principle of cross-compliance means that payment of subsidies to farmers will be linked to compliance with EU environmental standards. Farmers benefiting from agri-environment payments under their country's rural development plan (see Box 7.5.1) are required to follow 'good farming practice', defined in EU law as 'the standard of farming which a reasonable farmer would follow in the region concerned'.

Box 7.5.1 *Agri-environment schemes under the England Rural Development Programme (ERDP)*

There are seven agri-environment or land based schemes under the ERDP:

- Countryside Stewardship Scheme;
- Energy Crops Scheme;
- Environmentally Sensitive Areas;
- Farm Woodland Premium Scheme;
- Hill Farm Allowance;
- Organic Farming Scheme;
- Woodland Grant Scheme.

Defra describes their purpose in these terms:
   Land based or agri-environment schemes focus on promoting environmental awareness and good practice with farmers. They are an important tool in compensating farmers for income lost when establishing or improving environmentally beneficial aspects of farmland (www.defra.gov.uk/erdp/schemes/default.htm#land).
   In addition, Defra is piloting an entry level scheme which, if successful, will be available across the country to all farmers, and which will aim to encourage as many farmers as possible to engage in simple but effective environmental management systems. The entry level scheme is scheduled to be rolled out across England in 2005.

Note: As an aspect of devolved government, England, Northern Ireland, Scotland and Wales each have their own, tailored rural development plan. They all share the same broad objectives, and have many similarities in the instruments they use

---

The verifiable standards which each member state sets out in its own definition of good farming practice form the baseline of the minimum acceptable environmental performance for which no agri-environment payments are eligible. In addition, farmers are encouraged to abide by the codes of good agricultural practice for soil, air and water (MAFF, 1998a, 1998b, 1998c). And of course, any other (primarily EU) legislation that sets relevant environmental standards must be adhered to (see Box 7.5.2).

Box 7.5.2 *EU environmental legislation of relevance to agriculture*

The Habitats Directive aims to provide strong protection of designated sites – it establishes special areas of conservation (SACs). Its principal impacts on agriculture and farming practice are to restrict actually or potentially damaging operations in or near an SAC. Council Directive 92/43/EEC of 21 May 1992 on the conservation of natural habitats and of wild fauna and flora.

The Birds Directive aims to provide strong protection of designated sites known as special protection areas (SPAs). Its major impact on farming is to restrict actually or potentially damaging operations in or near an SPA. Council Directive 79/409/EC of 2 April 1979 on the conservation of the wild birds.

The Water Framework Directive introduces a requirement to prevent deterioration of, and to achieve good status for, all waters, with a new focus on ecological status for surface waters. It will tackle diffuse pollution for the first time. It is accepted that farming is a major source and cause of diffuse pollution. Directive 2000/60/EC of the European Parliament and of the Council of 23 October 2000 establishing a framework for Community action in the field of water policy.

IPPC Regulations identify prescribed installations that cannot operate without an authorization – which governs the materials and technology used, discharges to the environment, energy efficiency, best practice operation and maintenance and accident prevention. The regulations apply to certain sized intensive pig and poultry farming units. Council Directive 96/61/EC of 24 September 1996 concerning integrated pollution prevention and control.

The Waste Framework Directive determines that a cradle to grave, duty of care responsibility for waste lies with producers of waste. Farms both produce and use waste; trends suggest exemptions for some processes, which are deemed beneficial to agriculture, may be withdrawn. Council Directive 75/442/EEC of 15 July 1975 on waste.

The Nitrates Directive restricts use of N-based fertilizers on agricultural land, via the designation of nitrate vulnerable zones (NVZs). The area designated as NVZs has increased from 22 to 55 per cent of England and Wales – many more farmers will be affected in future. Council Directive 91/676/EEC of 12 December 1991 concerning the protection of waters against pollution caused by nitrates from agricultural sources.

The Groundwater Directive imposes a requirement for authorization of use, storage and disposal of dangerous substances where actual or potential risk of escape would result in groundwater pollution. Council Directive 80/68/EEC of 17 December 1979 on the protection of groundwater against pollution caused by certain dangerous substances.

The Landfill Directive creates an obligation to reduce biodegradable waste going into landfill; it places restrictions on hazardous wastes going to landfill and establishes a requirement of pre-treatment. The application to agricultural land may well be the most likely option for biodegradable waste that can no longer go to landfill. Opportunities arising may include cheap soil conditioning material and development of composting businesses. Council Directive 1999/31/EC of 26 April 1999 on the landfill of waste.

The Environmental Liability Directive is currently a proposal from the European Commission that proposes to codify civil liability for environmental harm caused by prescribed activities (e.g. under IPPC) and waste disposal (e.g. paying for clean up). Strict liability could apply for harm to the public but not for harm to biodiversity. In this context intensive pig and poultry farming is a prescribed activity under IPPC. COM(2002) 17 final, 2002/0021(COD). Proposal for a directive of the European Parliament and of the Council on environmental liability with regard to the prevention and remedying of environmental damage. Brussels, 23.1.2002.

The prospective **Soils Directive** will provide protection against soil degradation in all its forms. Liability could apply to farmers who adopt poor land use or farming practices that result in soil erosion and soil quality degradation.

Following the reform of the CAP, farmers will be required to meet these baseline standards of environmental practice, regardless of their participation in any agri-environment schemes.

Meeting baseline standards, however, is not of itself enough to ensure the sustainability of agricultural systems. It can perhaps be likened to ensuring that all car engines are properly tuned so as to minimize emissions, but doing little to minimize the actual use of those cars, or to reduce their fuel consumption. There is still an extremely lively debate, therefore, as to what sustainable agriculture and food production really means.

Sustainable agriculture and organic farming

Sustainable agriculture has many definitions. One useful attempt, from the Biotechnology and Biological Sciences Research Council, is this: 'a sustainable system is one whose state remains within a defined acceptable range', and that a sustainable agricultural system 'is one in which agricultural activities are environmentally, ethically and economically sustainable'.

Of course, there is much disagreement over what is acceptable and what activities can actually be sustained without degrading environmental, ethical, social and economic structures in the long term. And so intensive, modern farming systems which pursue integrated farm management (IFM) principles (see the next section) may be considered sustainable by their adherents, whereas an organic farmer may consider any system which is not fully organic to be environmentally unsustainable in the long run.

In fact, there is much conflicting evidence about the relative merits, in environmental and conservation terms, of different farming systems. Pretty (1998) provides an accessible summary of the principles of sustainable agriculture, which is well worth exploring. The EU strongly supports the case for organic farming as one viable route to sustainability for individual farms (http://europa.eu.int/comm/agriculture/qual/organic/index_en.htm).

In the UK there are a number of organizations involved in supporting and certifying organic agriculture, of which the most prominent is arguably the Soil Association (www.soilassociation.org). Organic farming 'severely restricts the use of artificial chemicals and fertilisers' and avoids the 'the routine use of drugs, antibiotics and wormers common in intensive livestock farming' according to the Soil Association. The Soil Association and other organic certification schemes extend beyond prescriptions for agricultural practice to stipulate standards for processing, packaging, distribution and retailing of foods as well.

Indicators

In order to estimate the environmental performance of the agricultural sector as a whole, or indeed at the local level, the UK Government has produced some draft indicators. Some of these are more developed and easier to measure than others. In 2000 MAFF developed a complementary set of 35 pilot indicators (Table 7.5.1), which it has classified according to the Organisation for Economic Co-operation and Development's (OECD) pressure–state–response model. Thus we can measure pressures, such as the use of pesticides on farms (e.g. indicators 15 and 16), which lead to particular measurable states such as levels of pesticide in groundwater or in rivers (indicators 13 and 14), which in turn require responses, such as government payments to farmers for agri-environment purposes.

Table 7.5.1   MAFF pilot indicators (2000)

Issue	Area	Indicator
A. Agriculture within the rural economy and society	Structure of the agriculture industry	1 Agricultural assets and liabilities 2 Age of farmers 3 Percentage of holdings that are tenanted
	Farm financial resources	4 EU producer support estimate (PSE) 5 Payments to farmers for agri-environment purposes 6 Total income from farming 7 Average earnings of agricultural workers
	Agricultural productivity	8 Agricultural productivity
	Agricultural employment	9 Agricultural employment
B. Farm management systems	Management	10 Adoption of farm management systems
	Organic farming	11 Area converted to organic farming
	Codes of practice	12 Knowledge of codes of good agricultural practice
C. Input use	Pesticide use	13 Pesticides in rivers 14 Pesticides in groundwater 15 Quantity of pesticide active ingredients used 16 Spray area treated with pesticides 17 Pesticide residues in food 18 Nitrate and phosphorus losses from agriculture
	Nutrients	19 Phosphorus levels of agricultural topsoils 20 Manure management 21 Ammonia emissions from agriculture
	Greenhouse gas emissions	22 Emissions of methane and nitrous oxide from agriculture
	Energy	23 Direct energy consumption by farms 24 Trends in indirect energy inputs to agriculture
D. Resource use	Water	25 Use of water for irrigation
	Soil	26 Organic matter content of agricultural topsoils 27 Accumulation of heavy metals in agricultural topsoils
	Agricultural land	28 Area of agricultural land 29 Change in land use from agriculture to hard development
	Non-food crops	30 Planting of non-food crops
E. Conservation value of agricultural land	Environmental conservation	31 Area of agricultural land under commitment to environmental conservation
	Landscape	32 Characteristic features of farmland
	Habitats	33 Area of cereal field margins under environmental management 34 Area of semi-natural grassland
	Biodiversity	35 Populations of key farmland birds

Source: MAFF, 2000

The national concept of agricultural sustainability in policy terms has been fertilized by a more global analysis. The OECD published a framework for agri-environmental indicators (1999–2001), and a substantial worldwide literature has examined the subject (e.g. Pannell and Glenn, 2000; Rigby et al, 2001).

The indicators identified by MAFF and some of the changes in them over time have been measured and published, suggesting base and trend lines. However, although much of the data is available as source material, considerable further work is required to evaluate the state of the indicators at the regional and local levels, depending on the degree of detail required.

MAFF (2000) claims that these indicators are showing positive progress towards sustainability. However, not everyone agrees and others claim that farming is failing in key performance tests such as soil conservation, use of renewable energy sources, air pollution, biodiversity and social capital.

Food production, environmental performance and the supply chain

When it comes to the supply chain, the primary environmental concerns of the food industry are dominated by the concept of food safety. In large part this issue is not explicitly a concern of environmental management practice – avoiding food poisoning by the imposition of stringent hygiene regulations, for example, would appear to be a technical health and safety matter. However, many food safety issues are integrated with environmental concerns. The BSE (bovine spongiform encephalopathy) crisis and genetically modified crops have both raised food safety issues, and both raise fundamental questions about environmentally sound agricultural practice.

Thus a major driver of farm practice is the need to meet the food safety requirements imposed by legislation (such as maximum permissible pesticide residues in food), and by the food chain itself, where major customers of farmers and other suppliers, such as the multiple supermarket chains, require food production to be undertaken in accordance with their own rigorous standards.

The British Retail Consortium (BRC) has developed a range of food production standards which typify this supply chain approach, and which aim to ensure that the food retailed by BRC members is safe for human consumption (mainly by imposing a requirement to implement hazard analysis and critical control points – HACCP – systems). As indicated above, food safety issues and environmental management go hand in hand in many cases. In terms of direct environmental management performance issues such as energy efficiency, however, the BRC works with suppliers on the basis of best practice guidelines. In this respect the food industry can be examined in the same light as any other manufacturing or distributive sector, and thus other sections of this handbook are equally relevant here.

Farmer responses to these food safety and environmental improvement drivers include formalized approaches to the adoption of IFM. IFM can be summarized as:

a whole farm policy providing the basis for efficient and profitable production which is economically viable and environmentally responsible. IFM integrates beneficial natural processes into modern farming practices using advanced technology. It aims to minimize environmental risks while conserving and enhancing that which is of environmental importance (Boxall, 2000).

One of the highest profile, farmer driven initiatives in support of this principle is Linking Environment and Farming (LEAF). LEAF brings together government departments, farmers, supermarkets, conservation, environmental and consumer groups, educational establishments and industry bodies to promote IFM on British farms.
    According to LEAF, the principles of IFM are:

- a commitment to good husbandry and animal welfare;
- efficient soil management and appropriate cultivation techniques;
- the use of crop rotations;
- minimum reliance on crop protection chemicals and fertilizers;
- careful choice of seed varieties;
- maintenance of the landscape and rural communities;
- enhancement of wildlife habitats; and
- a commitment to team spirit based on communication, training and involvement.

Farmers who join the LEAF scheme may achieve certification to LEAF standards, by way of demonstrating their adherence in practice to IFM principles (see Figure 7.5.1),

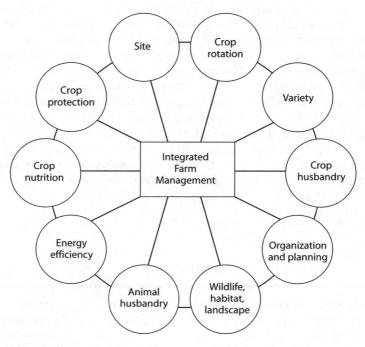

Note: This figure shows the various management processes that need to be integrated effectively for successful environmental and economic outcomes
Source: Boxall, 2000

Figure 7.5.1   The IFM wheel

and the good environmental practice that this implies. This good practice is ensured and verified by audit, and helps farmers meet the standards required by customers such as BRC members.

By aiming to resolve the potential conflicts between economic, environmental and safety factors at the primary food production level, IFM allows food to enter the supply chain in conformity with the principles of best practice which also need to be imposed throughout the chain – up to the retail point. There are many sector specific and regional quality control schemes in operation that aim to promote high quality, safe food into the supply chain – whether it is on the basis of high standards of food safety, animal welfare, or environmental protection.

The best example of this approach is the British Farm Standard (www.littleredtractor.org.uk), better known for the little red tractor logo. Governed by an umbrella body, the Assured Food Standards, each sector has a scheme tailored to ensure appropriate certification to environmental and food safety standards. These schemes, of which there are ten covering six production sectors, depend on a process of independent inspection.

One of the biggest drivers of environmental performance on the food chain (and indeed of initiatives such as the British Farm Standard) is the influence of the major multiple retailers. For example, Sainsbury's aims to 'influence our suppliers to reduce their direct environmental impacts and improve the environmental quality of own brand products through more sustainable sourcing'. Pleasing customers of the size of Sainsbury's and Tesco is a substantial incentive for suppliers to comply with their stipulations about production methods and product quality. The retailers themselves are motivated by consumer demand, which translates into competitive pressures. Increasing consumer concerns about the issues discussed in this chapter represent both a threat to those retailers who do not respond to those concerns, and an opportunity to differentiate their offering for those who can offer more reliable produce and supply chains.

These consumer perceptions about and expectations of the supply chain are developing to embrace wider environmental issues as well as food safety. Customers want to know that animal welfare is satisfactory on the farms producing animal products; they are increasingly concerned about food miles, and are beginning to realize that the environmental advantages of eating organic vegetables may be outweighed by the environmental costs of air-freighting them in from the other side of the world. In general, they are becoming more sophisticated in their understanding of the environmental issues behind the food industry. The entire supply chain is having to respond to those more sophisticated concerns.

Summary

Making real progress in environmental management requires agreement not only on the appropriate indicators of environmental performance and the means of measuring them, but on the systems and technologies that will promote improvement.

The mechanisms for making this progress are principally the reforms to agricultural policy on the one hand, and the commercial incentives presented by the nature of the supply chain on the other. Policy is moving away from rewarding volume of production for its own sake to a system of rewarding the protection of public goods (such as environmental benefits, or more rural jobs). The dominant players in the supply chain (the multiple retailers) are pressing the entire chain, including farmers, to produce better quality food at less environmental cost.

There are too many unanswered questions about the real impacts on the environment of modern agricultural and food production systems to confidently predict the eventual nature of a genuinely sustainable food industry. However, it is certainly one of the most dynamic and interesting economic sectors about which to ask those questions in the first place.

References and further reading

Boxall, J. (2000) 'LEAF, Demonstrating a Way Forward for British Agriculture and Horticulture', *APRC News*, no 24, August, Apple & Pear Development Council

Carson, R. (1963) *Silent Spring*, Hamilton, London

Defra (2003) 'Agriculture in the United Kingdom', Department for Environment, Food and Rural Affairs, London

LEAF The LEAF website is www.leafuk.org/leaf/

MAFF (1998a) 'Code of Good Agricultural Practice for the Protection of Air', available at www.defra.gov.uk/environ/cogap/aircode.pdf

MAFF (1998b) 'Code of Good Agricultural Practice for the Protection of Soil', available at www.defra.gov.uk

MAFF (1998c) 'Code of Good Agricultural Practice for the Protection of Water', available at www.defra.gov.uk/environ/cogap/watercod.pdf

MAFF (2000) 'Towards Sustainable Agriculture – A Pilot Set of Indicators', Ministry of Agriculture, Fisheries and Food, London

OECD (1999–2001) *Environmental Indicators for Agriculture*, vols 1–3, Organisation for Economic Co-operation and Development, Paris

Pannell, D. J. and Glenn, N. A. (2000) 'A Framework for the Economic Evaluation and Selection of Sustainability Indicators in Agriculture', *Ecological Economics*, vol 33, no 1, pp135–149

Pretty, J. (1998) *The Living Land*, Earthscan, London

Pretty, J. (2002) *Agri-culture: Reconnecting People, Land and Nature*, Earthscan, London

Rigby, D. et al (2001) 'Constructing a Farm Level Indicator of Sustainable Agricultural Practice', *Ecological Economics*, vol 39, no 3, pp463–478

Royal Society of London et al (2000) 'Transgenic plants and world agriculture', National Academies Press, http://books.nap.edu/catalog/9889.html?onpi_webextra

Section 8

Environmental Futures

Chapter 8.1

The Sustainability Challenge

The sustainability transition

The global sustainability challenge facing us is simply stated: it combines an empirical assessment and a normative claim. The evidence-based assessment, as shared by numerous scientists, is that current society–nature interactions are not sustainable – they are negatively affecting both vital ecological systems and human welfare in ways that threaten irreversible, long-term damage (UNEP, 2002). Attached to this empirical claim is the normative position of sustainable development – that societal development paths should meet fundamental human needs, within and between generations, while maintaining the planet's life support system and living resources.

Of course, the most well known vision of sustainability has been the one promoted within the United Nations (UN), from the Brundtland Commission to the 1992 Rio Conference and, more recently, the World Summit on Sustainable Development held in 2002 in Johannesburg. It is broadly a social democratic understanding, which states that a durable commitment to poverty eradication, delivered through inclusive governance structures and more equitable economic growth, must run alongside measures to reverse the continuing degradation of the global environment.

The achievement of the Johannesburg Summit was to have reinvigorated this self understanding of sustainability, with an action plan targeting priority areas of concern for the economically disenfranchised in developing countries – for example halving, by 2015, the proportion of the world's people living on less than US$1 a day and the proportion lacking access to safe drinking water or proper sanitation; as well as slashing child mortality rates by two thirds and maternal mortality rates by three-quarters. These anti-poverty targets accompany a more diffuse mix of environmental protection commitments addressing such areas as the regulation of hazardous chemicals, fisheries management and investment in renewable energy.

Given the novel governance thrust of the Johannesburg action plan – opting, instead of international rule making, to embrace voluntary partnership initiatives between public and private actors – some commentators (particularly environment and development activists) pointed to a marked gulf between the moral imperatives expressed and the political actions promised. Yet at the close of the meeting the UN Secretary General, Kofi Annan, identified a new political will among governments:

> This summit makes sustainable development a reality ... [it] will put us on a path that reduces poverty while protecting the environment, a path that works for all peoples, rich and poor, today and tomorrow.

General recognition of the nature of the global sustainability challenge masks significant disagreements about the means of addressing it effectively (Juma, 2002). As the mainstream candidate for a 21st century paradigm of sustainability, the Johannesburg implementation plan attempts to bypass this obstacle by favouring diverse modalities of action, pulling in multiple actors and decision-making processes across a range of scales. And this is more than a political adaptation to a global governance arena where consensus on international environmental rule making is proving more elusive. It pinpoints the comprehensive transformation of daily economic and social practices needed to make the transition to sustainability.

The crucial challenge to the Johannesburg vision of public–private partnership initiatives is whether these are sufficient to overcome unsustainable structures and trends in what is now a global political economy. Above all, this means production and consumption patterns driven by economic output growth fixated on short time horizons and compelled to externalize environmental costs. This chapter presents in outline a view of the necessary economic–technological, regulatory and participatory democratic framework conditions for the transition to sustainability. The argument, ultimately, is that sustainability proponents can no longer avoid facing the far-reaching political character of this transition – that enabling individuals and peoples freely to meet their needs in an equitable, ecologically sustainable fashion is compatible neither with free market fundamentalism (Anglo-American neoliberalism) nor its illiberal alternatives (e.g. religious fundamentalist regimes and movements).

Economic and technological conditions for sustainability

Undoubtedly the greatest challenge in the transition to sustainability is the structural realignment of our dominant economic development paths away from energy- and material-intensive processes and an unyielding fixation with rapid output growth of commodities. Shaped by academic debates and policy choices in northern European countries, the most influential perspective on the economic and technological conditions conducive to sustainability is 'ecological modernization'. This approach advocates the greening of production processes through technological innovation, offering 'win–win' solutions: to corporate actors from more efficient resource and energy use; to employees and communities from less pollution; and to governments from investment patterns in line with ambitious productivity and regulatory targets. Ecological modernization gains have been significant in many industrialized states, but fall short of the economic dematerialization gains necessary for delivering environmental sustainability.

The advances are observable in the widespread embrace of eco-efficiency by businesses – that is, strategies for creating economic value with less environmental impact. Eco-efficient corporations aim to decouple resource consumption, energy use and pollution emissions from economic activity, as well as capture productivity increases from knowledge based innovation. As promoted by organizations such as the World Business Council for Sustainable Development, the eco-efficiency perspective has brought a growing repertoire of practical solutions for moving corporations towards sustainability. Allen et al (2001, pp29–80) present a range of examples attesting to the influence of the concept in multinational companies. These include:

- the reduction of chemical usage in the production of semiconductors by Hyundai Electronics, utilizing non-chemical cleaning, process conditions effective for minimal chemical inputs and the recycling of discharged waste chemicals;
- the waste-free strategy of the Xerox Corporation, introduced in the early 1990s, which has evolved from print cartridge recycling and equipment remanufacturing programmes to encompass a more ambitious dematerialization goal, whereby online knowledge management solutions are geared to the value-added service function of the Xerox products rather than the provision of office based equipment;
- the innovative green procurement policies of the Canon group, which entail eco-efficiency demands imposed on 1500 companies involved in its worldwide supply chain. These environmental standards not only cover product characteristics (e.g. resource conservation and recycling potential) but also the corporate structure of the suppliers themselves (e.g. the presence or absence of an environmental management system).

That these large corporations can push through eco-efficiency strategies is evidence that the business community can meet significant environmental challenges, although effective diffusion of these practices requires a supportive cross-national bedrock of regulatory norms and green taxation incentives. There is a concern that ecological modernization is designed to maintain the economic advantages of existing global business elites, and blunts a more far-reaching sustainability challenge, which would include corporate social responsibility demands. To be sure, recent developments like the Global Reporting Initiative (GRI) demonstrate that many major corporations are willing to be subjected to public scrutiny for their economic, environmental and social performance.

Sustainability reporting, under GRI guidelines, has already been undertaken by more than 110 companies, including BASF, the Co-operative Bank, Electrolux, Ford, GM, Interface, Nike, Nokia and Shell (see www.globalreporting.org). However, such voluntary commitments to sustainability assessment of corporate performance, while promoting relevant business engagement, do not address the growing scale of production and consumption in the global economy. Indeed, there are grounds for anticipating that the efficiency gains arising from less intense energy and material use in economic production will, over time, be wiped out by the resource demands of increased consumption. This so-called rebound effect highlights why the ecological restructuring of production must be accompanied by an assault on overconsumption in affluent societies. Ultimately, the sustainability transition means a far-reaching reform of economic activity, such that wealth creation drivers are tamed by shared social and ecological needs (e.g. reduction of working time, investment in public goods, community self determination).

Regulating for sustainability

The transition to sustainability will not be achieved without recourse to extensive forms of legal and social control. To pretend otherwise is naïvely to suppose that those dominant free-market incentives favouring short term private benefits will, without regulatory steering, somehow register collective environmental and social needs. Or that those groups profiting from unsustainable resource use, whether legally or illegally, could be persuaded to forfeit their material gains for the good of more vulnerable communities or future generations. Neither scenario is realistic: the challenge to regulate for sustainability is thus formidable. It necessitates the introduction of creative and flexible regulatory practices that are problem led, rather than anchored in fixed organizational or ideological structures. These regulatory forms are best thought of as networks – they protect and promote sustainability at multiple scales, bringing actors together in new configurations of mutual learning and collective control.

Some recent trends in environmental policy making within industrialized countries offer a sense of the types of regulatory networks likely to be both effective and democratically legitimate in any sustainability transition. Their starting point is the acknowledgement that government command and control regulation in pursuit of public interest goals is often, by itself, not sufficient to lever durable changes in behaviour. Rather, direct state intervention is more likely to be effective when used strategically and selectively: the pivotal role of government is to facilitate the creation of regulatory networks which recruit affected parties to shape and participate in sustainability rule making and enforcement.

Regulation, broadly defined, would be guided by overriding principles of sustainability (intra- and intergenerational justice, prevention of social and ecological harm), but in practice would draw pragmatically on a wider range of policy tools than traditional standard setting: these may include economic instruments (e.g. tradable pollution credits, taxes or fixed charges), voluntary undertakings (e.g. corporate codes of conduct) and communicative approaches (e.g. community right-to-know provisions, product certification). Above all, it is smart regulation (Gunningham et al, 1998) insofar as it devises and implements complementary combinations of policy tools tailored to specific contexts. By favouring policy adaptation to particular environmental and social pressures, harnessing the problem solving capabilities of multiple actors, it invites the level of open experimentation in regulatory development necessary to meet the complex demands of the sustainability transition.

A fundamental shift in regulatory emphasis is called for to secure this transition – a move away from reactive, incremental policy making towards anticipatory, integrated approaches. For example, the focus of strategic environmental assessment on avoiding negative ecological impacts forecast to arise from policies, plans and programmes indicates the preventative thrust that, when extended also to social and economic effects, constitutes the scope of sustainability assessment systems. To be effective, integrated assessment in support of sustainability decision making must blend natural and social scientific data, taking into account plural human preferences.

Some of the more promising methods share a preoccupation with stakeholder participation in sustainability modelling and evaluation, in order to facilitate an inclusive dialogue on possible futures: this is designed both to incorporate information on what people want to be sustained and also, through a common ownership of the decision making process, to boost incentives for behavioural change. Leading examples include the Dutch TARGETS (Tool to Assess Regional and Global Environmental and Health Targets for Sustainability) model and the Canadian QUEST (Quite Useful Ecosystem Scenario Tool) system (Abaza and Baranzini, 2002).

Both approaches have been developed with a view to enabling citizens to learn about the social and environmental consequences of multiple future scenarios. A key educative ambition they share is to demonstrate that the forms of regulatory restraint required to meet the sustainability challenge are actually conditions for the long term flourishing of more healthy and meaningful forms of life.

Democratizing sustainability

The full political implications of the sustainability transition have yet to be grasped. Inherent to the conception of sustainable development championed by the UN is a commitment to intra- and intergenerational justice, which highlights the inequities of current resource allocation patterns around the globe. It is clear that ensuring an equal opportunity for all to satisfy their basic needs is not possible without a deepening of democratic decision making in governance forms (local to global), nor without a significant redistribution of resources from affluent groups to the world's poor people. Of course, the principle of equal opportunity also implies that individuals should not systematically be made socially vulnerable or exposed to human induced environmental hazards. In considering possible civic–political conditions for promoting sustainability, the critical benchmark is the extent to which they empower individuals to identify and claim their sustainability entitlements as planetary citizens; that is, their equal rights to economic security and socio-environmental wellbeing.

What constitutes legitimate sustainability constraints on political economic structures is by no means straightforward to specify, as much depends on the particular institutional contexts. However, as we already grant, through the ascription of rights, strong moral and legal protection to the civic–political conditions under which persons can freely and equally determine their life paths, it seems logical that this protection should be extended to sustainability constraints that relate to vital conditions of existence – for example economic subsistence and livelihood opportunities, social welfare entitlements, clean air and water and ecologically sustainable land use.

The universality of human rights captures well the sustainability principle that conditions of life should be maintained that keep open the fullest range of options for the future, while meeting fairly the needs of everyone in the present – that is, political choice and economic development paths should not be making the socially marginalized or our successors worse off. Unlike civic–political rights, which are widely embedded in national constitutions and international human rights conventions, the notion that critical social and ecological conditions of existence should be recognized in this way remains controversial. It also sits uneasily with that Anglo-American market fundamentalism which perceives only individual liberty rights to be relevant to human wellbeing. Nonetheless, the sustainability challenge here is for concerned citizens to build political support for rights protection of vital social and ecological conditions of existence.

Beyond moves to entrench core sustainability entitlements in resource allocation decisions, there remains the less salient, but no less demanding, task of fostering a widespread socio-cultural identification with sustainable development. As Tim O'Riordan (2001, p239) notes 'sustainability has not properly entered into the realm of social connectedness – namely, the bonding of trust and accepted rules of behaviour that ensure a society holds together.' A preoccupation in policy circles with economic and regulatory reform has neglected the potential role of civic education and socialization in transmitting pro-sustainability values. In a highly interdependent world, a necessary political source of identification with sustainability is that those facing threats to their wellbeing from particular material transactions are able collectively to perceive these as adversely affecting their interests and therefore in need of regulation. They are able, in other words, to attribute responsibility to external actors or structures, and identify with others whose sustainability entitlements are being eroded. Empathy with the socially excluded is key to the cultivation of values and norms in support of sustainability; as of course is consideration of the needs of future generations. Yet all that is required here is an extension outwards of social norms already operational in all durable human cultures – for example positive concern for the young and other vulnerable groups, mutual understanding and the expectation of secure, stable community relations.

Planetary futures

This discussion, albeit necessarily brief, has highlighted several pivotal framework conditions for the sustainability transition:

- a structural realignment of economic development objectives, combining dematerialization and eco-efficiency with a disciplining of wealth creation incentives by social justice considerations;
- the effective integration of regulation for sustainability across policy sectors as well as political borders;
- the routine employment, in decision making, of sustainability assessment informed by extensive stakeholder participation;
- the ascription of rights protection to critical sustainability entitlements for all planetary citizens (e.g. economic security, social welfare provision, vital ecological conditions of existence); and
- the promotion of altruistic, ecologically enlightened social identities.

To repeat, the specific institutional designs in support of these conditions will be shaped by local and regional contexts: there is no simple template for change. While the global spread of democracy offers grounds for anticipating governance forms sensitive in principle to the social and environmental needs of populations, recent geopolitical developments demonstrate that political consensus on sustainability is far from strong even in the liberal democracies.

In its recent comprehensive appraisal of the state of the global environment, the UNEP suggests four possible futures over the next 30 years (2002, pp319–400). The most familiar to us, on the basis of the established hold of neoliberalism on leading industrialized states and international economic organizations, is the 'markets first' scenario, which anticipates economic liberalization continuing as the main driver of development paths around the world. Deference by states to market forces acknowledges their innate capacity for technological innovation and wealth creation, but not their failure to register, let alone address, the new risks and inequalities generated.

With national economic interests associated with unimpeded market liberalization, systems of governance for sustainability are likely to remain poorly developed, for collective policy measures will be reactive rather than proactive. The potential sustainability gains of this market fundamentalist trajectory are minimal, prompting consideration of an alternative 'policy first' scenario where there is international political consensus that governance institutions at all levels are strengthened to address environmental and social goals. This planetary future finds resonance in existing trends towards ecological modernization, although no provision is made for the rebound effect already mentioned, not for the levels of citizen participation and identification needed to ensure a successful sustainability transition.

Indeed, as the UN report makes clear, to realize the latter requires an unprecedented recasting of governance institutions according to sustainability criteria. The 'sustainability first' scenario encompasses a full application of the framework conditions outlined in this chapter. Above all, human development and environmental quality priorities, as collectively shaped by local and transnational publics, steer market forces.

The many examples of innovative environmental management practices found in this handbook attest to the real possibilities for advancing policies for ecological sustainability. Such policies, conjoined with development goals, move us towards and beyond the Johannesburg vision. However, they demand a level of international cooperation and civil society engagement at odds with the prevailing geopolitical climate – one that is best captured by the 'security first' scenario in the UN appraisal. Recent geopolitical trends have signalled a worrying move away from multilateral cooperation for sustainability, and away more generally from consensus based international rule making and enforcement.

Religious fundamentalist movements and violent criminal networks represent a threat to the global order unforeseen by earlier sustainability analyses. The 'war against terrorism' they have triggered has revived Cold War notions of power politics, although now of course one country, the US, is internationally dominant. Whether the sustainability challenge will be met in future decades depends largely on the political commitment of the US governing coalition. Sustainability advocates across the world have, as their challenge, to impress on this and other centres of power that their long term security and prosperity rests on them embracing a more inclusive, ecologically rational planetary future.

References

Abaza, H. and Baranzini, A. (eds) (2002) *Implementing Sustainable Development: Integrated Assessment and Participatory Decision-making*, Edward Elgar, Cheltenham

Allen, P., Bonazzi, C. and Gee, D. (2001) *Metaphors for Change: Partnerships, Tools and Civic Action for Sustainability*, Greenleaf Publishing, Sheffield

Gunningham, N., Graborsky, P. and Sinclair, D. (1998) *Smart Regulation: Designing Environmental Policy*, Oxford University Press, Oxford

Juma, C. (2002) 'The Global Sustainability Challenge: From Agreement to Action', *International Journal of Environmental Issues*, vol 2, nos 1–2, pp1–14

O'Riordan, T. (ed) (2001) *Globalism, Localism and Identity: Perspectives on the Transition to Sustainability*, Earthscan, London

UNEP (2002) *Global Environment Outlook 3: Past, Present and Future Perspectives*, United Nations Environment Programme, Earthscan, London

Chapter 8.2

Integrated Thinking and Governance

Introduction

Most environmental professionals will look at the phrases 'integrated thinking' and 'corporate governance' and consider them to be at best fashionable buzzwords or at worst oxymorons. Their pedigree is not inspiring. Integrated thinking is prompted by the awareness that there has been a less than coordinated approach to business functions and management systems within organizations and government. In addition, many are seeking an integrated approach to environmental, social and economic issues under the umbrella of sustainable development. The recent emphasis on corporate governance and accountability, on the other hand, is largely inspired by the breakdown of trust between such organizations and their many stakeholders.

The two phrases do, however, afford an opportunity to look at the future of environmental management from two outcrops of (slightly) higher ground. For, if nothing else, the very act of management integration requires a fundamental understanding of the disciplines being merged, while issues of governance require that all participants, from director to shareholder, confront the issues of personal and collective responsibility.

But can and should environmental professionals embrace these different concepts? Integration, for example, is fundamentally mechanistic. It conjures up elements in a Newtonian universe that can be fanned together like two decks of cards in the hands of an expert dealer. The current expression of concern about governance, too, has a similarly reductionist ring to it. Accountability is either there or it isn't, and it's usually proven to be there when one can identify an individual or group of individuals at whose door one can lay the irrefutable blame and thus seek legal redress.

Both these approaches support the idea of society and industry as a kind of hugely complex calculating engine. There may be some bent or missing teeth among the vast array of gears and cogs, admit the experts, but when these problems are identified and rectified through the dual prisms of governance and accountability, all will mesh smoothly and untold benefits will spew forth at the turn of a handle.

The context

Sustainable development and environmental management, however, posit a very different kind of organizational universe, diametrically opposed to this Newtonian corporate model. It is a universe that is as baffling and all-embracing as Einstein's space/time continuum, itself a doorway into further concepts that share the counter-intuitive characteristics of chaos and quantum theory. The nature of this different model is essentially ecological, leading the way into a new appreciation of interdependent factors affecting social, economic and environmental corporate performance. Unlike the mechanical universe, the more we explore, the more confusing things become.

In the first universe, one cannot be comfortable with ambiguity; in the second it is that same ambiguity, an emphasis on relativity, which is the motivating force of the things around us. Just as space/time is a single continuum, so too is sustainable/development. In the future, environmental professionals will increasingly find themselves in the untenable position of straddling both worlds.

For example, environmental management systems (EMSs) (whether ISO 14001, BS 8555, EMAS or own brand) are seen mostly in mechanical terms, but the concepts that drive them are forever shifting and evolving. The links between The Natural Step and a management system like ISO 14001 are probably the most illuminating here. The most mind-expanding vision prompted by the first will simply remain a pipe dream unless it is harnessed to a device for delivering it like the second. The device itself lies dormant until brought to life by the power of the vision.

This then is the context for an examination of how integration and governance will be blended into the existing scope of environmental management. At heart, because environmental issues interact with all other business factors and disciplines, these changes were always going to affect the Institute of Environmental Management and Assessment's (IEMA's) members and other environmental practitioners. However, being on nodding terms with such developments is very different from understanding them, and that is what this section of the handbook attempts to achieve; exploring how non-environmental concerns will affect future developments within both the IEMA's remit and that of its members.

The trend towards integration

There's nothing new about the trend towards integration of topic focused management systems, usually quality, health and safety and environmental. Any corporate management team juggling these issues within the framework of legal requirements, corporate codes of practice and trade sector initiatives soon identifies the overlaps. It becomes equally clear that the benefits will include:

- avoidance of duplication;
- simplified systems;
- reductions in costs;
- reductions in formal procedures and bureaucracy;
- reduced certification costs; and
- potential to embrace other wider issues, i.e. sustainability.

On the surface, the basics of the systems are extremely similar no matter what the topic. Overlaying international standards like ISO 14001 and ISO 9000 for quality management, with internationally recognized specifications like OHSAS 18001 for occupational health and safety reveals a commonality of approach among both writers and implementers.

As corporate actions lead to consequences both within and without the organization, identifying the actual and potential consequences (impacts) in advance allows for the preparation and execution of an appropriate management plan. This plan will include specific objectives and targets, be realized by a set of related operational controls, then checked through auditing and given a top-down review on a periodic basis. Whether the consequence is expressed in terms of quality, occupational health and safety or the environment, the pattern – otherwise known as 'plan–do–check–act' – is much the same. Align this pattern with a willingness to improve on a continual basis, prevention of negative impacts and obedience to the rule of law and you have the basis of the systematic approach.

There are, however, several factors that hold back faster take up of integrated management systems overall. The first is the complexity of any guidance associated with integration projects. At the time of writing this chapter, the Danish Standards Association in response to an identified need within the country has announced that it will begin an ambitious programme to develop a standard covering integration of systems. The aim of the new standard is to integrate the management of energy, quality, corporate social responsibility, occupational health and safety, ISO 14001 and EMAS.

Meanwhile, in the UK, the Department of Trade and Industry has been funding the creation of the SIGMA Guidelines (BSI, 2003) – SIGMA is an acronym standing for Sustainability: Integrated Guidelines for Management. Published in September 2003, the guidelines of more than 80 pages are the product of a three year project. Though it may have at its heart a management framework based on the 'plan–do–check–act' cycle, it also comes with its own burgeoning toolkit, including a 'backwards compatibility tool' which allows organizations to see how the integration of sustainability might interlink with their existing systems.

Though informative and no doubt needed, such potentially daunting guidance and standards are certainly more likely to appeal initially to larger organizations than smaller ones. For smaller enterprises, there is still the possibility of developing a less complex, more streamlined system that will integrate a lesser number of management issues. Yet even here, there is another factor that may slow uptake of integrated systems.

In a European-wide survey of EMS related integration initiatives for small and medium sized enterprises, it was noted that 'although experience so far is very limited and most efforts are ad hoc, cost savings have not been as forthcoming as hoped' (Hilary, 2003). The general lack of experience of integrated systems among operators can be matched only by the lack of the requisite broad knowledge base among certifiers and verifiers.

In many countries, occupational health and safety has been supported for many years by a specific and well developed regulatory framework. By comparison, quality does not figure specifically in legislation, though fitness for purpose is often cited in product regulations, while areas like social responsibility have yet to make much of an appearance on the regulatory horizon.

To complicate matters even further, in the environmental arena, particularly in the UK and to a lesser extent in Europe, the regulatory framework is itself going through a period of integration and consolidation. In the immediate future, UK process operators can expect to see further integration of performance requirements with management system requirements by regulators. Combine this with the continued but gradual extension of the principles of integrated pollution prevention and control across processes, environmental media and trade sectors in the next five years, and the push towards 'joined up thinking' within the environmental sector itself will be hard to avoid.

With such a breadth of issues to cover, attempting to find certification and verification teams (let alone individuals) with the appropriate competencies and training has been hard. Both in the UK and in Sweden, where work is probably more advanced than anywhere else on the subject, the initial high expectations for the take up of integrated systems have been revised downwards.

The changing regulatory framework, lack of experience, lack of a supporting verification framework and sheer complexity all point to a 'slow but sure' take up of integrated systems overall. Yet even if progress was not slowed by these complications, there are still more fundamental challenges to realizing potential benefits; challenges that perhaps the environmental professional is better placed than any other to take on. To investigate these more closely, we need to confront some essential truths about integration as a management principle and about environmental work as a whole.

Searching for the benefits of integration

An underlying negative characteristic of integration work is that it can harden the very boundaries between management functions that it seeks to make more flexible. In a case of 'lowest common denominator' rather that 'greatest good for the greatest number', senior management can often view their new integrated system as handling issues and producing benefits only at an operational level. Not only have many managers merely paid lip service to quality as a strategic issue for many years, even fewer really believe that occupational health and safety is anything more than an operational issue.

All too often, integration leads to environmental management being dragged down to the same 'operational only' level, with strategic decisions taken on the basis of economic performance alone. Environmental managers, just like health and safety managers, are then brought in to ensure that the negative operational consequences of the decision are minimized. The possibility of inclusion during the strategy-forming sessions – thereby obviating the negative impacts at source – is never even considered, let alone the possibility of optimizing the positive potential for resource efficiency.

As long as environmental management is kept outside boardroom strategy sessions and away from financial decision making, the inevitable consequences will be damage limitation instead of integrated thinking and optimization. Integrated systems are more likely to continue this unrealistic stance unless the environmental profession takes steps to prevent it. Those steps include overcoming more subtle obstacles to integrated thinking.

Sadly, many directors expect the benefits of integrated thinking (indeed perhaps even of sustainability itself) at the strategic and operational levels to be an emergent property of integrated systems. 'Emergent property' is a phrase often employed when the user is unsure as to the link between an action and an outcome – thus human intelligence is often said to be an emergent property of the mechanical links between neurons in the brain. Replicate the human brain's complexity and size in a large enough mechanical model, the argument then follows, and intelligence will surely result.

Thus, there is a general expectation that somewhere during the process of integrating three or more strands of management at the system level, managers will undergo an as yet unspecified change and through a magical transformation be capable of thinking both strategically and operationally at the same time. In addition, they will be able to extricate themselves from any number of organizational and mental constructs that constitute the current reality for that particular organization.

Experience and empirical evidence point to the opposite. Corporate executives who owe their relative success to a pre-existing framework of specialisms and silo management have been slow to embrace anything as untested and as unformed as a generalist integrative approach. In system integration, the focus is still on the mechanism and not on the desired outputs. Thus, consciously or unconsciously, the difference between functional integration (on an operational level) and systemic integration (at a strategic level) is preserved. All, however, is not lost.

Embracing such an inclusive subject as sustainable development, or the environment, moves the focus away from the 'how' and onto the 'why'. Experience in the SIGMA Project confirms that when an organization is attempting to establish its contribution to sustainable development, it does not start by looking at its structures or even its outputs, but struggles instead to have a more precise definition of the vision it is seeking to realize.

The environment as the entry point

As one of the three recognized 'legs' of sustainability, and the subject of much recent thought, policy making and regulation, the environment – as opposed to social or economic impact management – has an important contribution to make in breaking down the mental and organizational barriers already identified.

Models of sustainability may be based on the 'triple bottom line', on The Natural Step's 'four system conditions', or on the 'Five Capitals' model (natural, human, financial, manufactured and social). Whatever is used, it is hard to escape from an aspect of the models that finds its best expression in the Orwellian style phrase 'all capitals are created equal except natural capital, which is more equal than others'.

This is not simply an argument for environmental specialists to maintain their status in a world of wavering business fashion. The basis for the assertion is the irreducible fact that without a fully functioning and healthy foundation of natural capital, the other capitals will not last very long at all. Let any of the other capitals serve as a foundation for development and sooner or later the model fails. Although everyone would agree that a balance between the capitals is the best way forward for sustainability, unless mankind as a biological species overcame the need for environmental support, then weighting in its favour makes good, rational, precautionary sense.

Yet where does that leave the environmental profession as a whole? Even if the argument is unimpeachable, if the corporate focus has moved on, what happens next?

Worse, if directors think that they have 'done' environment simply because they have an ISO 14001 certificate or carried out a pre-acquisition audit and local government officers and elected members are content with environmental impact assessments on individual developments, then how do those who work with environmental concerns get access to the boardroom, local authority 'cabinets' and strategic planning meetings?

Instead of fighting to be included under the limiting banner of the latest management trend, the professional bodies and individuals concerned should be seeking the preeminence for environmentalism in the sustainability debate that it obviously deserves. The environment may no longer be fashionable at public and private sector policy making level, but it may be all the better for it. Now it has to prove that it has a right to serious strategic attention beyond the confines of operational novelty, political correctness and the zealotry of the recently converted.

More than most professions, the environmental sector has been obliged to mature and develop rapidly. From being a relatively low profile specialism associated mainly with utilities or civil engineering to being on the brink of recognition by Royal Charter within a few decades is spectacular progress by anybody's standards. It is also a testament to the efforts of the constituent bodies of the emerging Society for the Environment. However, along with maturity comes not only power and influence but also a need to develop an understanding of the nature of responsibility; the ability to respond with both knowledge and wisdom.

Knowledge of an environmental specialism is still only effectively utilized through an appreciation of its relationship to the whole, the fundamental ecology of the subject matter itself. Thus, environmental work has at its heart a necessity to synthesize, and it is this that could help in the future to generate a type of corporate gestalt on the subject of sustainability and all allied strategic decision making.

If integration within organizations is to lead to anything more than cost savings and less bureaucracy, it is those familiar with environmental and ecological subjects who will help make the whole greater than the sum of the parts. It is their clarity of thinking and depth of understanding that will be needed if sustainability is to help mankind successfully avoid the unappealing alternatives.

Let there be no mistake as to the size of the challenge that lies ahead in the next decade if this path is chosen. Companies became legal entities in the first place in order to give them recognition as individuals under the law. These individuals can then be recognized separately from those who make up their managing boards. As such, a company can borrow more money than a collection of individuals, helping to spread individual liabilities. As a way of fuelling investment and subsequent commerce, the move was second to none, and as economic engines, there is little to rival modern companies. This economic function is intrinsic to their nature, and attempts to retrofit other, broader responsibilities, such as environmental management or sustainability, are doomed to fail if they do not work at the same fundamental level.

One attempted short cut to this deeper level has always been expressing the benefits of a particular course of action in terms of the financial. How many environmental managers have been exhorted to express the annual review of their activities in terms of money saved by their actions? At policy making level, fiscal instruments are symptomatic of the same approach – grab them by the wallet and their hearts and minds will follow.

The challenge of governance

The relatively recent emphasis on governance as an issue is no different. Side stepping any meaningful debate on ethics, and preserving the current emphasis on competitiveness as a principle in both public and private sectors, governance and the concomitant narrow definition of accountability are more closely allied to finance than many prefer to acknowledge.

Companies need inward investment, preferably at not too onerous a price and across a spread of investment sectors. Investors, on the other hand, need reassurance that their money will be appropriately managed, and the more of them there are, the more the definition of 'appropriate' may vary. Add to this the confusion in the pension scheme markets, the increased complexity of finance, the dual pressures of globalization and technological capacity, and, as a result, both sides of the investment equation increasingly see governance as a critical part of enhancing and maintaining value.

In what way then, does the recent emphasis on the establishment of good governance affect the environmental profession? From the Cadbury Report (Cadbury, 1992) through the Turnbull Report (ICA, 1999) to the Higgs Review (DTI, 2003), directors in the UK are not short of guidance on best practice when it comes to confronting new demands on transparency and accountability. The emphasis of the reports, however, is firmly on the field of financial management with a few nods towards the environment as a compliance and liability issue. The Higgs Review is perhaps the most forthright in asking for further clarification of responsibilities and liabilities for directors in this area. Yet even here, one has a sense of minimizing exposure to harm rather than maximizing potential for good.

For many, the best practice principles espoused by reports of 'risk assessment' and 'comply or explain' has led directors to a familiar response. They undertake a gap analysis followed by a tick-box review of current procedures, sensing that investors currently need reassurance rather than details. However, it will not be long before rapidly educated and increasingly sophisticated investors begin to ask more detailed and more searching questions about the overall effectiveness of boards. The Higgs Review does, after all, include recommendations on director development, board and director performance evaluation and an enhanced role for the company secretary – these are not matters that are traditionally brought up during the annual general meeting.

As we have seen, this box-ticking or mechanistic approach often precedes a deeper understanding and a more integrated approach to a given subject. The optimist will see the current response of directors as a positive sign for the future. It is possible that where a greater understanding of corporate governance, values and ethics exists, there might be an entry point to the strategic planning process for those whose environmental experience has led them to a broad and inclusive approach to management issues in general. The pessimist, however, will observe that directors only respond to the pressures imposed by regulatory compliance and exposure to liability.

Promoting the first scenario and avoiding the second is in the hands of the current generation of emerging environmental professionals. The challenge in the next ten years or more is to demonstrate that ecologically based thinking is at the very heart of business sustainability. In order to achieve this, however, the profession itself needs to consider the benefits of a little integrated thinking.

Concluding thoughts

Bernard Shaw expressed the opinion that 'All professions are conspiracies against the laity.' If those they seek to serve increasingly regard the established professions such as law or medicine this way, then the obstacles faced by a relatively new group are even greater. Luckily so are the opportunities, chief among them being the chance to discover the nature of the shared vocation.

For the most part, the environmental sector spends too much time indulging in specialization to the exclusion of exploring commonalities. Is it any wonder that senior executives, when faced with a barrage of jargon and technicalities do not see the contribution that the sector may be able to make over and above the single minded pursuit of competitiveness?

Perhaps what is common to all those who work in the environmental area is the wish to profess something, even if the need for a collective articulation of it has not yet been recognized. Many environmentalists see their work as being more than the simple acquisition of money, or the exercising of particular specialist knowledge. At heart, and though the cynics may blush at its expression in this manner, what drives environmental practitioners is a championing of something that goes beyond the partial interests of organizations, government or individuals, for the general betterment of all. Environmentalists argue for the inclusion of the environment as a major factor in everyday decision making, and for ecological thinking as a whole.

It is easy to characterize directors, whether private or public sector, as having sold their souls to market forces. They thus continue their short-termist approach and have little time for those who choose to worship other idols. Yet what if those involved in industry or in the management of public sector institutions also have something they wish to profess, have a calling that expresses itself through the mechanism of an organization? Would they not welcome those who aid in that expression?

Unfortunately, given the fact that the environment has long been ignored or sidelined in the progress of societal development, much of the environmental sector's work involves conservation or remediation of environmental resources under threat or already damaged. It is this that gives the profession its limiting, retrospective character in the eyes of Shaw's laity. When the majority of the profession is involved in work that is essentially 'after the fact' rather than engaged in actively shaping the future, there is no wonder that our role is seen as operational rather than strategic.

This is more than a mere presentational issue. We need something more fundamental than a public relations drive to re-present what we do to others. Instead, as an identifiable profession, we need to come to a better common understanding of the environmental sector's collective motivation and allow our actions with our clients and wider stakeholders to become its living embodiment. Those actions should be informed in turn by the capacity to understand the relationships between organizations, their environment and their long term sustainability; to move from 'clean up' (valuable though that function is) to rethinking the ecology of the future in its broadest sense.

References and further reading

Barden, P. et al (2002) 'Is Integration the Holy Grail of Management Systems?' *the environmentalist*, no 11, June, pp24–25

BSI (2003) 'The SIGMA Guidelines: The SIGMA Project', British Standards Institution, London, see also the SIGMA web site at www.projectsigma.com

Cadbury (1992) 'The Report of the Committee on the Financial Aspects of Corporate Governance', chaired by Sir Adrian Cadbury, *Gee Publishing*, London, see also the web site of the European Corporate Governance Institute, www.ecgi.org/codes/country_pages/codes_uk.htm#cadbury

DTI (2003) 'A Review of the Role and Effectiveness of Non-executive Directors' (the Higgs Review), Department of Transport and Industry, see also the department's web site at www.dti.gov.uk/cld/non_exec_review

Hilary, R. (2003) *BEST Project Report on Environmental Management Systems and SMEs*, Scott Wilson, London

ICA (1999) 'Internal Control: Guidance for Directors on the Combined Code' (the Turnbull Report), Institute of Chartered Accountants in England and Wales, see also the institute's web site at www.icaew.co.uk/internalcontrol

Shaw, O. (2003) 'An A to Z of Integrated Management Systems', *the environmentalist*, no 16, pp32–33

Smith, D. (2001) *Integrated Management Systems: The Framework*, British Standards Institution, London

WWF-UK (2001) *To Whose Profit – Building a Business Case for Sustainability*, WWF-UK, Godalming, Surrey, see also the WWF web site at www.wwf.org.uk

Chapter 8.3

The Future of the Environmental Profession

No problem can be solved at the level of thinking that created it. – Einstein

Introduction

The job title environmental manager sounds simple enough. After all that may be said, isn't it simply management of an organization's environmental compliance and performance? And isn't this what it will always be? Well, sort of – but in reality, it is not that simple.

A quick look through the articles and occasional working diaries of environmental managers in professional journals such as the *ENDS* report and *the environmentalist* shows how wide and varied the role already is. Managers may find themselves working on compliance, health and safety, pulling together the annual environmental or corporate social responsibility report, or scouting around for a new bit of technology to reduce emissions or improve energy efficiency – and more.

It is worth casting back; 15 years ago the job was very different. As researcher John Morelli writes:

> Originally, the activities of the environmental manager in industry were performed at the loading dock, at the end of the pipe, at the top of the smokestack. His or her purpose was to capture the waste, treat it to the extent feasible to reduce potential impacts on human health and the environment, discharge what could be discharged, and isolate what could not (Morelli, 1999).

It was a practical job and, perhaps unfairly, not very different from being a plumber.

Environmental managers' responsibilities were not defined clearly and dealt mostly with ensuring compliance with legal requirements. Their role was perceived by their work colleagues as constraining production to achieve externally imposed environmental limits, and they were often opposed by other managers and offered little support.

One of the main reasons their role was so restricted then was that regulation dealt with significant emissions, effluents and discharges that had to be controlled. Little or no attention was paid to indirect effects such as from purchasing or transport, or to thinking that proactive approaches to environment, ethics or corporate social responsibility could be a source of significant cost reduction or competitive advantage. There was very little possibility that the environment might soon be a strategic issue for management.

For the most part, environmental managers were focused on least-cost compliance and occupied relatively low-status positions compared with (say) sales and marketing managers or company accountants. Even by the late 1980s, with some notable exceptions, very few corporate businesses and even fewer governmental organizations felt the need, for example, to work out, let alone publish, an environmental or ethical policy.

By the early 1990s, the number of environmental managers in the UK was counted in the tens or low hundreds. Now they number several thousand and the majority of them are members of the Institute of Environmental Management and Assessment. The job has become much more complex. It is already possible to discern some of the shape of the future of the profession.

It helps to analyse the work into a number of levels, each with a different time span, and each with its own characteristics and increasingly wide range of responsibilities at higher levels of business organization. Each level needs an increased level of human capability which, given reasonable levels of challenge and support, may continue to develop naturally in one person over a lifetime. This practical approach, which captures a great deal of what we observe in others as they grow through the normal developmental passages of adult life, has been developed for management notably by Jaques (1996). The different developmental levels have also been observed by many others and characterized in various ways that can provide useful understanding for the practitioner's own development. We will look at career progression in the light of this 'levels' model.

Working at Level 1: task focus

Jaques' first level, Level 1, is the earliest and deals with day to day operations. The focus is on delivering direct output and quality. The work here involves responsibility for direct operating tasks such as: practical prevention and control of risks; collecting and compiling compliance report information for management or regulatory authorities; assisting operatives map their possible environmental effects and risks; and interviewing, observing and advocating shop-floor opportunities for improvement. Here the person is working in the largely predictable environment of the task in hand. This is the level at which the practical work of ensuring regulatory and policy compliance gets done.

Typically the person working at this level will have, at most, a time span perspective of three months. If they do not achieve results within this period, they will tend to feel demotivated and quite stressed.

Level 2: first line management

The next level, Level 2, is still operational, and includes first line management or supervision of a group of operatives who are producing the outputs. This would include responsibility for routine actions within any existing environmental or wider management systems, starting with routine compliance issues. It would include facilitating awareness of the potential environmental consequences of a company's activities and promotion of that awareness throughout the workforce. It could include responsibility for a team of technical or compliance auditors, and for coordinating predetermined training within the organization. It would include the drafting of routine internal and external monitoring reports, and it would include practical responsibility for coordinating and delivering planned environmental programmes and performance improvements.

The person routinely working at this level will have, at most, a time span perspective of one year. If a job does not show results within this time, the same thing will tend to happen – loss of motivation and excessive stress. The environment or space of immediate interest is the internal environment of the work group.

Level 3: department and system management

At Level 3, the responsibilities are again wider, the time span for achieving objectives again longer, now two years. This is still, however, an operational level. Typically, managers will be dealing with the development, implementation and improvement of systems, starting with compliance systems, as well as ensuring that managers, staff and operators at the first and second levels work with and through the system. In the 1990s this meant integrated pollution prevention and control (IPPC) and ISO 14001, but the sustainable development agenda has made progress and this now means starting to deploy or develop systems to support corporate social responsibility and business ethics.

At this level, we find responsibility for energy management systems, manufacturers' safety data sheets systems, best practice research and incorporation, waste minimization programmes, organization of supplier and customer environmental management systems and organization of industrial ecology opportunities. In other words, the role is making use of existing systems, and adjusting, modifying and tuning to make the most of the systems they have and to cope with changing trends.

The manager here will be part of or fit into the corporate core planning, budgeting, implementation, monitoring and reporting system and cycle. They will have much more autonomy for creative development of activities to contribute towards improving environmental performance.

Level 4: general management of a division or function

Level 4 is, for example, head of function, within general management, for a division or department. It is the first level at which management can be comprehensive and tactical. Only by being comprehensive in its systems can an organization release genuine focus and attention for tactical thinking and projects, and the coordination of tactical projects is the beginning of strategic thinking.

The time horizon is now about five years. The work at this level includes coordinating the activities of operating units on different sites. Each of these will tend to have differences in approach and programme, and the coordination leads to reflections on strategy. This level of work involves considering and developing alternative processes to maximize efficiency and performance.

At Level 4, the manager is translating the mission into actuality via design and coordination of objectives, systems, appointments, practices and approaches. The environment of thought will normally include networks within and without the organization, for example, in the UK, the IEMA regional network.

The capability needed now is modelling: maintaining contact with what currently exists and detaching to conceptualize ('model') something completely different – not merely a modification, but a point of departure. It involves comparing and contrasting alternative operating systems, for example the various ISO and similar systems – as well as alternative ways of deploying or modifying them. It involves naturally maintaining an existing approach within which new hypotheses are tested. And more recognizably, the manager will be easy with handling a number of interactive projects or programmes, each adjusting in relation to the others.

Currently, the work of environmental managers at this level includes scanning the regulatory and other environments for early warning of relevant changes, and monitoring environmental and sustainable design for innovations in products and processes. It involves support and coordination of site environmental managers, and the function's projects and programmes, including risk and loss prevention management, internal and community communications, operations, staffing, education and facilitation.

Making level sense

At each level, there is a need to build increased environmental competences and the environmental manager needs to be able to offer it. An analysis of the current range of responsibilities in this way shows the width of the role, the extent to which it is expanding, and possibly becoming too big in flatter organizations.

'Work levels' analysis also provides an appropriate tool to align the number of levels with the required and planned responsibilities. But there are practical limits; where top management requires a flatter organization, the function may have to cut its coat according to its cloth. Environmental managers will have to become skilled in organization design, or face more dysfunctional work as the number of new tasks increases.

The key to making sense of all of this is an appreciation of the possibilities of management development and how human capability tends to develop – unless it is blocked. Under stimulating and supportive conditions managers tend to grow through the levels from Level 2 in their early twenties, at a rate of about a level every five years. Well designed management development programmes can and should provide this kind of stimulating and supportive environment.

Environmental managers are having to tackle a growing number of new issues, including take-back legislation, sustainability, corporate social responsibility (CSR) since the mid to late 1990s, emissions management, integration of Health and Safety Executive (HSE) and environmental systems with core management processes, sustainable design and product development, supply chain development, customer support, and the requirement for environmental and sustainability leadership in their organization.

Tom Bramley, environmental supply chain adviser to LandRover, says that even at Level 3, the job is too broad:

> Within the automotive sector, environmental managers still spend the major part – too much – of their time on compliance issues, when they should be more engaged in collaborating with their customers to reduce environmental impacts through design. For many, a lot of their time goes into education, persuasion and lobbying senior management to take environmental and sustainable development issues seriously, and into catching up on lost ground. It is notable that companies in the Far East seem to have accepted the need for both systemic environmental performance improvement and for a strategic approach – if only to safeguard exports (Bramley, 2001).

Level 5: the real challenge and opportunity

> Can we move nations and people in the direction of sustainability? Such a move would be a modification of society comparable in scale to only two other changes: the Agricultural Revolution of the late Neolithic age and the Industrial Revolution of the past two centuries. These revolutions were gradual, spontaneous and largely unconscious. This one will have to be a fully conscious operation, guided by the best foresight that science can provide… If we actually do it, the undertaking will be absolutely unique in humanity's stay on the Earth.

This quotation by William D. Ruckelshaus, formerly EPA Administrator in the US under Presidents Nixon and Reagan (Meadows and Meadows, 1992, p218) is a stark reminder of the scale of the challenge of sustainable development. David Ballard (Ballard, 1998) showed that this view is widely shared among leading UK practitioners in the field of sustainable development. A more formal UK study in Lancashire (Macnaghten et al, 1995) suggests that the population at large is largely in agreement.

Level 5 typically involves management of a business unit containing divisions or departments (or some equivalent) and a contribution to the creation of corporate policies, strategy and culture through shaping vision and mission. The framework for thinking about environmental and sustainability issues is national or regional. There is a further expansion of time horizon, to ten years – and of responsibilities.

The management capability required at this level involves making relationships between previously unrelated material. It is about creating general rules and redefining fields of knowledge and experience. It involves engaging in an open context and deciding when it should be closed – the manager will be modifying the boundaries of any discussion, operating a complex, tiered system below this level, reframing and modifying it and coping with second- and third-order consequences and feedback. Elements will be seen as interdependent, to change one part is to change the whole.

At Level 5 the work includes strategic risk management, coordinating hierarchical plans, external annual environmental management reporting, compiling and assessing performance data, coordinating external technical and due diligence audit programmes and related negotiations, annual environmental conferences, internal training and empowerment across all business functions, levels and processes. It is here that board demands for activity on CSR are having an impact, with little agreed or settled at the time of writing on how this is to be turned into an integrated management process.

At this level, responsibility for leading and managing becomes unavoidable. Examples could include: take-back legislation; emissions management; integration of HSE and environmental systems with core management processes; sustainable product development and sector leadership; and the next steps along the path to the possibility of real ecological sustainability. The most difficult task at this level for some time to come is the education of boards of directors, other senior management and investors, and their commitment to take environmental and sustainable development issues seriously, as part of business as usual.

Seeing the whole at Level 6

At Level 6 we are looking at the international level, with a time span of 20 years within which management can tolerate waiting for a result. This is the level at which corporate citizenship normally has to be the concern of the whole top team in an organization. At this level the environmental manager will probably have acquired other responsibilities and will be at the top table, expected to lead and support discussion on corporate citizenship. Level 6 capability does exist for international corporate organizations, but is very difficult to find and retain in the present US/UK stock-market driven business environment where the share price reacts to every quarterly result, and analysts appear to only work with a time horizon of two to four years.

Responsibilities at this level require understanding and judgements about the world environment (ecological, economic, political, social, technological, cultural), generating a range of perceptions of complex Level 5 systems and their contexts and selecting options and determining priorities. It includes filtering instabilities to give national and regional business units some level of stability and continuity.

At this level, there is a requirement to support and maintain corporate international management systems and their local country coordinators. At present many leading global organizations have board level committees trying to get to grips with CSR and their relationships with corporate citizenship, governance, ethics, environmental management and sustainable development. This is the level at which progress can be made in meeting the next logical item of the sustainable development agenda, that is addressing the gap between environmental performance improvement and real ecological sustainability. Work is taking place on this, for example, in the UK via the BSI SIGMA Project (BSI, 1999–2003).

At this level we see advocacy and lobbying at work around potential legislation, and interaction with country and international political systems and processes, for example legislatures and the World Trade Organization. Those with top environmental responsibilities in organizations are also faced with the daunting task of acting as an internal 'guru' on ethical and sustainable development issues, including corporate values, ethical issues, carbon management, biodiversity, far future forecasting and more.

The job at this level has at least 25 to 30 possible components and requires appropriate human capability to handle this much complexity, together with a great deal of management skill.

The future

It is important to remember that the picture of different levels is derived from the experiences of many people working in many organizations. Very few organizations have all of this happening presently. What does emerge, however, is an evolving and interesting profession in the future.

At the lower levels, there will continue to be the traditional compliance work. But while brands continue to reside in the developed world, manufacturing and (now) service aspects are likely to continue to migrate to the lowest labour cost economies. This means that compliance work is now likely to span home and supplier country locations. Outsourcing to newly industrializing nations will limit the responsibility for compliance but it will still have to be managed and risk assessed – merely to consider risks to supply. Consumers and interest groups will probably continue to demand more.

The last two decades have been characterized by the removal of layers of management in organizations. It will often be the case with international organizations that those with environmental responsibilities will only have three or four tiers of management between the 'people on the ground' and the people carrying the responsibility in the boardroom. In other words, they may have two less than they may need. This suggests that existing environmental professionals in the hierarchy will, in many cases, be quite overloaded with responsibilities.

Again, logically, this suggests that the future of the profession will involve requirements for highly developed professional management capability and technical skills, and these will need to include contracting skills to contract the resources needed to handle the many and varied responsibilities.

In the future, it is probable that environmental managers will see their jobs evolve as the sustainable development agenda is reconceptualized as sustainable management. The recognition that sustainable development has an economic, an environmental and a social dimension paves the way logically to a management role that includes these responsibilities. This is a new kind of professional, combining the understanding of an MBA graduate with a rethinking of all aspects of this knowledge from the perspective of sustainable development.

In other words we are likely to see the evolution of environmental managers during their working lives from very practical work 'on the ground' to professionals with growing in-service management development and training, probably in the form of modular management development masters and doctoral programmes, focused on sustainable management.

What this seems to amount to is that, towards the top end, we need to be developing not glorified plumbers but philosopher kings. Philip Sadler, OBE, former CEO of Ashridge Business School, Patron of the Tomorrow's Company Programme, and notable business author has said:

The responsibility of management developers for those with very senior environmental responsibilities is to equip them for a 'guru' role if this is what they are called on to offer. This is, apart from the CEO, the Chairman and the Board, the place where the future of sustainability is best understood – and this is the future. And this function's role is to be an informed support for the CEO, Chair and Board.

At this professional level there is a need for those who can answer the call towards responsibility and leadership and can guide their organizations and sectors through the multiple environmental challenges which will press back ever more strongly unless business becomes part of the answer. At this level the professional will need to be able to contribute to the future by playing an active part in reconciling the demands of the environment and society for sustainability by bringing into being new configurations of thought, markets, ideologies and social institutions.

This should be enormously interesting work for those ready for it. This level of capability is also very rare – and there has always been a shortage. It generally arises when there has been good potential with many favourable circumstances. A great many such people will be required for the global transition to real ecological sustainability and there is a need for all educational institutions responsible for executive development to put their shoulders to the wheel – by yesterday!

Having said all this, quite clearly, the future of the profession will not be only one unified, inclusive senior management capability; for example, many organizations will choose to separate the roles of environment and CSR. There is already the separation at the lower levels of health and safety and frequently energy management. Environmental managers are not all going to want to move away from their origins. At board level, however, there are few seats, and someone will carry the environmental and sustainable development responsibilities.

It seems, therefore, important for the future of this work, which can certainly be thought of as 'right work' in Buddhist terms, that the profession gears itself to provide a management development process that produces people of the requisite capability and education.

This leads to the issue of the need for chartered status for the top end of the environmental profession. This is a longish career path and the early work has been concerned with developing the syllabus and quality control of training and educational establishments. Clearly, the Institute of Environmental Management and Assessment has gone a long way with this since 1991. The focus has initially been practical and skills oriented – producing environmental auditors, management systems auditors, soil specialists and members (affiliate, associate, full and fellow) – mainly focusing on legal compliance and management systems capability. But to meet the needs of Levels 4 to 6, we now need to extend their management development to the whole organization, and this means every business function (operations, marketing, purchasing, logistics, etc.), at every level.

If we do this, environmental professionals will have covered the normal MBA syllabus and a great deal more. We also need to develop managers who are not overwhelmed by the traditional MBA graduate – to quote the proud principal of one of these institutions, 'with shareholder value branded on their foreheads and written through them like Brighton rock'. In other words, the profession needs to develop managers with a new kind of MBA syllabus, covering the conventional MBA areas but upgrading their treatment where there needs to be more, better, different or transformational change to meet the real needs of the sustainable development agenda.

Beyond this, the future involves a smaller number of similarly educated doctoral level managers, who have extended their MBA (which may well be called an MSc) to cover more of the crucial higher level knowledge – for example, corporate ethics, government and media relations, and the conditions and processes for real, competitively advantageous ecological sustainability. The Institute of Environmental Management and Assessment will need to find ways of communicating with the boards of organizations, non-executive directors, analysts and investors in a language that they can understand. The message is that the need for sustainable management is fully justified, and they need to be working together for a genuinely sustainable market economy.

Finally, the future of the profession will need the development of the qualities of its members. If at the top end there is a need for impeccable leaders and 'gurus', then those coming through the profession need to be developing suitable qualities to avoid the temptations and the corrupting influences of security, office, belonging, esteem and power.

In the past the inculcation of the relevant virtues and values came from schools supportive of the socially positive messages and requirements of major religions. Given the turbulence of thought and material orientation of the major source of current management, US and US-influenced European and Asian business schools, then as they currently are, these institutions will tend not to inculcate the values and virtues required.

The best source of the integrity that will be required to 'carry the day', is deliberate personal growth and development by the managers themselves. This does not begin without honesty and needs increasing integrity. It is a great journey and adventure with great support along the way from those who have gone ahead.

The profession offers, in the future, a career path that at higher levels needs development of the personal qualities of its members – real growth similar to that which you might hope to find, for example, in mid- and later-career psychologists. This will support and go hand in hand with, and is not separate from, real growth of work capability. It is also a path to real leadership since there is an age-old recognition that those who are further along the road have this naturally.

It helps to have more than one 'road map' to help us to find our bearings on developmental stages – wherever we start. Wilber (2000) sketches several such maps, with reasonable academic standing, and some further reading is provided for those who wish to pursue this subject in more detail.

Some lucky few (very few) will grow naturally through these stages, however labelled. For the rest of us, the path of growth involves more effort and some committed work. The pay off is very worthwhile personally, for our work capability and for our colleagues, family and friends. Beyond this, without taking ourselves in hand and facilitating our own greatest growth and transformation, the work out in the world that our profession now needs to do – will very probably not be done.

References

Ballard, D. (1998) Paper presented to the UK Round Table for Sustainable Development, Defra, London

Bramley, T. (2001) Cited in King, Ross 'The Future of the Profession', *Environment Business Magazine*, December, p24

BSI (1999–2003) For further information on the SIGMA Project go to www.project-sigma.com

Jaques, E. (1996) *The Requisite Organization: A Total System for Effective Managerial Organization and Managerial Leadership for the 20th Century*, Cason Hall & Co, Massachusetts

Macnaghten, P. et al (1995) *Public Perceptions and Sustainable Development in Lancashire: Indicators, Institutions and Participation*, Lancashire County Council, Preston

Meadows, D. M. and Meadows, D. (1992) *Beyond the Limits*, Earthscan, London

Morelli, J. (1999) *Voluntary Environmental Management: The Inevitable Future*, CRC Press, London

Wilber, K. (2000) *Integral Psychology*, Shambahala, Cambridge, Massachusetts

Further reading

Argyris, C. and Schon, D. (1996) *Organizational Learning II: Theory, Method & Practice*, Addison Wesley, Reading, Massachusetts

Bateson, G. (1972) *Steps to an Ecology of Mind*, Chandler, San Francisco

Crosbie, L. and Knight, K. (1995) *Strategy for Sustainable Business*, McGraw-Hill, Maidenhead

Jaques, E. and Cason, K. (1994) *Human Capability: Study of Individual Potential and its Application*, Gower Publishing, Aldershot

Jaques, E., Clement, S. and Lessem, R. (1994) *Executive Leadership: A Practical Guide to Managing Complexity (Developmental Management)*, Blackwell, Oxford

Kuhn, T. (1962) *The Structure of Scientific Revolutions*, University of Chicago Press, Chicago

Rossan, S. (1994) 'Management Levels and Capability Model', BIOSS 1994 at www.csem.org.uk

Rossan, S. (2001) 'IRIS – Initial Recruitment Interview Schedule', BIOSS 1994 at www.omnicor.co.za/assessments/iris.htm

Sheahy, G. (1997) *New Passages: Mapping Your Life Across Time*, HarperCollins, New York

Torbert, W. R. and Fisher, D. (2000) *Personal and Organizational Transformations*, McGraw-Hill, Maidenhead (gives extensive literature on developmental stages)

Index

Page numbers in *italics* refer to figures, tables and boxes